ROADSIDE HISTORY OF
ARKANSAS

ALAN C. PAULSON

Cover art:
The Arkansas Traveller, by Edward Payson Washbourne
Courtesy of Arkansas Territorial Restoration
Department of Arkansas Heritage, Little Rock

Maps by Jennifer Hamelman

Printed in the U.S.A.

Library of Congress Cataloging-in-Publication Data

Paulson, Alan C.
  Roadside history of Arkansas / Alan C. Paulson
      p.   cm.
  Includes bibliographical references and index.
  ISBN 0-87842-335-4 (alk. paper). — ISBN 0-87842-334-6 (alk. paper)
  1. Historic sites—Arkansas—Guidebooks.   2. Arkansas—History,
Local.   3. Arkansas—Tours.   4. Automobile travel—Arkansas—
Guidebooks.   I. Title.
F412.P38   1998
917.6704'53—dc21   98-14017
                                                                          CIP

Mountain Press Publishing Company
Missoula, Montana
1998

To
J. Stephen Lay

CONTENTS

PART 5, THE OZARKS

FOREWORD

Perhaps no state has neglected its history as much as Arkansas. We did not get a state archives until well into the twentieth century. Our state historical society was not founded until 1941. A university press was not established until the 1980s. When Arkansas celebrated its statehood sesquicentennial in 1986, we were forced to face the fact that we did not even have a state history textbook for use in the secondary schools of the state!

This historical neglect was not due to a failure to notice the problem. As early as 1868, Robert Ward Johnson (1814–1878), a former U.S. senator and scion of a pioneering family in the state, spoke of the tendency of Arkansans to overlook their heritage. Arkansans need a state pride, he wrote, adding, "The state that cherished no distinct 'state pride' must have a meager and barren history. . . . Her people, without it, will have few incentives to honor, toleration and noble efforts. Her children will grow up without memories or proud ambitions, as it were without a home. . . . It is time we begin to cherish such thoughts."

Nor was this historical neglect due to Arkansas having a boring or uneventful heritage. How could a land that witnessed the exploits and subsequent death of Spanish conquistador Hernando de Soto have an uneventful history? Our state has produced a host of interesting sons and daughters—ranging from David O. Dodd, the "Boy Martyr of the Confederacy," to Hattie Caraway, the first woman elected to the U.S. Senate, to President Bill Clinton.

Arkansans have witnessed some of the most searing and tragic episodes of U.S. history. Thousands of Cherokee, Choctaw, and other Native Americans lie buried in unmarked Arkansas graves, the victims of the Trail of Tears. Fort Smith was the home of federal judge Isaac Parker, widely hailed as "the Hanging Judge" during the last quarter of the nineteenth century. More recently, Central High School in Little Rock was the scene of perhaps the most important confrontation between federal and state authority during this century.

Fortunately, the days of neglecting Arkansas history seem to be at an end. Museums of Arkansas history are numerous, and they attract large crowds of visitors. A growing number of counties now have local historical societies, many of which publish journals. At last we have a requirement that state history must be taught in Arkansas schools. More important than anything else, Arkansans now have access to more and better books about the state.

As a recent emigrant to Arkansas, Al Paulson brings a fresh and unbiased perspective to viewing our state's past. For example, in looking at the incredibly complex history of the city of Hot Springs, he sees beyond the beautiful bathhouses and the exciting Oaklawn Race Track. We learn about the earliest days of the city, when it was known far and wide for its hot, healing waters. We meet the gangsters, the gamblers, the preachers, and the reformers. Paulson's Roadside History introduces us to the entire cast of characters. Some were a bit eccentric, like Wild Bill Hickok serving as a spy during the Civil War. Some, such as Miss Laura Zeigler, who ran an elegant bordello in Fort Smith, were a little less than law-abiding. Some were hardworking and prosperous—Nathan Warren, an African American who owned a popular candy store in Little Rock before the Civil War, is a case in point.

This book is more than a mere guidebook to popular historic sites in Arkansas. As a "roadside history," it is organized in such a way that readers can use it to plan tours of the state. Such well-known places as Eureka Springs and the Crater of Diamonds are included, along with obscure but interesting places like Mount Ida, Conway, and Brinkley. Even places that no longer exist, including Hopefield (which was destroyed during the Civil War), are discussed.

This admirable inclusiveness is aided by the author's decision to structure the book around the natural divisions of Arkansas. Therefore, we are introduced to the often neglected Delta and Coastal Plain areas of the state, as well as the better-known Ozarks.

Academic historians should not be put off by the author's decision to include some folklore in a book of history. This is not intended as a textbook. It is, rather, a book that will encourage readers to get out and explore Arkansas, to become familiar with the nooks and crannies of the state, and, most important, to understand the unique aspects of our personalities.

Arkansans will benefit from the publication of *Roadside History of Arkansas*. If Robert Ward Johnson were alive today, he would read this book, and I think he would view it as a step toward developing that "cherished state pride" in our collective heritage.

Tom W. Dillard, Archivist
University of Central Arkansas
Conway, Arkansas

ACKNOWLEDGMENTS

I thank J. Stephen Lay for suggesting I write this book and Dan Greer for guiding the project. Few writers are lucky enough to have such a remarkable friend and colleague as Stephen Lay. Few writers are lucky enough to work with such a gracious and competent editor as Dan Greer. I also appreciate the outstanding critique and copyediting by Larry Barowsky, and the invaluable help of editor Gwen McKenna, who picked up the gauntlet after Dan Greer moved on to other pastures.

Journalist, friend, and wife Polly Walter took copy negatives of nearly 300 historic photos for this project, contributed her own photos, critiqued the manuscript, and tolerated the excessively long hours I invested into the six-year obsession that produced this book. Henryetta Vaneman volunteered the use of her darkroom and helped with printing. Tom Dillard, the archivist at the University of Central Arkansas, and his staff provided enthusiastic help throughout the project. I'm particularly grateful for Tom's skilled critique of the manuscript and his insightful foreword to this book.

Inez Cline, the Garland County historian, provided a great deal of information on Maxine Temple Jones, helped us locate important photos on diverse subjects, and gave us hugs when we needed them. Bobbie McLane, who is the director of the Garland County Historical Society, provided gracious and invaluable help with the project. Linda Pine, who is the head of Archives and Special Collections at the University of Arkansas at Little Rock, provided enthusiastic assistance and stimulating discussions.

Historian Greg Urwin at the University of Central Arkansas donated the use of his substantial files on the Civil War. Sammie Rose, who is coeditor of the *Boone County Historian*, graciously volunteered the fruits of her research before she had a chance to publish them herself and provided photographs from her personal collection. Carolyn Ann Joyce, director of the Fort Smith Convention and Visitors Bureau, provided the material on Miss Laura and a photograph from her personal collection.

Jeanne Clements, director of education at the Arkansas Oil and Brine Museum in Smackover, provided valuable help in sleuthing out interesting stories about the oil boom in Arkansas. G. Lamar Smith, the museum's archivist, helped locate photos from the museum's collection. My writing on the oil boom drew heavily from the scholarship of Don Lambert, who is the director of the Arkansas Oil and Brine Museum.

Director Lucille Westbrook and Magdalene Collums of the Southwest Arkansas Regional Archives provided enthusiastic assistance in researching information and photographs. Assistant director Mary Parsons and assistant librarian Manon Wilson of the Shiloh Museum of Ozark History in Springdale provided generous hospitality and help finding valuable photographs. Andrea Cantrell and her staff at the Research Services Department, Special Collections Division at the University of Arkansas Libraries in Fayetteville helped me locate useful information and photographs. Mary McGimsey at the University Museum in Fayetteville provided several photographs.

I am particularly indebted to Desmond Walls Allen, who is the editor of *Arkansas Historical and Genealogical Magazine*, for her intensive and insightful critique of the manuscript.

To these folks and to everyone else who helped with the project, I offer my heartfelt appreciation.

Readers who would like to learn more about Arkansas history will benefit from the section on recommending reading at the end of this book. More serious students of Arkansas history will enjoy reading the *Arkansas Historical Quarterly* and the many historical journals published by county historical societies throughout Arkansas. A number of community and county histories have been published locally as limited editions, and can be found in community or university libraries. Finally, the determined researcher will also benefit from visiting museum and university archives to seek out rare manuscripts and peruse microform copies of relevant Arkansas newspapers. Together, such sources provided much of the information that went into *Roadside History of Arkansas*. I offer my profound appreciation to all of the authors, amateur and professional historians, journalists, and archivists who made *Roadside History of Arkansas* possible. This book is merely a personalized synthesis of their work.

ABOUT THE AUTHOR

Al Paulson has lived in Arkansas since 1990. Before that he spent twenty-one years in Alaska, where he worked as a writer, editor, photographer, and biologist.

In 1977 Paulson was voted Alaskan Writer of the Year. He has written hundreds of articles on varied topics in science, art, and technology, including the historical aspects of those subjects. Museums have purchased his fine art photographs for their permanent collections, and fine art galleries continue to offer his images to the public. His wife and partner, Polly Walter, teaches journalism and photography at the University of Central Arkansas. Together, they are now working on *Roadside History of Alaska,* forthcoming from Mountain Press.

Paulson is a member of many professional organizations, including the Ozark Writers League and the Institute for Research on Small Arms in International Security. He asserts that his most satisfying adventure since moving to Arkansas has been the six years he spent researching and writing *Roadside History of Arkansas.* This is his second book.

ARKANSAS CHRONOLOGY

1541	Hernando de Soto begins exploring Arkansas
1643	Father Jacques Marquette and Louis Joliet explore the Mississippi River
1686	Henri de Tonti establishes *Poste d'Arkansas* (Arkansas Post)
1718	French establish New Orleans
1756	French and Indian War begins
1764	French establish St. Louis
1776	America declares independence from Britain
1803	Louisiana Purchase
1811	New Madrid earthquakes
1817	Cherokee council declares war on the Osage Nation
1817	U.S. Army establishes Fort Smith
1819	*Arkansas Gazette* becomes the first newspaper west of the Mississippi River
1819	Congress establishes Arkansas Territory
1820	The first steamboat lands in Arkansas
1832	President Andrew Jackson begins relocating all Indians to areas west of the Mississippi River
1836	Arkansas becomes the twenty-fifth state in the Union
1861	Arkansas secedes from the Union following outbreak of the Civil War
1862	Battle of Pea Ridge is the most significant Civil War battle fought west of the Mississippi
1863	Federal troops seize Fort Hindman
1863	Federal forces occupy Little Rock
1864	Arkansas ratifies a pro-Union constitution and abolishes slavery
1865	General Robert E. Lee surrenders at Appomattox
1872	Congress passes Amnesty Act, restoring voting rights to Confederate veterans
1874	Brooks-Baxter War
1874	New state constitution ratified

1875	Isaac Parker, the Hanging Judge, arrives in Fort Smith
1898	Father Pietro Bandini establishes Tontitown
1902	Parnell-Tucker feud erupts
1915	Legislature prohibits the sale of alcoholic beverages in Arkansas
1917	State legislature allows women to vote for the first time in a primary election
1919	Eighteenth Amendment to the U.S. Constitution prohibits the production and sale of alcoholic beverages in the United States
1919	Nineteenth Amendment to the U.S. Constitution allows women to vote in all elections
1921	Oil discovered in Arkansas
1929	Stock market crash starts the Great Depression
1935	Liquor sales again become legal in Arkansas
1950	Sam Walton, founder of Wal-Mart, opens his first store in Bentonville
1957	Central High in Little Rock is desegregated
1958	Daisy Manufacturing Company moves from Michigan to Rogers
1966	Winthrop Rockefeller wins gubernatorial election
1974	Arkansas Nuclear One begins commercial production of electricity
1978	Bill Clinton wins his first gubernatorial election
1980	Bill Clinton loses his bid for reelection
1981	The flawless 6.25 carat Newman diamond discovered at Crater of Diamonds State Park
1982	Bill Clinton returns to the governor's mansion
1991	*Arkansas Gazette* goes out of business
1992	Bill Clinton wins U.S. presidential election
1996	Governor Jim Guy Tucker resigns after being convicted on two felony counts of mail fraud and conspiracy
1996	Bill Clinton wins a second term to the U.S. presidency

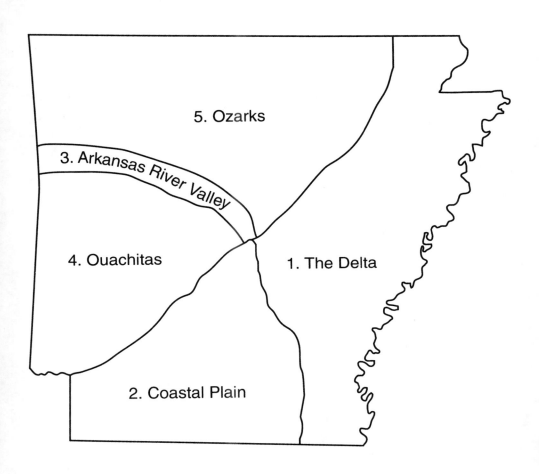

An Introduction to Arkansas
—Its Land and People—

Arkansas is a beautiful land with a rich, if turbulent, history. The state can be viewed as highlands and lowlands. Similarly, the pioneers who settled here can be viewed as highlanders and lowlanders, who had different lifestyles and different aspirations from the 1830s onward. These differences, in large measure, drove the ebb and flow of Arkansas history.

Roadside History of Arkansas tells the story of the Natural State, from the establishment of the earliest permanent outpost along the Mississippi River—through territorial days, statehood, secession, and civil war—to the rise of modern corporate moguls such as Don Tyson and Sam Walton. Since this book is part of the Roadside History series, these diverse and compelling stories are tied to particular spots along the highways and waterways of Arkansas. For the most part, these stories are told as community histories. Historic places are grouped into tours of manageable size, and the tours are grouped into five regions of highlands and lowlands. The chapter on each region begins with a map showing all of the tours, highways, and communities discussed in that region. This is not a stodgy academic history heavily salted with formal citations of primary sources. Rather, my goal has been to write good history in a gentler style, spiced with carefully selected smidgeons of folklore.

Before striking out on the roadways of Arkansas, let's look at a general picture of the highlands and lowlands, the Indians who once thrived in the region, and the settlers who transformed a wilderness into the Natural State.

—THE LAND—

Admitted to the Union in 1836, Arkansas became the twenty-fifth state and is now the twenty-seventh largest state. About the same size as Alabama or Wisconsin, Arkansas covers 53,104 square miles, or roughly 34 million acres.

Roadside History of Arkansas is subdivided into five geographic regions based on the state's topography: the Delta, the Coastal Plain, the Arkansas River Valley, the Ouachitas, and the Ozarks. Understanding the land provides the foundation for understanding the ebb and flow of history generated by the pioneers who settled here.

Arkansans refer to the lowlands in the eastern third of their state as "the Delta." From a geological perspective, however, this area is not a true delta but rather the alluvial plain of the Mississippi River. Not just a feature of Arkansas, the Mississippi Alluvial Plain actually extends from Missouri to Louisiana. While the Delta is flat and poorly drained, its rich soil proved ideal for the cultivation of cotton, as planters and ambitious farmers turned their eyes westward to Arkansas Territory in the early 1800s.

The Coastal Plain occupies the southern portion of Arkansas, south of the Ouachita Mountains and west of Bayou Bartholomew. These lowlands are actually part of the West Gulf Coastal Plain, which extends south through Texas and Louisiana to the Gulf of Mexico. The terrain ranges from flatlands and rolling hills of sand, gravel, and clay to the rich bottomlands of the Red, Ouachita, and Saline Rivers. It was these bottomlands that first attracted cotton planters to Arkansas.

The Arkansas River Valley slices through the Arkansas highlands, separating the Boston Mountains of the Ozarks from the Fourche Mountains of the Ouachitas. The valley averages thirty to forty miles in width through the mountains, and then continues through the foothills to open onto the Mississippi Alluvial Plain at Little Rock. The soils and topography of the valley vary widely, ranging from fertile bottomlands to the rocky slopes of Magazine Mountain, the highest point in the state. The Arkansas River was a major artery into Arkansas and points west until the advent of the railroad, so the history of this valley really encompasses the march of people, politics, and change between the highlands and lowlands of Arkansas, and between the western frontier and the states east of the Mississippi River.

The Ouachita highlands occupy the west-central portion of Arkansas between the Arkansas River Valley and the West Gulf Coastal Plain. The ridges and valleys of these highlands trend east-west from the Mississippi Alluvial Plain into Oklahoma. The Fourche Mountains occupy the northern portion of these highlands, the Ouachita Mountains stand in the central portion, and the Athens Plateau lies in the southern portion. The soils support rich stands of timber but quickly become infertile when subjected to cultivation.

The Ozark highlands rise in the northwestern part of Arkansas north of the Arkansas River Valley and west of the Mississippi Alluvial Plain. But the Ozarks are not merely a feature of northern Arkansas. The Ozarks stretch across much of southern Missouri, all or part of eight counties in northeastern Oklahoma, and a wee bit of

Cherokee County in southeastern Kansas. While the Ozark Mountains may be small compared to the Rockies, they are a great deal older. The Boston Mountains border the Arkansas River Valley, and the Springfield Plateau occupies the central and northwestern portion of the Ozarks in Arkansas, while the Salem Plateau extends northward from the Springfield Plateau to the Missouri border.

For the most part, the relatively infertile soils of the highlands support stands of timber but not sustained agriculture. Therefore, the area tended to attract fiercely independent hunters and subsistence farmers rather than land speculators, social climbers, and pioneers with aspirations to raising cotton and other market crops on large farms and plantations. The fertile lands near Fayetteville, however, did attract cotton farmers for a time.

—THE PEOPLE—

The earliest pioneers found a land rich with game and promise. Relatively few Indians lived in the area, so settlers faced little competition for land and resources. Yet Arkansas was once *densely* populated by impressive Indian civilizations with large communities and well-developed agriculture, when the first European explorers ventured into the area. It is hard to overstate the impact of those first few Europeans, for they waged high-tech war and brought with them dangerous diseases.

Spanish steel and pestilence together wiped out perhaps 90 percent of the Indian population in the years following Hernando de Soto's arrival in 1541. So many Indians perished during this apocalypse that the population in Arkansas did not rebound to its earlier level for centuries. If Charles Bolton correctly estimates the precontact Indian population at 75,000, then the Arkansas population did not return to previous levels until 1840. If Elliot West is correct in accepting de Soto's estimates as accurate, then the modern population did not equal the former Indian population until the twentieth century—perhaps as late as 1950.

Pioneers

Spanish and French trappers and traders who maintained a small station usually known as Arkansas Post had a long history in Arkansas. But the first significant wave of permanent settlers in the Arkansas wilderness prior to 1840 came from the highlands of Scotland, Ireland, and Wales via Tennessee, Kentucky, and other southern states. Few came from northern states, and few were born in foreign countries. Their highland Celtic culture was both distinctive and well adapted to the requirements of life on the frontier. In fact, these high-landers had long provided the pioneers for opening up the lands east of the Mississippi River.

Grady McWhiney, in his book *Cracker Culture*, describes these Celtic highlanders as clannish people who loved whiskey, gambling, hunting, and fighting. They preferred the leisurely raising of livestock to labor-intensive agriculture. And they despised fences, almost anything to do with government, and everything English. These traits characterized the highlanders of Arkansas in the early 1800s. Furthermore, McWhiney suggests that these values became the foundation for white culture throughout the South during the antebellum years.

It is interesting to note that many Indians of the antebellum South practiced lifestyles that were remarkably similar to those of the Celtic highlanders who pioneered places like Arkansas. John Dederer points out that African tribal culture and folk traits strongly resembled Celtic clan culture and folk traits as well. He makes a persuasive case that these similarities enabled slaves to "fit Celtic characteristics around their African practices" with little adaptation. Some authors suggest that white southern pioneers had more in common with their Indian and African neighbors than with the English and European residents of the northern states.

I should point out that the Celtic culture of the Old South should be compared only to the culture of British Celts *before 1800*. Most of the emigration from Ireland, Scotland, and Wales to the Old South took place before that date. Moreover, Celtic culture in the British Isles began to change profoundly in the late 1700s. This change was driven by an aggressive English program to "civilize" and subjugate the rebellious Celts once and for all, after many centuries of border conflicts and full-scale wars. So do not equate *modern* Celtic culture with the Celtic culture of the pioneers who pushed the American frontier westward.

Most Celtic pioneers came to Arkansas for cheap land and the opportunity for a better life. But their lives were dominated by two other sorts of people who also looked upon Arkansas Territory as a land of opportunity. Land speculators and swindlers quickly tied up the best agricultural lands in the lowlands, using family connections and outright fraud as necessary. Others with more wit and ambition than financial resources saw opportunity in terms of politics, which provided a fast track to upward mobility, power, and profit. But most pioneers were simply single men and young families looking for cheap land. Relatively few wealthy planters moved west to Arkansas, with the exception of some Virginians who settled in the Red River Valley.

Hunter-trappers, livestock raisers, and subsistence farmers spread throughout Arkansas. This was a time of tremendous economic opportunity and peril. Some people made fortunes. Others lost fortunes. Most carved a good life out of the wilderness and saw at least the possibility of significant upward mobility.

By the 1830s, when Arkansas became a state, cheap government land (which included former Indian lands) spawned a large influx of farmers who began to amass large farms and slaves for the large-scale production of cotton. The aspirations and lifestyles of highlanders and lowlanders rapidly diverged.

Highlanders Versus Lowlanders

The highlanders developed small but prosperous subsistence farms, raising diversified crops, hogs, and a few cattle. Few of these farmers had slaves, and the lifestyle of highlanders who had slaves differed little from that of their neighbors who had none. They raised a surplus, but few marketed their goods in places like New Orleans because transportation was not available to the highlanders. Based upon taxable property, the highlanders held their wealth primarily as land and livestock.

The lowlanders built larger farms and raised cotton as a cash crop. They also ran larger cattle herds than the highlanders, although cattle raising gradually declined in favor of cotton cultivation. Both the lowlanders and highlanders raised corn and potatoes for their own use. Based on taxable property, the lowlanders held their wealth primarily as land and slaves.

The differences between highlanders and lowlanders started to become volatile upon the attainment of statehood, when Arkansans had to draft a state constitution. Since more voters (free white males) lived in the highlands than in the lowlands, the lowlanders feared they would be dominated politically by the highlanders. In reality, that was quite unlikely.

By 1836 the planters had influence far beyond their numbers. Planters constituted only 1 percent of the population, but they provided 16 percent of the constitutional delegates. Slaveholders constituted 19 percent of the population, yet they provided 73 percent of the delegates. The lowlanders argued that they held most of the state's wealth and most of the population when the slaves were factored in. They argued that the highlanders and lowlanders should get an equal number of senators in the state legislature. This apportionment plan, based on the "principal of sectional equality," became incorporated into the constitution.

The lowlanders used this arrangement to consolidate an increasing share of political power during the coming decades. Eventually, this power enabled the planters and other slaveholders to vote for secession from the Union.

Shelby Foote has said that the Civil War fundamentally defined who we are as Americans. This is even more true in terms of defining who we are as Arkansans. Arkansas was a land of tremendous opportunity for upward social and financial mobility before the war. The average income level in Arkansas was higher than half of the thirty-four states in the Union, including fourteen Northern states. The war took 600,000 American lives and destroyed the Southern economy.

By 1880, the average Southerner was earning less than half as much as the average Northerner. The average Arkansan earned even less. Known as a land of opportunity before the rebellion, Arkansas became a land without opportunity after the war. That was one factor that helped foster a somewhat negative national impression of Arkansas.

It can be argued that Arkansas never recovered economically from the Civil War. Even by 1940, the average Arkansan earned a mere 43 percent of the national average income. Many Arkansans left the state during World War II to work in defense plants in northern and western states. The postrebellion perception of Arkansas remained unchanged, as suggested by *Readers Digest* in late 1945. The magazine's humor section reported on a sign allegedly posted in a northern defense plant: "One pair of shoes for sale. Owner returning to Arkansas."

While the income of Arkansans improved considerably between World War II and 1970, the average income has since stagnated at about 74 percent of the national average. Only three states have lower average incomes. Many Arkansans believe the state's economy has always been poor, yet Arkansas was a land of dynamic economic opportunity before 1860. In recent decades, Arkansas has spawned a number of corporate success stories, demonstrating that the state can still be a land of opportunity. The late Sam Walton, for example, built his Bentonville dime store into a national empire of Sam's Wholesale Clubs and Wal-Marts. This likeable Arkansan became the wealthiest man in the United States. In 1993 Wal-Mart created more new jobs than any company in the nation. That same year, the forty-second governor of Arkansas, Bill Clinton, took the oath of office as the forty-second president of the United States. Arkansas is finally shaking off the residual effects of the Lost Cause.

The state's substantial economic progress in the 1950s and 1960s set the stage for a cultural revival that began in the Ozarks and spread throughout the lowlands. Arkansans began to rediscover their rich heritage and to share that history proudly with the world through facilities such as Old Washington Historic State Park and the Delta Cultural Center. *Roadside History of Arkansas* is a celebration of that rich heritage.

—Part One—
THE DELTA

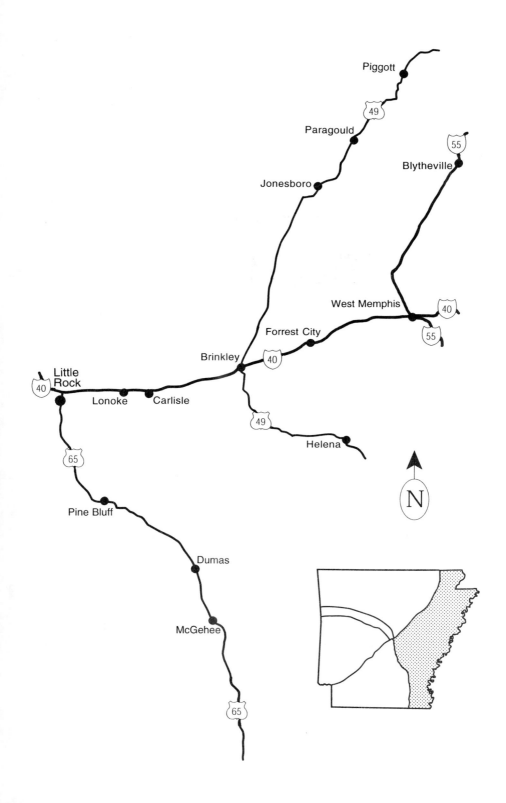

Louisiana State Line–Little Rock
149 miles

US 65 provides a popular route to Little Rock for folks traveling north from eastern Louisiana and for Arkansas snowbirds heading to Florida for their winter vacations. The Arkansas portion of US 65 generally parallels Bayou Bartholomew, which winds through the Delta a few miles west of the highway. The bayou was once the route of the Arkansas River, when the Mississippi ran down the present course of the Arkansas. Approximately 300 miles long, the bayou extends from Pine Bluff to southwest of Wilmot, where it enters Louisiana and then joins the Ouachita River. Bartholomew is probably the longest bayou in the world.

Bayou Bartholomew figured prominently in the early European history of the area, since it bisected what was then known as the Great Wilderness. Many early settlements were established along the bayou. While many settlers were subsistence farmers, others planted cotton in the rich bottomlands. Some of these villages faded away when the

Sharecropper in the 1930s. –Arkansas History Commission

11

railroads came to southern Arkansas in the 1890s and early 1900s, and country folk moved to the railroad towns for cash employment in the young timber industry or in local stores. Scores of towns dried up throughout southern Arkansas along the bayou, including Bartholomew (near Boydell), Hawkins Landing (near Wilmot), Holly Point (north of Parkdale), and Lightfoot (near Wilmot). Some bayou towns survived.

The origin of the bayou's name is shrouded in mystery. The term *bayou* is commonly used throughout Arkansas, Louisiana, and Mississippi to denote a stream of dead water, with little or no observable current. (Thus the term is incorrectly used in the name *Polk Bayou*, which is a swift stream near Batesville.) *Bayou* comes from the French word *bayouc*, which has the same definition as the English word. Some people suggest that *bayouc*, in turn, may be a corruption of the French word *boyau*, which means gut (or, by extension, a long narrow passage). But *bayouc* was probably an adaptation of the Choctaw word *bayuk*, which meant a stream of dead water.

While the word *bayou* probably came to us from the Choctaws via the French, Bayou Bartholomew was probably named after French trapper Joseph Bartolomé, who had an Indian wife and six children in the area during the 1760s.

The Arkansas portion of US 65 also passes near the site of Arkansas Post, which was the first European settlement in the lower reaches of the Mississippi valley. Even older than New Orleans, Arkansas Post played a key strategic role on the western frontier from the 1600s until the Civil War, spawning a number of battles for control of this important outpost throughout this period. Then, as the fortunes of Arkansas Post began to wane, Pine Bluff emerged as the new power on the lower reaches of the Arkansas River.

This part of the Arkansas story begins, however, with the history of a railroad town that appeared near the Louisiana border in the early days of the twentieth century.

—McGEHEE—

Located 105 miles southeast of Little Rock and 44 miles north of Louisiana on US 65, McGehee is named after Abner McGehee, who came to Arkansas from Alabama in 1858 at the age of seven. While his father was one of the most successful planters in Desha County, Abner became even more successful. By 1889 Abner McGehee owned over 12,000 acres, producing cotton, corn, cattle, and hogs. After building a cotton gin, McGehee also opened a mercantile. He founded the town in 1905 along the route of the Memphis, Helena & Louisiana Railway, which was completed in 1906. The train refueled at McGehee, and

The Arkansas River flooded McGehee and many other communities in 1927. McGehee continued to suffer floods into the 1990s. –Arkansas History Commission

passengers ate dinner at Colonel McGehee's plantation home. Railroad shops performed maintenance on the railroad stock and provided an additional economic base for the town.

–DUMAS–

Located eighty-six miles southeast of Little Rock and sixty-three miles north of Louisiana on US 65, Dumas is named after W. B. Dumas, who was the county surveyor. Dumas purchased a large tract of land in 1851 for $1.25 an acre, where he built a general store and cotton gin. This served as the nucleus for a small agricultural town, which was eventually incorporated in 1904. The town's baseball team inspired a popular ragtime tune in the 1920s, "Ding Dong Daddy from Dumas." The Desha County Museum is located in town on Arkansas 54. Most of the area's history, however, was written just to the northwest of Dumas at Arkansas Post, on the eastern bank of the Arkansas River.

A woman picking cotton in the Delta, circa 1938. –Arkansas History Commission

—ARKANSAS POST—

Arkansas Post National Monument sits about eighteen miles northeast of Dumas via US 165 and Arkansas 169 on the highlands called *Écores Rouges* (Red Bluffs) by the French. The monument commemorates the first permanent European settlement in the lower reaches of the Mississippi River valley.

Established by Henri de Tonti as a French trading post in 1686, *Poste d'Arkansas* was born before New Orleans and Natchez. Arkansas Post was more of an idea than a place, changing its location at least six times when changing circumstances or a rambunctious river mandated a move. Yet Arkansas Post played a major role in controlling the vast interior of the continent for nearly two centuries, as its ownership and mission evolved. Battles were fought from well before the Revolutionary War to the Civil War for control of this strategic outpost. Remarkably, this important chapter in American history remains largely unknown.

To understand the forces that led to the establishment of *Poste d'Arkansas*, it is necessary to understand the struggle among three major European powers for control of the Mississippi valley during the seventeenth and eighteenth centuries: France, Spain, and Britain.

14

This rivalry remained unresolved until a newly established power—the United States—occupied the region in the nineteenth century.

The Spanish initially claimed both North and South America, and the pope sanctioned these claims. In 1539, Spanish explorer Hernando de Soto left Florida with 600 men, 200 horses, fighting dogs, and a drove of hogs in search of gold. The Spaniards dealt harshly with the tribes they encountered, killing at least 4,000 Indians along the way. The frequent fights depleted de Soto's forces by the time they reached the banks of the Mississippi River, which he called the *Rio Grande*. The Spaniards crossed into what is now Arkansas a few miles south of present-day Memphis in May 1541, according to the scholarship of Charles Hudson.

The Spaniards explored into the Ouachita Mountains in a vain attempt to find native villages rich with mineral wealth. They circled back toward the Mississippi River, where de Soto died from a fever on June 20, 1542. After an abortive attempt to reach New Spain

Hernando de Soto and party on the banks of the Mississippi. —H. L. Stephens drawing, Arkansas History Commission

(Mexico) through Texas, the survivors of de Soto's expedition returned to the Mississippi and spent the first half of the following year building boats so they could descend to the Gulf of Mexico and continue on to New Spain. The Spaniards finally left Arkansas in June 1543. About three months later, 311 survivors reached a Spanish settlement near present-day Tampico, Mexico. The Spanish explorers of this era left no permanent settlements anywhere in the Mississippi River valley. It would be 130 years before Europeans visited Arkansas again.

Spain was having trouble consolidating its hold on claims throughout the vast area of North and South America. So France occupied eastern Canada, and Britain occupied the eastern coast of the northern continent, while Spain struggled to keep control of Florida and Mexico. England then began to push westward toward the Mississippi valley, and France began to push southward from the Great Lakes into what would become Ohio and Illinois.

The French would soon provide the first permanent European presence in what is now Arkansas. Unlike the Spaniards, the French did not come as conquerors. The typical pattern of French settlement started out with a few explorers who would make friends with the Indians. They would be followed by a small number of trappers, traders, priests—and perhaps a handful of soldiers. The first *Français* to reach Arkansas were a trapper and a priest.

Les Français

Father Jacques Marquette and Louis Joliet began exploring the Mississippi River in 1643 with two large canoes and five men. Joliet was interested in establishing fur trade, and Marquette wanted to convert new tribes to Catholicism. The explorers also hoped to find a water route through the continent to the Indies. The Illinois Indians gave *les Français* a long-stemmed pipe made of red stone as a kind of passport to guarantee safe passage through the territories of other tribes. The French called the stone passport a "calumet," or peace pipe.

The Illinois Indians, who spoke Algonkian, called the downstream tribes the Akensa (or Akensea or Akemsea), which meant the "Downstreamers." When the Frenchmen finally met the Downstreamers, they learned that the tribe called itself the Ugakhpa. The neighboring Osage tribe called them the U-Ga-Xpa, which meant the "Pushed Off the Hill People." These latter names evolved into "Quapaw."

The Quapaw told the French explorers they were only ten or twelve days from the mouth of the Mississippi, which did not empty into the Pacific Ocean or Sea of Cortez. As disappointing as that news was,

Quapaw warrior, circa 1700, from a drawing by Charles Banks Wilson.
—University of Arkansas Fayetteville Museum

the Quapaw also warned that the explorers were very close to Spanish lands. That spelled danger to the Frenchmen, so they returned upriver to Canada. Marquette lost his notes and the map he had made when his canoe overturned, so he prepared his report from memory. That report inspired René-Robert Cavelier, Sieur de La Salle, to launch an expedition to secure the entire Mississippi River valley for the king of France. Perhaps he could even challenge the Spanish for control of the mouth of the mighty river. In any event, he could establish a highly profitable fur trade with the Indians of the vast region.

La Salle launched his fifty-man expedition in 1682. His lieutenant, Henri de Tonti, was an Italian by birth. After receiving a friendly reception in what is now Arkansas, two Quapaw guides led the

17

Henri de Tonti. In 1686 he established the French Poste d'Arkansas, *which preceded the settlements of New Orleans and Natchez.*
—Arkansas History Commission

Frenchmen to the mouth of the Mississippi. La Salle returned to France to stage a larger, two-pronged expedition to the Mississippi. La Salle planned to sail to the mouth of the Mississippi and work his way upriver while Tonti headed downriver again from Canada.

Tonti eventually made it back to the land of the Quapaw. La Salle didn't. He sailed past the mouth of the Mississippi, and a storm wrecked his ship off the Texas coast. La Salle marched the survivors eastward toward the Mississippi until his disgruntled men murdered him. Meanwhile, Tonti bivouacked near the future site of St. Louis and waited for word from La Salle for two years. Then he set out to find his boss.

When Tonti once again reached the realm of the friendly Quapaw, he took advantage of La Salle's permission to claim a large amount of land for himself around the mouth of the Arkansas River. He set up a fort and trading post twenty-seven miles above the confluence of the Arkansas and Mississippi Rivers. Tonti called his settlement *Poste d'Arkansas*—Arkansas Post. Leaving six men at the first European settlement on the west bank of the Mississippi, Tonti returned to Canada and then to France, where he learned of La Salle's death.

The king of France was preoccupied with a war in Europe, so France did not send a lot of settlers to solidify its claim to the Mississippi. The French did, however, try to head off English and Spanish claims by establishing several settlements along the Gulf Coast, including Mobile in 1702 and New Orleans in 1718. The French also established a trading post on the Mississippi in 1764, which they called St. Louis.

Poste d'Arkansas never attracted many settlers during this period. Throughout the first half of the 1700s, the settlement averaged perhaps fifty hunters, trappers, traders, and their families—plus a dozen or so slaves. The adjacent fort averaged a dozen soldiers. During this time, British traders pushed deeper into the Mississippi valley and began to exert influence on the Choctaws and Chickasaws, who became increasingly hostile toward the French in Arkansas. The Quapaw remained quite friendly.

A Chickasaw raiding party of 150 braves attacked and destroyed the French settlement in 1749, killing six men and taking eight women and children prisoner. The Chickasaws then attacked the nearby fort, but the dozen soldiers garrisoned there drove off the attack. The French promptly reinforced *Poste d'Arkansas* with fifty soldiers, as part of a larger plan to reinforce the Louisiana Territory with about

Arkansas Post. –Arkansas History Commission

19

2,000 troops. The fifty soldiers stationed in Arkansas managed to repulse an attack by the Osages late in 1752. Then the French and Indian War erupted (also called the Seven Years' War, since it lasted from 1756 to 1763), pitting the French and their Indian allies against the British colonists. The Spaniards sided with the French too late to influence the course of the war, which the British won.

Besides the problems with pro-British Indians, the French settlement had a running battle with floods created by high waters in the Arkansas, White, and Mississippi Rivers. The original post was destroyed by flooding, so the French moved their settlement closer to the Mississippi to better function as a trading post. The new *Poste d'Arkansas* lay ten miles above the Mississippi, where repeated flooding destroyed crops and rotted wooden structures. After the terrible Chickasaw raid destroyed the settlement in 1749, Arkansas Post moved back upriver, and then relocated again even farther upriver in 1752. The settlement at that time included five cabins, and the walled-in fort measured 180 feet on a side. While the houses were built on posts to protect them from flooding, the structures had decayed into ruin by 1758. Arkansas Post moved again, this time very close to the Mississippi at a place known as Napoleon Landing. Here, the French rebuilt *Poste d'Arkansas* just in time for France to lose its war against the British colonists.

In that war, France lost its American empire. The Treaty of Paris granted all lands east of the Mississippi to the British. Facing bankruptcy at home, the French government ceded all lands west of the Mississippi to Spain, ostensibly as compensation for Spain's loss of Florida to the British during the war. In reality, Louisiana had cost the French government 800,000 livres a year without returning a single sou to the treasury, so this was a convenient excuse to rid the government of a serious financial burden. An intangible result of the French defeat was that it freed the British colonials from their fear of French encirclement. Now these American colonists could turn their undivided attention to confronting the British government over their rightful relationship to the Crown.

Spain now owned Louisiana, which included the land of the Quapaw and Arkansas Post. Word of the new Spanish control of the area took two years to reach Louisiana, and the first Spanish officer did not reach Arkansas Post for five years.

Los Españoles

Little changed in Louisiana when the first Spanish governor, Antonio de Ulloa, arrived in New Orleans. Since a big part of his task was to cultivate friendship with the Indians, the Spaniards adopted the

French method of controlling the tribes through licensed traders and purchasing the loyalty of important Indian leaders with gifts. Governor Ulloa sent twenty-three Spanish soldiers to occupy Arkansas Post under the command of Captain Alexandre DeClouet, who had been a French officer. Spain employed many former members of the French army in Louisiana, but the Spaniards changed the garrison's name from Arkansas Post to Fort San Carlos III, after the king of Spain.

When the Spaniards reached Arkansas Post in 1768, the settlement had about 140 residents. They discovered a strong Anglo-American presence on the east bank of the Mississippi. European wars and diseases had reduced the number of the Quapaws, allowing the fierce Osages to push their territory closer to the outpost on the Arkansas.

As soon as Spanish Captain Fernando de Leyba assumed command of the post in 1771, he found himself facing increasing depredation by the Osages. After several hunters died at the hands of the Osages, Leyba began to fear that an attack on the post was only a matter of time. Besides trying to protect local hunters, trappers, and traders from the Osages, the soldiers were also required to intercept and arrest any British hunters or traders west of the Mississippi. While the commanders of Fort San Carlos changed repeatedly over the years, the central reality did not. The garrison simply did not have the manpower to control the Osages or to keep British adventurers from penetrating the White and St. Francis Rivers, much less maintain the fort. The garrison decayed into an appalling state of disrepair, even as British pressure on the area increased.

The British established a trading post on the eastern shore of the Mississippi, just opposite the mouth of the Arkansas River. Called Concord or Concordia, the settlement consisted of hunters and trappers who subverted the local Indians by supplying them with abundant merchandise. While their incursions into the lands west of the Mississippi provided considerable heartburn to the Spanish garrison at Fort San Carlos (Arkansas Post), the Spaniards made no move directly against Concordia.

British pirate James Willing, however, had no compunctions about direct confrontation. Willing pillaged Concordia's eighteen huts in 1778, driving the survivors away. The hunters and trappers returned, but then fire destroyed the settlement, and the British abandoned the place once and for all.

Meanwhile, the grievances of the American colonials against the British Crown had erupted into violence at Lexington and Concord in 1775. British colonials declared their independence in 1776, spawning the American Revolution. Since France and Spain had substantial grievances against Britain, they declared war on Britain too. As a

Spanish garrison, this technically pitted Arkansas Post against any British forces in the Mississippi River valley. But the fort's new commandant, Captain Balthazard de Villiers, had become more concerned with the frequent flooding of his outpost than the prospect of fighting the British.

Captain de Villiers wrote his boss, the Spanish governor of Louisiana, that "*Écores Rouges*, nine leagues from here seems to be the most propitious place [for relocating the fort]. On the edge of a vast plain, the inhabitants, families of hunters and others who would be protected, would voluntarily go there to establish a land which would produce for the state, excellent tobacco, as good wheat as the Illinois, and for them all the advantages of life."

When the governor failed to reply, de Villiers wrote another letter complaining about the flooding every spring. This time he also emphasized that the settlement was much inconvenienced by not being close to the Quapaw village. The governor finally agreed, and the outpost moved to the left bank of *Écores Rouges* in March 1779, on a curve of the river that formed three shores.

The Quapaws settled on one bank. British-American settlers occupied another. And the Spanish-Americans established their fort on the third shore, which featured a slight prominence that enhanced the fort's defenses. Actually building the fort took several years, with the funding coming from the settlers themselves rather than from the Spanish government. About eighty hunters and local residents formed a militia in the summer of 1780 to protect the outpost. The fort was not completed when war erupted in the Mississippi valley between Spain and Britain.

War erupted in the Mississippi valley the following year, when British residents in the Natchez district revolted against Spanish rule. Later, Tory sympathizer James Colbert captured a Spanish flatboat on the Mississippi, seizing passengers, money, and supplies. Colbert, a trader who had lived with the Indians for years and held the rank of captain in the British army, launched a series of raids against Spanish trading interests in the Mississippi valley using a force comprised mainly of Chickasaws.

By this time Captain de Villiers had died, the official name of Arkansas Post had become Fort Charles III, and the temporary garrison commander—Lieutenant Louis de Villars—proceeded to upgrade the defenses of the outpost. Eventually, Captain Jacobo Dubreuil assumed command of the garrison, and Lieutenant de Villars became his second in command. The garrison included a complement of two officers, sixty-seven soldiers, and several cannon when a storm destroyed the lieutenant's hut and four others inside the fort. The lieutenant moved his family into the unfortified village, just four days before Colbert's 130 raiders hit Arkansas Post without warning.

Colbert's Raid

Colbert's raiders arrived several miles below Fort Charles III early on the morning of April 17, 1783. They marched to *Écores Rouges* and slipped into the settlement about 2:30 A.M. without alerting a ten-man patrol. They seized Lieutenant de Villars and his family, but a shot alerted the patrol, which attacked the more numerous raiders. Colbert's men killed two members of the patrol and scalped one of them. The raiders also wounded a soldier and a slave and took six soldiers prisoner. Sergeant Alejo Pastor managed to fight off three raiders and dive through a gun port into the safety of the fort.

The gunfire alerted Captain Dubreuil and the rest of the garrison, but the fight outside the walls was so confused that the garrison troops couldn't fire for fear of hitting their own people. Within a half hour the raiders had withdrawn to a ravine about "a half cannon shot" away from the fort. The raiders quickly reorganized and attacked the oak stockade, trying to batter down the gate. The fort responded with cannon and musket fire. The battle raged for six hours.

By 9 A.M., the defenders had fired their cannon about 300 times and the Spanish troops had fired their muskets so many times that they had expended nearly all of their powder and ball. While the enemy musket balls penetrated only an inch into the oak stockade, the depleted stock of Spanish munitions—combined with Dubreuil's fear that the British were about to bring up cannon—suggested that a more aggressive defense was now required. Captain Dubreuil asked for volunteers to counterattack. Ten Spanish soldiers and four Quapaws (who happened to be in the fort at the time of the attack) stepped forward. Under the command of Sergeant Pastor, the volunteers stormed out of the fort screaming like Indians on the warpath.

The lively covering fire from the stockade abruptly died almost as soon as it began when Señora María Luisa Vallé de Villars (the lieutenant's wife) appeared with one of Colbert's officers under a white flag. The fusillade and war cries frightened off the officer, allowing the Spanish to bring Señora de Villars into the fort. She delivered a message from the raiders.

Colbert claimed to have a force that included 500 Chickasaws, two boatloads of British militia, one cannon, and four swivel guns. If Captain Dubreuil did not surrender the fort by noon, Colbert warned that he would destroy the outpost. Furthermore, Colbert said he would kill all of his prisoners if the Quapaws from the neighboring village attacked in support of the Spaniards. That message, however, reflected

Colbert's views before the counterattack that rescued Señora de Villars. The war cries of Sergeant Pastor's volunteers had so frightened Colbert's men that they abandoned the ravine and fled downriver with their prisoners toward their boats. Pastor continued the fight until Colbert released the women and children he had taken prisoner. Colbert then launched his boats, taking the remaining prisoners with him.

Chief Angaska of the Quapaws did not appear at the fort until several hours after the fighting was over. Dubreuil complained about the lack of help. The chief replied that his men had been afield hunting, and considerable time had been required to assemble his warriors. The Quapaws then pursued the retreating raiders and caught up with them near the mouth of the Arkansas River. The chief intimidated Colbert into releasing Lieutenant de Villars and almost all of the remaining prisoners, including nine people taken during the capture of a pirogue (a large freight canoe). But Colbert kept four Spanish soldiers, the son of Ansemo Layones, and three slaves. The Quapaws did not attack because of the remaining hostages, thus ending the only battle of the American War of Independence fought west of the Mississippi River. A final touch of irony is that the battle for Arkansas Post was fought after the war officially ended in January 1783, following the British surrender at Yorktown.

During the decades following the war, a strong rivalry developed between the Americans and the Spaniards for domination of the lower Mississippi valley. Meanwhile, the French Revolution led to the rise of Napoleon, who had become the virtual master of Europe by the end of the century. Spain gave Louisiana back to France, and Napoleon promptly sold Louisiana to the Americans in 1803.

The American Years

Under U.S. dominion, Arkansas Post began to play a much more important role than it ever had under the French and Spaniards. By 1805 the settlement included a trading post, sixty to seventy families, and sixty slaves. The settlement's most important period began in 1819, when Arkansas Post became the capital of Arkansas Territory and the *Arkansas Gazette* was established there, becoming the first newspaper west of the Mississippi River. (The *Gazette* remained the oldest newspaper west of the Mississippi until its demise on October 18, 1991.)

The settlement's heyday lasted only a few years. The territorial capital moved to Cadron briefly and then to Little Rock. The *Arkansas Gazette* moved to Little Rock, too. Nevertheless, Arkansas Post remained an important garrison, port, and postal center.

When Arkansas seceded from the Union in 1861, the Confederates dramatically improved the fortifications and reinforced the garrison with 3,000 men. In January 1863, Union gunboats and 30,000 troops crushed Confederate resistance and obliterated the post.

Then a rambunctious Arkansas River washed the site away. The visitor's center at Arkansas Post National Monument provides a fascinating glimpse into the rich history of this important outpost on the colonial and early American frontier. History buffs will also want to visit the Arkansas Post County Museum, a few miles northeast of Dumas via US 165 and Arkansas 1. Established in 1960, this was the first county-supported museum in Arkansas. Exhibits span local history from the Stone Age to the present day.

When Arkansas Post's importance as a port began to wane, the fortunes of Pine Bluff began to eclipse its older rival to the south. Perched on bluffs that rise above a deep bend in the Arkansas River, Pine Bluff sits at a natural geographic boundary between the sweeping oak and pine forests of the Coastal Plain to the west and the wide expanse of cotton fields that dominated the Delta to the east for generations.

—PINE BLUFF—

Located 42 miles southwest of Little Rock and 107 miles north of the Louisiana border on US 65, Pine Bluff's history and culture suggest that the community has closer ties to the Delta than the more northerly reaches of the Arkansas River valley or the forested Gulf Coastal Plain to the west.

The first settler of the area was Joseph Bonne, whose father was French and mother was Quapaw. When the spring flood of 1819 devastated the farming community of New Gascony, Joseph Bonne became quite discouraged. He left his wife, Mary, and their children in the care of his father-in-law, François Imbeau, a prosperous farmer capable of providing safe and comfortable accommodations to the Bonne family indefinitely. Bonne then loaded his canoe and paddled up the Arkansas River in search of higher ground. He pitched a wigwam under one of the few oaks in a forest of giant pines.

When the water receded, Bonne discovered that his camp sat atop a bluff overlooking the river. Soon the bluff erupted with flowers as well as muscadine grapevines, making the campsite an attractive location for a permanent home. Bonne built a cabin before the onset of winter, then relocated his wife and children to their new home.

Joseph Bonne got along very well with the Quapaw. Not only had his mother belonged to that tribe, but he had served as the translator during negotiations for the Quapaw Treaty of 1818, which he signed. Bonne set up a trading post on the high, dry ground atop the bluff. Most European Americans who visited the bluff for the first few years were hunters and trappers. Soon, settlers began to appear and the little community became known as Mount Marie. Most of the newcomers cleared the land and began to raise cotton.

When the territorial legislature created Jefferson County (in honor of Thomas Jefferson) out of Arkansas and Pulaski Counties in 1829, the legislators established the temporary county seat at the home of Joseph Bonne, until the residents of the county could find a permanent location. The county seat then moved three miles below the bluff to the home of Antoine Barraque, a planter who had fought under Napoleon and then came to the land of the Quapaws as a trader.

That same year, the settlement changed its name from Mount Marie to Pine Bluff, and a county election made Pine Bluff the permanent seat. Then the legislature funded the building of a jail, which made the move more or less official.

This county seat was very much a frontier town. James Robinson shot and killed Jefferson County's first judge, William P. Hackett, during a duel on a sandbar just outside of Pine Bluff. The judge was broke when he died, so the county spent $8 to buy a coffin and $3 to pay Sheriff Stanislaus Dardenne to dig Hackett's grave. Pine Bluff grew slowly over its first two decades, reaching a population of 460 by 1850. The population tripled in the 1850s, however, as steamboat traffic docking at Pine Bluff increased dramatically to transport cotton from the burgeoning plantations of the area. Many families moved into Jefferson County from Kentucky, Tennessee, the Carolinas, and other southern states. Bavarians also came to the area to work as farmers and merchants.

By 1860, the official (white) population of Pine Bluff had increased to 1,063 people living in 182 homes. The local population also included about 300 slaves who lived, for the most part, on farms outside the city limits. Then Fort Sumter fell, and life in Pine Bluff turned upside down.

War Comes to Pine Bluff

Months before Arkansas seceded on May 6, 1861, Pine Bluff had raised two companies of secessionist militia. Captain Charles Carlton and L. Donaldson probably raised the Jefferson Guard the previous year. And Captain Joseph Bocage organized the Southern Guards in February 1861. The militia trained every Saturday, as the pro-Union and pro-secession citizens of Pine Bluff argued among themselves until secessionist forces captured the U.S. Army Arsenal at Little Rock without a fight.

Under the command of Captain Bocage, these two companies from Pine Bluff may well have fired the first shots of the war. In April, possibly before the fracas at Fort Sumter erupted, the Pine Bluff militia fired musket balls across the bow of the steamboat *Sky Lark*, which was carrying supplies up the Arkansas for the U.S. Army. The musketry forced the captain of the steamer to put ashore at Pine Bluff and allow the militia to off-load the material.

Once Arkansas seceded on May 6, many men of military age (who were not slaves) promptly joined the Confederate army and were shipped off to fight far from home in Virginia and other places east of the Mississippi. The defense of Arkansas fell to Confederate troops from Texas, Missouri, and Indian Territory (later Oklahoma). The first Federal did not enter Pine Bluff until the summer of 1863, when he rode brazenly into town as a spy rather than as a conqueror. Dressed as a hillbilly, the unlikely spy was actually James Butler "Wild Bill" Hickok.

Wild Bill Hickok, the Spy

Pine Bluff should have seemed an unusual destination for a hillbilly riding a jackass, but the man really looked the part, according to Frank Wilstach's 1926 book *Wild Bill Hickok, the Prince of Pistoleers*. His long whiskers were unkempt, and his hair fell nearly to his waist from beneath a big, decaying hat of unbleached straw. He wore faded denims and an indigo vest with flaming crimson stripes. His coat was ragged and torn, but its huge brass buttons hinted at more prosperous times. An old shotgun dangled from the hillbilly's saddlebags, and a stringy old hound followed behind the jackass. The rider spit tobacco juice from time to time as he rode slowly down to the end of Main Street, where he dismounted and walked to the nearest saloon.

The hillbilly presented such a remarkable vision that patrons of the saloon simply gawked in amazement as he ordered a drink. Hickok figured he was completely safe in his disguise, so he spent the rest of the day meandering around town to see what he could see. The next day, Hickok walked right into the Confederate headquarters, with his antiquated shotgun and scrawny hound, to volunteer his services. The recruiting sergeant laughed, in spite of himself.

"Where the devil did you come from?" asked the sergeant.

"I've got a little cabin up here in the Ozarks," Hickok replied, "where I've been livin' in a patch o' clearin' with this here jack and Bowlegs for the past twenty years."

"Who is Bowlegs?" asked the sergeant.

"Why, look here, mister," Hickok said, "haven't you never heard o' Bowlegs, the greatest wildcat and bar killer in the whole o' Arkansas?

Bowlegs is my dog. And ef you'd seed him two months ago tackle a catamount up on Huckleberry Hill, bigger'n my jack, you'd bet the last bristle on yer back that he could whip anything that ever wore hair. . . ."

"Never mind the dog," the sergeant growled. "Can you fight as good as Bowlegs . . . if we should set you on a drove of Yankees?"

"I think I might make a full hand of them," Hickok replied, "ef you'll fernish me with amernition. I got plenty of caps jest now, but my powder an' shot is kinder low."

The whole room of soldiers laughed at that, as Wild Bill stood looking thoroughly confused as to what was so funny.

"You don't suppose our soldiers fight with shotguns, do you?" the sergeant asked.

Wild Bill opened his eyes wide with wonder. "On course I do, cause hain't shotguns better'n squirrel rifles by a durn'd sight?" The conversation ended with the sergeant enlisting the hillbilly, more as a potential source of amusement than as a good potential soldier.

The whole outlandish enterprise was spawned by Union Brigadier General Samuel Curtis, who had been using Hickok as a scout behind Confederate lines since soon after Curtis took command of Union troops in southern Missouri in early 1862. At first, Curtis was reluctant to use Hickok as a spy since he was rather young for such work— a mere twenty-five years old. Yet Hickok had impressed Curtis with his valor under fire as a wagon master, sharpshooter, and leader of men. So Curtis allowed Hickok to become one of his five spies. Hickok quickly became the most successful and fearless of the lot. Few figures associated with the Old West live up to American mythology, yet Hickok's career does meet the archetypal expectations about the Wild West. Hickok's exploits, including his remarkable adventures during the war, are chronicled in a number of books. Unfortunately, many early portraits of figures prominent in the Old West and the Civil War are painted with a broad brush; it can be hard to sort out hyperbole, faulty memory, and outright fiction from fact. *They Called Him Wild Bill,* by Joseph G. Rosa, manages to sift fact from folklore.

The Federal campaign had reached a critical stage when Hickok left Union lines for Pine Bluff in 1863. Brigadier General Curtis, with Major General Frederick Steele, marched down the White River from Missouri, capturing everything from Batesville to Helena. On a second front to the west, General James Blunt drove the Confederate forces from northwestern Arkansas, across the Boston Mountains to Van Buren. Now Curtis had to decide if the Federals should continue their drive into the heart of Arkansas in an effort to capture the entire Trans-Mississippi, a department of the Confederacy. Or were the

*James Butler
"Wild Bill" Hickok.*
—Colorado Historical
Society

Confederates trying to lure the Federals south, so Confederate cavalry could strike deep into Missouri? Curtis sent Hickok to Pine Bluff in an effort to learn Confederate dispositions and intentions.

Hickok decided the safest approach was a circuitous one. He rode cross-country into western Kansas, turned south, and crossed through Indian Territory into Texas, where he began to represent himself as a cattleman. From there, Hickok entered the southwestern corner of Arkansas, well inside Confederate territory. He stayed with an elderly black family, where he rested and discovered the fixings for his remarkable disguise. Hickok swapped his horse for a very old jackass and continued on to Pine Bluff, where he became a private in Company A under Captain Leverson.

After Hickok had spent several weeks at Pine Bluff, about 300 reinforcements joined the Confederates as they prepared to strike out at the Federal advance from Helena toward Little Rock. One of the new men recognized Wild Bill and raised the alarm. Several minutes later, twelve armed men arrested Hickok.

Brigadier General Earl Van Dorn convened a court-martial, which convicted Hickok of spying in less than an hour and sentenced him to death the following morning. Soldiers tied Hickok's arms securely and left him in a small log hut. Two guards just outside the cabin door kept a constant watch on Hickok, peering through one of the two windows frequently to check up on him. The Confederates were determined that there would be absolutely no chance for Hickok to escape. Yet Wild Bill remained optimistic that he would find a way, even though the ropes were so tight that any attempt to twist his hands drew blood. Lightning from a thunderstorm about 3 A.M. enabled Hickok to study the room. He noticed the handle of a battered folding knife stuck in the auger hole of a log near the door. The knife was obviously used to lift the old handmade door latch. Meanwhile, one of the guards sought shelter from the rain under the roof of a nearby shed.

Hickok quietly got to his feet, skulked to the wall, and withdrew the knife from the hole with his bound hands. He opened the blade and stuck the handle in the crack between two logs, so he could rub the ropes against the blade. As soon he severed the ropes, Hickok grabbed a piece of firewood laying next to the cabin's stove, used the knife to gingerly unlatch the cabin door, and clubbed the guard, knocking him out. A flash of lightning revealed a number of sleeping and drowsy soldiers under the roof of the nearby shed, so Hickok quickly dragged the unconscious guard into the cabin. Wild Bill donned the man's uniform, grabbed his musket, then stood guard outside the cabin door until he got his bearings. He finally disappeared into a nearby canebrake, stole a horse, and made his way back toward Union lines.

Hickok found the advancing Union column the next day, and his information helped General Steele establish a critical supply depot at DeValls Bluff, where riverboats could off-load supplies for the short overland march to seize the Arkansas capital. That ended the Confederate attempt to interdict Steele's march on Little Rock, which fell to the Federals on September 10, 1863. The spy's harrowing escape added considerable stature to the reputation of Wild Bill Hickok, who continued to work behind the Confederate lines in spite of the fact that an ever-increasing number of Arkansans recognized him.

The withdrawal of Confederate forces from Pine Bluff in 1863 left the town residents and Jefferson County farmers quite defenseless from the paramilitary marauders who were laying waste to a third of Arkansas by this time. In what may have been an utterly unprecedented move by a Confederate community during the war, a committee of local citizens met with General Steele in Little Rock and asked him to send Union troops to take over the county. Martial law under enemy occupation was infinitely more desirable than mindless murder and mayhem at the hands of Bushwhackers and Jayhawkers.

Steele sent a battalion of the 5th Kansas Cavalry to Pine Bluff on September 14. He then reinforced Pine Bluff with the rest of the 5th Kansas as well as the 1st Indiana Cavalry. Confederate Brigadier General John Marmaduke tried unsuccessfully to drive the Federals from Pine Bluff on October 25, and Union forces continued to control the area for the remainder of the war.

After the war, those planters of Jefferson County who had not lost their farms began to rebuild, using contract labor rather than slaves to work the fields. The residents of Pine Bluff mourned its many young men who had died in the war, and the town tried to get on with life by establishing a system of public schools. Progress came slowly. The population of Pine Bluff finally reached 3,000 in 1880. The local economy really began to improve in the 1880s due to the advent of rail service through Pine Bluff, and the town's population tripled by the turn of the century.

One of Pine Bluff's most influential citizens during this difficult period was a former slave, who started as a barber and then worked his way up the political ladder from alderman to legislator, assessor, circuit clerk, and, finally, the head of the Republican Party in Jefferson County. While Wiley Jones was the wealthiest black man in town (and probably in all of Arkansas), the Ferd Havis story provides a particularly fascinating glimpse at life in Pine Bluff during the last half of the nineteenth century.

Ferdinand Havis

Ferd Havis was born on November 15, 1846, in Desha County. His father was white planter John Havis and his mother was a slave owned by his father. So Ferd was born into slavery. When John Havis later moved to Jefferson County, he arranged for Ferd to learn the barbering trade, which gave young Havis his start after the war. By the time his first wife, Dilsa, died in 1870, Ferd owned his own barber shop across the street from the county courthouse in Pine Bluff. During the city election of 1871, Havis became one of two black aldermen to win in that election. Havis kept his day job, however, moving his shop to Barraque Street, next to Murphy's Saloon, where he employed a number of additional barbers.

The next year, Havis won election to the legislature as the representative from the Twentieth District, which included Jefferson, Bradley, Grant, and Lincoln Counties. A year later, Governor Elisha Baxter appointed Havis to the post of assessor for Jefferson County.

That same year, 1873, Ferd Havis also ran for alderman in Pine Bluff, since it was relatively common in the latter half of the nineteenth century for a popular individual to hold two elected offices simultaneously. Havis not only won the election, he actively participated in the work of the council. He was a hands-on kind of guy, as a story in *The Press* demonstrated. "Our worthy councilman, Honorable Ferd Havis," the newspaper began, "is now engaged with a number of hands at work upon the streets in Bellwood Cemetery. This work is much needed and Mr. Havis deserves especial thanks from the public for his persistent efforts in this laudable undertaking."

It should not be surprising that Havis was a strong supporter of Elisha Baxter, when the governor was forcibly removed from office by Joseph Brooks in April 1874, spawning the Brooks-Baxter War (described in the section on Little Rock). Havis wrote Baxter on April 16, "Old Jefferson [County] all right. We will furnish 1,000 men if necessary to reinstate you." The letter was signed by Ferd Havis, H. King White, A. J. Wheat, and D. A. Robinson.

Baxter had earlier commissioned Havis a colonel in the state militia, so Havis embarked 500 black troops onto the steamer *Hallie* four days later, accompanied by John Thomas and a company of white troops. When the steamer landed at Little Rock, Havis and Thomas marched their troops smartly off the wharf "with drum and fife playing, colors flying and yelling like wildcats," according to John Harrell. Baxter decided that these troops could best be used back at Pine Bluff to counter the Brooks militia there.

Troops led by Havis and another black officer, Captain A. Montaque, subsequently engaged in a skirmish with pro-Brooks forces, taking several officers prisoners and forcing the members of the opposing militia to disband and return to their farms. *The Press* published the official report of the engagement, and went on to observe that "no braver or better men . . . live in our land" than Colonel Havis and Captain Montaque.

An engraving from Frank Leslie's Illustrated Newspaper *(May 23, 1874). The caption read: "Anarchy in Arkansas—Baxter's forces under General King White, embarking at Pine Bluff near Little Rock, for New Gascony, to attack Brooks troops."*
—UALR Library

Once the Brooks-Baxter War was over, Havis ran again for alderman and was reelected. Throughout this time, he continued to work in his barber shop as well as to participate actively in the Republican Party, serving several times as a delegate to the Republican National Convention. But the Brooks-Baxter War heralded a time of political change. The Democrats began to gain power, and the Republicans began to lose it. Since the black vote was solidly Republican at the time, the black community began to lose political power as well. Nevertheless, Colonel Havis was an immensely popular man who could win elections in spite of changing political momentum. He was elected to the office of circuit clerk in 1881 and eventually served five terms. Havis also served as the county chairman of the Republican Party for many years. The colonel's political fortunes continued to rise, and his personal fortunes kept pace.

He owned his own home at 920 West Barraque as well as several tenements. He and partner Essex Bellamy ran an "elegant new brick [establishment called] Havis and Bellamy, wholesale and retail whiskey dealers," according to *The Press-Eagle*. Then Ferd's second wife, Geneva, died from consumption. Ferd's problems deepened when Bellamy decided he wanted out of the partnership. So Havis mortgaged the bar and its property for $5,000 to buy out Bellamy's interest. The following year, forty-year-old Ferd Havis married twenty-year-old Ella Cooper.

While family life took a turn for the better, his political career took a strange twist. An argument with longtime friend and political associate Wiley Jones escalated into a serious confrontation on August 6, 1885, when Havis and Jones "exchanged a few pistol shots," according to *The Weekly Commercial*. Both men were skilled marksmen, so folks assumed the men must have viewed the gunfire as a means of expressing themselves rather than a means of harming their opponent. The two combatants patched up their differences, and both men attended the Republican National Convention the following year. Ferdinand Havis was at the peak of his political power.

A story in the February 1, 1890, issue of *The Press-Eagle* described Colonel Havis: "In personal appearance Mr. Havis is a handsome well-proportioned man and owes much of his success as a politician to his ability as an orator. He is a good parliamentarian and has a memory so retentive, and is so logical a speaker that he rarely fails to carry his point in debate. He is a member of the Masonic fraternity, the G.U.O.O.F. (Grand United Order of Odd Fellows) and the United Brothers of Fellowship. He owns 2,000 acres of land in addition to valuable city property."

Wiley Jones, circa 1890, an important Pine Bluff businessman and politician.
—UCA Archives

While Colonel Havis was widely respected, he did develop some substantial enemies, since he always used his considerable political influence to defeat any candidates whom he disliked. After Havis helped defeat David Parks in his bid to be elected constable of Vaugine Township, Parks, who ran a saloon, vowed that Havis "would never be in his way again." In February 1890, Parks tried to hire Gilbert Baker to assassinate Havis. Parks told Baker that he wanted to eliminate the circuit clerk so he could assume the leadership of the county's black community and control local patronage.

Parks did not know, however, that Gilbert Baker was a detective for the P. R. Burns Agency, which worked for the St. Louis, Arkansas & Texas Railway (which later became the Cotton Belt). Baker wrote his boss about the matter, and the detective agency sent John Williams to Pine Bluff to consummate the deal and gather evidence against Parks. Williams was once the marshal of Texarkana and now worked for the detective agency.

After a long series of negotiations, Parks gave Williams a handsome gray stallion worth about $450 to kill Havis. Instead, the detective informed local officials, who arrested Parks. But somehow Parks was never brought to trial, which disappointed Colonel Havis considerably. But perhaps the colonel's biggest disappointment came eight years later, when he failed in his attempt to be named the postmaster of Pine Bluff in 1898.

While many prominent white citizens backed his appointment, opponents deluged the Senate Committee on Post Offices with statements that the appointment of Havis would offend the white residents of Pine Bluff. In spite of the fact that more than fifty white community leaders backed Havis (including legislators, two former mayors of Pine Bluff, a bank president, and key businessmen), the senators bowed to the growing disenfranchisement of black voters in the South, and appointed a white postmaster.

This did not end the political career of Ferd Havis, however. He continued to serve as the county chairman of the Republican Party until 1908, when he declined the nomination to continue at that post. Twenty years as party chairman was enough, as far as the colonel was concerned. He retired, after a fashion, to a life of farming, managing his many commercial interests, and participating in the activities of local fraternal organizations.

When Ferd Havis died at his home in 1918, the *Pine Bluff Commercial* ran the following obituary:

> Ferd Havis was a born leader and forged his way into public life by methods that were conservative and looking toward the greatest good for his race. He was loyal to the South and especially the state of Arkansas. As opportunities opened for a possible broader career in public life he refused to be tempted to leave the state to whose interest he was anxious to give his service.
>
> During the Brooks-Baxter War and at other times when tense situations tended to mar the harmony of the races, he cooperated with the leading white citizens of Pine Bluff to quell any feeling that would bring strife. He was a politician that kept abreast of the times and his pride in the advancement of his race was ample reward for the labor he contributed to the cause.
>
> Ferd Havis had acquired ample means to be called a man of wealth and with increasing fortune he gave an increase to charities. The educational advantages that had of late been offered the young Negroes of Arkansas gave him a hope that there would be many leaders for his race to take the place of the faithful ones that had risen by their own efforts to positions of trust.

Ferdinand Havis wrote a lot of history in Pine Bluff during his fifty-year struggle to help his community adapt to a changing world. As the new century dawned, the process of change seemed to accelerate, providing Pine Bluff with a host of new challenges and opportunities.

Tales of the Twentieth Century

Pine Bluff's economy began to slow around the turn of the century, after the period of rapid growth spawned by the railroads during the two preceding decades. This downturn was offset in part by the growth of the lumber industry, which began to harvest virgin timber on a grand scale. Not all change improved life in Jefferson County, however. The growth of so-called populism—with its foundation based in large part upon racial intolerance—led to the disenfranchisement of blacks, segregation, and increasing racism. Then, in 1914, prohibitionists enacted legislation that closed the saloons. Pine Bluff lost some of its vitality and joy.

Nevertheless, the community continued to strengthen its position as a transportation center. The appearance of automobiles and electric streetcars stimulated road improvement. U.S. Army engineers dredged the Arkansas River, which increased commercial river traffic through Pine Bluff. After years of tribulations, the city finally built a bridge over the Arkansas to link the northern and southern portions of Jefferson County. Then tremendous floods in 1908 and 1916

Riverboats C. B. Reese *and* Arkansas *at Pine Bluff, circa 1910.* –UCA Archives

37

rampaged through the county, changing the very topography of Pine Bluff.

Yet the economy rebounded quickly, thanks in large measure to the tremendous worldwide need for cotton generated by the Great War in Europe. The end of the war, however, signaled an end to the unprecedented demand for cotton, and the market crashed. A lot of local farmers and cotton buyers went bankrupt. The Pine Bluff economy finally recovered in the mid-1920s and began to boom once again. After Pine Bluff industrialist Harvey Couch listened to the first radio station in the United States to broadcast on a regular basis (KDAK in Pittsburgh, Pennsylvania), he decided to establish his own radio station as a means of advertising his business interests. Pine Bluff's WOK became the first commercial radio station in Arkansas.

The economy became so strong that the stock market crash of 1929 did not begin to affect the local economy for nearly a year, when both the National Bank of Arkansas and the Merchant and Planters Bank closed their doors. A disastrous drought that same year, combined with reduced demand for agricultural and forest products, led to reduced railroad traffic, which in turn spawned more layoffs. The amount of human suffering in Jefferson County became appalling. As part of the New Deal, the Farm Security Administration sponsored two projects to relocate farm families from unproductive land elsewhere in Arkansas and help them start farming the rich lands in Jefferson County. The economy was beginning to turn around when World War II erupted, bringing rapid change to Pine Bluff.

The Army Air Corps promptly built a large flight training facility on some of the best farmland southeast of Pine Bluff. The army named the facility Grider Field, in honor of Lt. John Grider, an Arkansas pilot who died fighting as a member of the British Royal Air Force in 1918. Soon thereafter, the army purchased 15,000 acres north of town, which eventually became a major chemical warfare plant called the Pine Bluff Arsenal. Most folks don't realize that the United States government spent more money to develop chemical and biological weapons during World War II than it spent on the Manhattan Project to develop the atomic bomb.

While the young men of Pine Bluff went off to war, the community filled to capacity and beyond from a steady influx of construction workers, the subsequent appearance of civilian workers at the arsenal and airfield, plus military cadre and student pilots. Sharecroppers left the fields and entered the cash economy, which led to the establishment of larger farms and more heavily mechanized production of cotton and rice.

Cotton pickers board a field-bound truck in Pine Bluff during the 1930s.
—Arkansas History Commission

GIs returning to Pine Bluff found a healthy economy eager for their labor. The Pine Bluff Arsenal continued to operate when the hot war turned into the cold war, although some of the equipment was converted to produce fertilizer and chlorine for the commercial market. The facility employed about 1,000 people. The Ben Pearson Company expanded into the largest manufacturer of archery equipment in the world, and industries such as Pinecrest Mills and the Central Transformer Company relocated to Pine Bluff. The biggest economic boost came from the growth of the paper industry, with the addition of three major plants to the area.

Pine Bluff Arsenal was expanded during the Korean War to include the production of biological warfare agents until President Richard Nixon halted the production of biological weapons. The arsenal continued to house much of the nation's chemical weapons until a treaty with the Soviet Union mandated the destruction of all chemical weapons, an expensive process that will continue at the Pine Bluff Arsenal into the early part of the twenty-first century.

The completion of the McClellan-Kerr Navigation System on the Arkansas River Navigation Project in the 1960s made Pine Bluff the only slack-water harbor on the Arkansas River. Local residents voted for a $1.2 million bond issue to build appropriate port facilities on the east side of town, and soon Pine Bluff was handling more tonnage of barge traffic than any other port on the Arkansas. Today, the University of Arkansas at Pine Bluff, rather than the city's economic strength, gives the residents of Pine Bluff their greatest source of civic pride.

I-40
West Memphis–Little Rock
127 miles

This 127-mile stretch of interstate between West Memphis and Little Rock provides a somewhat shorter and infinitely more efficient passage than the old Military Road that joined the two communities in the mid-1830s. At that time, West Memphis was called Hopefield, and this eastern terminus of Military Road provided a gateway to the West for most of the hardy, hopeful pioneers seeking a better life in Arkansas and Texas.

–WEST MEMPHIS–

The establishment of West Memphis dates back to a time when Arkansas Post was the only European settlement of any size in Arkansas. The story actually begins in 1792, when Benjamin Fooy settled where Memphis now stands. Born in Holland, Fooy moved across the Mississippi three years later and established a settlement that came to be known as Fooy's Point, where he became a successful trader and merchant. A book called *Early Western Travels* describes the settlement as the "most healthful, moral and intelligent community between the south of Ohio and Natchez" due to the influence of its first settler.

The Spaniards established a fort at the present site of Memphis in 1795. Called *San Fernando de las Barrancas*, the plan was to protect Arkansas Post and provide a link to New Madrid. The fort never really lived up to its mission, so the Spaniards abandoned it two years later and established a small garrison at Fooy's Point, which they called *Campo del Esperanza*, or Field of Hope. It wasn't much of a garrison, averaging about eight soldiers at any given time. Nevertheless, *Campo del Esperanza* qualifies as the first naval base in Arkansas, since it supported one or two cannon launches. A crew of three operated each boat, which patrolled the Mississippi River to interdict invaders and illegal immigrants.

Benjamin Fooy operated a store on each side of the river, although he maintained his residence at Fooy's Point. He also owned a flatboat, which he used to bring supplies upriver from New Orleans. The trip from New Orleans to Fooy's Point usually took forty days, although the crew once made the trip in a mere thirty days. The United States took over the garrison in 1804 after the Louisiana Purchase, and changed the name of the settlement to Hope Encampment, which subsequently became Hopefield.

When Benjamin Fooy died in 1823, the character of the town changed abruptly. Gamblers and thieves who had been banished from Memphis gravitated to Hopefield. And a place just south of town became the traditional place where the gentlemen of Memphis settled their serious differences with dueling pistols.

Nevertheless, the community soon became a gateway into the heart of Arkansas. Congressman Sam Houston pointed out the military need for a good road into Arkansas from the east. One proposed route went from Hopefield to Little Rock, while another crossed the Mississippi at Helena. The Military Road was eventually built along the more northerly route, which roughly parallels the present path of US 70 from West Memphis to the L'Anguille River. Military Road reached Little Rock by traversing the infamous Great Mississippi Swamp, a fearsome task hardly fathomable to us in the twentieth century in light of modern engineering principles and massive earth-moving machinery available for such purposes today.

The battle to build the road was launched by Secretary of War John Calhoon, and the initial fight was led by Lieutenant Charles Thomas of Pennsylvania. Building the road was not even half the battle, however, because the road refused to stay built. The story of Military Road is a prime example of the American struggle to tame a wild land.

The Battle to Build Military Road

The army decided to build a road through the middle of the Great Mississippi Swamp, because the route was convenient to the community growing atop the Chickasaw Bluffs on the eastern shore of the Mississippi River. Memphis was developing political as well as economic muscle. In 1824, the army sent surveyors Joseph Paxon and Thomas Mathers to develop a route to Little Rock. Two years later, the army dispatched Lieutenant Charles Thomas to supervise the civilian contractors, Anderson Carr and William Irvine, who would actually build the road.

When Lieutenant Thomas arrived in Memphis, he found that the contractors had only hired seventeen men, and many of them were too sick to work. Anderson Carr had contracted to build the first sixty miles of road (from Hopefield to four miles shy of the St. Francis River). Carr had already made some progress on the first ten miles of road, including the roadway itself plus a dozen log bridges and a dozen causeways. But he had not begun the major bridges needed over three bayous, which put the project behind schedule. In exasperation, Thomas ordered the contractors to hire more men, and then he set out on horseback to inspect progress on the road.

Thomas quickly began to wonder if the survey team had even set foot on the proposed route, which ran right through Blackfish and Shell Lakes, and then continued through an impassable bog between the White River and Bayou De View. The lieutenant returned to Memphis, where he hired an experienced woodsman as a guide, borrowed a compass and chain, and set out to survey an alternative route between the St. Francis and White Rivers.

Late the following summer, Lieutenant Thomas arrived in Little Rock and asked the territorial delegate to Congress, Henry Conway, about the possibility of changing the route to the one he had just blazed. Conway assured Thomas that Congress had only mandated the building of a road between Memphis and Little Rock, not the actual route. Conway did say, however, that Thomas should prepare a full report to the quartermaster general, because the president would have to approve a route change.

The report Thomas wrote suggested that the road be moved southward to avoid the great swamp. The new route would cross the White River at a place that already had an established, year-round ferry with a boat stationed on each side of the river (the crossing is now known as Clarendon). The route would then angle north to intercept the original route from Two Prairies to Little Rock. The lieutenant's proposal was eventually approved.

Meanwhile, William Strong finished a bridge across the L'Anguile River, and Anderson Carr completed his section of road. With the eastern section of Military Road completed, work began on the easier western half of the road. The future seemed bright, but this was literally the calm before the storm. A prolonged period of unprecedented rainfall in 1828 began to wash away all of the hard-won progress.

Floodwaters attacked causeways, embankments, and log bridges all the way from the Mississippi to the St. Francis, destroying years of work and the lieutenant's will to continue the battle.

Lieutenant Charles Thomas asked for a transfer north. The War Department sent him south, to fight Indians in Florida. Thomas went on to fight in the Mexican War and the Civil War, and eventually retired long after his battle to build a road through 200 miles of Arkansas swamps and wilderness. Meanwhile, the great flood of 1828 rendered the eastern stretch of Military Road quite impassable for the next five years. The delay finally spawned renewed interest in building a road to Little Rock from Helena.

In 1832, the secretary of war sent Indian agent Edwin Clark to explore the possibility of building a road from Helena to Little Rock. Clark sent a detailed report that described an old, well-traveled Indian trail that went from Helena to the confluence of the Cache and White Rivers. Clark observed that the Memphis route cut through uninhabited wilderness, while the Helena route passed numerous farms and three gristmills, which could provide food and other supplies to travelers, and forage for their stock. He concluded, "Compare it as described with the Memphis and Little Rock road and even unimproved it is far superior."

Meanwhile, Arkansans led by Samuel Dickens sent an impassioned plea to Congress to repair the road from Memphis to Little Rock. They contended that it would be cheaper to relocate the Indians from east of the Mississippi by road than by riverboat. Furthermore, they argued, the road would dramatically improve mail service, encourage settlers, and enhance the army's ability to protect the residents of Arkansas Territory. Congress appropriated $20,000 to fix the road but gave Governor John Pope the responsibility for effecting the repairs.

After a year of active oversight, which included numerous trips to the home of William Strong on Bench Creek (the site of an old Cherokee village near the St. Francis River), the governor capitulated to the overwhelming might of the Great Mississippi Swamp. He enlisted the help of the territorial legislators, who wrote Congress for more money, saying that the difficulty of repairing the road between Memphis and Strong's house "transcends all the calculations which have been made."

Congress appropriated $100,000 to complete the road between Memphis and Strong's home, but required a new survey prior to launching a new attack on the Great Mississippi Swamp. The survey by Doctor Howard took a year. Several alternative routes proved impassable, and previously built log bridges had already rotted into ruin. Wooden structures simply would not survive in the swamp. Howard proposed building an earthen embankment at least eight feet higher than the surrounding terrain to successfully cross the swamp, replacing wooden corduroy, bridges, and causeways.

The new assault on the great swamp was led by Lieutenant Alexander Bowman, who rejected the massive effort required by Howard's detailed proposal. After a year battling the swamp himself, Bowman began to realize that an earthen embankment made more sense than traditional road-building methods, and proposed a suitable plan to Washington. The army's assistant chief engineer, Robert E. Lee, approved the plan in November 1835 and named contractors. But the workers made little progress over the following year.

A 300-man crew tried to build an embankment across Mound Bayou in July 1837, after a long delay caused by spring flooding. But disease cut down nearly 75 percent of the workforce, and the contractor responsible for building that first four miles of roadway abandoned the attempt. Lieutenant Bowman hired a new contractor to complete the entire road from Hopefield to the St. Francis. The new contractor used oxen and scrapers to move dirt, instead of the man-operated shovels and wheelbarrows used by the previous contractor. They moved 1,021,994 cubic yards of fill to complete that stretch of roadway at a cost of about 14 cents per yard.

Congress then gave Governor Pope another appropriation to repair Military Road between the St. Francis and Little Rock, which completed the project begun fourteen years earlier. The road from Memphis finally tied in with the previously built portion of Military Road that connected Little Rock with Fort Smith, and then continued on to Fort Gibson in Indian Territory. Another road connected Strong's crossing at the Cache River to Batesville, while a road called the Old Southwest Trail ran from the northeastern border with Missouri, through Little Rock, to Fulton on the Red River.

Alexander Bowman shifted his attention to the Great Raft, which blocked navigation on the Red River. Bowman supervised Henry Shreve's effort to clear the ancient logjam from the river, and later died in 1865 with the rank of lieutenant colonel.

While only traces remain of Military Road, the fact remains that it provided the only passage through the Wilderness (as the Mississippi bottoms were once known) for many years. From its completion until the outbreak of the Civil War, long trains of wagons could be seen traversing the miles of swamps and continuing on beneath overhanging trees toward the heart of Arkansas, Texas, or Indian Territory. Throughout those eventful years, Hopefield remained the gateway to the wilderness, a role that increased profoundly with the coming of the railroad in 1858.

Train tracks threatened by floodwaters between Memphis and Forrest City.
—Arkansas History Commission

The Memphis & Little Rock Railroad

When rails were completed between Hopefield and the St. Francis River in 1858, the Memphis & Little Rock became the first railroad to actually lay tracks in Arkansas. The railroad completed another section of roadway between DeValls Bluff and Argenta (now called North Little Rock) by 1860, but then war derailed future construction. While the trip between Memphis and Little Rock was now more direct and more efficient, especially for hauling freight, the journey was by no means nonstop. The trip began with a ferry ride from Memphis to Hopefield, where the traveler boarded a train to Madison. Then the traveler transferred to stagecoach for the trip to Clarendon. A ferry then transported the passenger to DeValls Bluff, where a train once more transported the traveler to Argenta, where a ferry provided passage across the Arkansas River to Little Rock. Continuous tracks to Argenta were not completed until 1871. Interstate 40 now takes essentially the same route between West Memphis and Little Rock.

When construction of the railroad to Little Rock began in 1858, the enterprise seemed to promise a bright future for Hopefield. But history proved to be unkind.

The Death of Hopefield

While many towns have come and gone in Arkansas, Hopefield was the only town to disappear in a single day. That fateful day was February 19, 1863. The instrument of destruction was the Union army.

When the Civil War halted completion of the tracks to Little Rock, the Confederate authorities converted the railroad shops in Hopefield into an armory for modifying and repairing guns for the army. When Memphis fell to Union forces in June 1862, most of the vanquished

Confederates crossed the Mississippi to Hopefield, where they boarded trains and headed west. The military situation remained relatively quiet until December, since frequent patrols of Union troops, based out of Memphis, forced the residents of Hopefield to take an oath of allegiance to the Union.

Then Confederate Lieutenant General Theophilus Holmes ordered Captain James McGehee to take his cavalry to Crittenden County "for the purpose of scouting and burning cotton in that country, and annoying the enemy on the Mississippi River." McGehee would demonstrate an exuberant genius at annoying the enemy.

Captain McGehee immediately began his guerilla operations by capturing the steamer *Joseph Musselman*, and ran the boat fifteen miles upriver to Bradley's Landing, where he captured a heavily ladened flatboat. After off-loading anything of use, McGehee torched the boats. Five days later, he captured the steamer *Grampus No. 2* right in front of the Federals in Memphis. McGehee scuttled the five coal barges being towed by the steamer, and then took the steamboat upriver to Mound City and burned it to the waterline. A month later, McGehee captured a Federal flatboat thirty miles below Memphis that was packed with critical medicines, as well as some weapons and munitions. McGehee's remarkable run of luck ended the following day, February 17, 1863. Hopefield's luck would run out two days after that.

Severe fog the next day forced the skipper of the steam tug *Hercules* to put ashore between Mound City and Hopefield. As soon as the crew secured the tug and its seven coal barges to the shore, McGehee and fifty Confederate cavalrymen immediately appeared and captured the crew. Or at least most of the crew. One died in the skirmish, and one escaped downriver and raised the alarm in Memphis. Soon a hail of shellfire began to fall on the tug from the far side of the Mississippi, preventing McGehee from moving his prize. So the Confederates torched the tug and tried to off-load coal from the barges.

But the fog lifted, exposing the Confederates to accurate bombardment from a fleet of mortar boats that had moored in the Wolf River above Memphis. The Confederates retreated as the steamer *Wisconsin* approached the blazing *Hercules*. Major General Ulysses Grant, who commanded all of the Federals in western Tennessee and northern Mississippi, became convinced that the residents of Hopefield were helping and even harboring the Confederate guerillas. Burning the *Hercules* became the final insult.

The next day, Brigadier General James Veatch, who commanded the Federals around Memphis, dispatched four companies across the river to deal with Hopefield once and for all. They crossed the

Mississippi on the steamer *Mill Boy* under the covering bombardment of the gunboat *Cricket*, which shelled the woods where the troops were about to land. The Federals surrounded the town and gave the residents one hour to grab what they could and get out of town. Then the Federals torched every building in Hopefield.

Hundreds of Memphis residents assembled on the opposite shoreline to watch as flames engulfed handsome little white houses with green shutters. Then a barn exploded when flames reached a store of gunpowder hidden there. The dispossessed women and children of Hopefield huddled without hope near their remaining possessions and wept as their homes burned to the ground. The Union captain in charge of destroying Hopefield offered to transport the Arkansans to Memphis, but not a single person accepted his offer.

The burning of Hopefield generated a firestorm of outrage throughout the Southern press, which heatedly condemned the "abolitionist Yankees" for their retaliation against innocent civilians "who had nothing to do with the affair."

After the war, Hopefield arose from the ashes to become a rollicking river town known for its cockfights (which were banned in Memphis), boxing matches, horse races, and high-stakes pool games. Hopefield boasted more saloons than churches, a large wharf, boardinghouses, two hotels, brick sidewalks, and even kerosene street lamps. Then the town suffered a quadruple whammy. Yellow fever devastated the community in 1878. New bridges allowed the railroad to bypass the town. Southbound steamers plying the Mississippi between Cincinnati and New Orleans discontinued the practice of stopping at Hopefield to off-load westbound passengers and freight, stopping instead at Memphis. The crowning indignity was delivered by the new levee system, which raised the water level and produced a plague of mud and mosquitoes.

Another inexorable problem had begun to eat away at the very foundation of Hopefield in the 1880s, when the mighty Mississippi began to change its course. The final blow came in 1912, when spring floods swept away Hopefield's pool rooms, saloons, and boardinghouses—actually washing away the land itself. Some folks say that Mud Island, which appeared at the Memphis waterfront about that time, was born from the silty remains of beautiful downtown Hopefield.

The Birth of West Memphis

The area revived just before World War I, when Zack Bragg moved from Mississippi to Arkansas and opened a sawmill next to the former location of Hopefield. Called Bragg's Spur for the next decade, the town changed its name to West Memphis when incorporated in 1927.

Boat landing at West Memphis in the 1930s. —WPA, Arkansas History Commission

The logic for the name change was that foreign lumber buyers paid a premium price for wood shipped out of Memphis. The local economy profited from the name recognition generated by the big neighbor to the east.

Today, West Memphis is best known for Southland Greyhound Park, which attracts tourists from throughout the South to wager on pari-mutuel dog races. The development of riverboat casinos along the Mississippi River in the 1990s has severely undermined Southland's success, however.

–FORREST CITY–

Spread across the western slope of Crowley's Ridge, Forrest City is thirty-eight miles west of West Memphis and ninety-three miles east of Little Rock on I-40. Forrest City sprang to life in 1867 as a construction camp of the Memphis & Little Rock Railroad. Initially called Forrest Town, the camp was named after Nathan Bedford Forrest, who had been a Confederate general and later became the contractor for cutting the railroad through Crowley's Ridge. The town was laid out in 1869, incorporated in 1871, and became the county seat in 1874.

Born dirt poor in Tennessee, Nathan Bedford Forrest had made himself a wealthy, if barely literate, gentleman in Memphis by the

N. B. Forrest. –J. H.
Moyston, Arkansas
History Commission

outbreak of the Civil War. When he joined the 7th Tennessee Cavalry, Forrest was probably the only millionaire private in the Confederate army. He soon organized a cavalry battalion and was promoted to lieutenant colonel. Forrest's cavalry unit left Columbia, Tennessee, on a December 1862 raid armed mainly with flintlocks and shotguns, rather than contemporary military weapons. Nevertheless, Forrest went on to capture 1,200 Union soldiers and then simply paroled his prisoners on the spot. Forrest quickly became a brilliant, self-taught strategist in the use of cavalry. He also believed in leading his men from the front, rather from a more secure position at the rear of his troops.

His aggressive and fearless leadership placed him in tremendous peril, personally coming under fire more than a hundred times. A contemporary general, James R. Chalmers, reported that Nathan Bedford Forrest had twenty-seven mounts shot out from under him during the course of those fights. Not only was that a record for any officer during the Civil War, subsequent research suggests that Forrest actually had thirty horses killed out from under him.

Forrest was not only brilliant and fearless, he was tough. When a musket ball finally caught up with him and lodged close to his spine, he refused anaesthetic before a surgeon removed the bullet. Forrest also suffered recurrent bouts of boils so severe that he could barely mount a horse, much less ride. But ride he did, becoming the most feared cavalry leader of the war. Nathan Bedford Forrest led with such style and success that one of his adversaries, General William Tecumseh Sherman, called Forrest "the most remarkable man our Civil War produced on either side." Forrest was also the only man in either the Confederate or Union armies who started the war as a private and ended the war as a lieutenant general. His simple rule for achieving victory was "get thar fustest with the mostest!"

With the collapse of the Confederacy, Nathan Bedford Forrest once again found himself dirt poor. But his reputation as a leader of men enabled him to win the job of completing a considerable gap in the Memphis & Little Rock line. Forrest employed about a thousand poor Irish immigrants to complete the massive task of cutting through Crowley's Ridge with hand tools and mule-drawn wagons. The first train crossed Crowley's Ridge during the winter of 1868–69. Nathan Forrest is also known as the founder of the Ku Klux Klan, although his participation with that group took place in Tennessee before he came to build a railroad in Arkansas.

Forrest City is now known for the Crowley's Ridge Vocational Technical School and the East Arkansas Community College.

—BRINKLEY—

Located sixty-three miles west of West Memphis and sixty-eight miles east of Little Rock on I-40, Brinkley began life—like so many Arkansas towns—as a railroad construction camp. The Irish laborers were such hard workers that the camp was called Lick Skillet, since "licking the skillet clean" meant to do a thorough job. The Irishmen faced substantial obstacles, including malaria, as the bridge contractor for the line observed in his memoirs:

> There was a dense canebrake a large part of the way from Cache River to the high land west of Brinkley. The [bridge construction] force numbered about twice as many men as needed, owing to sickness from chills and fever. I wrote the assistant chief engineer . . . and asked him to send me one barrel of good whiskey, and two dozen ounces of quinine. I had the barrel mounted in my office . . . put an ounce of quinine in a jug of whiskey and sent it up to camp three times a day. By the time I had used up the quinine, there was not a sick man on the job.

The town began as three or four stores in a clearing created by two small lumber camps. The stores served the railroad construction workers and provided the nucleus for a small community that was named after Robert Brinkley, who was the president of the railroad.

The town developed into a center for the lumber industry. As loggers cleared the dense stands of trees, farmers arrived to cultivate cotton, so Brinkley also developed as a market town for the local cotton industry as well. Two other railroads later crossed through town, enhancing Brinkley's progress as a transportation center. Disaster struck in 1909, however, when a tornado tore through town and killed sixty people. Only a church and six or eight homes remained standing. Brinkley thoroughly recovered by the 1930s, and the town developed a distinctive culture.

A writer sponsored by the federal Works Projects Administration described a typical scene in the business district:

> The man on the street wearing overalls and brogans is a small cotton farmer; if he wears gum boots, he is from the Cache River bottoms. The man in work shirt and pants is probably from the lumber mill, and if he is slightly stooped, with glasses and a studious look, he is probably a foreman, or perhaps a sawyer who glances at the bark and waves for the carriage man to 'turn her over' before the carriage runs the log back into the whirling saw.

While the importance of railroads to the local economy has waned, the presence of the interstate highway has helped to maintain the economic health of the community. Brinkley remains one of the fortunate fraction of railroad towns in Arkansas that continues to prosper after the demise of railroading's golden age.

—CARLISLE—

Carlisle stands ninety-seven miles west of West Memphis and thirty-four miles east of Little Rock on I-40. The community was born in 1871, when Samuel McCormick laid out a town on the property he owned along the right-of-way for the Memphis & Little Rock Railroad. The origin of the name remains a mystery. Some folks believe McCormick named the place after his hometown of Carlisle, Pennsylvania. Others suggest he named the town after a friend who was a state senator in another state.

One of the town's first citizens was Albert Emonson, an immigrant from Norway who brought Holstein cattle and superb draft horses to Lonoke County, enabling Carlisle to develop as a trading center for the dairy industry (as well as the cotton industry). Carlisle began to develop a literary reputation when a young printer named Opie Reed came to town. With partner H. C. Warner, Reed opened a newspaper called *The Prairie Flower*, in honor of the nearby prairie called *Gran Maris* (Grand Prairie) by early French explorers. The motto on the

Workers in Carlisle's Turrentine Hotel, August 1901. —Arkansas History Commission

masthead of the paper read, "If you have to talk, be sure to start on time." The newspaper gave Opie Reed the opportunity to develop his skills and reputation as a humorist.

According to Fred Allsopp, *"The Prairie Flower* was pretty, but frail and lonely, and soon withered and died." Undaunted, Opie Reed continued to write, becoming a highly successful novelist thanks to books like *A Yankee from the West, Emmett Bonlore,* and *An Arkansas Planter.*

The area's agricultural industry began a shift to rice farming at the beginning of the twentieth century, and Carlisle had the distinction of producing the state's first rice crop in 1904.

Today, a thirteen-mile stretch of original prairie survives along US 70 and the Rock Island Railroad. The original *Gran Maris* stretched from the White River to the Arkansas. Twelve miles southeast of town on Arkansas 86 is a two-mile remnant of original tupelo swamp and bottomland forest. Each of these tracts provides a fascinating peek back in time into the long-gone Arkansas wilderness.

—LONOKE—

Lonoke lies 26 miles east of Little Rock and 105 miles west of West Memphis on I-40. George Rumbough originally named this spot Lone Oak after a large, solitary red oak used as a landmark when he surveyed the county. At the suggestion of several railroad engineers, Rumbough changed the name to Loneoak. By the time the town site was surveyed in 1867, the name had evolved from Loneoak to Lonoak to Lonoke.

The railroad bypassed nearby Brownsville, which was the seat of Prairie County, and passed instead through Lonoke. The residents of Brownsville packed up their belongs and moved lock, stock, and barrel to Lonoke. They moved their houses, their businesses, and even their brick courthouse to Lonoke. Then the legislature formed Lonoke County from portions of Prairie and Pulaski Counties in 1873, and named this growing railroad town as the county seat.

By 1889, only the town cemetery and several frame houses remained at Brownsville. The tall tree that gave Lonoke its name was cut down in 1900. About this time, Lonoke's most prominent citizen ascended to the national political stage. Joseph Robinson served in

Joseph Robinson served as Arkansas governor and U.S. senator. –Arkansas History Commission

Congress, became governor, and then served numerous terms in the U.S. Senate. Known simply as Joe T to his constituents, Robinson made an unsuccessful bid for the White House in 1928 as the running mate of presidential candidate Al Smith. Joe T is fondly remembered as a big man with a powerful voice who championed causes like providing relief to poverty-stricken farmers and fighting against religious prejudice. While Joe T never made it to the White House, his thirty-five-year political career did a lot of good for a lot of folks. Joseph T. Robinson continued to serve in the U.S. Senate until the day he died in 1937.

During World War I, the army built Eberts Field at Lonoke to train aviators. Named after Captain Melchior Eberts, who was killed in a crash in New Mexico, the 960-acre facility bustled with as many as 1,500 personnel, making it the second largest training field in the United States. Lonoke residents could sometimes see several hundred biplanes in the air at a time. The government dismantled the airfield after the war.

Then Lonoke became the home for the first warm-water fish hatchery in North America, and today the Joe Hogan State Fish Hatchery is one of the largest warm-water hatcheries in the world. Lonoke can also boast about the largest minnow farm in the world. Featuring 200 miles of levees and 6,000 acres of ponds, the Anderson Minnow Farm ships 300 million fish a year throughout the United States.

The gunner and pilot posed for this photo at Eberts Field. –Arkansas History Commission

The northern terminus of US 49 is Piggott, Arkansas, on the eastern slope of Crowley's Ridge near the Missouri border. This highway strikes southeast through the heart of the Arkansas Delta, more or less paralleling Crowley's Ridge to the Mississippi River. US 49 then continues a short distance into Mississippi, where it connects with US 61.

Crowley's Ridge provided Arkansas pioneers with both a landmark and a dry trail from Cape Girardeau, Missouri, through the intimidating morass of the St. Francis valley, all the way to Helena. Many pioneers settled along the rolling, narrow strip of hills that rise from the surrounding flatlands of the Delta. Geologists speculate that the 150-mile-long ridge, which is a loess drift glacial deposit, developed because the Mississippi River once flowed west of the ridge. According to that theory, the course of the river changed at the northern edge of the ridge to follow the present path of the St. Francis River. Then the Mississippi moved again and cut its present course to the sea.

A boy fishes at Crowley's Ridge State Park, circa 1948. –Arkansas History Commission

The ridge is named after Benjamin Crowley, who was a veteran of the War of 1812. Crowley moved to the ridge with his family and slaves after mustering out of the army, and he became a prominent local citizen. A state park near Paragould contains his homesite and grave, and bears his name like the ridge he loved.

—PIGGOTT—

Located 11 miles south of the Missouri border via Arkansas 139 and US 62, and 110 miles north of I-40 at Brinkley via US 49, Piggott is one of two functioning seats for Clay County. Piggott serves as the eastern county seat, while Corning serves as the western seat. Dual county seats were established in Arkansas when substantial natural barriers, like the nearly impassable Black River bottoms, divided one part of a county from another.

The most northeasterly county in Arkansas, this is also one of the youngest counties in the state. Originally called Clayton County when formed by the legislature in 1873 from parts of Greene and Randolph Counties, legislators changed the controversial name two years later. The county was initially named after Powell Clayton, who was a pervasive if controversial figure in Arkansas history. Clayton served as a Union soldier during the Civil War, a Reconstructionist governor from 1868 to 1871, a U.S. senator from 1871 to 1877, and finally the U.S. ambassador to Mexico. Widespread public dislike of Powell led the legislature to change the county's name by dropping the last three letters of "Clayton." The new name—Clay County—honored Henry Clay, one of the most noted statesmen of the South.

Soon after the creation of the county, local commissioners selected Corning as the county seat. Originally a logging camp, the community was called Carpenter's Station after the man who ran the depot for the St. Louis, Iron Mountain & Southern Railroad. Later Jay Gould, the eastern financier and railroad builder, suggested that the name be changed to honor H. D. Corning, an engineer who helped build the railroad. Since the Black River bottoms made it extremely difficult for residents of eastern Clay County to visit the county seat, local officials began to look for a likely community to serve as a dual seat of government.

They selected Piggott, which was originally called Houston. The community was built on a tract of land originally settled by D. Throgmorton, who came to Arkansas from Tennessee. When Throgmorton wanted to become postmaster of the new post office, Dr. J. A. Piggott pulled some political strings and secured the appointment for Throgmorton. In return, the new postmaster changed the

Logging train, circa 1905. —Southwest Arkansas Regional Archives

A logging crew and children in Pike County, circa 1910. —Southwest Arkansas Regional Archives

name of the post office from Houston to Piggott. The town naturally changed its name to match the post office.

The coming of the railroads through the area fueled explosive growth of the timber industry, and farmers began to settle in the clearings about 1910. Ernest Hemingway came to Piggott, where he wrote *A Farewell to Arms*. When the book was made into a movie starring Gary Cooper and Helen Hayes, Piggott hosted the world premier of the movie in 1933.

Today, Piggott and Corning continue their role as shared seats of Clay County.

—PARAGOULD—

Located thirty-one miles southwest of Piggott, twenty-two miles northeast of Jonesboro, and seventy-nine miles north of Brinkley on US 49, Paragould takes its name from two of the great railroad robber barons of the nineteenth century: J. W. Paramore and Jay Gould.

During the 1880s, both rival robber barons were laying track across Arkansas to link the businesses and industries of St. Louis with markets and resources in Texas. The two railroads crossed in Greene County, creating a logical place to build a town, which was surveyed in 1881. Officials of the rival railroads argued and argued about a suitable name for the embryonic community without any success at all, until some wag suggested naming the town after both rival railroad magnates. Thus Paragould, like Texarkana and Arkadelphia, was coined by combining several words into one.

Like Clay County, Greene County started out with a different spelling when the legislature lopped it off of Lawrence County in 1833. While the legislature named the county in honor of General Nathanial Greene, who was a hero of the Revolutionary War, the act creating the county misspelled the name without the final *e*.

Born in Rhode Island in 1742, Nathanial Greene operated an iron foundry and became active in colonial politics. When the Revolutionary War erupted, Greene commanded American troops with tremendous success. His militia participated in the siege of Boston. His outstanding strategic skills led to the capture of Charleston. He also stood by George Washington at Trenton, Brandywine, and Valley Forge. When the revolutionary government could not afford supplies for the Continental army, Nathanial Greene issued personal IOUs to the contractors. General Greene had to sell everything he owned to pay off those debts after the war.

It was embarrassing that the county named after such an illustrious national hero was not spelled correctly. So folks started spelling the name with the *e* at the end, and eventually even official state documents began to appear with the correct spelling. This change evolved without any legislation or other official approval. No one ever objected, and the change in spelling quietly became permanent.

After the formation of Greene County, the legislature established a temporary county seat at the home of pioneer Benjamin Crowley. Commissioners selected Paris (about five miles north of present-day Gainesville) as the first permanent county seat, which subsequently moved to Gainesville in 1848, and finally to the new railroad town—Paragould—in 1884.

—JONESBORO—

Located 53 miles southwest of Piggott, 57 miles northeast of Brinkley, and 108 miles northwest of Helena on US 49, Jonesboro was named after Senator William Jones, the legislator representing St. Francis and Poinsett Counties who ramroded the legislation creating Craighead County from portions of Mississippi, Greene, and Poinsett Counties in 1859. In an interesting twist of politics, the county was named to placate Senator Thomas Craighead, who was the one legislator who most profoundly opposed carving up Mississippi County and giving away some of the best stands of hardwood timber in Arkansas.

The Pioneers

European pioneers came relatively late to what is now known as Craighead County. The terrible series of earthquakes that destroyed New Madrid and vast areas of southern Missouri in 1811 and 1812 also devastated the St. Francis River valley, so folks other than hunters and trappers remained shy of the area until the fear of renewed earthquakes finally dissipated. The fate of the first European pioneers who finally did journey down the St. Francis failed to inspire confidence.

The first four settlers departed from the Indian village of Chilicataw (now Kennett, Missouri) in two pirogues and paddled down the St. Francis River to a place called Deep Landing at the foot of Maumelle Prairie. (The early Frenchmen who explored the Mississippi basin seemed to name geographic features after the human breast at every conceivable opportunity, for the name "Maumelle" appears routinely throughout the Mississippi and Great Lakes regions.) A man named Rittenhouse and his wife decided to settle there, and started to build a cabin at the landing.

The other two members of their party returned to Chilicataw to pick up the rest of their gear. The Rittenhouses had nearly completed the cabin when the two men returned. They found Mr. Rittenhouse dead next to the cabin, a roofing tool in his hand and a bullet hole in the back of his head. They searched the surrounding area, and found Mrs. Rittenhouse, who had been beheaded. After burying the couple, their friends packed up what they could and paddled back to Chilicataw. That grizzly discovery discouraged any subsequent settlement for fourteen years.

Then in 1829, Daniel Martin moved about six miles southwest of present-day Jonesboro. A veteran of the War of 1812, Martin cleared a small patch of land adjacent to a spring at the foot of a hill and planted Indian corn. He got along well with the local Indians, who moved out of the area in the 1840s as more Europeans began to arrive. One of the earliest settlers was Rufus Snoddy.

By the time the legislature created Craighead County in 1859, Snoddy's son had acquired a great deal of land in and around the future site of Jonesboro. Fergus Snoddy acquired most of his 480 acres by purchasing the bounty warrants Congress issued to veterans of the War of 1812. These warrants entitled veterans to 80 acres of land in Arkansas. Several other people—including Amzy Gayley, John Nicholas, Alfred Erwin, and L. Berry Mangrum—owned 160-acre plots in what would become Jonesboro.

The Birth of Jonesboro

Fergus Snoddy donated fifteen acres on the crest of Crowley's Ridge as the location for the county seat of the newly created Craighead County. He selected this site because it was a natural clearing, thus eliminating the need to cut down a lot of trees. The clearing did support a great deal of scrub, making it prime deer habitat. Men in coon-skin caps and homespun clothes came with axes to brush out the site for the new town, gathering scrub and a few rotted logs into great piles for burning. Unfortunately, the old logs contained large colonies of yellow jackets, which objected with painful persistence when the brush piles were set ablaze. Many of the volunteers had killed deer in the clearing, and some of the old-timers had killed bear there. In fact, they later built the first courthouse at the junction of well-used deer and bear trails.

Jonesboro and Craighead County grew slowly during those antebellum years. By 1861, the area still supported a small population without major roads, industries, or navigable rivers. The county had 2,979 free and 87 slave residents, and remained largely virgin forest. The social structure and attitudes of the area more closely resembled the Ozarks than the Delta and the Gulf Coastal Plain, where the explosion of cotton plantations had generated a slave-based economy. With only about thirty slaveholders in Craighead County, the average slaveholder was a small farmer with three slaves. So most local residents had little sympathy for the growing secessionist movement elsewhere in Arkansas where plantations were the norm.

Jayhawkers and Bushwhackers

Attitudes changed after Arkansas actually seceded from the Union, however, since most residents of the area emigrated from Tennessee, Kentucky, and other southern states. So Craighead County did raise three companies for the Confederacy, plus about a quarter of another company. While no companies were raised for the Union army, many residents who did not hold slaves remained hostile to the Confederacy and joined bands of pro-Union guerillas known as Jayhawkers. For the most part, however, Jonesboro and Craighead County remained a forgotten backwater during the war.

That changed somewhat in the spring of 1862, when a mob of more than a hundred people stormed the home of "Old Man Williams," an outspoken supporter of the Union. The mob tried and convicted the silver-haired septuagenarian and sentenced him to serve three years in the Confederate army "in front of Van Dorn's army." General Earl Van Dorn sent Williams back to his home, but an assassin's bullet soon silenced Williams and his politically incorrect views. Roving bands of pro-Confederate guerillas became known as Bushwhackers.

Between the Bushwhackers and Jayhawkers, wanton violence and depredation steadily increased. But perhaps the greatest hardship facing the typical farm family of Craighead County was the lack of salt, which was essential for preserving meat. Families began to trek into Union-held Missouri as far as Cape Girardeau in search of this elusive, expensive, and essential commodity. They traded wool, lint cotton, and dried fruit for the salt—but that was only part of the bargain. The only way Arkansans could obtain Union salt was to take an oath of allegiance to the Union, so loyalty to the Confederacy began to crumble in Craighead County.

The first real clash with Union troops in Craighead County came in the summer of 1863, after Federals came up Crowley's Ridge from Helena and captured Wittsburg, which is between Jonesboro and Forrest City on the St. Francis River. The Federals used Wittsburg as a base of operations for striking out into the Delta to seize as much cotton and liberate as many slaves as possible. During one of these forays, the Union commander, Captain Henry Eggleston, sent a detachment of Federals to collect a number of sick soldiers and take them back to Helena. As the Federals passed through Jonesboro, they encountered a small unit of Confederates and beat them in a skirmish that netted twenty-four prisoners, thirty horses, and thirteen wagons. The Federals locked their prisoners in the Jonesboro court-house and set out pickets for the night.

Survivors of the skirmish who had escaped the Federals earlier in the day returned that night with a considerable Confederate force. They slipped past the Federal pickets and attacked the sleeping main force without warning. Only a few Federal pickets escaped to tell the tale. Subsequent Federal forays into Craighead County were few and far between. But atrocities committed by lawless bands of maraud-ers—plus hardships created by the lack of salt, seed, food, clothing, mules, and horses—conspired to make the residents of Jonesboro and Craighead County mightily relieved when the war finally ended.

Jonesboro Grows

While Jonesboro had about 150 residents at the start of the Civil War, the population had only grown by about 50 people by the mid-1870s. Nevertheless, the town could boast of four lawyers, three sa-loons, three stores, two doctors, two drugstores, one school, and a church that used part-time preachers. Fire had destroyed the origi-nal courthouse, and all of the businesses were located on courthouse square, so officials held court in one of the stores whenever that was necessary.

The coming of the railroads in the 1880s created a population ex-plosion in Jonesboro. The number of residents jumped from about 250 in 1880 to about 2,500 by the mid-1880s. Then a great fire on April 27, 1889, swept through about forty businesses and homes north and northeast of the courthouse square. Jonesboro quickly rebuilt, for the town's economic growth appeared to be unstoppable.

The railroads spawned the birth of a major timber industry as well as related companies, such as the Jonesboro Stave Company, the Jonesboro Wagon Manufacturing Company, and the Indiana Match Company. Other industries developed that depended on good, cheap transportation. The Henry Wrape Company produced 1,600 carloads of products per year, the Jonesboro Brick Company produced 50,000 bricks per day, and several lumber companies began clearing the vir-gin forests at a prodigious rate. In the 1890s, landowners began to import sharecroppers to till the land after it was cleared. Cotton became the crop of choice, since it produced the greatest income per acre.

The Jonesboro economy took a nosedive in 1907 when cotton prices declined. F. M. Richardson, who had purchased recently cleared land in Craighead County, began to experiment with raising rice, which had never been grown in Arkansas before 1904. Richardson devoted 10 percent of his land to his rice experiments. His success quickly spawned the largest sale of land in the county's history; Alex Berger

Workers in a cotton field on the Tate farm in Ouachita County, circa 1900.
—Southwest Arkansas Regional Archives

bought 3,500 acres of cleared forest and devoted the entire parcel to rice production.

While Jonesboro's rate of growth slowed both abruptly and dramatically when cotton prices plummeted and lumber companies began to run out of trees, the value of farmland in Craighead County tripled from 1900 to 1910 as lumber companies accelerated their disposal of cleared land and rice became a major cash crop. Manufacturing companies that used wood as their raw materials disappeared, and agriculture replaced industry as the backbone of economic life in Jonesboro and Craighead County. While many of the industries brought about by the coming of the railroads disappeared during this first decade of the twentieth century, one such industry continued to thrive.

Jonesboro's Red-light Districts

While Jonesboro supported several sporting houses such as Arrington's Rooming House and Central Rooming House on Main Street, the town also supported several red-light districts such as two blocks of Cotton Belt Avenue just west of Culberhouse, and several blocks along Cate Street east of Main. But the most colorful district even had its own name: Swamp Poodle.

Swamp Poodle was a cluster of little red houses perched on posts sunk into a swamp between Main Street and the American Handle Mill. Each house in Swamp Poodle had its own boardwalk that connected to the high boardwalks along Johnson Street. After a heavy rain, the water rose until Swamp Poodle looked like a fleet of houseboats riding at anchor.

The ladies who lived in Swamp Poodle rarely ventured into downtown Jonesboro, since that might upset the more sensitive members of the community. So any time they needed to go shopping, the madam who ruled Swamp Poodle would telephone the appropriate store, which would send a driver to bring an assortment of goods so the ladies could select their purchases at home. Sometimes the Meyer Department Store would open up after hours so the ladies of Swamp Poodle could come and browse. R. H. Meyer would ask for volunteers from his female clerks and pay them overtime to work late. The clerks drew the shades and turned off the outside lights. Hacks with drawn curtains conveyed the ladies of Swamp Poodle to a back door in the alley, where they could discretely arrive and depart. Such forays always went off without a hitch.

LaFayette Sammons wrote eloquently of his memory of the red-light districts when he was growing up in Jonesboro. "I can remember as late as 1919 standing on the corner of Main and Huntington," Sammons wrote, "watching a street parade of the Haggenbach & Wallace Circus at the corner of Main and Huntington, and seeing gaily dressed young women out on the upstairs veranda that fronted on Main Street. From this veranda of the Central Rooming House, they waved to the clowns on the Band Wagons," and the clowns waved back. Many sporting houses particularly prospered during World War II, thanks to the new air base at Walnut Ridge.

Throughout their reign, the sporting houses of Jonesboro never did attract rough characters or underworld figures. Only an occasional fistfight between patrons disturbed the peace. Novelist Douglas Faulkner would have understood and relished the red-light districts of Jonesboro. Those days ended, however, with World War II. The 1950s heralded Jonesboro's emergence as a college town.

College Town

Jonesboro began its role as a college town in 1909, when one of the four state agricultural schools established by the legislature was slated for Jonesboro. The institution opened the following year as an agricultural high school, and reorganized as a two-year junior college in 1918. The school officially became a four-year program authorized to grant baccalaureate degrees in 1925, when the name changed to the State Agricultural and Mechanical College. The school awarded its first baccalaureate degree in 1931, and the name changed to Arkansas State College in 1933. Thanks to the GI Bill, the college began to grow so rapidly in the 1950s that, by the end of the decade, college officials began to develop aspirations of achieving university status. They began a serious program of improving their faculty and their facilities. The sheer size of the campus by the mid-1960s supported those aspirations as enrollment approached 5,000 students.

The 1966 election installed a new crop of legislators and a new governor—Winthrop Rockefeller. Within a year, Arkansas State College had become Arkansas State University. The university has subsequently earned the respect of educators and students alike, and has secured Jonesboro's reputation as an outstanding college town.

—HELENA—

Ten miles below the spot where the St. Francis River enters the Mississippi, the great river swings west to within 400 yards of the southern end of Crowley's Ridge. Numerous springs flowed out of the eastern base of the ridge, providing abundant drinking water. The rich land begged for crops, and the canebrakes begged for cattle. The Indians were friendly. And the Mississippi provided easy access. These were the riches that attracted the first Anglo-American settlers in the late 1700s to the place that would soon become a pioneer settlement called Helena. This town would figure prominently in the history and culture of the Delta.

Using modern highways as the frame of reference, Helena is 161 miles south of Piggott and 51 miles southeast of Brinkley on US 49.

The Pioneers of Helena and Phillips County

The first Anglo-American to settle in the area was Sylvanus Phillips, who came from North Carolina with his family in 1797 and settled a mile below the mouth of the St. Francis River at a place that came to be known as Little Prairie. Phillips arrived at the end of Spanish rule. Then Spain gave the land back to France, which immediately sold the lands to the United States as part of the Louisiana Purchase. The few settlers who arrived at the southern end of Crowley's Ridge before 1810 tended to be cattlemen and traders.

Ironically, the two events that paved the way for large-scale migration to the area were disasters: the New Madrid earthquakes of 1811 to 1812, and the War of 1812 (which ended in 1815). Congress made free land allotments available to victims of the earthquakes and to veterans of the war. These allotments could be used in lands of the Louisiana Purchase that were not already bound by Spanish land grants or Indian treaties.

Arkansas was then part of Missouri Territory, and a fair amount of land had already been purchased by the time Congress provided the New Madrid and war allotments. So some of the best lands had already been taken by the time the new wave of immigrants arrived. Immigrants entitled to an allotment could settle the land themselves or sell it.

Sylvanus Phillips and his neighbors were cattlemen, traders, and land speculators who were well positioned to profit from the onslaught of settlers. When Congress carved Arkansas Territory out of Missouri Territory on July 4, 1819, President James Monroe appointed James Miller of New Hampshire to be the first territorial governor. An election later that year installed a territorial legislature, which included Sylvanus Phillips as one of its members. The legislators proceeded to build the body of laws, make political appointments, and create the infrastructure necessary to govern the new territory.

In 1820, the legislature began to divide the territory into counties to facilitate the establishment of local government. Phillips County (named in honor of Sylvanus Phillips) became the second county created by the territorial legislature. The first county seat was Monticello, which was probably located close to the mouth of the St. Francis River where Sylvanus Phillips originally settled. That same year, Phillips, William Russell, and Nicholas Rightor surveyed a town site at the southern edge of Crowley's Ridge and named the embryonic town Helena, after Phillips's daughter.

Within a decade, Helena was prospering to the point that voters moved the county seat to Helena in 1830. From its earliest days, the waters of the Mississippi River governed the ebb and flow of life in Helena.

Whether it was spring floods or the coming of the steamboats, the Big Muddy was the Big Reality for Helena. "We have almost as big a river in our rear as in our front," a Helena editor wrote in the spring of 1836. Folks used ferryboats to get around town. "One foot rise in the river now," the editor wrote, "and we should require a lead and line to find the town." The waters rose to within six inches of topping the levee that year.

Levees and Steamboats

Levees have been such an integral part of the landscape in Phillips County since territorial days, that most folks take these remarkable structures for granted, never realizing the grueling work that went into building them by hand, or the scores of floods that washed away the work and dreams of pioneer families. Before the levees were built, spring floods rushed across the Mississippi valley on a regular basis. Twenty-four major floods between 1799 and 1864 inundated towns and farms along the Mississippi.

Local farmers and some communities began to protect themselves by building earthen embankments with shovels and wheelbarrows. These primitive levees tended to work as long as the opposite river bank did not have a levee. The embankment deflected floodwaters to the opposite shore, where the water washed over the land, dissipating its energy without raising the water level at the levee. But these isolated levees were not high enough or strong enough or long enough to effectively protect the farms and towns along the Mississippi, so few farmers risked planting the alluvial plain. Then Congress joined the fray in 1850.

Congress did not throw any money at the problem, but it did donate the swamps and flooded lands of the Mississippi valley to the states. Congress also gave state governments the authority to sell these lands to finance the construction of levees and drainage systems. Arkansas received about a million acres under this program. Governor Elias Conway seized upon the opportunity to build levees that would open up the state's alluvial lands to intensive agriculture. By 1854, simple levees protected almost all of the agricultural lands

Working on an Arkansas levee in the 1930s. —WPA, Arkansas History Commission

fronting the Mississippi and a considerable part of the lands fronting the Arkansas River.

By 1860, an almost continuous line of levees ran along the entire Arkansas shoreline of the Mississippi. The state had by then issued $2.5 million in public bonds to build 10 million cubic yards of levees. A lot of that money went into the pockets of corrupt government officials, con men, and dishonest contractors. But the levees changed the face of Arkansas and permitted large-scale agriculture on the alluvial lands of the Delta. The growth of agriculture stimulated the growth of steamer traffic to Helena, which prospered like Natchez, Vicksburg, and Memphis during the golden age of the steamboat.

Bernard De Voto believed that understanding the steamboat's impact on American life was to understand America. He revelled in the energy of the waterfront, where every aspect of life "was vital and eloquent." De Voto loved "the dens at Helena and Natchez and all the waterfront slums; the shanty boats with their drifting loafers; the boats of medicine shows, daguerreotypes, minstrel troupes, doctors, thugs, prophets, saloon keepers, whoremasters. . . . It was a cosmos." This colorful scene did, however, have a dark side.

While most people imagine Dodge City, Kansas, or Tombstone, Arizona, when they think of wild and woolly frontier towns, the reality of life in Helena equalled the legends of the Old West. Newspaper accounts of the day abound with shootings, organized robberies, murders, gamblers, counterfeiting, and sundry mayhem. The bayous, canebrakes, and swamps of the Delta provided a handy refuge for brigands and blacklegs (swindlers).

While Helena was clearly a lusty town, it also supported a number of schools, churches, and newspapers. The long tradition of land speculation supported so many lawyers doing title searches and land litigation that one wag observed that early Helena positively swarmed with lawyers. Many lawyers, merchants, and other professionals were also planters, and farming was certainly the principal enterprise of the Delta during the antebellum years.

Antebellum Life

A significant feature of the antebellum economy was that a small number of residents—the landed aristocracy—controlled most of the wealth. In 1860, for example, only twenty-five people owned 57 percent of the land in Helena. A mere seven people owned 37 percent of the land. Contrary to popular belief, however, most of the landed aristocrats in this area were not transplanted tidewater planters with old money from the southern colonies. Most were people of humble means who were the first fearless pioneers of the area and subsequently became successful land speculators.

Furthermore, Delta culture was not cleanly divided into a society of wealthy old plantation families, poor whites, and slaves—as Southern mythology seems to suggest. Delta society was a continuum from wealthy planters to successful farmers with medium-to-small holdings, to people who owned no land and worked as tenants and tradesmen, to unskilled laborers. Only 17 percent of the white male population owned slaves.

The wealthy planters who owned a thousand acres or more did control 48.5 percent of the land, but they represented only about 4 percent of the adult white males in Phillips County. Another 4 percent of the planters competed in the cotton market at a much lower level, with holdings of 600 to 999 acres, while 8 percent were large farmers, holding 300 to 599 acres. Together, these planters and farmers controlled all but 15 percent of the land. Most of the remaining territory was owned by yeoman farmers, who made up about 20 percent of the adult white male population.

The most illuminating statistic is that 65 percent of the county's adult white males held no land at all. Perhaps that explains the strong antisecession sentiment in Helena and Phillips County during the crisis of 1860 and 1861. Few men held land or slaves, so few supported leaving the Union. But the wealthy secessionists controlled local politics and sent a prosecession delegate to the convention held in Little Rock to determine how Arkansas would respond to the crisis.

Plowman with team. –Jesse L. Charlton, Special Collections, University of Arkansas Libraries, Fayetteville

Once the Union tried to reinforce Fort Sumter and shots were fired, and Lincoln called for volunteers to suppress Southern insurrection, sentiment in Helena and the rest of the Delta changed abruptly. Since the Little Rock convention voted to join the Confederacy and war was now inevitable, most men chose to fight with their kith and kin.

This decision would bring hardship and violent change to Helena and the Delta, which already had experienced tremendous change in the short time between the initial survey of Helena and the outbreak of the Civil War. The Delta evolved from frontier culture to cotton culture in a single generation. While the war and its aftermath would change the Delta forever, this brief period before the war established the cultural and historical foundation for Helena, Phillips County, and the Delta.

War in the Delta

War fever spread rapidly through Phillips County during the summer of 1861. About 400 of the 2,000 adult white males of the county quickly joined the Confederate army and soon found themselves fighting in battles far to the east at places such as Bull Run (Manassas) in Virginia and Shiloh in Tennessee. The Union threat to Arkansas came from the west.

After a big battle at Elkhorn Tavern on Pea Ridge in northwestern Arkansas, Federals under the command of General Samuel Curtis advanced into Arkansas along the White River in a bid to capture Little Rock. As the Union supply lines became stretched to the breaking point, Curtis concluded he needed a supply base somewhere on the Mississippi River. Helena was the logical choice, since it was ideally suited for sending gunboats and supply steamers up the White, St. Francis, and Arkansas Rivers.

General Thomas Hindman called up the local militia and requested additional volunteers to stop the advancing Federals. Hindman threw the state into chaos. The time was March 1862, and most of these men were the small farmers who produced the grain and meat that fed the people of Arkansas. A reporter for the *Arkansas Gazette* observed that "the plows are rusting in the furrows; the hoes rusting in the corners of the fence; the horses, mules, and oxen are browsing in the commons, and the men who were left to cultivate the soil are absent from home."

The situation was even more serious for the yeoman farmer himself, who needed this cash crop to pay off the loan on his land. Answering the call of patriotism meant ignoring the economic security of the farmer and his family. This was a time of difficult decisions.

The editors of the *Arkansas Gazette* called upon planters to start producing food instead of cotton. Hindman couldn't mobilize enough men quickly enough to stall the Federal advance, so he called upon every Arkansan to conduct a guerilla war against the Union supply lines. He further asked Arkansans to destroy every ounce of stock-piled food and forage, fell trees across all the roads, and burn every bridge in an effort to slow the Federal juggernaut. Human nature being what it is, most folks preferred to save what little they had rather than destroy everything in sight.

Hindman's scorched-earth policy never came to pass, and the Union army easily captured Helena in July 1862. Ironically, the taking of Helena marked the real beginning of the war for the residents of Helena and Phillips County. Small Confederate units (commonly only ten men) began an aggressive campaign of harassing Union troops and supply lines at every opportunity. Soon these guerillas pretty much controlled the countryside, while the Federals only controlled Helena and major encampments in the area. Snipers constantly shot at the Federals, and pickets along major roads came under constant fire from small bands of Confederates at night. These guerillas also dealt most harshly with anyone who cooperated with the Federals in any visible way.

Neither the Federals nor the Confederate guerillas could establish clear control, which put the civilian population square in the middle of all the violence and uncertainty. The Federals began to employ increasingly repressive measures in an effort to halt the guerilla attacks. Foraging parties from both sides liberated anything of value

Union troops of the 13th Illinois Infantry in Helena during the late summer of 1862. –Arkansas History Commission

from the surrounding farms—including the tools, livestock, and seed necessary for farming families to even support themselves. On top of all this misery, the Federals imposed a war tax.

Those who couldn't pay had their lands confiscated. It didn't matter if the property owner failed to pay because he was away fighting for the Confederacy, or because Union foraging parties destroyed his crops and stole everything that wasn't nailed down. No tax payment meant forfeiture of the land. By 1863, the Federals had seized 6,000 acres in Phillips County.

The economic nightmare continued to worsen in Helena and Phillips County. Inflation skyrocketed, so locals spent any cash on the necessities of survival, which did not include such things as the payments due on mortgages and other debts. Since many yeoman farmers only had four-year mortgages, the 1861 secession convention in Little Rock had passed a law prohibiting lenders and creditors from collecting debts for the duration of the crisis. But then the lenders and creditors couldn't pay their own bills, and the financial crisis rapidly cascaded throughout the society. Things really got crazy after the Federal occupation, since it was not clear if this law protecting debtors was still legally binding.

The misery visited upon the residents of Phillips County worsened once again in the spring of 1863, when large Confederate units began to arrive in preparation for an attack on Helena. They appropriated what little food and forage remained on the local farms. The Confederate plan was to recapture Helena as a means of loosening the Federal stranglehold on the Confederate garrison at Vicksburg. The attack came in July, but the Federals repulsed the Confederate attempt to take the city. The main Confederate force withdrew.

Helena remained a strategically critical Union stronghold, so the Confederates resumed their guerilla campaign in the area throughout most of 1864. The only thing these raids accomplished was to bring a rash of Federal reprisals upon the hapless civilians of the county. Eventually, the guerilla activity stopped, and Phillips County remained relatively quiet for the rest of the war.

An old soldier's saying declared that the Civil War was a rich man's war and a poor man's fight. Historian Carl Moneyhon studied how the war changed Phillips County in an effort to test the accuracy of that old truism. Here's what he found.

How the Civil War Changed Helena and Phillips County

In complete contradiction to folklore, which says that the wealthiest families lost the most from the war, Carl Moneyhon found that landed aristocracy (my term, not his) actually gained more than they lost. Most of the land the Federals seized during the war was returned to the original owners within five months of the Confederate surrender at Appomattox. While some families would lose their plantations due to tax problems during Reconstruction, the war itself did little to alter the ownership of land and wealth. Many families with land and old money actually improved their holdings after the war. Neither the planters nor the plantations disappeared.

Furthermore, Moneyhon observed that "all landowners below the great planters lost proportional shares of local wealth, suggesting that many of them had to pay the price of the war. Ultimately, however, it was the bottom, the landless, who paid the greatest price." Rather than being a great social leveler as Southern mythology suggests, the war actually produced an increasingly wide chasm between successful landowners and the rest of society.

Thus the frequent complaint that this was a rich man's war and a poor man's fight appears to be "much more than simply the grousing of the common soldier. It appears . . . to have been a true estimation of the impact of the American Civil War on Southern society."

An interesting development after the Civil War was the emergence of a black middle class, as former slaves entered the trades, professions, and politics. Black Arkansans began to exert their own influence on the reshaping of Southern society. This was by no means a universal black experience throughout the South. For many years after the Civil War, as historian Tom Dillard has pointed out, many blacks came to Arkansas because they viewed this state as a haven from social and economic oppression. "Emerging as it was from its primitive frontier isolation," Dillard observed, "Arkansas had a great labor shortage and black immigrants were eagerly welcomed."

One of the most notable immigrants to Helena after the war exemplified the forces that shaped the emerging black leadership in Phillips County and the rest of Arkansas during the last half of the nineteenth century.

Elias Camp Morris

Born in the hills of northern Georgia on May 7, 1855, Elias Morris lived with his mother and siblings. His father, who was owned by another farmer, was a skilled craftsman who could read and write. He taught these skills to his children when he visited them twice a week. When Union troops liberated his family, Elias enrolled at schools in Georgia, Alabama, and Tennessee until his parents died when he was fourteen. An Alabama shoemaker, Robert Carver, took in Elias as an apprentice. After completing his apprenticeship three years later, Elias opened a small shoe-repair business.

Life in Alabama for a young black businessman must have been less than ideal, so Morris joined thousands of other blacks who were leaving Alabama during the 1870s for the promised land of Kansas. At the age of twenty-two, Morris traveled by steamboat to Helena and planned to continue overland to Kansas. But he never continued the journey, for he found a community that was a hotbed of black political activity. J. N. Donohoo was a state legislator. H. B. Robinson was serving his second term as sheriff, and William Gray was county clerk. Helena showed great promise to a young shoemaker from Alabama.

Morris opened a shop, joined the local chapter of the Republican Party, and earned his credentials as a minister. The double income from his shop and ministry enabled Morris to buy land and rental properties. As his interest in real estate expanded, Morris also formed the Phillips County Land and Investment Company.

When he was only twenty-five years old, Morris was elected secretary of the Baptist State Convention. Two years later, he became president of the organization, an office he would continue to hold for

*Elias Camp Morris,
circa 1895.*
—UCA Archives

thirty-six years. Morris was not shy about mixing religion and politics whenever an issue moved him to action. He worked hard in the political arena, where he had enough political clout to be appointed an alternate delegate to the Republican National Convention in 1884. That same year he helped establish Arkansas Baptist College in Little Rock, where he served as president and later chaired the board of trustees.

By the time Helena built the first public library in Arkansas (1891), some white Republicans wanted to segregate the party of Lincoln, and Elias Morris helped lead the fight against the segregationists in his party. He became so exasperated with the Republican leadership, however, that he eventually urged his fellow blacks to abandon the GOP. Five years later, Morris was elected president of the National Baptist Conference, which was a newly created union of three competing black Baptist conventions.

Morris greatly broadened the scope of that organization to include a women's auxiliary, a union for young people, a retirement fund for ministers, and a publishing house. Even as segregation became the law of the land in Arkansas, Morris helped foster cooperation between black and white Baptists. Like other black leaders who emerged in the last half of the nineteenth century, Elias Morris worked tirelessly and at every opportunity to improve life for his fellow citizens.

Music on the Big Muddy

Besides the emergence of black leaders and a black middle class during the life of Elias Morris, Helena also developed a reputation for music. The town built a grand opera house in 1870 that was one of the three most elegant in the South, and performances always drew large crowds. Over the following century, local musicians moved onto the national stage, playing such diverse venues as the Metropolitan Opera Company, Radio City Music Hall, and the Grand Ol' Opry, among others.

A football player from Central High, for example, started singing and playing his guitar at local functions and talent shows. After a stint in the army, Harold Jenkins decided he preferred Twitty to his own last name when he resumed his musical career. After a performance in Conway, Arkansas, he found a new first name. Conway Twitty quickly rose to the national stage.

But perhaps Helena's greatest contribution to Southern culture was its fostering of a grassroots musical form indigenous to the area: the Delta blues. One of the first bluesmen to emerge from the cotton fields of Phillips County was Robert Junior Lockwood, who was born in 1916. One of his friends, Rice Miller, became a local character and a national legend as Sonny Boy Williamson. Once these two friends were

"King Biscuit Time" with Sonny Boy Williamson, announcer Sam Anderson, and Junior Lockwood. –Special Collections, University of Arkansas Libraries, Fayetteville

arrested for vagrancy and thrown in jail. Then a big storm destroyed part of the building and set them free. They had places to go and an art form to create.

Williamson used to play every day for Helena's Radio Station, KFFA, on a legendary program called "King Biscuit Time." For one glorious hour every day, Sonny Boy Williamson raised the spirits of folks throughout the Delta. Williamson and Lockwood helped develop a new form of uniquely American music that people around the world still find utterly compelling. That's a remarkable legacy for two friends from the cotton fields of Phillips County.

The Delta Cultural Center

Today, Helena is known as the historical and cultural heart of the Delta, thanks to the wide variety of events the community sponsors throughout the year. On the second weekend of October, for example, the town hosts the famous King Biscuit Blues Festival, which draws tens of thousands of enthusiasts from around the country. Helena supports an active program of historical preservation, which reached a new level in 1990 with the creation of the Delta Cultural Center. The center offers exhibits on Delta culture for the public and archives for the serious researcher.

Helena has figured prominently in Delta life for the better part of two centuries. Now the community is bringing that rich heritage to life for a new generation of Arkansans. Historic Helena continues to be the heart and soul of the Delta.

US 55
West Memphis–Blytheville
62 miles

US 55 connects West Memphis with Blytheville, the Missouri boot heel, and points north, stretching through rich Delta farmland that was once covered with almost impenetrable underbrush and frequently flooded forest. The principle community along this highway was named after the Methodist minister who came to Mississippi County in 1853, precisely twenty years after the state legislature carved the county out of Crittenden County. Mississippi County is bordered by Missouri to the north and Tennessee to the east, and the Big Muddy gives the county its name.

–BLYTHEVILLE–

Born in Virginia in 1816, Henry Blythe went through a lot of changes before settling at Crooked Lake in Mississippi County. His family moved to Tennessee in 1826, and he struck out on his own at the age of eighteen, living in northern Mississippi for several years before returning to Tennessee in 1841, where he began to farm and also earned his credentials as a minister. His wife and son died in 1844, and he remarried in 1851. But his new bride died a year later.

Needing a fresh start, Blythe moved to Arkansas, where he cleared sixty acres and remarried. He began preaching during the dark days of 1862, and his third wife died around the end of the Civil War, leaving no children. Blythe married yet again in 1868, but his new wife died a year later, leaving him a daughter. Henry Blythe married Milly Murry five years later, and they shared a good life together that produced seven children.

Soon after this fifth wedding, Blythe moved to another tract of land, which he had purchased in partnership with a friend named Mosely. He built a home in a small clearing on a slight rise and then added a sawmill. He surveyed part of this land for a town site in 1880, where he established a store and church, and he also served as the first postmaster. He wanted to call the new town Blythe, but friends prevailed upon him to call it Blythesville instead. Blythe later served a term in the state legislature at the end of the decade. Blythesville grew very slowly during that first decade, since the only roads to the town were so boggy as to be nearly impassable.

The town finally began to prosper after L. W. Gosnell installed a steam-powered gin in 1888, and cotton buyers began coming to town from Memphis. The s was dropped from the name "Blythesville" in 1890, when the post office moved for the third time. The town incorporated in 1891 and got a real shot in the arm toward the end of the decade, when a driller brought in an artesian well that finally provided the town with a source of good water.

The burgeoning railroad network in Missouri and Arkansas finally reached Blytheville in the first several years of the new century, drawn by the profitable virgin forests of Mississippi County. A new timber industry spawned a frantic explosion of activity. As loggers cleared the land and exposed the fertile soil, landowners drained the flooded land and sold it to aspiring cotton farmers.

The coming of World War II started a boom-and-bust cycle generated by military spending. The economy boomed when the federal government built the Blytheville Army Air Field in 1942. The economy then suffered a bust when the field closed in 1947. The base reopened in 1957 as a B-52 bomber base under the Strategic Air Command, and then closed again as the cold war ended. Today, Blytheville has returned to its roots as a transportation hub and supply center serving the farmers who work the rich soil of the northern Delta.

–Part Two–
THE COASTAL PLAIN

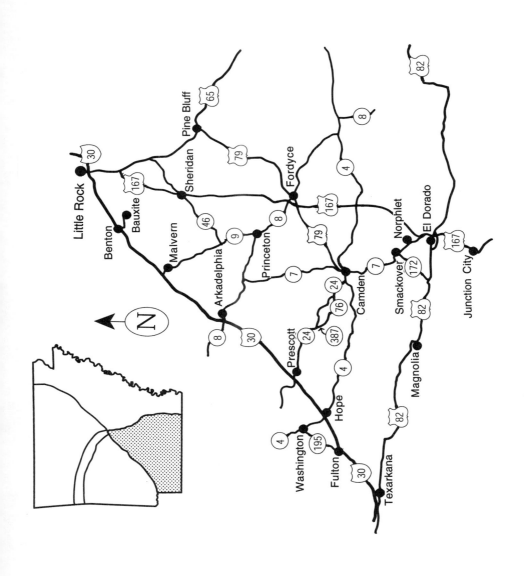

Little Rock–Texarkana
143 miles

Interstate 30–Washington–Fulton
23 miles

I-30 traverses the historical heart of the Coastal Plain along an ancient Indian path that became known as the Southwest Trail. In a very real sense, the story of the trail and the bottomlands of the Red River tells the story of the Coastal Plain. The history of Washington, in particular, provides a superb microcosm of life in territorial and antebellum Arkansas. The town's fortunes peaked during Fulton's heyday as a steamboat landing. Washington's fortunes fell when the railroads passed it by in favor of Texarkana, Hope, and Arkadelphia. And Washington found renewed vitality with the birth of the interstate highway system.

Yet Washington's history provides much more than a capsulized view of Arkansas history. For in many ways, Washington was one of the most remarkable and unique communities this country has ever produced. It has affected life in these United States more than any other community of comparable size.

The compelling history of Washington really begins with the Southwest Trail. I will then explore the histories of Washington, Hope, Fulton, Arkadelphia, and Benton. The Texarkana story appears later, in the section covering US 82 and Arkansas 172 from Texarkana to Smackover. Little Rock's history is told in part 3, and Malvern is discussed in part 4.

–SOUTHWEST TRAIL–

US 67 and I-30 roughly follow an ancient route along the eastern edge of the Ozark and Ouachita Mountains. State highway 195 precisely follows the Southwest Trail from Washington (eight miles northwest of Hope on Arkansas 4) to Fulton. The entire route extended from the Mississippi River through what is now Texas to the Great Southwest. Called the Chihuahua Trail by the Spanish and later the Southwest Trail by the Anglo-Americans, the route began as a narrow Indian path carved out in time before legend. The path skirted hills, avoided swamps whenever possible, and crossed rivers at the best fords. At the end of the eighteenth century, this was the only public road cutting through the wilderness that would become Arkansas.

The trail began on the Mississippi River at St. Louis, entered Arkansas at Hix's Ferry on the Current River, and headed southwest about 300 miles to the Red River, which at that time constituted the border with Spanish territory. The route bisects the state diagonally. Rocky, forested uplands and mountains lie above the trail. Flat, fertile alluvial and coastal plains lie below. The very disparate geology and topography of these two regions helped create two different cultural traditions, and two different patterns of economic development.

After the Louisiana Purchase in 1803, Congress financed the removal of brush and tree limbs along the trail, and folks began to refer to it as Congress Road or National Road. Prior to the establishment of Arkansas Territory in 1819, the trail would only accommodate traffic on foot or horseback. Travel by wagon or stagecoach was impossible.

Commerce and military traffic increased in the new territory, and the road was gradually improved. In 1832, President Andrew Jackson used army troops to widen the trail to sixty-one feet to facilitate his plan to remove all Indians east of the Mississippi. Now the trail could be used by wagons and stagecoaches, although the trip was still arduous. Hooves and wagon wheels churned the trail into muddy mires after a rain. Tall stumps still studded the road at inopportune places. Forty-five fords crossed rivers, streams, and bayous, and travelers ran a very real risk of losing wagons, livestock, or lives. Yet the upgraded Southwest Trail represented real progress.

The upgraded trail was commonly called the Military Road, but the Indians being evicted from east of the Mississippi called it the Trail of Tears. Hardships and disease along this route would claim 22 percent of them.

In its heyday, the liveliest spot along the Southwest Trail was known as the Hill of the Five Trails (now the site of Washington). Here, a day's trek northeast of the Red River, four Indian trails intersected with the Southwest Trail. Sam Houston, Davy Crockett, Stephen Austin, and Jim Bowie knew the area well. Three tiny settlements developed nearby. Fulton, located fifteen miles southwest of the hill on the Red River, developed as a landing for keelboats bringing in supplies from New Orleans. Mound Prairie developed five miles down the western Indian trail, and a few log cabins clustered around Ozan Creek on the Southwestern Trail seven miles above the hill.

Settlers in this area of gently rolling hills generally fell into one of three categories. Some were veterans of the Revolutionary War who had received land grants from a grateful government. Others received land grants for fighting in the War of 1812. And some came from

Missouri after they had lost everything to the terrible New Madrid earthquake in 1811. They came with cottonseed and a few slaves to plant the rich black soil of the bottomlands, which were formed by small rivers and creeks. Few settlers followed the two more southern Indian trails, which led to a treeless tangle of canebrakes where springs were quite uncommon.

At this time, there was only one real town in the entire Arkansas Territory, Arkansas Post, which had been established by Tonti in 1686 on the Arkansas River near the Mississippi. At the time when folks began to settle around the Hill of the Five Trails, Arkansas Post plus all the trappers and fur traders it served numbered about 400 people. As wagon traffic became possible down the Southwest Trail, the flow of settlers increased. Pioneers drove cattle ahead of their wagons, and some brought a family or two of slaves. Each sought prime bottomland somewhere in the wilderness. Small towns began to appear at fords along the many rivers that crossed the trail.

When the railroads began to penetrate Arkansas in the 1870s, they followed the same ancient pathway as the Southwest Trail. New towns began to grow along the railroads. Older towns at fords and riverboat landings began to fade away. Then the automobile made its imprint upon the land, and paved roads became the standard a half century later. The general route of the Southwest Trail became a ribbon of concrete. From prehistory to the modern day, the Southwest Trail has provided many Arkansas travelers with the best way to "get there from here."

—WASHINGTON—

Located nine miles northwest of Hope on Arkansas 4, Washington has a rich history dating from the dawn of the nineteenth century. Here James Black created the Bowie knife and one of the most compelling love stories of the period. Davy Crockett told tall tales at the tavern. Sam Houston planned the Texas Revolution. And Washington's courthouse served as the Confederate capitol of Arkansas after Little Rock was captured in 1863. Today, much of the old town remains preserved in a state park.

The Pioneers

Methodist minister William Stevenson brought the first settlers west to the area in 1812. They traveled down the Southwest Trail from Missouri, cutting the trail a little wider along the way to accommodate their pack mules. The families who came with Stevenson made their homes around the future site of Washington, which was called the Hill of the Five Trails according to local folklore. When Congress established Arkansas Territory in 1819, the southwestern part of the territory was organized as Hempstead County. The log home of John English near Ozan Creek (about eight miles northeast of what is now Washington) became the Hempstead County courthouse; the community that formed around it became known as Hempstead Courthouse.

In 1822, the Reverend Stevenson built a large log shed to serve as a centrally located meeting place to hold Methodist services. He selected a spot on the Hill of the Five Trails by Black Bois d'Ark Creek, and called it the Ebenezer Camp Ground. The site was ideally located, for folks from the surrounding settlements could reach the camp in less than a half day by oxcart.

The oxcart had become a prime means of travel in the area, thanks to an intensive road improvement effort spearheaded by the Court of Common Pleas at Hempstead Courthouse. The court appointed local freemen and their slaves to work on roads from Hempstead Courthouse to Ozan, which was a new settlement on Ozan Creek. Other roads were improved from Ozan to Mound Prairie, from Mound Prairie to Columbus, and from Columbus to Fulton. The work involved removing underbrush and whacking stumps to within six inches of the ground.

John Ragland in 1976 drives his horse cart in front of the Hempstead County Courthouse, built 140 years earlier. —Southwest Arkansas Regional Archives

Meanwhile, a steady stream of travelers rode down the Southwest Trail toward the Red River and Mexico, in spite of the substantial danger from desperados and Indians on the far side of the river. Elijah Stuart built a tavern on the Hill of the Five Trails, where the weary traveler could get a hot meal and a room for the night. William Shaw and his two sons built a blacksmith shop, where they repaired wagons and shoed horses.

Log homes began to appear on the hill, followed by a mercantile store featuring fine fabrics and coffees from New Orleans. Soon a trading post appeared. A town was beginning to grow all around the Ebenezer Camp Ground.

The surrounding settlements were growing too. Folks heading down the Southwest Trail to Texas became seduced by the rich bottomlands of Hempstead County, and they stayed. Soon new settlers spread out from Mound Prairie toward the Red River, bringing with them three to twenty slaves per family. Here Kentuckian Daniel Witter opened a one-room log schoolhouse. Nearby, in Mound Prairie, Dr. Nathan Smith opened a hospital on his farm, where he grew mulberry trees to feed his silkworms.

Local cotton farmers got a big boost when John Johnson cut a road—at his own expense—across *Prairie d'Ane* to *Écore à Fabri* (Fabri's Bluff; now called Camden), which was a settlement on the Ouachita River. From there, the river provided easy access to cotton

Cotton bales on a steamboat of G. L. Koons and Bros. –Southwest Arkansas Regional Archives

buyers in New Orleans. This new route avoided the infamous Great Raft, which choked the Red River with miles of tangled trees swept into the water by centuries of flooding.

Meanwhile, Stephen Austin's fortunes had improved since he had left the area (see Fulton). Newly independent Mexico honored Spain's grant to Moses Austin (Stephen's father) to establish a colony on the Brazos River in the Province of Texas. Moses Austin died, so Stephen Austin led 300 families to the Brazos himself. Illnesses raged through the Hill of the Five Trails about this time, spurring many local residents to join Austin in Texas.

In the fall of 1824, the Court of Common Pleas for Hempstead County moved to Elijah Stuart's tavern on the Hill of the Five Trails. Thanks to a small land grant from Congress, a permanent log courthouse was built at the highest point of the hill in 1825. That same year, the hilltop settlement took the name Washington. Perhaps the most interesting resident of Washington during this period was James Black.

James Black and the Bowie Knife

James Black was born in 1800, and his mother died when he was very young. His father remarried, but James could not bear to live with his stepmother, so he ran away to Philadelphia at the age of eight. He claimed he was eleven so he could apprentice to a silversmith. Unfortunately, by the time Black became a journeyman seven years later, British competition had virtually destroyed the U.S. silversmithing industry. So he worked his way down the Ohio and Mississippi Rivers to New Orleans in search of possibilities.

Black worked on a ferryboat for a time, but quickly grew bored, so he signed on as a deckhand on a steamboat headed up the Red River to Fulton. Upon reaching Fulton, he hiked fifteen miles up the Southwest Trail to have a look at the growing settlement on the Hill of the Five Trails. There he found odd jobs until he was hired by William Shaw to work in his smithy. Black learned his new trade quickly, and soon he was repairing guns and making knives.

Blacksmiths were essential to the survival and growth of communities in those days. They were highly respected, and they earned more than doctors. Within a year, James Black had become indispensable to the Shaw smithy. He got along well with William Shaw's large family, forging a particularly close friendship with Shaw's eldest daughter, Anne. William Shaw wanted Anne to marry into a prestigious plantation family and became outraged when he learned that James Black had won her heart.

Yet Shaw needed Black's skills in the smithy, since the apprentice had become the best blacksmith in the county. Shaw made Black a full partner in the business to keep him from opening his own shop. Business boomed. But Shaw would not allow his daughter to marry Black. The daily torment of unfulfilled love took a terrible toll on Anne and James.

Finally, they could no longer stand the pain and the frequent arguments with Anne's father. Black sold his share of the blacksmithing business back to William Shaw, who said he didn't have the money but would pay it as soon as possible. Black set off on foot westward into the wilderness, after Anne promised to await his return.

After five years of hard work, James Black returned to Washington for the woman he loved. But Anne's father still vigorously opposed the marriage. He also claimed that he didn't owe Black any money from the old partnership. But Black got what he really wanted; Anne married him over her father's objections. William Shaw never forgave his daughter. Black added injury to insult when he opened a smithy in Washington, competing directly with Shaw. Soon Black had all the work he could handle, and he had made an enemy for life. Even after Shaw's daughter had borne three sons and a daughter, he still hated Black.

Black used a superior process for tempering steel, which enabled his knives to stay razor sharp after an unusual amount of work or abuse. The market for such implements was large. Every man in the territory carried a large knife for both utility and self-defense. A knife was reliable and could be used against several opponents, whereas a flintlock pistol only afforded one shot—if the powder in the priming pan would ignite, which was problematic in damp conditions.

Black's knives gained renown as the best made anywhere. He designed each knife to satisfy the needs and taste of the particular customer. Many were fighting knives featuring a long stiletto blade that tapered evenly to a fine point. So many men in Arkansas began to carry this knife that it became known as an Arkansas Toothpick.

It was at this point in Black's career when James Bowie came to town. This knife fighter and ruthless land speculator from Louisiana came to Washington in December 1830 to consummate a deal involving several thousand acres in Arkansas. Bowie had carved himself a reputation as the frontier's premier knife fighter years before in the Battle of the Vidalia Sandbar, where perhaps as many as a dozen men died. Black and Bowie had not met before, but each knew the other very well by reputation.

Bowie asked Black to build a knife based on a pattern originally developed by Bowie's brother Rezin. He left town, saying he would return in several months for the completed knife.

Black built the knife his customer had requested. He also built one of his own design that he felt would make a far superior fighting knife. When Bowie returned, Black showed him both knives and explained the advantages of his own model. He then offered to let Bowie try them and select either one at the same price. Bowie picked Black's design.

Soon thereafter, Black's knife established its permanent place in history. An enemy Bowie had presumably swindled hired three well-armed desperados to kill Bowie as he was traveling to Texas. They ambushed Bowie and managed to wound him in the leg. According to newspaper accounts of the day, Bowie drew the knife Black had just made and completely severed the head of one ruffian. A vicious up-thrust disemboweled a second attacker. Bowie concluded the fight by striking the third desperado with a single blow which split the man's skull to the shoulders. Newspapers throughout the country published all of the lurid details, and orders poured into Black's smithy.

Davy Crockett was mightily impressed when he had occasion to see Bowie draw this knife. Crockett said in his autobiography that "many a time I have seen a man puke at the thought of the point touching the pit of his stomach." The knife had become the most effective implement for personal protection on the frontier.

Henceforth, every customer who came to Black for a knife asked him to make a knife just like Bowie's knife. Soon they simply asked for a *Bowie knife*. The knife's design and superior tempering made it a peerless weapon.

The feature that really set Black's design apart from all the others was the scimitar-like curve on the top third of the blade just behind the point. This concave edge was razor sharp, as was the more traditional bottom edge of the blade. The point of the knife hooked upward well below the level of the top edge of the blade, adding a new deadliness to knife fighting that was ideally suited to Bowie's fighting style, which he described as "reach and disable."

The reason Black's blade was so deadly was that a short thrust with this knife would create a vicious, elongated puncture that made it much easier to withdraw the blade and continue the fight. Some sources say that Bowie may have fought fifteen to twenty duels with the knife Black made before Bowie died at the Alamo, but others believe that number may be a bit high.

Black continued his successful career, amassing a comfortable fortune to support his wife and four children. Then Anne got sick and died. William Shaw seemed to blame Black personally for the death of his daughter. His years of simmering manic hatred were about to

The original Bowie knife made by James Black, now owned by Burt Moore.
—Southwest Arkansas Regional Archives

boil. In the summer of 1839, a protracted fever kept Black bedridden, and his children cared for him.

One dark night, Shaw snuck into Black's bedroom with a club and began to bludgeon the helpless blacksmith in the head. Black was nearly dead when the noise of the assault alerted his dog, which seized Shaw's throat. Shaw somehow managed to break free and escape. He was lucky to survive. Black survived too, but the resulting infection left him blind.

After regaining his strength, Black headed east to a specialist, but a quack in Cincinnati took all of his money and permanently destroyed his sight. He returned to Washington to discover that William Shaw had sold off everything Black owned and disappeared into Texas with the proceeds as well as Black's children. Black was penniless, blind, and alone.

John and Jacob Buzzard, two planters on the Red River, soon learned of Black's plight and invited him to live with them. Black accepted. Several years later, Dr. Isaac Jones examined Black and told him there was a slight chance his sight could be restored in the right eye, but there was no hope for the left. Black declined the offer, however, on the grounds that he had no way to pay the doctor for his services. Dr. Jones wouldn't take no for an answer, so Black moved in with the Jones family and began a long series of painful procedures. The effort failed, but Jones asked Black to stay with the family and look after his four boys when the doctor was away from home.

The explosion of a steam boiler on his plantation killed Dr. Jones in 1858. The family insisted Black stay. After Mrs. Jones died in 1876, Black moved in with the doctor's son Daniel, who wrote an account

Daniel Webster Jones, circa 1875. –Southwest Arkansas Regional Archives

of Black's recollections. Daniel Webster Jones wrote, "my earliest recollections are connected with him. His kindness and fatherly advice
to me, and my brothers, endeared him to us all, and my father felt
that he was sufficiently compensated by the manner in which he executed the trust in looking after us." He continued:

> I slept in the same room [as a child], read to him light literature and
> history, and led him about when he desired to go anywhere from
> the place. He was a man of extraordinary memory and was always
> made the referee in all the controversies among the old settlers when
> they failed to agree to any occurrence of the early times. He was
> universally respected as a man of the strictest integrity and upright-
> ness. Night after night, I have listened to him until midnight, recit-
> ing to me incidents of the early days of that section of the state, and
> I have often regretted that I did not write them down as he told me.

James Black took the secret of his tempering process to the grave.
He was buried in what is now called the Old Presbyterian Cemetery

in Washington. The wooden marker has long since rotted away, so the grave is now unmarked.

Washington bustled during the decade when James Black crafted a knife for James Bowie. Davy Crockett livened up the place. Indians evicted from east of the Mississippi by Andrew Jackson began to stream down the Southwest Trail, dying in droves from cholera along the way, and making many Washington businessmen wealthy in the process. One of the most interesting developments occurred when Sam Houston hatched the Texas rebellion.

Sam Houston and Davy Crockett

Wearing a Mexican poncho, Sam Houston rode into town on a horse sporting silver plates on the saddle. This tough hombre of imposing stature stayed for a time in a room over the tavern. According to local legend, handed down from parent to child, Stephen Austin and James Bowie met with Houston in December 1832 to develop a plan for liberating Texas from the tyranny of Mexican rule. While this meeting cannot be documented, records show that the three men were indeed in the area at this time.

Houston returned to Washington two years later, to meet with friends above the local tavern. Austin had been imprisoned in December 1833 by the new president of Mexico, when Austin delivered a petition requesting that Antonio Lopez de Santa Anna recognize the independence of Texas. Austin would remain imprisoned for nearly two years.

In his book *Excursion Through the Slave States of North America* (published in 1844), G. W. Featherstonhaugh—an English writer and snob who visited Washington during this time—provides a firsthand, if somewhat condescending, description of the revolutionary spirit pervading the town in those days:

> After breakfast, we made an agreeable excursion in the neighborhood, calling for a short time at the little insignificant wooden village of Washington, where government land-sales were holding.
>
> I was not desirous of remaining long in this place. General Houston was here, leading a mysterious sort of life, shut up in a small tavern, seeing nobody by day and sitting up all night. The world gave him credit for passing his waking hours in the study of *trente et quarante* and *sept a lever*, but I had been in communication with too many persons of late, and had seen too much passing before my eyes to be ignorant that this little place was the rendezvous where a much deeper game than *faro* or *rouge-et-noir* was playing. There were many persons at this time in the village from the States lying adjacent to the Mississippi, under the pretence of purchasing government lands, but whose real object was to encourage the settlers

of Texas to throw off their allegiance to the Mexican government. Many of these individuals were personally acquainted with me; they knew I was not with them and would naturally conclude that I was against them.

Featherstonhaugh left town, "having nothing whatever in common with their plans, and no inclination to forward or oppose them."

Davy Crockett and a half-dozen companions arrived in Washington from Tennessee in November 1835. Crockett spent a week partying with the local folks before continuing on to join Sam Houston's army in Texas. He really liked the people of Arkansas. "If I could rest anywhere," Crockett observed, "it would be in Arkansaw where men are of the real half-horse, half-alligator breed such as grows nowhere else on the face of the universal earth." That weeklong party was the grandest occasion in the town's history. People poured into Washington from the outlying settlements and plantations. Speeches from the

Davy Crockett, from an engraving by S. S. Osgood used as the frontispiece in Col. Crockett's Tour of 1835. —Southwest Arkansas Regional Archives

courthouse steps were greeted by huzzahs and a flurry of coonskin caps thrown into the air. A formidable storyteller, Crockett regaled the folks with many humorous tales. A favorite involved his recently failed attempt at reelection to Congress.

Crockett had told folks in Tennessee, "If you re-elect me to Congress I will serve you faithfully; if you don't, you may go to the Devil and I will go to Texas!" Andrew Jackson disliked Crockett and did what he could to foil the woodsman's campaign. Old Hickory succeeded, and Crockett soon met his destiny at the Alamo.

The month after the Alamo fell, Houston's army annihilated 1,600 Mexican soldiers at San Jacinto, winning independence for the Republic of Texas. Six months later, Houston became the president of the new republic. By the end of the year, Stephen Austin had died. His imprisonment in Mexico City had broken the man beyond repair.

The winds of political change were not confined to the Republic of Texas, however. Three months after Texas achieved its independence from Mexico, Arkansas became a state. Washington residents loomed large in the political process of the territorial government at Little Rock, and their influence continued after statehood. But the town rapidly changed from a frontier outpost to a community of lawyers. Ruffled shirts became as common as coonskin caps. Law offices seemed to sprout on every sandy street. Washington's barristers prospered, and many became influential judges and prosecuting attorneys. Daniel Ringo, for example, was appointed chief justice of the Arkansas Supreme Court. And Washington's Judge Cross was elected to the U.S. House of Representatives. Not all folks who had lived in Washington brought pride to the community, however.

A Duel to the Death

In December 1837, one of the Washington's most respected former residents killed a man on the floor of the state House of Representatives. Colonel John Wilson, who was Speaker of the House, used a Bowie knife to conclude a long-standing political disagreement with Colonel J. J. Anthony during a heated debate about a bill establishing a bounty on wolves.

Anthony proposed an amendment that would require the president of the State Bank (who happened to be Wilson) to inspect every pelt before the bounty was paid. Angered over a proposal that entailed such an obvious waste of his time, the speaker asked Anthony if he intended an insult. Anthony rose from his chair to speak, but Wilson asked him to take his seat. Anthony remained standing. Wilson again asked him to take his seat. Anthony heatedly replied that he had a right to the floor, and he would keep it. In a fit of passion,

Wilson stormed down the aisle toward Anthony with Bowie knife in hand. Anthony drew his own knife and closed on his attacker.

According to a letter from James Snell to his father on December 5, 1837, Wilson took a swipe at Anthony, but failed to connect. Anthony severely sliced Wilson's right arm, and another powerful blow nearly severed Wilson's left hand at the wrist. Somehow, the mutilated Speaker of the House was able to retaliate with a powerful strike to the center of Anthony's breast, killing him instantly. Wilson immediately fainted from his wounds.

According to local Washington legend, however, the flow of events was slightly different. In this version of the fight, Washington resident Grandison Royston tried to prevent the incident by pushing a chair between the two men. Wilson knocked the chair aside with one hand and buried his knife in Anthony's chest with the other.

In any event, such behavior tended to be frowned upon on the floor of the legislature. So it was no surprise when Wilson was expelled from the House. Royston was elected Speaker of the House, and local officials reluctantly brought Wilson to trial. While duels were illegal, they were nevertheless a common indulgence. Wilson was acquitted, and later reelected.

The fight paled into insignificance, as far as the general public was concerned, next to the mismanagement and chicanery that undermined the state's two banks, throwing Arkansas into an economic funk that was only worsened by the nationwide Depression of 1837. Both banks had been plagued with bad luck, folly, and embezzlement. The state government completely failed to grapple with the problem, and the banks closed their doors in 1839. That same year, William Etter brought a printing press to town from Pennsylvania and started a newspaper, which he called the *Washington Telegraph*.

Antebellum Washington

The bank failures hit Washington hard. Editor William Etter wrote in the *Telegraph*, "nearly one-fourth of the town was tenantless, some having grown tired of the unprofitable monotony, and moved away, and others having caught the Texas fever." Washington's experience was a microcosm of the entire state, as many Arkansans left for Texas, Oregon, and California.

The town began to prosper again as the whole area around Washington began to change. The first stagecoach rumbled into Washington in 1838, providing unprecedented speed and comfort to Little Rock. The stage covered the 120 miles in an astonishing 38 hours. Ten stores provided a dizzying array of products. Slaves poured into the plantations via Fulton, and a wealthy class of planters arose in

Grandison Royston.
—Arkansas History Commission

the bottomlands around Washington. Slaves, cotton, and riverboats brought prosperous times to Fulton. Columbus evolved into a prosperous village. Hempstead Courthouse took the name Marlbrook from the name of the plantation owned by Judge Edward Cross.

Yet the warm frontier spirit remained. Mothers told their children to go visit Uncle Jimmie Black. "He's a lonely old man," they would say, "and he needs the company." Grandison Royston took a pocketful of magnolia seeds and planted them in his neighbors' yards. The year was 1839. The seed planted near his law office grew into a particularly fine tree that is still alive today. It remains the largest magnolia in Arkansas.

Young children were taught on each plantation by a resident schoolmistress during the growing season. Many plantation families wintered in Washington, where their children attended one of two subscription schools. Planters' older sons were sent to schools east of the Mississippi to complete their educations, while older daughters attended academies in the South. Soon Washington established

Author Al Paulson is dwarfed under the canopy of this magnolia tree planted by Grandison Royston near his law office in 1839. It remains the largest magnolia in Arkansas. —Polly Walter

its own academies to educate local sons and daughters. A year later, in 1848, the man who had built the first house and tavern on the Hill of the Five Trails made the local newspaper. Elijah Stuart had died.

But King Cotton lived, and Washington prospered. Aside from the failure of the state's two banks, the antebellum years were kind to the Anglo-American residents of the Washington area. Texas was filling up, and Arkansas had the only supply of good cotton land left in the South. The Washington area had a lot of prime bottomland.

Both large plantations and small farms profited from the booming cotton trade. On a quiet night, folks in Washington could sometimes hear the mournful whistle of a steamboat leaving Fulton ladened with cotton headed for New Orleans, or arriving with a load of supplies and slaves.

Slavery in Washington

Nearly every white adult in the area owned slaves. Slaves worked the fields, ran the households, and raised the children. Trusted young female slaves went to New Orleans by steamboat to learn haute cuisine from the finest French chefs. Others might learn dressmaking or hairdressing. Slaves attended one of the four local churches with their masters, sitting in the balcony with all the black and white children. Every service—whether Baptist, Methodist, Presbyterian, or Episcopal—included a special time when a spiritual was sung from the balcony. But slaves they remained. They were bought and sold. They were commonly given as wedding presents by doting parents. Slavery was woven deeply into the fabric of life in antebellum Washington.

Bob Lancaster wrote eloquently in *The Jungles of Arkansas* about the hardships, grotesque treatment, and brutality that slaves faced throughout Arkansas. His essay was based on interviews of more than 800 former slaves conducted by the WPA Federal Writers Project in the 1930s. The former slaves remembered the whip and the auction block quite clearly, and set to rest the myth of the happy, contented slave. Nevertheless, a sizeable minority of former slaves spoke highly of their former masters.

Most slave owners around Washington only owned a few slaves, and small farmers worked the fields side by side with their slaves. Yet working on a small farm in other areas of Arkansas did not ensure kind treatment. In Ashley County, for example, William Daniels was hauled into court *for being too kind to his slaves.* That was considered obnoxious behavior in the Ashley County of 1849.

The environment and attitudes of Hempstead County in general, and Washington in particular, were apparently different. There seems to have been a sense of community among the blacks and whites in Washington that would become evident when war came, and Federal and Confederate wounded streamed into the town after the Battle of *Prairie d'Ane.* That sense of community would become strained in the turmoil immediately following the fall of the Confederacy.

Although the history of Washington is really the history of southern Arkansas (the Coastal Plain), several aspects of Washington life also set the community apart. The town's community spirit—the unprecedented involvement of its residents in regional social, political, and judicial issues—the traditions of fair play and cooperation—all of these things may have mitigated somewhat the hardships and alienation commonly experienced by slaves elsewhere in Arkansas. In that sense, the history of Washington may not be representative of the history of the Coastal Plain (or the Delta) in the nineteenth century.

War Clouds on the Horizon

Washington had matured by 1860. Old men who had once been young pioneers hobbled along the boardwalks. The Southwest Trail had become the town's main road, Franklin Street. The old-timers who had built Washington passed the torch to a new generation. Dr. Nathan Smith retired to the farm where he had started the area's first hospital. Daniel Witter, who had built and taught at the first school, retired after serving on two occasions as the county judge. Judge Edward Cross also retired after three terms in Congress and a few years as an associate justice with the Arkansas Supreme Court.

Washington residents continued to exert a powerful influence on Arkansas. Brothers Rufus and Augustus Garland represented the county in the state legislature. Alfred Carrigan served in the state senate. Edward Gantt, who was just about the youngest lawyer in

John Eakin.
—Arkansas History Commission

town, was elected to the U.S. House of Representatives—although the Civil War prevented him from serving. And Dr. Charles Mitchell was elected to the U.S. Senate.

Washington changed forever when Arkansas joined the Confederacy. William Etter's newspaper provided staunch and articulate support for the cause. While he filtered out opposing views and unhelpful news, Etter's reporting was honest. His new editor, John Eakin, was a lawyer and political activist who took a more active role both on the pages of the paper and on the political stump. Once a staunch Unionist, Eakin became an eloquent and tireless advocate for the Confederacy. He soon became the mayor of Washington, as well. His fiery oratory in the paper earned him notoriety as the "foremost oracle of Confederate propaganda in the Trans-Mississippi Department."

Soon after the firing on Fort Sumter, Washington raised a company of volunteers, called the Hempstead Rifles, for the Fourth Arkansas Regiment of the Confederate army. One of its officers was Daniel Webster Jones, who had worked for James Black as a child and cared for him in his later years. After the war, Jones would become governor of Arkansas. Hempstead County raised a second company of 86 men commanded by John W. Rawles.

John Eakin set himself the task of keeping up public morale and unifying the citizenry of southwest Arkansas in general, and Washington in particular.

The war soon heated up, and the Federal blockade of New Orleans began to take a heavy toll on Washington. Money dried up because there was no way to export cotton. Inflation soared. And critical commodities like salt, needles, and thread became scarce. But the real problem was the lack of medicine. The measles and congestive fevers began to claim the very young and the very old—and then people in the prime of life. Even Texan volunteers on their way to sign up in Little Rock succumbed to the disease and breathed their last in Washington.

Spirits plummeted to an all-time low in January 1863, when Eakin wrote in the newspaper that the "enemy is in possession of Fort Smith, Van Buren and probably Ozark. Our army has fallen back. We are ashamed of the Trans-Mississippi Department." This was the first time Eakin had ever published any dissatisfaction with the Confederacy.

Vicksburg fell, and Federal forces advanced on Little Rock from the east. To the north, Confederate forces fell back toward the Arkansas River. The war ground its way toward Hempstead County. The Federals had split the Confederacy in two, severing all communications between the states on either side of the Mississippi. Arkansas, Louisiana, and Texas were on their own—with most of their men

The courthouse in Washington served as the state's Confederate capitol after Union troops captured Little Rock. –Arkansas History Commission

fighting on the other side of the Mississippi. And the Confederate army east of the Mississippi lost a major source of pork, beans, forage, and other consumables. Yet "self-styled military genius" (as Eakin called him) Jefferson Davis placed little military importance on Vicksburg as far as folks in the Trans-Mississippi could tell. That proved to be one of the gravest strategic blunders of the war. Union General Frederick Steele captured Little Rock on September 10, 1863, and refugees began to appear in Washington.

Town residents and nearby planters sheltered and fed them. Soon exhausted refugees filled every spare room and attic in the area. Then barns and empty slave quarters were filled. Finally, tents were erected on local lawns. Governor Harris Flannigan moved the government records from Little Rock to the Hempstead County Courthouse (which still stands today), and Washington became the Confederate capital of Arkansas. Major General Sterling Price established the headquarters for the Arkansas portion of the Confederate army in nearby Camden, which lay at the end of the road John Johnson had cut to the Ouachita River when Washington was young.

Work on defensive fortifications took on a new urgency. The spring rains did not materialize in 1864, so the roads dried to a hard surface by March, enabling the Federals to launch their Red River Campaign (more on that later).

Soon suffering Union and Confederate soldiers packed every home and building in town. Dr. Nathan Smith came out of retirement to treat the wounded in the Baptist church. Smith was unusual among Washington residents in that he had strongly opposed secession. His family, like many throughout Arkansas, had been divided by the issue; Smith's son had joined the Confederate army (and eventually was one of the wounded his father tended).

Bitter cold settled onto the land, and soon the church's firewood was exhausted. Rains had soaked potential firewood in the forest, so the pine pillars inside the church were chopped up and burned to comfort the blue and gray wounded who sheltered there. When soldiers of either army died from their wounds, they were buried in the Presbyterian cemetery.

Times were oppressively hard in Washington, yet circumstances were far worse almost everywhere else. Anarchy, desolation, and depredation ruled most of Arkansas. Disease was lord over all.

Newspaper owner William Etter took a more active role in helping Washington's residents and refugees. He led a wagon train of cotton to Mexico, where it was traded for four wagonloads of desperately needed medicines and supplies. Judge Daniel Ringo joined Etter on the journey. By the time they returned to Washington four months later, many of their friends had died. Etter quickly departed with another load of cotton for Mexico.

Washington's population soared to more than 30,000 counting soldiers and refugees. Refugees living on the plantations around Washington helped with the work, since most slaves had been impressed by the authorities for military labor. Boys tended the fields. With no boys available to deliver the local newspaper, subscribers had to pick up their copies themselves. Women and girls scoured the woods for roots and leaves to make teas and poultices for the sick and wounded. Local blacks held a charity ball and raised $1,147 to help the sick and wounded of all races sheltering in Washington. This town on the Hill of the Five Trails somehow managed to remain a bastion of hospitality and civilization in a barbarous and devastated land, until events east of the Mississippi finally ended the war in 1865.

Eakin continued to publish his support of the Confederacy after Lee surrendered at Appomattox, focusing on the various battles that followed. He attempted to portray Lee's capitulation as merely another incident of the war. Finally, some five weeks after the surrender, Eakin had to admit that the war was lost. On May 31, he wrote, "The man who deserts a failing cause stands in quite a different position than one who, after it is irrecoverably lost, immediately does the next best thing. . . . All good men should . . . bury old animosities."

About this time, William Etter became Washington's last fatality of the conflict. Etter had been captured by Federals in Texas, and he died of pneumonia while imprisoned.

Washington Rebuilds

Refugees from Little Rock began to head back up the Southwest Trail toward home as Washington residents waited for Federal troops to arrive. Planters fed their former slaves until the Federals arrived and told them what to do with them. John Eakin published his epitaph for the Confederacy on June 7.

"With it dies all obligations of allegiance. Each man is free in conscience, without loss of dignity or self-respect, to take the oath of allegiance to the United States.

"We are satisfied that our single devotion to the Confederacy, during its existence, has fulfilled all the obligations of patriotism. With a conscience clear of offense, we are willing to transfer that allegiance, so left in abeyance, to the government of the United States, and hope to observe it quite as faithfully."

At that point, Eakin was the only community leader in Washington who was willing to forgive and forget, and get on with life. Local residents were still angry and stunned by the defeat of the Confederacy. Their mood darkened further when the bluecoats arrived two weeks after Eakin had published his epitaph. Yet Eakin fearlessly continued to publish his rather unpopular views.

The problems facing blacks and whites alike were substantial. Blacks needed food, clothing, shelter, and protection. Planters needed labor but had no way to pay laborers. Everyone lacked basic essentials and the means to pay for them. Eakin recognized the problems. He sympathized with townsfolk who had trouble dealing with the humiliation of defeat, the difficulty of presenting a friendly facade to an occupying military who had been the enemy for the last four years, and the difficulty of letting go of the past so they could rebuild their lives.

Eakin continued to urge everyone take the oath of allegiance and get on with rebuilding Arkansas in general, and Washington in particular.

Eakin left the *Washington Telegraph* in August to run for the legislature, where he felt he could do more good. In spite of their differences, his neighbors elected him to the 1866 legislature. This strident advocate of the Confederacy now turned his energies to rebuilding Arkansas. Eakin went on to help draft the new state constitution in 1874, and he later served as an associate justice of the state supreme court.

Washington fared better than much of Arkansas, for Reconstruction was not particularly traumatic around the Hill of the Five Trails. The carpetbagger sent to govern Washington, unlike many others visited upon the South, proved to be an honest and likeable man. Robert MacWhorter quickly earned the respect of everyone in the community, as well as the hand of a local belle.

Local blacks became key officials in the new administration, and looked after the community with skill and sensitivity. Archie Shepperson was elected county sheriff, and Richard Samuels represented Hempstead County in the new state assembly. A school for blacks opened in the Baptist church, and a school for whites opened in the home of Alchyny Delony. The town's two academies didn't reopen. Higher eduction was the last thing on anyone's mind. Everyone was bankrupt. Farm tools were worn out. Fields were barren. Every storeroom in the area was empty.

A major problem developed when Congress passed a law that disbarred every lawyer who had borne arms for the Confederacy. This threw Washington's ample supply of attorneys out of work. Augustus Garland single-handedly saved the career of every lawyer in the South by establishing before the U.S. Supreme Court that the disbarment of Confederate lawyers was unconstitutional. Garland became a local hero. Arkansans elected him to the U.S. Senate in 1867, but Congress wasn't recognizing delegates from all the southern states yet, so he became governor instead.

After completing a term as governor, Garland was elected to the U.S. House of Representatives, and later to the U.S. Senate. In 1885, President Grover Cleveland appointed Garland to his cabinet as attorney general, and another Washington resident—James Kimbrough Jones—left his seat in the House to take over Garland's Senate seat. Jones went on to chair the Democratic National Convention several times.

Another Washington attorney, Daniel Webster Jones, after representing the county in the state assembly and serving as state attorney general, went on to serve two terms as governor. Grandison Royston returned from retirement to become president of the state's constitutional convention. As the years passed, a steady stream of Washington residents continued to rise to high office. Members of the white establishment weren't the only people adding to the community's rich history.

Blacks also made Washington proud. Richard Samuels and Archie Shepperson were elected to the state legislature. Samuels also founded the Colored Methodist Episcopal Church. Shepperson later became a county judge. James Tyrus became the tax assessor. And John

Judge James H. Pilkinton and C. G. Crip Hall. Here Arkansas Secretary of State Pilkinton is registering to run for governor in 1958. He later withdrew from the race, after Governor Faubus created the integration crisis at Central High in Little Rock, and went on to ramrod the preservation and restoration of historic Washington. –Southwest Arkansas Regional Archives

Williamson founded an Episcopal academy, which drew students from five surrounding states.

Judge Abner Williams, who was working for President Grover Cleveland at the time, observed that "there is not a town between the seas of the same population that has ever turned out so many men distinguished for their ability in high and important positions which they have filled in the councils of state and nation."

The future seemed limitless to the residents of Washington. They built a new, bigger Hempstead County Courthouse in the town square on Franklin Street and added a new jail behind the Methodist church. The town's population peaked at 780. But this flurry of activity proved to be Washington's last huzzah, for the new railroad bypassed the town and a new community was established: Hope.

Then two huge fires devastated Washington, and the last of the pioneers began to die. When Daniel Witter, the first schoolmaster, died at the age of ninety-one, Judge Edward Cross became the last of the old-timers. At his request, he was buried on his old plantation (Marlbrook) under a headstone shaped like a tree stump. He wanted to be remembered as "one of the stumps of Arkansas."

Washington merely faded away. Few homes and shops remained. Vacant lots and decaying buildings exuded the ambiance of many other small towns bypassed by the flow of history. But then the embers of the town's rich history and unquenchable heart flared into life in 1958.

Judge James Pilkinton called together the town's residents at the Baptist church. He showed them a filmstrip on the restoration of Colonial Williamsburg in Virginia and slides on the restoration of St. Augustine in Florida. He announced that a new highway, running from one coast of the United States to the other, would soon be built and would pass within a few miles of Washington.

Pilkinton proposed to create a private foundation to renovate the town's significant number of antebellum buildings and reconstruct important landmarks lost to fire and weather. Then they could create a "Williamsburg of the Southwest." The assembly was quite enthusiastic. They formed two organizations that very night: a nonprofit group called the Foundation for the Restoration of Pioneer Washington, and the Community Improvement Club. Raising money with a chicken dinner and tours of old houses, volunteers began restoring old buildings of historic interest. The flow of tourists and donations accelerated.

Continuing donations and bequests fueled the restoration, which expanded so much by the early 1970s that the foundation no longer had the resources to sustain the project. The group donated a number of building assets to the state in 1973, forming the nucleus of Old Washington State Park. The local foundation continues to help the state with the restoration process and helps fund the Southwest Arkansas Regional Archives. More than 90,000 people a year come to bask in the warmth of Washington's rich history.

—HOPE—

Located 34 miles northeast of Texarkana and 112 southwest of Little Rock on I-30, Hope was born in 1873, when the Cairo & Fulton Railroad surveyed and platted a new town site named after Hope Loughborough. Her father, James M. Loughborough, was the railroad's land commissioner. He would figure prominently in the establishment of Texarkana on the Arkansas side of the state line the following year. Hope was incorporated in 1875.

Hope's economy boomed while the economic fortunes of Washington began to stagnate and then decline. Residents of Hope began a sixty-year struggle to move the county seat from Washington to Hope. But Washington had held the title for half a century and fiercely resisted the change. The big fire of 1884 nearly destroyed Hope's entire business district, but every man and woman in town turned out

The first school bus in Hempstead County. The converted Model T Ford is open for the driver and has no sides for the riders. When the bus went uphill, the kids sometimes had to get off and push. –Southwest Arkansas Regional Archives

to fight the fire. By 1888, Hope boasted an opera house, six churches, two banks, lumber and planing mills, a wagon factory, a cotton compress, an abundance of stores and smithies, and a population of about 2,000. The beautiful little prairie had become a prosperous town.

As Washington continued to wither on the vine, Hope residents became so confident of gaining the county seat that they built a new courthouse in an attempt to sway the next election. They failed. The courthouse was eventually used as the city hall. An election in 1938 finally settled the struggle between Washington and Hope that had been waged for generations. Hope became the county seat the following year. Since the courthouse was now being used as the city hall, Hope had to build yet another courthouse for Hempstead County.

For most of the twentieth century, Hope's principal claim to fame has been its annual watermelon festival. The festival and its seed-spitting contest were commonly the only thing outsiders knew about Arkansas. Large-scale cultivation of watermelons began soon after the introduction of a new variety that grew much larger than any others in Hempstead County. Until the early 1920s, the Gibson Drug Store offered a prize for the biggest watermelon (the store sold seeds and schoolbooks as well as drugs). Farmer interest in this crop skyrocketed. Hope sent a 136-pound giant to President Calvin Coolidge in 1925, and the town soon became known as the "watermelon capital" of Arkansas. Folks flocked to Hope every August from 1926 to 1930 to watch a parade and eat free slices of iced watermelon. A special train brought people from Little Rock until a blight destroyed the crop and the festival for several years.

The watermelon industry received a boost in 1935 when O. D. Middlebrooks produced the largest watermelon up to that time. It weighed 195 pounds, and that world record held for 44 years. Middlebrooks sent this watermelon to movie star Dick Powell, who was a native of Arkansas. Today melons commonly exceed 200 pounds, although most are marketed in the 20 to 40 pound range, since they make the best eating.

While watermelons put Hope on the state map, Hope's favorite son—Bill Clinton—put Hope on the national map when he entered the 1992 presidential campaign as the Democratic answer to President George Bush.

Clinton's political ascendency began in 1978, when he became the youngest governor in the country at the age of thirty-two. A former Rhodes scholar and attorney general, Clinton focused on school reform, building highways, and supporting industry. But many voters

President Bill Clinton's boyhood home in Hope. –Polly Walter

became upset by a variety of events, such as more expensive car licenses, which they saw as manifestations of Clinton's loss of touch with grassroots Arkansans. Folks were particularly angered by the housing of Cuban refugees at Fort Chaffee, although Governor Clinton had nothing to do with the relocation of these refugees to Arkansas. Republican Frank White beat Clinton in the following election, which has become known as the Car Tags and Cubans Campaign. This was one of the most bitter contests in the annals of Arkansas politics. Clinton was reelected in 1982 and remained governor through the presidential campaign of 1992. Hope received national television exposure during the 1992 Democratic National Convention as the birthplace of Bill Clinton.

—FULTON—

Located fifteen miles southwest of Washington on Arkansas 195, Fulton began life as the point where the Southwest Trail entered Spanish territory, and as a landing for keelboats bringing in supplies from New Orleans. Both Indians and seventeenth century explorers had crossed the Red River here, and many key figures in the early days of Arkansas and Texas passed through. Stephen Austin, for example, figured prominently in the development of the settlement and went on to play such an important role in the Texas revolution that he is regarded as the Father of Texas.

The first deed for property in this area was recorded in 1808. The first mention of the community's name appeared in an 1819 advertisement in the *Arkansas Gazette* that offered lots for sale in "a town named Fulton." This was the same year that Congress created Arkansas Territory from the southern half of Missouri Territory. No records document where the town name came from, but one historian speculates that the settlement may have been named after Robert Fulton, who invented the steamboat. Fulton died about the time the town began to grow as a keelboat landing, so this is probably a pretty good guess.

Stephen Austin's father, Moses, drew the plans for building a community and supply depot at this location. He believed that hundreds of cotton farmers would flock to the bottomlands of the area, since the U.S. government was encouraging people to settle the new Arkansas Territory. He also hoped to convince Spain to allow 300 more families to settle in the bottomlands on the Texas side of the Red River. Once established, Moses reasoned, those settlers would draw hundreds of additional families through Fulton to the Texan side of the river. Spanish cooperation was essential to build a large economic base centered on Fulton.

Austin's desire to civilize the area was further complicated by rampant lawlessness in what became a sort of no-man's-land just west of the Red River. Neither Spanish nor U.S. authorities ventured into the area, where outlaws and Indians reigned. Farmers and families stayed east of the Red River. Until these problems on the Spanish side of the river were resolved, Fulton served as a gateway to nowhere, except for well-armed adventurers.

Implementation of Moses' plan began in June 1819, when Stephen Austin and his brother-in-law James Bryan left Missouri by keelboat.

River Travel

Keelboats were one of three kinds of craft common to the rivers of the day. The bargelike flatboat could carry a great deal of cargo cheaply, but it could only travel downstream with the current. Upon reaching its destination, the flatboat would be disassembled and the lumber would be used for local home-building or other construction. The keelboat, however, featured a round bottom, keel, and pointed bow that allowed the craft to maintain a straight course as its crew poled it upstream. Horses or men walking along the bank were sometimes used to pull a keelboat upstream. Barring any snags or other difficulties, a hard day's work could move a keelboat about ten miles upstream per day.

The canoe was the only other option for moving upstream until the first steamboat began working the Mississippi in 1811. (The first steamboat didn't land in Arkansas until 1820, when the *Comet* stopped

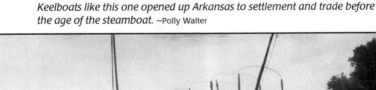
Keelboats like this one opened up Arkansas to settlement and trade before the age of the steamboat. –Polly Walter

109

at Arkansas Post.) The keelboat could work in shallower and narrower waters than the steamboat, however, so it continued to play a major role on Arkansas rivers for many years to come.

Stephen Austin and James Bryan reached Fulton in a matter of weeks, despite having to negotiate the infamous Great Red River Raft, which was a tangle of floating logs that jammed the river for seventy-five miles. Years of floods had swept countless logs into such a tangle that a fearless individual could walk down the middle of the river. The logs even formed floating islands that trapped silt, which supported living trees and vines.

Austin and Bryan tried to establish successful plantations and consolidate their other land claims after Austin sold his interests in Fulton to William O'Hara and Robert Anderson, among others. Austin's other land dealings in Arkansas soon failed, and he returned penniless to Texas (see also Washington).

O'Hara and his partners in the Fulton enterprise tried selling lots through the *Arkansas Gazette*, but they found no takers. Part of the problem was the Red River's reputation for fearsome and frequent

Captain Henry Shreve on the Red River, circa 1836.
—Southwest Arkansas Regional Archives

A snag boat works to clear the Great Red River Raft. –Arkansas History Commission

floods. Moreover, the land had not been surveyed. Finally, the Great Red River Raft made commercial use of the Red River impractical, until Captain Henry Shreve and his army engineers used specially designed steamboats to clear the infamous seventy-five miles of snags from the river. A town fifty miles downriver from Fulton was named after the captain: Shreveport, Louisiana. Fulton became attractive as a steamboat landing, and in 1831 the *Enterprise* became the first steamboat to reach Fulton.

Fulton Begins to Bustle

Soon side-wheelers regularly plied their way upriver from New Orleans, past daunting shoals and snags, to deliver essential supplies and exotic luxuries such as bananas and wines. The steamboats off-loaded to freighter wagons, pulled by six mules each, which transported this bounty to Washington and returned to Fulton weighted down with bales of cotton.

Lots finally began to sell. A post office was built in 1836, and Fulton finally began to feel like a real town. By 1839, Henry and Augustus Block were selling slaves as fast as they could be brought in on the weekly steamboat. Their father, Abraham, owned the largest mercantile store in Washington. The steamboats returned to New Orleans

The Fulton Union Church was built in the 1870s. Four denominations still use the old clapboard church for services on alternating Sundays. −Polly Walter

piled to the smokestacks with bales of cotton bound for export to foreign markets.

Fulton bustled with commercial activity in those antebellum days, gaining a reputation for drinking and gambling. In a single game of stud poker, for example, a local entrepreneur lost $2,200, a cotton plantation, and the steamboat *Waukesha*.

The Fulton Union Church was built in the 1870s, and four denominations still use the old clapboard building for services on alternating Sundays. Steamboat traffic increased so much that the Cairo & Fulton Railroad was completed to Fulton in 1874. Soon, however, Fulton was eclipsed by Texarkana, located eighteen miles to the southwest. Texarkana had become the terminus for both the Texas & Pacific and Cairo & Fulton railroads.

With the advent of the automobile, Arkansas began a program of building gravel highways. The road completed through Hempstead County in 1920 ran from Emmet through Hope to Fulton. It was part of a gravel highway called The Broadway of America, which stretched from New York to San Diego. A ferry at Fulton transported cars across the Red River.

Fulton during the flood of 1927. –Southwest Arkansas Regional Archives

The ferry did not have an engine; manpower muscled the raft across. The boat was attached by pulleys to a cable strung across the river. Ropes at each end were anchored to the opposite banks. By pulling on one rope and letting out the other, the operators could work the raft across the river, dodging trees floating downriver.

The Red River continued to flood Fulton and the surrounding countryside for miles, so a levee was built. A recently reprinted book called *The WPA Guide to 1930s Arkansas* describes Fulton's 485 residents walking around town while the Red River raged thirty feet above their heads on the other side of the levee. By inference, that would mean a levee looming thirty-six to forty feet above the streets of Fulton. That makes for dramatic reading, but it may be a bit exaggerated. While the top of the Fulton levee might be thirty feet above the river level in late summer, the levee only rises half that distance above the quiet streets of Fulton. Now the Dennison Dam controls the Red River, so the spectre of flooding no longer haunts the residents of Fulton.

Where Sam Houston and Davy Crockett once crossed the Red River—where steamboats once departed for New Orleans piled to the smokestacks with cotton—two highway bridges, a railroad bridge, and a pipeline now span the river. One of these bridges carries I-30, but there is no access from Fulton. Once the gateway to the wilderness and then the transportation hub of the region, Fulton landing has become a quiet backwater with a population of about 300 people.

As Fulton's fortunes faded over the years, Arkadelphia's fortunes blossomed.

Floodwaters of the Red River, higher than the levee but held in check by sandbags, threaten the town of Fulton. —Southwest Arkansas Regional Archives

—ARKADELPHIA—

Located sixty-seven miles southwest of Little Rock and seventy-eight miles northeast of Texarkana on I-40, Arkadelphia's history dates back to 1541, when Hernando de Soto crossed the Mississippi River into what is now Arkansas. Many believe de Soto traveled down an Indian trail in what is now Clark County, where he encountered brackish water and salt deposits on the south bank of the Ouachita River just below the site where Arkadelphia was built. These salt deposits were used by the Indians and would become an important resource three centuries later, when settlers began to appear soon after the Louisiana Purchase.

The first settlers arrived in 1839 and found forested hills of giant trees festooned by wild grapevines, and rich alluvial bottomlands burgeoning with almost tropical vegetation. Three Indian tribes hunted and trapped these lands. The Caddos lived along the banks of the Caddo River. The Quapaws lived along the Ouachita River and elsewhere. And the Delawares lived on the Ouachita near present-day Camden. The Indians eagerly traded furs, hides, and tallow with their white neighbors for blankets, bridles, guns, and ammunition. The settlers, in turn, used these furs and related commodities to establish a flourishing trade with New Orleans. They called their outpost Blakeleytown after the first pioneer in the area.

John Hemphill introduced manufacturing to the settlement in 1812. He made several small kettles for boiling brine at the salt springs three miles from town. This process produced salt, which was essential for preserving meat. Salt was a valuable commodity on the frontier. The demand for it grew and the business thrived until the Civil War, when the Confederate government leased the enterprise to provide salt to the army in the Trans-Mississippi Department. Union troops destroyed the saltworks during the Red River Campaign.

Jacob Barkman figured prominently in the early development of Blakeleytown, establishing a thriving plantation. He started the first freight service between the region and New Orleans using a huge dugout fashioned from two giant trees. The trunks were hollowed out and fastened together, and six of Barkman's slaves operated oars.

Barkman soon used his influence to win the community a post office, which was only the second one established in the territory. A

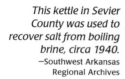

This kettle in Sevier County was used to recover salt from boiling brine, circa 1940.
–Southwest Arkansas Regional Archives

year after the territorial legislature carved Clark County out of Arkansas County, Barkman's home served as the first courthouse in 1819. His house remained the temporary county seat until 1825. Biscoeville served as the county seat for the next two years, followed by the home of Adam Stroud in Blakeleytown until 1930, when the county seat moved to Greenville (present-day Hollywood).

Keelboats began to ply the Ouachita River and Blakeleytown bustled. The Calloway Hotel was built in 1824 and served the community until it burned to the ground a half century later. A brickyard, cotton gin, and tannery boosted the local economy in 1830, and gristmills began to appear in the area. Then Jacob Barkman built the first steamboat to service the town. The small side-wheeler, called the *Dime*, profoundly altered the quality of life in the community. Keelboats could only bring a few necessities such as saws, gunpowder, and cotton cards. The steamboat brought luxuries. Real furniture of walnut, rosewood, and mahogany began to appear in the more prosperous homes. Much of the town turned out when the first piano arrived. The *Dime* could carry 400 bales of cotton plus hides, pelts, tallow, and lard to New Orleans to finance the rising aspirations of the community.

Blakeleytown had grown so much by 1839 that the settlement was finally surveyed, divided into lots, and incorporated. That's when the residents changed the town's name to Arkadelphia.

The origin of that name remains open to debate, but local folklore provides a plausible explanation. Ever since the first settler had appeared on the banks of the Ouachita, traveling Indians and settlers were always welcome to warm themselves at each other's fires. Everyone got along, even though the Delawares sometimes exhibited a rather frisky sense of humor. Perhaps it was this agreeable and brotherly tradition that stimulated early residents of Blakeleytown to think of their community as "Arkansaw's Philadelphia" or Arkadelphia.

The only rub with this explanation is that early court records spelled the town *Arcadelphia*—with a c. Even maps used this spelling into the 1870s. Some suggest alternative explanations based on the French word *arc*, meaning a circle or rainbow. But one must remember that standards of spelling were less precise in those days. The second territorial governor, George Izard, spelled the territory's name *Arkansas* since he was fluent in French and wished to honor their original spelling. The act of Congress establishing the territory spelled the name *Arkansaw*. And when the territory became a state in 1836, it was spelled *Arkansas*. Even the pronunciation of the state's name varied until an act of the state legislature settled the matter in 1881. So I'm inclined to accept this community as "Arkansaw's Philadelphia."

116

The eccentric who surveyed Arkadelphia merits some discussion. Dr. Haddock was highly educated but rather lacking in refinement. He hated to spend a cent on food or lodging; he preferred to mooch meals from local residents and sleep in the forest. If the weather was bad, however, he would try to mooch a bed as well. Haddock only accepted gold for his services and buried his horde in the forest, so people thought he was poor. He dug up his accumulated wealth after the Civil War and moved to Colorado, but he perished in a hotel fire his first night there.

Arkadelphia's importance as a steamboat landing grew dramatically in the antebellum days. The *Dime* soon faced competition from the *Bluelle*, *Joe Jakes*, *Will S. Hayes*, *O. K.*, and *Arkadelphia City*. A legendary barbecue was held on the banks of the Ouachita in 1842, at which the county residents voted to make Arkadelphia the permanent county seat. Arkadelphia continued to prosper, thanks to King Cotton and a fleet of steamboats. The future was bright until war came to Arkansas. Arkadelphia survived capture by Union General Frederick Steele fairly gracefully, since the five skirmishes in the immediate area occurred eight to twenty miles away. No fighting took place in the town itself.

Corrupt officials who came to power after the war, however, adversely affected the community for years after they finally left. Arkadelphia struggled and then prospered. The arrival of the Cairo & Fulton Railroad enabled the community to retain its vitality as the days of the steamboat passed into history. Over the coming decades, the fortunes of many communities would depend on the presence or absence of a railroad. Ouachita College was founded at the site of the old Indian village. The timber industry developed soon after the railroad arrived, while cotton remained important to the local economy. Henderson-Brown College began in 1890, and the first county fair was held a year later. By the 1930s, Arkadelphia was known as a college town.

Arkadelphia is still a college town, which thrives on the rivalry between Ouachita Baptist University and Henderson State University. Only a ravine separates the two campuses.

Ouachita Baptist University has traditionally drawn Baptist students from Arkansas, Louisiana, and Texas. OBU branched out in the early 1990s to develop a substantial foreign student program. Within three years, OBU tripled the number of foreign students and more than doubled the number of languages that they offered. The number of American students going overseas from OBU increased by more than twentyfold. The goals of this program are to increase foreign understanding of America's heartland and to help shape the future leaders of other countries, especially fledgling democracies. In 1992, for example, a journalist reported that OBU had more students from republics that were once part of the Soviet Union than any other university in the country. About 7 percent of OBU's 1,300 students come from overseas, representing every continent except Australia.

About the same time, Henderson State immersed itself in the local effort to revitalize the sagging economy in Arkadelphia. The 1980s had not been kind to business in the community, so local leaders launched a campaign to attract industry and to foster the development of small business. The community reclaimed its downtown core and cut the number of empty storefronts in half in less than two years. Henderson State got into the act by establishing a small business program in cooperation with the federal Small Business Administration. The university puts students and local businesspeople together so the students can learn how a small business operates in the real world,

Although this 162-pound watermelon grown in Arkadelphia set a world record one year, Hope is now known for producing the largest watermelons. –Southwest Arkansas Regional Archives

and the businesspeople can receive assistance directly from the Small Business Administration.

The approach has been quite successful. A book called *Fifty Fabulous Places to Raise Your Family* lists Arkadelphia as one of the best communities in the United States to find a safe family environment with excellent educational opportunities and a wholesome atmosphere.

Henderson State also has a fascinating museum, which occupies a thirty-room Victorian mansion on 10th Street. The museum features an excellent exhibit of artifacts from the Caddo Indians, who occupied much of southern and western Arkansas (as well as parts of Texas, Oklahoma, and Louisiana) when European explorers first ventured into the area. Other exhibits highlight the area's natural history.

The town contains excellent examples of antebellum, Victorian, and Romanesque Revival architecture. The county courthouse features a five-story clock tower, nine-foot windows, eighteen-foot ceilings, and original furnishings, making it a prime example of a nineteenth century court building.

Arkadelphia has survived war, the demise of the steamboat, and the changing fortunes of agriculture and railroads and business to eclipse the jewel of the Southwest Trail—Washington. Yet the community remains faithful to the traditions of the Indians and pioneers who first lived on these banks of the Ouachita. "Arkansaw's Philadelphia" lives up to its lofty legacy.

—BENTON—

Soon after the territorial legislature established Saline County in 1835, residents elected commissioners to a find a permanent county seat. They selected a site about two miles north of Saline Crossings and proposed that the town be named Benton, after Senator Thomas Benton of Missouri. The site was surveyed, and the commissioners ran advertisements in the *Arkansas Gazette* announcing that lots would be sold on June 10 and 11, 1836. To attract a big crowd, the promoters staged a big barbecue with free food and drink over the two days. Bidding was lively on the 114 lots sold that weekend, and Benton's future as the permanent county seat seemed assured.

Benton began as a trade center two years before the site got its name, when Joshua Smith opened a store in his house. Within three years, Smith took on a partner and built a large storehouse. Soon two mercantiles and a hotel provided some substance to the settlement, and Benton grew rapidly for several years. The town was incorporated in 1839 on eighty acres that the county purchased for $33. Life continued quietly until Arkansas seceded from the Union. About 1,300 local men volunteered for service in the Confederate army. Only about 20 percent would survive the war.

Although no major battles were fought in the immediate area, both armies actively operated in the region after 1863. Skirmishes did erupt at Benton and in the surrounding area. Patrols and foraging parties of both armies picked local farms clean. Worse, irregulars—who were little more than lawless bands of desperados—robbed, burned, and murdered their way through the countryside. Richard Brownlee would write in *Gray Ghosts of the Confederacy* that "vicious guerrilla activity directed against the civil population created such fear and disorganization that in many areas normal society collapsed entirely." Certainly, parts of Saline County and much of what became Garland County suffered such a fate.

The rural population suffered tremendous hardships. With the men gone to war, the women and children were easy prey. As a result, little food, forage, or livestock remained to support the families. Women often banded together, with three or four families staying in a single house to better protect themselves. They hid their food in logs and caves. They buried their valuables in the woods. Yet a resident of what is now Garland County wrote that many people in the neighborhood were in danger of starving that winter. There was no corn to be had nearer than the Arkansas River. By the end of 1864, the area around the Ouachita River was practically stripped clean, too.

With the surrounding farms barren and most of the local men dead, recovery after the war was slow and painful. A deposit of clay suitable for producing pottery was discovered in the central part of Saline County in 1866, and a company began to manufacture ceramics in Benton that same year. The business prospered, so the company greatly enlarged the plant in 1873. By the late 1800s, producing pottery had become Benton's principal industry, with seven major plants operating at the time.

The Cairo & Fulton Railroad (later called the St. Louis, Iron Mountain & Southern Railroad; and then the Missouri Pacific Railroad) ran through town, providing the transportation links necessary for industry to prosper. The timber industry blossomed after the railroad came to town. Two mills with gin and grist machinery, a planing mill, a tannery, and two shoemakers fueled the lively economy for Benton's 900 residents. The town boasted three hotels, two boardinghouses, ten general stores, two groceries, a butcher, two barbers, one livery, four blacksmiths, a saddle and harness shop, three drugstores, four physicians, seven resident preachers, and not even a single saloon. Liquor licenses had been freely granted in Saline County until about

Crew working on the St. Louis & Iron Mountain Railroad, which later became the Missouri Pacific. —Southwest Arkansas Regional Archives

1872, when the temperance movement appeared. The county voted itself dry a within a decade.

In 1887, a road contractor made what seemed to be a trivial discovery a few miles east of town. Yet Ed Weigel's find would ultimately lead to a multimillion-dollar industry employing thousands of people in its heyday. Weigel had unearthed a vast deposit of crumbly, soft gray rock that made an excellent road surface. State geologist John Branner identified the mineral as bauxite, the ore that produces virtually all of the aluminum used in modern society. But no one had developed a commercially feasible process for removing aluminum from bauxite at that time, so the discovery had no impact.

A Frenchman had developed a process for removing aluminum from bauxite in 1854, but his technique was hardly economical. Aluminum cost $545 a pound using the process, making aluminum both a novelty and a precious metal. Kings would provide their most honored banquet guests with aluminum forks and spoons; lesser guests ate with utensils of gold or silver.

Then an American and a Frenchman independently discovered a relatively economical method for separating aluminum from its ore. Charles Martin Hall patented his process in 1888 and began producing fifty pounds of aluminum per day at a cost of $1 per pound. When Hall and his partners learned of the bauxite discovery near Benton, they purchased all the known deposits in 1889.

The Aluminum Industry in Arkansas

Columbus Brazil was the first miner of bauxite in Saline County. First he cut down all the trees on his land, stripped off the topsoil, and mined the ore by hand with a pick and shovel. Then he crushed the ore using muscle power and dried it with a roaring fire. Finally, he shoveled the ore into a wagon and drove it to the railroad three miles away in Benton. All this backbreaking labor earned him $1.25 per ton.

The railroad shipped the ore to Memphis, where it was loaded on barges bound for the refinery in Pittsburgh. The first barge sank. The bauxite aboard the second barge froze into a solid lump that had to be dynamited before it could be unloaded. Such difficulties limited the development of the mining industry over the following decade. Clearly, it would be much more practical to refine the ore in Arkansas. Some folks thought that once the Pittsburgh Refining Company had purchased all the deposits around Benton, the company would locate processing plants in Arkansas.

But processing bauxite required a vast amount of cheap electricity. The only place that could reliably produce enough power was Niagara Falls, New York. So the company built its refining plant in New York and a drying mill in Arkansas a few miles from Benton. Arkansas would have to wait another four decades to get its own refining plant.

In 1907, the company's Alcoa Mining Division built a large crushing, grinding, and drying plant along with housing for Alcoa's employees and their families, creating the company town of Bauxite, just a few miles east of Benton on present-day Arkansas 183. Production grew steadily if modestly until the outbreak of World War I, when demand tripled and yet imports quickly dried up to less than 1 percent of prewar levels. Arkansas production helped meet this unprecedented demand for aluminum in spite of substantial obstacles including the coldest winters in decades and killer flu epidemics.

The war gave many manufacturers their first experience using aluminum, and they quickly developed peacetime uses for the metal after the war ended. Demand remained so high after the war that Alcoa concluded the Arkansas deposits could not keep up with the U.S. demand indefinitely. So Alcoa decided to set aside half of its reserves for future emergencies, and began to import the other half of the company's ore from Suriname and British Guiana. This conservation policy, plus a short but nasty depression in 1920 and 1921, hit the aluminum industry in Arkansas hard. But employment in the company town of Bauxite began to recover, and the workforce gradually increased to about 1,200. Community services began to increase, too.

Bauxite boomed throughout the Roaring Twenties, but then the Great Depression hit the aluminum industry like a steel sledge.

Many workers lost their jobs. Those who kept them worked for 20 cents per hour. They worked only two days per week from 1932 to 1934. The company helped by growing vegetables and giving them free to employees, lowering rent, and sometimes even providing free housing and electricity. The company also subsidized hospital care and local schools. The industry began to revive in 1937, and more mining companies began operations in Arkansas. The demand for aluminum increased as war began to loom on the horizon, and new technology permitted refining lower-grade ore. These factors combined to increase the impact of the aluminum industry in Arkansas.

With the outbreak of World War II, German U-boats began to sink freighters within sight of American cities. Federal officials feared that

A "powder monkey" places a charge in an underground bauxite mine. —Arkansas History Commission

123

Germany might be able to cut off the importation of aluminum ore, so the government invested $672 million in Arkansas to build plants for refining the ore. Bauxite prospered and added a new school. Alcoa operated the plants during the war. Local employment would exceed 7,000 before the war was over. After the war, the government sold the plants to Reynolds Aluminum in order to foster competition in the industry.

The growth of unions after the war and the changing social climate made company towns go the way of the dinosaur. Companies offset higher wages and improved working conditions by eliminating company housing. Bauxite dried up as people moved to Benton. Meanwhile, the aluminum industry in Arkansas continued to grow, thanks to a new $54 million plant built to refine lower-grade ore. Postwar production of bauxite from Arkansas reached $22.5 million in 1972.

Although Arkansas led the nation's bauxite production for many years—providing as much as 95 percent of U.S. output—its dominance didn't last. Electricity became much cheaper in Third World countries that also had large bauxite deposits. Antiquated equipment and low-grade ore also made Arkansas less competitive. As a result, aluminum production shifted to overseas locations. The Arkansas industry declined through the 1980s and has now largely shut down.

Bauxite mining at Bauxite. –Arkansas History Commission

Arkansas 24, 387, and 76
Prescott (*Prairie d'Ane*)—Camden
46 miles

US 79, Arkansas 8
Camden—Marks' Mills Monument
44 miles

Arkansas 8, 9, and 46
Marks' Mills Monument—Jenkins' Ferry Monument
53 miles

These three routes pass through some of the most hallowed ground in Arkansas—the places where the major battles of the Union's Red River Campaign erupted during the Civil War. Here Arkansans, Louisianans, Texans, and Indians whipped the Federals (Union troops) and drove them out of the Coastal Plain, giving the Union army its greatest defeat west of the Mississippi.

—RED RIVER CAMPAIGN—

Union forces launched their Red River Campaign in the spring of 1864, not as a well-conceived military expedition against the Confederacy, but rather as an economic and political enterprise. The Federals sought to capture the vast quantities of cotton thought to be stockpiled along the Red River in Arkansas and Texas, so Lincoln could revive the moribund textile industry in New England. Union authorities estimated that the campaign would yield 200,000 to 300,000 bales of cotton. Using the lowest of these two estimates and a conservative value of $500 per bale, the captured cotton would not only pay for the Red River Campaign—it would turn a $100 million profit. That was enough money to underwrite the entire Union war effort for two months. A less tangible objective was to send a message to the French, who were about to install Maximilian on the throne of Montezuma in Mexico. Lincoln wanted a significant gesture in the Southwest to keep Maximilian at bay.

The two-pronged campaign would involve 20,000 men under the command of Major General Nathaniel Banks, who would attack up the Red River valley from Alexandria, Louisiana, supported by a flotilla of gunboats carrying 210 guns. Another army of 14,000 men from Little Rock and Fort Smith, under the command of Major General

Frederick Steele, would strike down the Red River. Together, their forces would capture Shreveport and destroy General E. Kirby Smith's army once and for all. They would then march on Texas. That would be the end of "Kirby-Smithdom," as many folks called the Trans-Mississippi Department.

Banks was the weak link in the plan. Although he was an accomplished politician who had been governor of Massachusetts and Speaker of the U.S. House of Representatives, Banks had no business leading troops. His men cynically called him Napoleon behind his back. General Steele, however, was a shrewd strategist and cynical veteran who could see beyond the campaign's superficial sensibility on paper. In the field, Steele knew the plan would prove both presumptuous and risky. He tried in vain to get General Grant to cancel the enterprise.

The Red River Campaign in Arkansas would cover about 275 miles of almost constant skirmishing over a period of about 40 days. Battles would erupt at Okolona, Elkin's Ferry, *Prairie d'Ane*, Poison Spring, Marks' Mill, and Jenkins' Ferry.

Steele advanced slowly southward from Little Rock with 9,000 men on March 23, and Brigadier General John M. Thayer left Fort Smith on the same day with the rest of Steele's force, the 5,000-man Frontier Division. Steele's objective was Camden, the second largest community in Arkansas and the most formidable Confederate stronghold in southern Arkansas at that time. Camden sat on a bluff along the southwest bank of the Ouachita River, a clear tributary of the muddy Red River. By 1860, the town had become a major commercial center on the frontier, because the Ouachita was often navigable when the Red River was not. Roads radiated from Camden in all directions, but they became impassable after prolonged rains, so the river remained the town's principal asset. The same qualities that made Camden an economic center also gave it strategic value, so the Confederate army occupied the town after the fall of Little Rock and began to fortify the community.

Steele planned to use Camden, which was about halfway between Shreveport and Little Rock, as his base to link up with General Banks in northern Louisiana. But Steele did not have the resources to take Camden by frontal assault. So he did not approach by the most direct route, which would have taken him though Jenkins' Ferry, Tulip, and Princeton. The Union general would use guile rather than brute force. He marched out of Little Rock down Military Road (formerly known as the Southwest Trail) toward Washington, which had become the temporary Confederate state capital after the fall of Little Rock. Steele linked up with Thayer near the Little Missouri River and feinted

Major General Sterling Price.
—Arkansas History Commission

toward Washington in order to play upon Confederate fears that his main goal was to capture the state archives and the area's huge stockpiles of cotton. He hoped this threat would draw the Confederate army out of its impregnable defenses at Camden to defend Washington. Steele would then use a screen of cavalry to occupy the rebels while he dashed to take Camden.

Major General Sterling Price met the feint, and a series of bloody engagements flared for four days at *Prairie d'Ane*. With the Confederates engaged, Steele made a break for Camden. Steele took the route now traced by Arkansas 24 to Bluff City, and Arkansas 387, 76, and 24 to Camden.

Brigadier General J. O. Shelby's cavalry managed to get between Steele and his objective. Shelby delayed the Union forces long enough for a detachment of Confederate cavalry to reach Camden before the Federals on April 15. The detachment destroyed stockpiled ammunition, supplies, and a large quantity of cotton to keep them out of Union hands. Many local residents hid at least one bale of cotton, as an economic hedge against an uncertain future. Hours later, Union troops entered Camden unopposed.

Steele's plans to launch his campaign into Louisiana from Camden were derailed when Confederate General Richard Taylor whipped Banks at Mansfield (Sabine Crossroads), Louisiana. Banks retreated to Grand Ecore and regrouped his forces. With the Federals in Louisiana entrenched in strong defensive positions, Taylor concluded that Steele was much easier prey. Steele had substantially fewer men, and his lines of supply stretched from Camden through seventy miles of enemy-held territory back to Pine Bluff.

Taylor turned his full attention to Steele and marched north. Steele consolidated his position in the excellent defenses built by the Confederates at Camden and awaited developments. He was still confident that gunboats could reliably deliver supplies to Camden via the Ouachita River.

Steele had requested more provisions on April 7. Steele's supplies left Little Rock aboard two Federal steamers, the *Adams* and the *Chippewa*. But the supplies were lost in a freak accident when the steamers collided en route to Pine Bluff. The *Adams* sank, and the *Chippewa* was crippled. Food for his men and forage for his horses and mules were now in extremely short supply. Steele would have to scour the area around Camden for sustenance.

But that was easier said than done. The residents of Camden were starving, so Steele could not confiscate supplies from the town. The population was in such desperate straits that the Federals, who were already on half rations, felt compelled to provide some food to the destitute townsfolk.

Foraging the countryside would not be easy either, because the Confederates had destroyed food and forage within easy reach of Camden. Federal Captain Charles Henry wrote that a "destroying mania had seized the rebels . . . ; by night the whole heavens were illuminated by reflections of the devouring flames." Steele's situation became desperate. A bit of luck on the night of April 16, however, bought him some time. A Federal patrol captured the Confederate transport *Homer* far down the Ouachita River and returned to Camden with its 3,000 bushels of corn. Steele's troops would have something to eat for awhile.

But then the water level in the Ouachita River suddenly dropped, preventing Union gunboats from reaching Camden. Confederate cavalry made overland resupply from Pine Bluff risky. Once again, Steele found himself in serious trouble. He needed provisions immediately and had no choice but to scour the surrounding countryside for supplies. His most obvious option was to go after a huge cache of corn his troops had discovered during their dash from *Prairie d'Ane* to Camden. They had been moving too rapidly to take the corn with them. On April 17, Steele sent 200 wagons and an escort to recover the corn at Poison Spring (about ten miles northwest of Camden), even though he had no idea where the Confederate cavalry was at the moment. That was a fatal mistake.

A simple reconnaissance around Camden would have revealed that Major General Price had established his headquarters just sixteen miles west of Camden near Woodlawn. Price was a likeable 290 pounds of Missouri vanity, who was more of a fatherly figure to his men than a military strategist. Affectionately called Old Pap by his men, Price had displayed the good sense to let Steele take Camden without a head-on confrontation. Instead, he let his men sleep, since they had not slept though a whole night in two weeks. Price understood his best chance to defeat Steele was to cut his supply lines and starve him out of Camden. Old Pap spread seven cavalry brigades out to cover all the roads from Camden west of the Ouachita River. The total Confederate force was about 6,000 men. If Steele had known about the presence of such a force, he would have sent a substantially stronger escort with his forage train.

Steele's foraging party was hit the next day at Poison Spring, losing 500 men and 200 wagons. The fighting was particularly bitter, since most of the Union troopers were black, and the rebels refused to take black prisoners. The horror facing the black soldiers was compounded when Choctaws fighting on the Confederate side began to take scalps.

After Steele's error precipitated the Union defeat at Poison Spring, it was now Price's turn to make a mistake. Old Pap failed to deploy cavalry east of the Ouachita River to block the road to Pine Bluff. Three days later, 150 wagons managed to reach Camden from Pine Bluff with enough supplies to provide the Union troops with half rations for ten days. Steele still desperately needed provisions, but now he had some prospects for relief. He added 90 of his own wagons to the 150 from Pine Bluff, and sent them back toward Pine Bluff for more stores. The Federals foraged as they traveled to feed the teamsters and their escort, filling the empty wagons with anything they could loot from the local folk.

Both sides commonly looted the civilians throughout Arkansas. Official reports document that Confederate troops at Camden plundered the country for miles around. One soldier wrote his wife to hide anything of value any time she heard that a military unit was nearby. It didn't matter if they wore blue or gray.

The Confederates were eager to capture this wagon train, because many of the troopers came from the very farms being robbed by the bluecoats. Using local guides through backwoods and swamps to overtake the wagon train, they ambushed the Federals at Marks' Mill—

killing, wounding, and capturing almost 2,000 bluecoats. The victors feasted that night on food stolen from the homes of many of the Confederate soldiers, and then they took great pains to return the recovered jewelry, quilts, and clothing to the rightful owners.

It became obvious to Steele that his position at Camden was untenable. The town's impregnable fortifications meant nothing if he could not feed his men, horses, and mules. The question was whether Steele could successfully retreat back to Little Rock, but he had no choice. Through guile and luck and the cover of darkness, the Federals evacuated Camden without alerting Confederate lookouts, achieving a substantial head start before the exodus was detected about 9 A.M. on April 27. Steele's retreat approximately followed the present-day route of US 79 to Arkansas 9, through Princeton and Tulip, and then to the Saline River via Arkansas 46.

Confederate forces were not well deployed to counter Steele's surprise. Brigadier General J. O. Shelby's cavalry spotted the retreating bluecoats, and the chase was on. General Kirby Smith, the head of the Confederate Trans-Mississippi Department, caught the Federals at Jenkins' Ferry on the Saline River.

Jenkins' Ferry was a hard-fought battle in which both sides displayed much grit and valor. Both sides also suffered heavy casualties. The bluecoats managed to cross the Ouachita River to relative safety and wearily marched back to Little Rock.

A Union battery opens up on advancing Confederate troops during a 1993 reenactment. –Al Paulson

130

Union forces falter as they assault Confederate positions during this 1993 reenactment. –Al Paulson

The Red River Campaign not only had failed to destroy the Confederate Trans-Mississippi forces, it had become the Union's greatest defeat in Arkansas. The rebels lacked the resources to exploit their victories. The Federals lacked both the materiel and resolve to regroup and renew their advance. So the Red River Campaign marked the end of large-scale military operations in Arkansas.

US 82, Arkansas 172
Texarkana–Smackover
100 miles

—TEXARKANA—

Located 143 miles west of Little Rock on I-30, Texarkana straddles the Arkansas-Texas border. The first known inhabitants came to the area about 1,500 years ago. Called the Cole's Creek people by archaeologists, these Indians made pottery and distinctive weapons. About the same time, a tribe wandered up the eastern coast of Central America until they reached the present site of New Orleans. There they encountered migrants from Florida. The two groups liked each other and merged, becoming known as the Caddo. They worked their way up the rivers to the lush forests and meadows where present-day Arkansas, Louisiana, Texas, and Oklahoma meet. Within a century, they had displaced the Cole's Creek people and settled in the rich hunting grounds.

The Caddo

Caddo men hunted bison, bear, deer, and turkey in the forests. They harvested fish, turtles, and frogs from the streams and lakes. Caddo women cultivated corn, melons, beans, calabashes (a gourd used for making utensils), and tobacco. They always kept a two-year supply of seeds on hand in case crops failed in a bad year.

Caddo villages were known for their excellent organization, large houses, and tidiness. Construction of a house was a community affair, much like barn raisings among Europeans. The Caddo would begin by erecting a large conical frame of willows. After weaving cane through the willows, they would cover the structure with clay. Tiers of dried grasses provided the outermost covering. Although the size of these homes varied, some accommodated as many as twenty families.

Each family had its own area with wood-framed couches, which were covered with reed mats and furs. The Caddo used the couches for seats by day and beds by night. Each family had its own tools and utensils, its own pots and baskets, and its own food stores. Everyone shared a fireplace built in a circular depression in the center of the house. An opening in the conical roof allowed smoke to escape. Houses were arranged in a circle around a central open area used for social gatherings and ceremonies.

Six Caddo hamlets stood near the future town site of Texarkana. French explorers found the Caddo to be warm hosts in 1719, when they welcomed the Frenchmen with a feast that lasted a full day. Ultimately, the Spanish would lay claim to the area. They enforced that claim with a garrison at Spanish Bluffs on the Red River.

Anglo-American Settlers

The first Anglo-American settlers came to the area about 1808. Many didn't know if they were settling in Mexico or in what would become the Arkansas Territory. Despite attacks from Indians and depredations by the increasing number of outlaws drawn to the area, farms began to appear in the fertile Red River valley. Newcomers began to arrive in increasing numbers after the War of 1812. Until 1825, most settlers were mountaineers and lowland farmers from Kentucky, Tennessee, Missouri, and Arkansas.

These were relatively poor folks of the highland subculture who rarely owned slaves and merely sought more productive land to feed their families. Fearless and fiercely independent, they devoted as much time to hunting as they did to farming. While they had little formal education, they understood the wilds as well as the Caddo and Osage Indians. These pioneers settled in the areas now known as Miller County in Arkansas and Bowie County in Texas, thanks to the efforts of Stephen Austin and the Scottish soldier of fortune General Arthur Wavell. Such hearty and hardworking folk made ideal frontiersmen.

Cotton plantations, with their completely different Southern subculture, began to arrive about 1835. The landed gentry who had first settled in coastal Virginia, Carolina, and Maryland now spread their plantations and lowland subculture throughout the southern lands. They brought slaves, a cash economy based on cotton, a different religious tradition, a love of education, and a penchant for large, grandly furnished homes. It should be pointed out, however, that there were only a handful of grand homes in all of antebellum Arkansas. The success of their plantations was limited by the Great Red River Raft, a seventy-five-mile tangle of logs that posed a substantial barrier to transporting cotton to market in New Orleans.

After Captain Henry Shreve cleared out the raft, side-wheelers and stern-wheelers began to bring a steady stream of essential supplies and luxuries upriver. The riverboats returned to New Orleans ladened with cotton, hides, furs, and tallow.

The most important steamboat of the day—at least for this story—was the *Texarkana*. The owner selected this name since his boat plied the Red River from *Tex*as to *Ark*ansas to Louisi*ana*. This stern-wheeler was later lost during one of its trips on the tricky Red River, but its name lives on as the lively town shared by Texas and Arkansas. At least that's one version of how Texarkana got its name. Six other legends give alternative possibilities of what inspired the name when the community was born in 1880. Some folks point to the patent medicine made by a Mr. Swindle (what a great name for a snake oil salesman!) of Bossier Parish, Louisiana. Since he marketed his concoction throughout Texas, Arkansas, and Louisiana—he named his patent medicine Texarkana Bitters.

Even as the settlers were succeeding, the proud and resourceful Caddo were failing. European diseases killed more than 70 percent of the population, and hostile Texans threatened to kill off the rest. The Caddo sold their lands to the U.S. government and retreated to Indian Territory. (Today, several thousand Caddo share lands with the Delawares and Wichitas about fifteen miles north of Anadarko, Oklahoma.)

Several stories on how Texarkana got its name relate to the coming of the railroad. Some folks claim that the Cairo & Fulton Railroad coined the name when it planned a line from St. Louis to a terminus somewhere around the place where Texas, Arkansas, and Louisiana came together. Others suggest that Colonel Gus Knobel coined the name. Knobel conducted the survey for the railroad. He reportedly painted "Texarkana" on a board with big red letters and nailed the board to a stump to mark the intended location for the railroad depot. Yet another story asserts that General Thomas Dockery planned to found a town that he would call Texarkana. Others point out that Colonel C. M. Harvey called his plantation Texarkana long before the town was established. Harvey was probably the owner of the riverboat *Texarkana* as well. Historian William Leet believes Dr. Josiah Fort probably named the town. His land grant lay just to the north of the future town site. In expectation of the Great Pacific Railroad, Fort reportedly erected a sign on his land that said "Texarkana." That railroad never did materialize.

The one thing that everyone can agree upon is that Texarkana was born a railroad town. Here's how it happened.

Birth of the Twins

The Civil War stalled efforts to build a railroad through Arkansas to Texas. The plan lay dormant for a dozen years, and then the railroads

Texarkana railroad yards. —Jesse L. Charlton, Special Collections, University of Arkansas Libraries, Fayetteville

sprang to life with a frenzy. The Texas & Pacific Railroad began laying tracks across Texas from Waco toward the border with Arkansas. The Cairo & Fulton Railroad stretched from Illinois through Missouri and Arkansas toward the Texas border. The two railroads originally planned to meet five miles west of the Arkansas-Texas border. But to lay track into Texas, the Cairo & Fulton would need a charter from that state, a costly and time-consuming proposition. As a result, the railroads decided to meet at the border, and Texarkana was born.

Forging a community that would straddle the state line would not prove to be easy.

Major Montrose of the Texas & Pacific auctioned off lots for the Texas half of Texarkana on the morning of December 8, 1873. With plat and mallet on a big pine log, Montrose sold lots to bidders who had slept the previous night on the table boards of a tent hotel run by Mrs. Underwood, who also bid on land. Much of the land was already occupied by squatters, and they were afforded the opportunity to buy the lots they occupied.

James Loughborough of the Cairo & Fulton sold the first lots on the Arkansas side of Texarkana in January 1874. Texarkana grew quickly as the Cairo & Fulton became the St. Louis, Iron Mountain & Southern (later known as the Missouri Pacific). Other railroads came to Texarkana as well, making the community a major transportation hub. Soon the Texarkana, Shreveport & Natchez; the Kansas City Southern; and the St. Louis & Southwestern (the Cotton Belt) helped

Texarkana street scene and town well, 1874. –Southwest Arkansas Regional Archives

make Texarkana a boomtown. Saloons, gambling dens, and bawdy houses sprang up on both sides of State Line Avenue, which ran right down the border between Texas and Arkansas.

The criminal element loved this arrangement. A thug could commit a crime on one side of State Line Avenue and then simply walk a few paces to the other side of the street, into another state and another jurisdiction. By 1881, more than fifty desperados had descended upon Texarkana for the easy pickings. The victimized and exasperated citizens of Texarkana held a mass rally on October 7 to deal with the problem. They left the gathering and made the rounds through town, "calmly and deliberately" inviting every crook to leave town within twenty-four hours or face the consequences, according to a newspaper account of the day. Although the procedure wasn't compatible with the rule of law, it did work for a time.

The independent governments of the two young towns called Texarkana chose to compete rather than cooperate. But the towns nevertheless continued to prosper and grow. In the 1880s, Texarkana became a mecca for newlyweds, who would honeymoon at the Benefield Hotel. The saloons of Texarkana thrived until the Volstead Act visited Prohibition upon the land.

Wagons clog this street in Texarkana, circa 1910. Note the circus bills posted on the Texarkana Carriage Company and Tilson Carriage Company. –Southwest Arkansas Regional Archives

The saloons closed, speakeasies opened, and stills sprouted like wildflowers around Texarkana. Stills in the bottomlands of the Red River valley began to manufacture corn whiskey of such quality and quantity that the area soon became a major supplier for the speakeasies in Shreveport, Little Rock, and Dallas. Some moonshine even found its way to Chicago. Black men fueled fires among the cypress trees with gasoline, which wouldn't produce smoke. Smoke brought lawmen, which was bad for business. Garland City (which lies on Long Prairie in Miller County, about seventeen miles east of Texarkana on US 82) became the headquarters for bootlegging operations in the valley.

The men who ran these operations were not mobsters from Chicago wielding Thompson submachine guns. They were local rednecks (a term of pride coined by three-term Arkansas governor Jeff Davis to distinguish the hardworking common man from the "high-collared" bankers and rich folk who oppressed them). These backwoods entrepreneurs conducted their negotiations in more traditional fashion— with buckshot. Freelance stills were frowned upon, and at least one would-be distiller was blasted in the alligator-infested swamps each month.

These bootleggers were most unusual in that they took pride in their work. They even went to the trouble of importing a vast quantity of charred kegs, which were made from oak staves produced at Henry Thane's mills at the other end of Arkansas. This extra effort gave Garland City Pride its color and its semblance of aging. Most old-timers remember Garland City Pride as the best bootleg whiskey of the day.

While Garland City bustled, and while the bottomlands boomed with the occasional shotgun blast, the streets of Texarkana got tougher. Texarkana came to be known as Little Chicago. The town's two halves continued their lack of cooperation. When a house caught fire on the Arkansas side of State Line Avenue—right across from a fire station on the Texas side of the street—the firemen simply sat in their chairs and watched the building burn. Agriculture and the timber industry provided most of the jobs in Texarkana into the 1930s, but the railroads continued to provide the real backbone of the economy.

The Great Depression hit Texarkana hard. People literally sold pencils and apples on street corners. But Texarkana fared much better than most cities. Churches, civic organizations, and the Salvation Army made sure that nobody starved. Most residents grew their own vegetables, and many began to raise fruit trees and chickens as well. Federal agencies such as the Work Progress Administration created jobs while building government facilities such as the most photographed landmark in Texarkana: the U.S. Post Office. It is the only federal building that sits in two states simultaneously.

The most significant federal project was the construction of the Red River Army Depot in Bowie County during the late 1930s. The undertaking virtually eliminated unemployment in the area, providing a payroll that peaked at 11,570 during the Korean War.

Perry DeMarce became one of the most influential Texarkanans of that era. Elected to the city council on the Texas side of Texarkana in 1946, he decided it was time to cut criminals off at the knees. The city only had one police car. He pushed for the addition of four more cars, which were all equipped with radios, a novel concept at the time. He got the police in Texarkana, Arkansas, to do the same. Both police stations installed transmitters on the same frequency. Suddenly, criminals could run, but they couldn't hide.

DeMarce then invited city and county officials from both sides of the border to a great fish fry at which he urged everyone to stop bickering and start cooperating. He single-handedly got the city and county police and the fire departments to start working together.

The United States Post Office on State Line Avenue in Texarkana is the only federal building that sits in two states.
—Polly Walter

The legacy left by DeMarce is that this spirit of cooperation continues to this day. Some competition remains, and the "curse of State Line Avenue" still plagues the two Texarkanas. But the people on both sides of the line have become known for their spirit, self-reliance, and altruism. Texarkana is much more than a collection of dignified edifices framed by stately oaks and beeches, more than the memory of sultry breezes ladened with the scent of crape myrtle, dogwood, and wisteria. Texarkana is a unique blend of culture and tradition that delights the soul like the delicious ragtime of Scott Joplin, who was born in the area.

—MAGNOLIA—

Magnolia lies fifty-three miles east of Texarkana and thirty-four miles west of El Dorado on US 82. In the early 1800s, the heavily wooded area was especially known for its substantial population of deer and bear. Large hunting parties, trappers, and traders came from Louisiana via an Indian trail. The biggest early exports to New Orleans were bear oil, bear meat, and bear skins.

A few subsistence farmers began to clear land in the 1830s, but settlers came to this area more slowly than other parts of southern Arkansas that had access to navigable rivers or established roads. Wild turkey and venison supplemented the crops and livestock farmers raised to feed their families. Later, settlers would grow a bit of cotton for cash. The rather isolated area became known for its hospitality, since strangers provided a highly prized diversion from daily routine.

Columbia County was carved out of corners of Lafayette, Union, Ouachita, and Hempstead Counties in 1852. The first county court was held at the Furgeson & Morgan Store, located about six miles west of present-day Magnolia. The new county needed a permanent, centrally located seat of government. Commissioners selected the present town site as a suitable location. While the commissioners were dining at the home of B. S. Harper, his daughter Elizabeth suggested the name Magnolia for the new county seat. The commissioners agreed that evening. Elizabeth went on to marry a future county commissioner and teach at the local grammar school.

Magnolia remained a small farming community. Cotton was Columbia County's only export, and getting it to market was an ordeal. Farmers would haul their crop by mule and ox team over primitive roads to Camden or Shreveport, but such ineffective transportation limited the amount of cotton a planter could raise for market. The residents of Magnolia rejoiced when the St. Louis & Southwestern Railroad (the Cotton Belt) planned a line from Texarkana to Bird's Point,

Mississippi. This line would connect tracks already running from Waco to Texarkana and from New Orleans to Bird's Point.

Local residents tried to entice the company to run its line through Magnolia. Instead, the company routed the rails six miles north of town. But Magnolia refused to take "no" for an answer. At their own expense, they built a railroad roadbed from Magnolia to intersect with the Cotton Belt near the present town of McNeil (named after Captain W. B. McNeil, a wealthy and prominent businessman in Magnolia). Local residents offered to donate the right-of-way, graded roadbed, and ten acres of land in Magnolia to the Cotton Belt if the railroad agreed to lay a narrow-gauge spur to Magnolia and to run two trains a day. The plan worked.

The first train pulled into Magnolia on September 3, 1883, amid great celebration. More than 300 of the town's 600 residents boarded flatcars for the train's first run to the junction at McNeil. The steam locomotive burned pine knots for fuel and showered the passengers with burning embers, choking them with smoke and dragging them through a steady drizzle. Folks returned to Magnolia with holes burned in their sodden, sooty Sunday best, eyes red from the smoke but

The Alexander Hotel in Magnolia on April 26, 1889. Guests stayed upstairs, while the downstairs featured a kitchen-dining room, lobby, and showroom. Note the pig wandering across the city square! –Southwest Arkansas Regional Archives

brimming with delight. The railroad ran more excursions until everyone in town had a chance to make the trip. It was a glorious day in the history of Magnolia.

The railroad opened agricultural markets and permitted the birth of a local timber industry, bringing a modest prosperity to Magnolia. While oil was first discovered in the county in 1922, the profitable Magnolia Oil Field wasn't discovered until the late 1930s. By then, the state government had instituted controls on the industry that prevented Magnolia from experiencing the trauma, waste, and environmental damage that characterized the oil booms at El Dorado and Smackover in the early 1920s. Today, the community is home of Southern Arkansas University and the Ethyl Corporation (one of the country's two biggest producers of bromine).

—EL DORADO—

Located 87 miles east of Texarkana on US 82 and 117 miles south of Little Rock on US 167, El Dorado was born soon after the decision was made to move the seat of Union County from Scarborough's Landing (about 9 miles northeast of El Dorado along the Ouachita River) to a more central location. Matthew Rainey brought a load of supplies from New Orleans and set up shop at a site facing the future location of the courthouse. That site was a pond frequented by migrating ducks (no sense wasting prime land on the government!). Rainey sold groceries and a great deal of whiskey. He and Judge Davis christened the town with a jug of hooch, merrily drinking the whiskey rather than anointing the ground according to local legend. They named the new county seat El Dorado after the mythical town of gold, hoping that such a grand name would draw settlers—and therefore business—to the embryonic community.

But El Dorado grew very slowly. The surrounding land only supported subsistence farmers, who grew vegetables for their own families plus a little bit of cotton as a cash crop. The soil was good enough to support more farming, but the land was hard to clear and harder to drain. Much of the acreage lay under water, and even more would be inundated for long periods after a moderate rain. In spite of the community's stagnant economy, El Dorado managed to remain the county seat after three more counties were carved out of Union County.

The coming of the railroads in the late 1800s finally kick-started the El Dorado economy by spawning the timber industry. This was a common theme throughout southern Arkansas around the turn of the century. Yellow pine flourished in the region's hot, damp climate. Railroads finally provided a means to ship lumber to distant markets.

Sawmill machinery. —Southwest Arkansas Regional Archives

Steady wages lured many subsistence farmers off their farms into the cash economy as lumberjacks or workers in the mill towns that sprang up throughout the region.

Wesson, located a dozen miles southwest of El Dorado, became one of the first big mill towns to spring up. Soon the sawmill supported a community of 20,000 people. The El Dorado & Wesson Railroad hauled finished lumber to El Dorado. From there, the Missouri Pacific and Rock Island Railroads shipped the lumber out of the Coastal Plain. By the time the population of El Dorado reached about 4,000, the industry had harvested most of the marketable timber. Wesson's fortunes and population began a steady decline. Because reforestation was not practiced in those days, mills simply went out of business once an area was logged out, or else the companies moved on to virgin timberlands. Today, Wesson is practically a ghost town.

Huttig, located about three miles north of the Louisiana border on Arkansas 129 (some thirty-one miles southeast of El Dorado), fared better. This mill town was established by the Frost Lumber Company, which was later acquired by the Olin Mathieson Chemical Company. Olin Mathieson instituted modern forestry practices and became one of the largest producers of lumber and wood by-products in the South. Huttig's most famous native, Daisy Bates, led the struggle to desegregate the Little Rock schools in 1957. Bates continued to work toward improving civil rights and went on to publish a black-oriented newspaper, the *Arkansas State Press*.

As the new century dawned in El Dorado, a smoldering feud flared into life, inflaming such passions in Union County that the governor would have to call out the state militia on several occasions.

The Parnell-Tucker Feud

With a name like El Dorado, one might expect the community's streets to be paved with gold. But in 1902 and 1903 the color of the streets turned to red—blood red. This was one rough and tumble town at the time. City Marshal Guy B. Tucker suspected that the Parnell family had killed his close friends Frank Newton and W. H. Lisbon. The Parnell family suspected that Harrison Dearing, who was a friend of Tucker, had shot and killed a family friend. Mutual distrust exploded into an open feud when the city council refused to allow Tom Parnell to build a sidewalk in "an unapproved manner" in front of his store.

The council asked Tucker to serve notice that the sidewalk would have to be level, rather than a series of steps as Parnell intended. The two men exchanged strong words and tempers flared. The bad blood simmered for several days and finally boiled over about 4:30 on the afternoon of October 9, 1902. The following eyewitness account was given by Jack Pendleton, who was twelve years old when gunfire erupted on the streets of El Dorado. Pendleton told this story when he was eighty-one years old, having worked for many years as the Union County tax collector.

Pendleton began by stressing his impartial attitude toward everyone who participated in the fight. "I saw it all very clearly," Pendleton said.

> I remember that day distinctly. My father owned a butcher shop where the First National Bank is located now, and I was his delivery boy. We kept our delivery horse in a corral on the east side of courthouse square. I had started to catch the horse, and when I got to the square, I reached to open the gate of the courthouse fence.
>
> As I struggled with the gate, City Marshall Guy Tucker noticed me and said, 'Jack, you had better get out of the way. It looks like there's going to be some trouble here.'
>
> Tucker was a tall, slender man, about 35 years old. That particular day, he was wearing a blue serge suit and a black Stetson hat. Turning away as he spoke, he pulled his coat back and drew his Colt pistol.
>
> I ran back to the butcher shop and called to Mr. Harrison, another employee, to come to the door. Just as he arrived, I saw Tom

Parnell walking toward the square with a drawn pistol. Tucker called out, 'Don't you come on me, Tom Parnell.'

Harrison L. Dearing, who owned a harness shop on the north side of the square, and Walter Parnell were talking in Dearing's doorway. Dearing, also being a constable, started across the square, Walter Parnell at his side. Both had guns, but theirs weren't drawn yet.

A small thorn bush had grown up on the court square, in the northeast corner of the iron rail fence. As we were watching these men converge on Tucker, a shot suddenly rang out. Someone, hidden behind that thorn bush, had fired at the marshall, but missed.

The square was instantly filled with men, guns popping in every direction. Mat Parnell ran a store on the southeast corner of the square; he ran into the street with a gun. Dr. Clarence Tucker, Guy's brother from Strong, was down there, but he didn't have a gun.

A restaurant owner, Frank Newton, hurried to the corner of the square with a gun, but I don't think he shot anyone. Dr. R. A. Hilton came out of his office on the east side of the square, but he didn't have a gun either. Mat Parnell's brother, Alvin, was out there shooting too.

All this took just a few minutes. When it ended, the streets were filled with injured and dead. Tucker had shot Tom Parnell, but Parnell walked to the east side of the square near Dr. Hilton's office. He fell dead on the sidewalk in front of Union Grocery Company.

When the first shot was fired, Harrison Dearing and Walter Parnell had drawn and emptied their guns at each other. They were so close, they fell across each other in the street. Both were dead when bystanders got to them. That much I saw, and I repeat it without malice toward anyone.

Pendleton remembered that Tucker received only a slight graze across the back of the neck, although the *Arkansas Gazette* claimed he had been shot six times and was on the verge of death. Fearing additional violence, County Sheriff W. G. Pendleton (Jack Pendleton's uncle) wired Little Rock requesting state militia. Governor Jeff Davis placed El Dorado under martial law until the following Wednesday, October 13.

Local residents finally relaxed on March 24, 1903, when Circuit Judge James Steel closed the books on the shootout. He accepted an offer from the attorneys of Mat, Jim, and Alvin Parnell. The three Parnells agreed to leave the state if the law would not prosecute them for murder and assault with intent to kill. The judge also dropped charges of carrying a pistol, simple assault, and disturbing the peace that had been filed against Dr. Hilton, Clarence Tucker, and Frank Newton.

The compromise calmed things down for awhile, but soon violence erupted once again on the streets of El Dorado when John Parnell came into town to conduct some business. Jack Pendleton's cousins, Frank and Boykin Goldsby, witnessed what happened. This enabled Pendleton to relate the following account:

> The date was August 8, 1903, about 4:30 in the afternoon. Marshall Tucker and my cousins were standing just inside the doorway of McWilliams Hardware, on the south side of the courthouse. Tucker had sworn to kill every Parnell as fast as he could. While Tucker was in the doorway, he saw John Parnell walking up the sidewalk, in the direction of the hardware store. Parnell, however, did not see Tucker in the doorway.
>
> As Parnell reached the doorway, Tucker stepped onto the sidewalk. Although the marshall pleaded self-defense in court, my cousins claimed it was anything but that. Allegedly, Tucker grabbed Parnell's collar and shot him several times in the chest. When Parnell fell to the sidewalk, Tucker spied a gun under the dead man's coat.
>
> Across the street stood Tucker's horse, hitched to a rail. He ran and jumped astride the horse, but, being frightened, it reared and threw him into the dust of the street. He rose and ran into the courthouse, his Colt .45 still in his hand.
>
> My uncle was still sheriff, and he told me later of Tucker's arrest. It seems Tucker ran upstairs to Circuit Judge Mahoney's office, scaring away at gunpoint the sole occupant, Mr. W. P. Goodwin. Goodwin met my uncle on the stairs and warned him Tucker was still armed.
>
> Tucker, evidently fearing for his life, had reloaded his pistol. Sheriff Pendleton told him to consider himself under arrest. Tucker replied, "I will, but I am not giving you this gun."

He didn't either—not until he was inside the jailhouse. Once again the sheriff wired the governor for the state militia, since rumors circulated that a mob of 100 to 200 individuals was planning to descend upon El Dorado with the intent of killing Tucker and dynamiting several houses. The funeral of John Parnell was held at his father's house, and a lot of folks stopped by to pay their respects.

The feud was by no means over. Before Tucker was released on bail pending his trial, he received a gift by special freight. The jug of whiskey turned out to be laced with strychnine, as Sheriff Pendleton discovered when he drank several swallows. He nearly died. Tucker was acquitted of murder on March 28, 1905.

Tucker turned in his marshal's badge and moved to Champagnolle, where he opened the Mink Eye Saloon. Several months later, he was ambushed while riding along the river. Severely wounded by several gunshots, his doctor had to amputate one arm. After his recovery, Tucker moved to Little Rock and immersed himself in state politics.

He soon became Democratic national committeeman from Arkansas. Tucker later served two terms as the commissioner of mines, minerals, and agriculture. He also was a member of the state highway commission for two years, and served as chief deputy auditor until his death in 1924.

As late as the 1970s, the Parnell-Tucker feud continued to conjure up strong feelings among the old-timers of Union County. Some folks would get downright testy when the subject came up; others would smile and then change the subject. Now those old-timers are gone, and the feud has become a bloodstained footnote in the history of El Dorado.

The Tucker family legacy lived on, however, in the person of Jim Guy Tucker, who is the grandson of Guy Tucker and was active in state politics. Jim Guy Tucker served as a prosecuting attorney, state attorney general, lieutenant governor, and governor. His political career ended abruptly in 1996 when he and codefendants James and Susan McDougal were convicted on twenty-four of thirty felony counts related to seven financial transactions that took place in the 1980s. Convicted on two counts (conspiracy and mail fraud), Governor Tucker rocked the political foundation of Arkansas by promptly resigning his office, to be replaced Mike Huckabee, who was lieutenant governor at the time.

For several decades after the Parnell-Tucker feud, El Dorado settled into relative obscurity as a typical small town in rural Arkansas. About 4,000 people lived in the quiet county seat in 1920. El Dorado served as the trade center for local farmers and lumbermen, but the economic future looked less than healthy. Most of the quality timber had been harvested, and the lumber business was declining. Local farmers harvested a fair crop of cotton from about 60,000 acres that year, but the value of a bale of cotton suddenly dropped to a third of the price farmers got the previous fall. The decline of the timber industry led to the decline of the railroads. Passenger and freight traffic plummeted on the town's two major railroads (the Missouri Pacific; and the Chicago, Rock Island & Pacific). Traffic on the local short line railroad, the El Dorado & Wesson, plummeted too.

Deputies working for Sheriff Finn Craig earned $75 per month, but each deputy had to provide his own horse for transportation. While the automobile had reached El Dorado, and the town boasted five blocks of paved road in 1920, hitching posts and livery stables were still commonplace around town. A three-story brick hotel on Washington Street catered to drummers calling on local businesses. Rufus Garrett had the hotel built about 1910, when the exploration for oil began in southern Arkansas. Here the terrain was similar to

Louisiana and Oklahoma, where explorers had discovered vast pools of oil. But exploration in southern Arkansas produced dry holes or natural gas, so interest waned and the oil men moved on. In 1920, several oil men stayed at the hotel, hinting at a boom that would rattle the very foundations of the community.

The Great Arkansas Oil Boom

The man who changed the history of southern Arkansas was Bruce Hunt. An oil speculator from Tulsa, Oklahoma, Hunt had worked in the oil fields of El Dorado, Kansas, during the 1915 boom. There he met a geologist named J. J. Victor, who believed the Gulf Coastal Plain of southern Arkansas would produce oil. Hunt didn't have time to think about the suggestion until he was laid up with rheumatism in 1919. The illness depleted his financial resources, even as he became obsessed with purchasing oil leases in southern Arkansas. Upon his recovery, Hunt borrowed $250 from his friend Sam Arrendale and hurriedly left for El Dorado.

The Barnes No. 1 began producing on June 19, 1919, in the El Dorado Field. The drilling contractor, M. Carl Jones of Shreveport, is third from left in the foreground. –Arkansas History Commission

Things did not start out well. Every attempt to lease land east of El Dorado failed. Then he met Mamie Smith of Little Rock, who happened to be visiting her father. Since she knew most of the local farmers from growing up in the area, she offered to drive Hunt around in her buggy and try to help him win their cooperation. After a number of unsuccessful attempts, Smith helped Hunt lease 12,522 acres for $229. Hunt returned to Tulsa and gave Arrendale the remaining $21 of the grubstake.

Then Hunt visited Victor, who was working as a consulting geologist. Together, they convinced the Constantin Oil & Refining Company to drill a test well entirely at the company's expense. In exchange, Constantin Oil would receive 75 percent of the acreage Hunt had leased. Numerous foul-ups delayed drilling the first test well; the railroad even lost the heavy rotary drilling rig being shipped from California. Hunt's agreement with the landowners of Union County required that he start drilling by December 31, 1919, or the leases would be cancelled automatically. Hunt weathered one calamity after another, and drilling finally began with only a day to spare.

Drilling progressed smoothly until April 22, when the bit penetrated a monstrous pocket of gas. The well blew. Gas and saltwater roared into the sky with such a fury that residents of El Dorado heard the commotion clearly from two and a half miles away. Capping the well didn't cure the problem. The bowels of the earth rumbled as poisonous gas worked its way to the surface, creating hundreds of craters. Water wells and streams within a four-mile radius began to bubble and boil, and farmers found that their traditional sources of water were undrinkable. Then a dimwitted sightseer struck a match near a small crater. Five people died instantly, and the well itself caught fire. The inferno raged for months before being extinguished.

The resulting newspaper headlines certainly caught the interest of other oil men, and soon more drilling rigs dotted the landscape around El Dorado. One rig, the Busey No. 1, worked within sight of town. Word raced through El Dorado on January 10, 1921, when the rig reached sand at 2,233 feet. A small crowd gathered as drilling stopped and bailing began. As the bailer was being lifted from the well for the sixth time that afternoon, an ominous rumble began to shake the ground with increasing intensity.

The crew ran from the rig as a black column of gas, oil, and saltwater shot out of the well with a deafening roar, drenching the delirious crew as well as the spectators. The huge cloud turned the sheep on the Murphy farm black, even though they were grazing a mile from the well. A black mist settled on El Dorado, which was also about a mile from the gusher. It was Monday—wash day—and the clothes on

People pack the El Dorado railroad station as they wait for the Pine Knot Cannonball during the oil boom. –Arkansas Oil and Brine Museum

every clothesline in town dripped with oil. El Dorado would never be the same.

Within forty-eight hours, five special trains a day were bringing folks to El Dorado. Wagons, buggies, horseback riders, and automobiles choked the roads, churning them into quagmires. A Laird Swallow landed in El Dorado with two men from Tulsa, who had flown the 310 air miles in an astonishing three hours and twenty-eight minutes. Within six days, regular air service had begun between El Dorado and Shreveport. Within weeks, the population had exploded from 4,000 to 15,000 people. People kept coming, with no end in sight.

The residents of El Dorado made a valiant effort to shelter and feed the hordes of people descending on the community. The town's four hotels filled their lobbies and halls with cots. Soon they were renting the chairs in their lobbies to people who needed a place to sleep. That didn't begin to fill the need. The chamber of commerce encouraged homeowners to take in borders, many of whom slept two to a bed. Barber chairs rented for $2 a night. People went house to house begging for a place to sleep, offering $10 for a bed. Some entrepreneurs erected large tents and filled them with cots, while others began to erect more permanent boardinghouses. Fifty ex-servicemen were allowed to sleep in the courthouse. The rest of the homeless slept in the Presbyterian cemetery. Places that rented for $50 per month now commanded $2,000.

During the early days of the boom, folks lined up for hours in front of the town's few restaurants. By the time many finally got to sit down, they commonly discovered that all the food had been sold. The city council decided to rent space for temporary mess halls. The first shacks near the Rock Island Railroad depot soon expanded to cover South Washington Street all the way to the town square. The ramshackle row of eateries and other businesses soon became known as Hamburger Row.

Speculators, lease hounds, and high rollers shouldered their way through the congested lobby of the Garrett Hotel, but roughnecks, teamsters, and job seekers sought whatever they needed on Hamburger Row. The row offered food, a place to sleep, army surplus clothing (the favored style in the oil fields), automobiles, and ladies who always described themselves to the police as stenographers or seamstresses. Most of these ladies were veterans of other oil booms. While the Volstead Act was in full force, the biggest source of revenue on Hamburger Row was probably alcohol. The selection of illegal spirits ran from moonshine to beer to imported Scotch.

Many people made their fortunes from rental properties. George James was a classic example. James owned a number of properties on El Dorado's South Washington Street. Times being what they were, he collected rents on a *daily* basis. Every day during the boom, James would take the train from his home in Bernice, Louisiana, to El Dorado's depot on South Washington Street. He would walk up one side of the street and down the other collecting rents, and then take the train back to Louisiana.

On March 7, the Rogers No. 1 well came in, with a daily gas flow of 20 to 25 million cubic feet. The Caddo Central Oil & Refining Company had some trouble capping the well, so W. F. Rogers—who lived nearby—moved his family and furniture out of his home. That proved to be remarkable foresight. Lightning ignited the gas four days later. Some wild geese flying over the farm had their feathers singed off, and down they came. Thanks to a heavy rain, the farm buildings resisted the intense heat for a time. But several hours later, the entire Rogers farm went up in smoke.

This roaring volcano of fire erupted only a half mile from the center of town. The earth convulsed and the townsfolk stuffed their ears with cotton or chewing gum for some relief from the painful roar. Nearby wells were shut down and evacuated, as workers surrounded the burning well with an earthen levee in an attempt to keep the inferno from spreading. The blaze towered 200 feet into the air, enabling the residents of El Dorado to read newspaper headlines at midnight. The plume of flame could be seen for thirty miles. The fire was finally

Smoke billows from a burning oil storage pit. –Arkansas Oil and Brine Museum

extinguished thirteen days later using the steam provided by twenty boilers.

The well that started the boom, Busey No. 1, produced for only forty-five days, but the frenzied search for oil had become unstoppable. By June 1921, more than 100 wells tapped into the El Dorado Field, and another 340 derricks were under construction. Local roads had become quagmires of mud or sand, and local farmers began to make a handsome profit pulling vehicles from mud holes. They soon built bridges and corduroy roads over the mires, and charged tolls for crossing them. This became so profitable, that man-made mires became a cottage industry. With an average toll of 25 cents (or 50 cents to extricate a rig from the mud), most farmers made more money from traffic than they did from oil leases. An eight-mile trip by automobile from El Dorado to an oil well could take fifteen hours and cost $20 in tolls. One oil man left El Dorado for Smackover with $32 in his pocket, only to go broke on tolls and towing a mile short of his destination. He abandoned his car and walked.

Most roads were impassable enough without any entrepreneurial intervention. Even many roads in town had stretches that were knee-deep in mud. One photo of the day shows a teamster driving a wagon around one of the town's mud holes, where parts of a drowned mule are sticking out of the mire. Once an entire rig—wagons, mules, and cargo—reportedly sank out of sight. But mud mattered little to the residents of El Dorado, compared to the rampant robbery, mayhem, and murder plaguing Union County.

The Quest for Law and Order

By the time that the population of El Dorado reached 32,000 crime had become so rampant that the new mayor evicted everyone from Hamburger Row. Finally, the law began to have an effect inside the city limits. So many people were arrested that the new county sheriff, Alan Hancock, built an open "circus-type cage" in the courthouse yard to hold the overflow. In bad weather, the softhearted sheriff placed the prisoners in leg irons and held them under guard in the Missouri Pacific Railroad depot. To keep the prison population as small as possible, Judge W. D. Hall held court every day, imposing very heavy fines.

Within weeks, the saloons, dance halls, bordellos, and gambling houses moved to outlying areas, where new establishments called "barrel houses" offered every form of entertainment under one roof. These cabarets supposedly got their name from the habit of some bartenders, who would take the clothes from a drunk who had run out of money, put him in a barrel, and roll him out the door. The most popular of the thirty or so barrel houses in the valley included Dago Red's, Blue Moon, Smackover Sal's, Big Casino, Cattle Gap, Barrel House Blues, and Jake's Place. These places sold a six-ounce Coke bottle filled with bootleg whiskey for $1.25 and a bottle of choc beer (local bootleg, *choc* being short for Choctaw) for 75 cents. "Fancy women" provided a more expensive diversion.

Fights and violent robberies became so commonplace in the valley that six or seven people might die in a single twenty-four-hour period. Lawmen avoided the liveliest areas, Pistol Hill and Shotgun Valley, if they wanted to survive until their next payday. People headed for town could be robbed unless they were well armed and traveled in groups. Women would hide their husbands' pay inside their elaborately piled hair when they walked to the bank in El Dorado, keeping just a few dollars in their purse to satisfy robbers. The ladies weren't safe until they actually entered the bank.

Meanwhile, Two-Shot Blondie imported more fancy women and bootleg whiskey. Two brothers, known only as Oscar and Joe, ran moonshine stills throughout Union County, but they made their best whiskey in Calhoun County. The most-feared desperado of the day was a man of average height in his mid-twenties who brought a band of thugs from Burkburnett, Texas. Prematurely gray and addicted to narcotics, everyone knew him as Silvertop. He was feared even more than his strongman, Big Ed. Mothers warned children to hurry home or Silvertop would get them, until the day he was found, murdered, on the road to Smackover.

Both Silvertop's and El Dorado's fortunes had become intricately woven with the sleepy little village called Smackover. Although nine refineries in El Dorado were processing a total of 20,000 barrels of crude a day by April 1922, El Dorado's oil industry was not as healthy as it appeared. Too many wells had been drilled too quickly in the El Dorado Field. Production soon began to fall after only a small portion of the oil had been recovered. Uncontrolled exploitation was about to ruin that oil field, even as a new bonanza was discovered in what would be called the Smackover Oil Field.

—SMACKOVER—

Smackover is located nine miles north of El Dorado and twenty-three miles south of Camden on Arkansas 7. The town's story started when Thomas Jefferson purchased the Louisiana Territory from France for 4 cents an acre in 1803. The following year, the U.S. government commissioned expeditions to explore these new lands. William Dunbar—a planter, astronomer, and mathematician from Natchez—led the expedition to explore and chart the Ouachita River. A physician from Philadelphia, Dr. George Hunter, accompanied Dunbar and a company of soldiers. The Dunbar-Hunter Expedition eventually reached a bayou they called *Chemin Couvert,* which means the "covered way" in French. The bayou banks formed a deep ravine so choked with underbrush and cane that the land was nearly impenetrable.

After following *Chemin Couvert* (now known as Smackover Creek) for several miles, the expedition returned to the Ouachita River and eventually reached the site where the town of Smackover was later built. French hunters and trappers of the day called the area *Sumac Couvert,* since the land was covered in sumac bushes. By 1857, the bayou's name had been corrupted to Smack Overt; by 1884, this had become Smackover.

The first settler in the area was Nathan Primm, who staked the claim for his Indian War land grant on the very spot where the town of Smackover now stands. Primm brought his wife, elderly father, and a few slaves to help work the land. His father died in 1836 and is buried at the Old Hicks Cemetery on Mount Holly Road. Other settlers armed with government land grants began to arrive. Then Bill Howard opened a trading post at Cooterneck (now known as Lewis Hill) about a mile north of Smackover Creek sometime before 1850. The post served as a stopover for the freight and stage lines from Camden that serviced French Port, Newport Landing, Lisbon, Mount

Holly, El Dorado, and Louisiana settlements as far south as Monroe. The trading post closed when Howard joined the Confederate army.

The Reconstruction period after the war hit the Smackover area hard. The indebtedness of the county was only $1,600 in 1868, but mismanagement and heavy taxation inflicted by the carpetbaggers increased that debt by eightyfold (to $128,892) in six years. The Smackover post office was established in 1879 at Newport Landing, five miles north of the modern town site. Although that improved the quality of life in the area, local residents had to travel to Lisbon to vote, and the deplorable state of that road made the journey quite arduous. The residents in the north-central part of the county requested the formation of a nearby township where they could vote, which they called Smackover.

Therefore in 1887, the name "Smackover" referred to a township, a post office five miles from that township, and a creek. But there still wasn't a town. T. C. Murphy opened a mercantile store just before surveyors for the Alexandria & Camden Railroad Company established a route from Camden to El Dorado through the township. Smackover was designated as a water stop on the railroad.

The modest economic boom that followed completion of the railroad in 1890 soon led to the building of another mercantile, a combination doctor's office and drug store, a "two-floor" hotel, and a blacksmith shop that later sold gasoline and repaired the odd automobile that began to appear. A. W. Friend, Smackover's railroad agent,

A dead mule has been cut loose from this team hitched to a wagon mired in the muddy streets of Smackover. –Arkansas Oil and Brine Museum

Smackover in August 1922, before the oil boom. –Arkansas Oil and Brine Museum

conducted business out of a boxcar. All the businesses were built along an unusually wide main street. Soon three churches, a one-room schoolhouse, and the McKenzie Drink Stand added additional services to the community. Smackover was finally a town, but the residents still lacked a post office.

There was already a Smackover post office at Newport Landing, and the U.S. government would not permit two post offices with the same name in the same state, so the local residents changed the town's name from Smackover to Henderson City, in honor of the president of the railroad. But the town's new application for a post office was rejected on the grounds that Arkansas already had a post office named Henderson, so the flabbergasted residents changed their community's name back to Smackover, and the government moved the Smackover post office from Newport Landing to the growing railroad town.

Thanks to the railroad, the timber industry blossomed and began to fuel the local economy. In 1890, J. S. Cargile moved his lumber mill from Okalona to a location between Smackover and Norphlet, that he named Anolako (Okalona spelled backward).

Smackover's population slowly increased to about 131 people by 1922. Most folks worked as mill hands or teamsters. The town's only elected official was Tom Gray, who worked at the mill and functioned as a part-time town marshal. While Gray owned a pistol, he never carried it. Smackover was a quiet little community. That would soon change.

By the spring of 1922, the El Dorado Field was in trouble, and wild-catters began drilling near the peaceful little village of Norphlet, which lay eight miles north of El Dorado and just four miles southeast of Smackover. The discovery well called Murphy No. 1 was being drilled with a huge, 112-foot wooden derrick powered by a monstrous boiler similar to the ones used on steam locomotives. The new oil boom began in spectacular fashion on May 14, when the Murphy No. 1 struck gas.

The Great Crater

A sudden rumbling deep in the earth sent the crew of Murphy No. 1 scampering for their lives. Moments later, murderous gas pressure destroyed the derrick, blew out the drill stem, and deafened rough-necks working a quarter mile away. Some 65 to 75 million cubic feet of gas screamed into the sky that day, throwing balls of hard-packed sand through the air. A local minister rushed to the scene and watched in horror as the ground began to belch and boil and swallow up the giant derrick and boiler. "It's the closest thing to . . . hell as I have ever seen," the minister remarked in awe. He hadn't seen anything yet.

Roy Stone watched what followed. "The boiler would go down. Then it would come back up and roll over, then go back down again." The explosion-like belches from beneath the earth covered the surround-ing area with about five inches of sand, and a large crater formed as

Murphy No. 1 well crater near Smackover. –Arkansas Oil and Brine Museum

the land around the well began to sink. By the next morning, numerous small craters had ignited from the friction of the rapidly escaping gas. The well itself ignited on the second morning, and flames screamed 300 feet into the sky. Black smoke and slate-colored dust boiled much higher as the burning crater grew ever wider and deeper, gobbling up lesser craters and anything else in its path.

Subterranean water finally extinguished the blaze after seven hours, revealing a crater some 100 feet deep and 350 feet across. The floor of the crater bubbled like an active volcano, spewing sand (actually pulverized shale), water, and oil out of the crater. Pulverized shale struck a pilot in the face at an altitude of 7,000 feet. The gasser threw debris as far as ten miles from the well. Sometimes, the giant boiler would appear, spin like a top, and then disappear once again. The crater repeatedly caught fire and burned itself out.

A reporter from the *Arkansas Gazette* described Murphy No. 1 as "one of the natural wonders of Arkansas." Tourists trekked over log roads to view the spectacle and purchase sandwiches, drinks, and ice cream at refreshment stands that surrounded the crater. (Today, the site is used as a garbage dump, and little remains to warrant a visit.)

Local Lumberman Strikes Oil

Smackover's big strike was yet to come. The key player would be Sidney Umsted, who came to the village about 1907 while in his early thirties to work in the timber industry. Umsted purchased and leased vast tracts of land from the Old Camden Road north to the Ouachita River. He opened a lumber mill. But he dreamed about oil. Umsted had worked as a lumberman in northern Louisiana before oil had been discovered there. His new timberlands contained identical surface characteristics to the Homer Oil Field in Louisiana. Umsted tenaciously tried for years to entice someone to sink a test well at Smackover without success, until the boom began at El Dorado.

Umsted finally interested four investors from Camden plus the VKF Oil Company of Shreveport to drill a well on land leased on the farm of Charles Richardson. Umsted reserved half of the profits for his investors and himself, while VKF got the other half. They struck oil on July 29, 1922. Unlike many wells in Union County, the Richardson No. 1 well produced an abundance of oil for four decades, making Sid Umsted a millionaire.

Within weeks, 25,000 money-hungry roughnecks, speculators, teamsters, laborers, gamblers, fancy women, and desperados descended upon the little village of Smackover. Marshal Tom Gray started wearing two pistols at all times as he and Deputy Tim Walls (a local

Part of the business district in Smackover during the oil boom. —Eddie Lewis
Collection, Arkansas Oil Heritage Center, Arkansas History Commission

teamster) struggled to keep the streets of Smackover safe. Railroad tracks ran down the middle of Smackover's unusually wide main street: Broadway. In the main business district, on the south side of the tracks, the marshal was able to maintain a semblance of order. Boardwalks ran the length of the street. "Crossing boards" periodically spanned the sea of mud called Broadway to the establishments north of the tracks. This low-lying area of lowlifes was called Death Valley.

The Smackover Journal warned readers about venturing into Death Valley, where folks openly carried guns in an atmosphere like the legendary Wild West. "Don't ever go there at night," the newspaper admonished. "If you must go, then take four or five men with you and go well armed!"

Yet Death Valley was positively genteel compared to the hastily constructed tent towns, and the clusters of cot houses, barrel houses, and food joints on the far side of Smackover Creek. Accommodations ranged from primitive hotels called "slap-ups" to cot houses, where three men would rent the same cot, sleeping in shifts to match their schedules. One slap-up advertised "more cots and less mice." Meals ranged from 10-cent hamburgers of doubtful origin to oysters on the half shell and lobster d'Anglaise. One barrel house provided the most notorious delights of the day: eight fancy women who could speak five languages fluently or curse like a marine drill sergeant, depending on the client's preference. These highly regarded ladies were known as Dolly, Swede, Louisiana Sal, Big 'Un, Oklahoma Kate, Kitty, Mimi, and Barrel House Sue.

No story of life in Smackover would be complete without Barrel House Sue. She was a somewhat large, less than handsome woman who didn't dress with a great deal of care. What earned her the respect and affection of the community was her happy-go-lucky attitude and her desire to help the unfortunate. Sue ate at the uptown cafes, and she would commonly befriend and feed a broke and hungry old man, a destitute woman, or a youngster without hope. Sickness ravaged the valley during that first winter, and local doctors could not begin to cope with the magnitude of the problem. Barrel House Sue sat beside the beds of countless sick that winter, earning the love of many folks despite her coarse character and her profession. Barrel House Sue eventually left her line of work and married well.

Back in those earliest days of Smackover's boom, wells and pipelines seemed to sprout overnight like mushrooms. So much oil was extracted so quickly that the crude was stored in open fields surrounded by levees. Lease hounds quickly bought up every scrap of land in the area, making million-dollar deals using a tree stump for a desk.

Chaos reigned. Fred McDonald, a local merchant and part-time postmaster, became inundated by mountains of mail, driving the beleaguered man to send the following telegram to Washington:

OFFICE OUT OF CONTROL (STOP) LETTERS ARRIVING 5,000 TO 7,000 DAILY (STOP) PARCEL POST BY THE TON (STOP) CAN'T OPEN MAIL ANY LONGER (STOP) ACCEPT MY RESIGNATION (STOP)

The entire village was out of control. Smackover required some serious hands-on direction, since the community had neither a mayor nor any city government. So twenty-five of the village's fifty-six registered voters petitioned for incorporation, and the City of Smackover was officially born on November 3, 1922.

Unfortunately, none of the petitioners was remotely interested in the job of mayor. Jett Murphy, who ran one of the three general stores in town, grudgingly agreed to serve until the special election in December. Then Murphy not only washed his hands of politics, he left town. Smackover would go through four mayors in a matter of weeks before finding salvation in the person of a local lad who had his right leg amputated at the hip after a wagon accident when he was seven years old.

Smackover's Boy Mayor

Losing his leg in 1907 didn't slow Clyde Byrd down. According to childhood friends, Byrd was faster than most kids in town through the adept use of his crutch. By the time the boom began in Smackover, Byrd was a student at Henderson-Brown College in Arkadelphia. He returned home to run for mayor after the city was incorporated. This special election would select a temporary mayor until a general election four months later. Byrd's opponent was A. W. Friend, the well-liked ultraconservative who ran the local railroad depot. Ironically, Friend didn't want the job, whereas Byrd desperately wanted to be mayor.

As Don Lambert would later observe, this became a campaign of experience versus inexperience, maturity versus youth, and reluctance versus exuberance. Friend even refused to campaign.

Furthermore, rarely would so few vote on behalf of so many. More than ten thousand people choked the community, yet Smackover only had fifty-six registered voters. This curiosity developed thanks to a state law that required residents to pay a poll tax a year before an election to become eligible voters. Only eight of the sixty-plus businessmen in town could vote. Ironically, most of the active campaigning was conducted by the disenfranchised majority.

Friend won the December election by six votes, even though he probably voted for his opponent. He conducted city business out of the railroad depot, where he held police court every night by the light of kerosene lamps. A steady stream of gamblers, cutthroats, and fancy women paraded through court, yet the quality of life in Smackover continued to worsen. Every time citizens requested improvements such as better streets (several mules had drowned in mud holes), a bigger school (students attended classes in shifts at the Baptist Tabernacle), or a sewerage and water system for the city—Friend replied that the boom would be over in three months, and he didn't want to saddle the old-timers with the bill.

Friend resigned after two and a half months and immediately left town, an exhausted yet wealthy man. Clayton Taylor tried his hand as mayor and lasted exactly one month.

Young Clyde Byrd decided to bide his time. He ran unopposed for the office of city clerk in the 1923 general election, in which L. G. Hurley defeated Tom Gray for mayor by a vote of thirty-five to eighteen. Hurley burned out three weeks into his term and resigned at the June meeting of the city council.

Clyde Byrd had been quite active in the community over the intervening weeks, working in the realms of property management and real estate in addition to his duties as city clerk. The city aldermen appointed him mayor, and editor B. W. Barnes published an article the next day in *The Smackover Journal* about the "Boy Mayor." Barnes managed to get his story on both national wire services, claiming that Byrd had just turned twenty-one. Most newspapers throughout the country carried the story, bringing both Byrd and Smackover much better press than the town was receiving as a lusty boomtown. It turns out that Byrd was about eighteen months older than the article reported, but twenty-two and a half was still mighty young to be major of any town—much less one that appeared to be utterly unmanageable and getting worse by the minute.

But Byrd proved to be the right man for the job. He quickly took command and earned the respect of the community. Byrd covered the main street with lumber and gravel to eliminate the treacherous morass. When the paving sank into the mire, he immediately covered the street again. He installed water and sewer systems, organized a volunteer fire department, and hired more policemen. As city judge, Byrd imposed massive fines on lawbreakers, which encouraged troublemakers to stay out of town and also helped to finance local improvements. An occupation tax provided another quick and even more substantial source of financing. Marshal Tom Gray instituted the Smackover Mounted Police, who used horses to negotiate roads that were frequently too muddy for a man on foot or in an automobile. Smackover began to change for the better, and civilization gradually seeped into Death Valley (or the anarchy gradually oozed out).

The paving of Broadway inspired the biggest town-wide celebration Smackover had ever seen. The entire population turned out for a picnic and danced into the wee hours of the following morning. The white folks danced on the south side of Broadway. The black folks danced on the north side. Everyone came to the middle of the boulevard for barbecue and all the fixings. It was a progressive party for the time.

Byrd easily won reelection in 1925 and 1927. By the following year, he had pretty well eliminated the rampant criminal activity in Smackover and brought an amazing level of basic services to the community. The folks of Union County knew a good man when they saw one. Byrd went on to serve as county clerk, county judge, and then state senator until 1952. He ran for governor in 1968, but ill health kept him from campaigning. It was the only race he had lost since that first mayoral campaign in 1922, when A. W. Friend beat him by a vote of twenty-seven to twenty-one.

Boom and Bust

The Smackover Oil Field did not fare as well as the City of Smackover. In fact, the Smackover Field became a textbook example of how *not* to exploit an oil deposit. Unrestrained development squandered the resource and ravaged the environment. During the early years of the boom, some wells were allowed to flow wildly, natural gas was burned off as a waste product, and the crude—commonly a combination of oil and saltwater—was stored in thousands of fields surrounded by earthen levees. The oil would be skimmed into tanks, and the brine was allowed to soak into the ground or run into streams.

Crude tended to escape from the open pits when levees broke or rain caused the pits to overflow. Soon the vegetation had died along streams and low-lying sloughs. In November 1922, for example, more than 100,000 barrels of crude oil escaped into Smackover Creek after heavy rains. The entire creek caught fire, spreading destruction down its watershed. A burning log floating down the creek even ignited a well.

By 1926, only three states produced more oil than Arkansas, and 28,752 open pits of crude oil dotted the Arkansas landscape. Lightning

Oil flowing from Otto Morris and Meyer well near Smackover.
–Southwest Arkansas Regional Archives

162

tended to ignite pits with appalling regularity. Perhaps 8 percent of the crude oil production from the Smackover Field was lost during the first twelve years due to fires and spills. A staggering quantity of natural gas was squandered as well. The incompetent exploitation of the El Dorado and Smackover Fields would stimulate the Arkansas legislature to enact laws to prevent similar problems in the future.

Nevertheless, the impact of oil on the economy of Arkansas was unprecedented. The investment in oil equipment and facilities alone exceeded the assessed value of all the taxable property in the entire state! Put another way, the value of oil equipment and facilities was worth twenty-four times more than the combined capital of all 500 banks operating in Arkansas at the time the boom began. Arkansas pumped an astounding amount of oil to market. The dollar value of Arkansas "black gold" dwarfed the legendary gold strike in the Klondike.

Companies like Murphy Corporation, Lion Oil Company, and Cross Oil and Refining brought order and responsibility out of the chaos. El Dorado settled down to an economy based on oil production and refining, petrochemical production, agriculture, and timber. Smackover slowly transformed itself from an unruly and boisterous boomtown into a community of substance.

As oil production plummeted, the production of natural gas increased and then eclipsed oil production. Today, Arkansas produces ten times more natural gas than it produced during the oil boom. Many oil wells still yield a modest amount of oil. Others lie dormant and will only be used again when the value of oil increases enough to offset the cost of recovery. Petroleum continues to provide a substantial source of revenue to southern Arkansas, but only three refineries continue to operate in Union County.

Even though more than half of the county's oil remains underground, the rapid exploitation of the field has made much of that oil inaccessible using present methods of secondary recovery. The oil fields behave like an aerosol paint can that has lost its pressure. Therefore, the local refineries supplement local oil with crude imported from other states.

The Bromine Boom

Ironically, the abundant brine in the oil fields that so irritated early oil producers has developed into a real moneymaker, thanks almost entirely to one man: Dr. Frank Soday of the Lion Oil Company in El Dorado. Soday wanted to find a way to more economically dispose of the massive quantity of brine that was a worthless by-product of oil production in Union County. He discovered that the Smackover brines contained the largest concentration of bromine in the world, except for the saltwater of the Dead Sea.

Bromine is a dark red liquid at room temperature that is used to make pharmaceuticals, light-sensitive photographic emulsions, and fuel additives. Dow Chemical in Michigan was the primary producer of bromine at the time. Dr. Soday found that a barrel of Smackover brine would yield a cup of bromine. And Arkansas had a lot of brine. In the mid-1950s, El Dorado's Murphy Oil joined forces with the Michigan Chemical Company to use the waste brine from Murphy's oil production.

With a modest investment of $600,000, the partners built a plant in 1957 that produced 3 million pounds of bromine per year. Within a dozen years, the nation's bromine industry (located in Michigan and Ohio) relocated to southern Arkansas. Today, the Ethyl Corporation in Magnolia and Great Lakes Chemical in El Dorado produce 41 percent of the world's bromine. That works out to 91 percent of the bromine produced in the United States. Union and Columbia Counties possess the largest subterranean source of bromine in the world. The proven reserves will last for more than a hundred years.

Smackover's Oil and Brine Museum

Do not allow yourself to be underwhelmed by the thought of an oil and brine museum! This is not a facility filled with bottles of crude oil and saltwater. The uncommonly friendly folks at the museum tell the compelling story of the roughnecks and desperados who struggled through the Smackover boom. Technology buffs will find working examples of every sort of derrick and pump used over the years. And viewing the free film about the oil boom in the museum's theater will fascinate everyone. Old-timers who were there tell the story in a compelling fashion, and the cinematography is exceptional. Just seeing the film is worth the trip to Smackover.

Although the museum is run by the Arkansas Department of Parks & Tourism, its development has been a real grassroots effort. Old-timers and modern oil men have donated a great deal of time and equipment to Oil Field Park and the museum's 25,000 square foot exhibit center. The facility has much to offer history buffs, students, and teachers, including a superbly archived and cross-indexed oral history section for serious researchers. The Oil and Brine Museum preserves a wealth of human drama from southern Arkansas.

This is the route most folks take between Little Rock and Shreveport, Louisiana. US 167 begins in the middle of Junction City, which straddles the border. The highway passes through El Dorado and continues north through the former Union County seat of Champagnolle, the railroad town of Fordyce, and the crossroads at Sheridan, reaching Little Rock near its airport.

–SCARBOROUGH'S LANDING (CHAMPAGNOLLE)–

Located off US 167 about nine miles northeast of El Dorado, at the southeastern corner of Calion Lake along the Ouachita River, this small community developed where Lawrence Scarborough had established a boat landing in 1829 for himself and his neighbors. That same year, the territorial legislature created Union County from a large chunk of south-central Arkansas Territory. The legislature established the first county seat at *Écore à Fabri* (later known as *Écore Fabre,* and then Camden). Scarborough's Landing began to prosper as a business and shipping center, and eventually became the new county seat when the legislature lopped off part of the county to form another.

When the legislature carved off yet another portion of Union County, residents petitioned for an election of commissioners to find a more central location for the county seat. The site was quickly surveyed and platted so construction of the new courthouse could begin. The new county seat would be called El Dorado.

Meanwhile, the residents of Scarborough's Landing changed the town's name to Champagnolle after Pedro Champagnolle, who traded with the Indians of the area in the 1770s. French explorers had named a local stream after him long before the area was settled.

Champagnolle's fortunes peaked during the decade preceding the Civil War, a conflict from which the town never really recovered. Only eighteen of the ninety-two men who joined the Confederate army survived the fighting and disease. After the war, local planters once again raised cotton and shipped it by river to New Orleans, although on a much smaller scale than before. Boats made the five-day trip to New Orleans twice each week.

Champagnolle survived as a small but reasonably prosperous town of about 100 people through the 1880s. Then the railroads came to southern Arkansas in the early 1890s, sounding the death knell of river transportation and many small communities that the railroad bypassed. Champagnolle was one of those casualties. By the 1930s, the historic community was less than a ghost town, since few ruins remained.

The Lion Oil Company bought the entire town site in 1939 and built a tank farm fed by pipeline from the refinery in El Dorado. Once again, Scarborough's Landing became a river port. But now its workers loaded oil onto barges rather than cotton onto steamboats. The Lion Oil operation lasted a short time, and its rusty remains—along with a bronze historical marker—merely hint at Champagnolle's glory days, when the town played an important role in the development and history of Union County.

—FORDYCE—

Located sixty-eight miles south of Little Rock and forty-nine miles north of El Dorado on US 167, the town site was once owned by former slave Henry Atkinson. A. W. Holderness bought the land in 1881 for $118 and sold it to the Southern Improvement Company the following year for a handsome profit. Within another year, the St. Louis & Southern Railroad had laid tracks through the land, which was platted for a town site named after the railroad's surveyor, Samuel Fordyce.

Princeton (located eighteen miles northwest of Fordyce on Arkansas 8) was the thriving county seat when Fordyce was born. In fact, Princeton had been surveyed as the seat of Dallas County a year before there even *was* a Dallas County. But when the railroad bypassed Princeton, the town began to dry up even as Fordyce began to grow.

Fordyce's fortunes mirrored many other railroad towns in the Coastal Plain. A lumber industry developed to exploit the oak and pine that abounded in the region, and the town became an economic focus for the surrounding area. The first plant to make plywood from Southern pine was built in Fordyce.

In a break with Arkansas tradition, Fordyce took over as the county seat in 1906, even though it lay at the very edge of the county. When other county seats were moved over the years, they usually went to more central locations. Dallas County moved its seat to the primary source of economic activity. Fordyce remains the focal point for commerce in the region.

—SHERIDAN—

Located twenty-nine miles south of Little Rock and eighty-four miles north of El Dorado on US 167, Sheridan has been the seat of Grant County since the days of Reconstruction. The area was part of the Quapaw hunting grounds until the late 1830s. The woods teemed with deer, wild turkeys, ducks, raccoons, and squirrels. The waters swarmed with fish. The few Europeans in the area hunted and trapped, until farmers and planters began to settle in the area about 1840. The planters began to export cotton to Pine Bluff within two years.

When Arkansas seceded from the Union in 1861, only about 4,000 people lived in what would become Union County after the war. This was not a region known for its grand plantations. About sixty families owned slaves. The largest plantation had fifteen to twenty slaves. This was an area of modest plantations, small farms, and steam mills. Some mills ran grist machinery for grinding corn. Others ran saws, planes, gins, and shingle-making machinery. Many mills ran several different kinds of equipment.

Local residents were deeply divided on the issue of secession. The region raised so many volunteers for both sides during the war that scarcely an adult white male of military age could be found by the end of 1862. Most joined the Confederate army. But Captains Patterson Dodd, John Helfin, and Aaron Hedden raised three pro-Union companies. Bands of pro-Confederate irregulars called "Bushwhackers" and anti-Confederate irregulars called "Jayhawkers" conducted raids throughout the region. Add both Confederate and Union foraging parties who would take anything they needed (or wanted), and the local folk suffered mightily.

Depredations by roving bands of former combatants continued after the war ended. Most were motivated by a desire for revenge, but some were merely desperados seeking to rob anything of value that still remained in the region. The fates of Dr. Richard Rhodes and one of his friends, Mary White, shed some light on why the Civil War—and the years that immediately followed—provided the defining period for Arkansas.

Richard Clinton Rhodes

Dr. Richard Rhodes practiced medicine in North Carolina, where he owned a substantial plantation and amassed a considerable personal fortune. When gold was discovered in California, Rhodes decided to move there to experience some adventure. With his wife and two children, household goods and livestock, plus numerous slaves, this became an expedition rather than a simple move. He purchased thirty-six sections of land along the Arkansas River at Rob Roy near Pine Bluff, where he left 160 slaves and enough equipment to start a plantation. The rest of the expedition continued on toward California in two carriages and two wagons.

Flooding prevented them from crossing the Saline River. Rhodes came to like the remote location and abundant wildlife of the area as he waited for the floodwaters to recede. He decided to settle in Arkansas. Rhodes purchased 480 acres and built a two-story log house. Then a storm in 1849 destroyed the plantation being built at Rob Roy. This was not an auspicious start to his life in Arkansas.

Rhodes supported the Confederacy when war erupted in 1861. He was too old to fight, so he traveled the countryside in his capacity as a physician and reported to Confederate authorities on the disposition of any Union patrols or encampments that he encountered. This activity eventually came to the attention of pro-Union families behind the Confederate lines—including his pro-Union neighbors. They would remember.

Soon after the end of the war, an armed band of ruffians rode down Princeton Pike to the big house where Rhodes lived. They demanded all his gold (part of the logic for this demand was probably to lay the blame for what would follow at the feet of desperados rather than Jayhawkers). The doctor replied that he had none. He explained that he had spent it all during the war.

The men tied a rope around the doctor's neck and hanged him from a tree in his yard. After the horsemen rode away, black members of the household came out of the woods and cut him down. Somehow, Rhodes was still alive. The horsemen eventually returned and hanged him again, this time with wire, which sliced through his throat. Satisfied with the gory spectacle, the horsemen disappeared down the Princeton Pike. Rhodes was barely alive when he was cut down once again. But the wire had severed his windpipe. The doctor survived for some time, holding his windpipe together with his fingers whenever he had to swallow. Rhodes died a lingering death.

The next day, the riders struck a wealthy family who were close friends of Rhodes. They brutally murdered Mary White, who told family members before she died that she recognized at least one of the men as a neighbor. Such was the climate in much of Arkansas at the beginning of Reconstruction.

Tales of this kind make it easy to understand how passions would smoulder throughout Arkansas for decades—and even generations—after the war. Old scores would still be settled with violence as late as the 1890s in those areas where neighbors stood on opposite sides during the conflict. The pervasive violence and depredation directed at civilians during and after the war created more widespread suffering in Arkansas than in any other state.

The Birth of Sheridan and Grant County

The postwar political violence in Arkansas diminished as Reconstruction began to impose a semblance of order on Arkansas. Bands of outlaws, however, would continue to wander the land for years. Although many parts of Arkansas suffered great hardships at the hands of incompetent or corrupt carpetbaggers, the new government was principally an inconvenience to the population of present-day Grant County. Nevertheless, the residents of the region very much needed more efficient and more responsive government. They needed their own county.

Yet those were difficult times politically. Many people remained disenfranchised because officials could reject an applicant for voter registration if the individual had been a conspicuous supporter of the Confederacy. Thus politics was dominated by folks who had been either pro-Union or neutral during the war.

In a remarkably wily bid for political empowerment in 1868, local folks decided to seek more control and secure their own county by appearing to be a bastion of republicanism and reconstructionist zeal. William Allison, John Harrison, and Thomas Morris hatched this re-markable plan in the storehouse owned by E. H. Vance Sr., about a mile northwest of present-day Sheridan. They asked the legislature to create a new county named after Ulysses S. Grant, who had just been elected president of the United States. They further offered to name the county seat after General Phil Sheridan, who was famous (or infamous) for his scorched-earth "March to the Sea." Although this plan mightily insulted backers of the Lost Cause, most suffered this indignity in silence. The scheme worked.

Both Grant County and its seat, Sheridan, were born the following year. Two people gave the county adjoining tracts of forestland for the county seat. L. M. Veazy donated forty acres from his farm, which he homesteaded before the Civil War. A. N. Harris (who lived in Illinois) donated eighty acres. Surveyors laid out blocks and lots in 1869, and buildings began to dot the embryonic community. The town grew slowly, gradually adding stores, a sawmill, and a hotel. Yet few of the principal streets were actually cleared of trees until Sheridan was incorporated in 1887 and the population reached nearly 200. There had been little need to do so.

Sheridan experienced substantial growth just after the turn of the century, when the raising of fruits and vegetables as a market crop began to take off. Sheridan became the transportation and commer-cial hub for the new truck farms, and the value of land in town doubled in a relatively few years. The thriving community boasted 800 residents by 1905, along with twenty-three retail and two wholesale companies, three sawmills, a stave factory, a shingle mill, a gristmill, and a cotton gin. Sheridan had become the classic incarnation of small-town America in the twentieth century.

Today, Sheridan's 3,000 residents can boast one of the best small historical museums in the region—the Grant County Museum. The present courthouse is Sheridan's fourth since 1871. Built in 1964, the structure incorporated recycled brick from the third courthouse (which was built in 1910). The clock from the old courthouse was installed in the seventy-six-foot cupola that crowns the current home of county government.

—Part Three—

THE ARKANSAS RIVER VALLEY

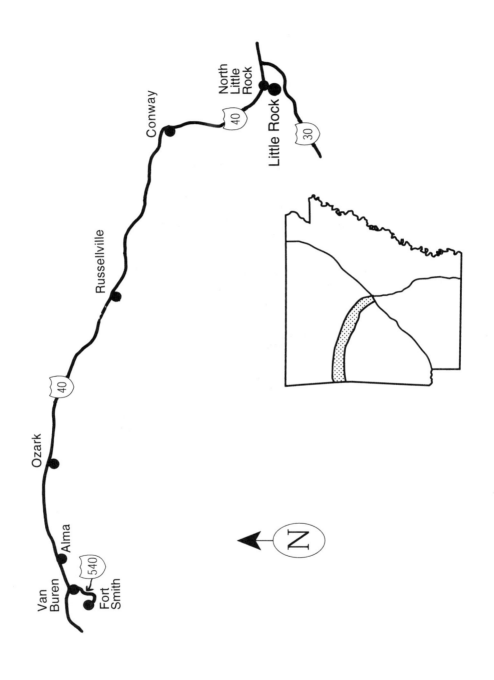

Fort Smith—Russellville

Traveling less than an hour and a half by I-40 covers more than the few miles from Fort Smith to Russellville, for this stretch of Arkansas spans history from the earliest days of the Wild West to the Nuclear Age. Indians, settlers, soldiers, lawmen, desperados, and the Hanging Judge provide the stuff of gritty nineteenth century life. From idealistic young army officers in Fort Smith to a charismatic reformer from Russellville who changed the face of Arkansas politics, this is a story of people conducting power politics at the most elemental level. This is the story of ordinary people doing extraordinary things, and extraordinary people changing the course of history.

A great deal of lively American history has been written along this short stretch of interstate in the Arkansas River valley. Much of it swirls around the establishment of Fort Smith, and the role this army post played in taming the continent.

—FORT SMITH—

The history of Fort Smith, which sits at the Oklahoma border 159 miles northwest of Little Rock on I-40, was largely written by soldiers, lawmen, and lawyers. Soldiers did their best to keep the peace between warring Indian tribes, and between the Indians and white settlers. Confederate and Union soldiers subsequently fought for control of Fort Smith during the Civil War. Both black and white lawmen, along with the Hanging Judge (Isaac Charles Parker), meted out stern justice around the turn of the century and finally tamed this seemingly untamable gateway to the Southwest. And then there were the lawyers. While lawyers made the little Arkansas town of Washington one of the most admirable small communities that this country has ever produced, a different caste of lawyers made Fort Smith one of the most depraved places in the United States during the antebellum era.

The tough, turbulent tale of Fort Smith is more than the story of northwestern Arkansas in the nineteenth century. It is also the story of how the southern West was won.

While it is part of American folklore, few people really understand that the army was the primary force in the opening of the southwestern wilderness. By 1817, the army had established a series of strategically placed posts along navigable waterways and Indian trails. Frequently the posts were garrisoned with no more than a company of troops (70 to 100 men), who still managed to make the surrounding area safe for settlers. As the land was secured and the frontiersman looked west, the post would move westward to where it was then needed. Few posts lasted for twenty years.

Each post played several roles: military, political, economic, even postal. The net result was that the soldier's role became that of a pioneer who literally and figuratively blazed the trails for the settlers who would follow.

These early posts actually had several military missions, which were in fact political missions as well. As far as the federal government was concerned, their most important responsibility was to guard the United States from Spain and Mexico. Within a few years, however, the most important objective became to pacify the Indian tribes. This task was usually complicated by the fact that the posts typically intruded on tribal hunting grounds. The pacification process was usually concluded when federal officials came to the posts to negotiate treaties with the tribal leaders. Such treaties always opened up new areas to white settlers.

The third military mission fell to army survey teams, who explored, surveyed, and mapped the wilderness as the posts pushed westward. The final task was building roads (using that term quite loosely by modern standards) to expedite the rapid deployment of troops to trouble spots on the frontier. These military roads frequently provided the first routes into an area other than scattered Indian trails, so they were used by the civilian settlers who followed closely on the heels of the soldier-pioneers. These roads were also used for the first mail service into an area. Soldiers on horseback were the first mailmen in the wilderness, and the forts were the first post offices.

A town would almost invariably spring up next to a new fort. Embryonic towns soon included taverns, trading posts, bordellos, shops, and a sprinkling of homes for the families of local entrepreneurs. Settlers would create farms to provide food for the soldiers and forage for their horses and mules. More stores would appear. The town would also grow, in part, because soldiers commonly took up residence in their post towns when they mustered out of the army.

When the fort was eventually closed and the garrison moved farther west, a lively town remained where there had been wilderness only a few years before. Except for the fact that Fort Smith remained an active post for a very long time, the origin of the adjacent town of the same name paralleled the birth of many other army towns. But few such towns would write such a wild and woolly history.

An early view of Fort Smith. —Arkansas History Commission

The history of Fort Smith really begins with two problems facing the federal government in 1817. The United States and Spain had overlapping territorial claims in the Southwest, so the border needed to be secured against Spanish patrols. The dominant problem along the Arkansas River, however, was a bloody feud between the Cherokee and Osage Indians that was spawned, ironically, by the incompetence of federal officials.

Clash of the Cherokee and Osage Nations

The problem began in the early 1800s when the federal government began to move the Cherokees and other eastern tribes (collectively known as the Five Civilized Tribes) from their traditional lands to make more room for Anglo-American settlers. The feds wanted to move these eastern Indians to the lower reaches of the Arkansas River. Because the Osage Nation claimed this area, the feds negotiated treaties in 1808 and 1809 in which the Osages ceded all of their lands east of a line running between the future site of Fort Smith on the Arkansas River and Fort Osage on the Missouri River. Cherokee scouting parties then explored this area and found it suitable for farming and hunting, so several thousand Cherokees left their farms and settlements in Georgia and Tennessee for a new life along the Arkansas. Federal agents continued negotiations with the rest of the Cherokees living east of the Mississippi.

Trouble erupted almost immediately after the first group of Cherokees arrived on the lands between the White and Arkansas Rivers. Anglo-American settlers soon began to encroach upon their lands, kill the buffalo, and steal Indian horses. These settlers had no respect for the Cherokees or their lands. They butchered buffalo solely for hides and tallow, leaving the meat to rot. They slaughtered bears just for their oil. Squatters burned down the forests and plowed the land. Renegade traders undermined Indian lives by smuggling in whiskey.

Yet as much as these renegade settlers outraged the Cherokees, the powerful Osage Nation provided the most serious threat to their existence. Their dispute erupted over game. Although many Cherokees were subsistence farmers, they still relied on hunting and trapping for much of their livelihood. In fact, it was the abundance of game along the Arkansas River that prompted them to cede their lands east of the Mississippi. When pressure from Anglo-American settlers depleted the wildlife along the Arkansas, Cherokee hunting parties pushed west across the treaty line and established hunting camps on the Cimarron and Canadian Rivers.

This was land claimed by the southern Osages. Osage war parties raided the Cherokee hunting camps and plundered traps, furs, and horses. It was not long before Cherokee hunting parties became war parties. Revenge fed one reprisal after another, and the violence quickly escalated.

Neither life nor property was safe for the Cherokees, Osages, and white settlers of the area. Cherokee leaders asked federal authorities for help. Indian agent William Lovely, who had worked with the Cherokees since their arrival along the Arkansas, did what he could. Lovely pleaded for help from his superior, William Clark, who was both the governor of Missouri Territory and the superintendent of Indian affairs. He admitted that both the Cherokees and Osages were equally to blame for the violence, but pointed out that "some whites of the Worst Character in this Country" had contributed a great deal to the problem. Lovely strongly argued that a military post on the Arkansas would exert a calming influence on everyone in the area.

The violence continued to escalate over the next two years, without any response from the federal government. Agent Lovely died before he saw a resolution to the chaos. Reprisals threatened to intensify into total war when the Cherokee council voted in January 1817 to annihilate the Osage Nation. Soon thereafter, a treaty brought still more Cherokees from their ancestral lands. The size of the

Cherokee Nation in Arkansas tripled. Cherokee war chief Tick-e-Toke sent word to Cherokees in Tennessee that he needed adventure-seeking warriors for a campaign against the Osages. He planned to launch his offensive as soon as the spring grasses were high enough to feed their horses. The war was delayed when Indian agents intercepted warriors coming from Tennessee, but this limited action did not prevent the Cherokee offensive.

One of the reasons for the lack of an effective federal response to this problem was that Governor Clark actually wanted war between the Cherokee and Osage Nations, since hostilities would inevitably reduce Osage power. He told the secretary of war that the tribe had recently become quite vicious. The Osages "have killed our Citizens and frequently whip, and plunder them," Clark said. "The war which the Cherokees & Osages are now engaged in . . . may produce . . . a favorable effect."

Nevertheless, terms of the most recent treaty with the Cherokees stipulated that the army would protect every Cherokee who moved to the Arkansas. Acting Secretary of War Richard Graham ordered General Andrew Jackson to establish a post at or near the point where the Arkansas River crossed into Osage territory. The primary mission of the post was to establish peace and harmony between the Osage and Cherokee Nations.

The Belle Point Garrison

A company to build and garrison the new fort was drawn from the most elite infantry unit in the army, which was called the Rifle Regiment. Major William Bradford, a veteran of the War of 1812, would command the post.

Even as Bradford began the arduous journey by keelboat toward his new area of operations with his men and supplies, Tick-e-Toke launched his offensive against the Osage Nation. Most of the Osage warriors and their families had left their villages to hunt buffalo along the Cimarron and Salt Fork Rivers. The Cherokees fell upon the villages with a vengeance, slaughtering the old men, women, and children who had remained behind. Sixty-nine died and many more were grievously wounded. Older boys were brutally emasculated. The Cherokees plundered huge quantities of jerked meat, buffalo robes, deer skins, furs, pumpkins, corn, squash, lotus roots, and cooking pots. They used Osage horses to carry their booty. And they took a hundred Osage prisoners, primarily young women and children. They burned the Osage lodges and anything else they couldn't carry back to their homes. This raid came to be known as the Battle of Claremore Mound.

Bradford subsequently reached Belle Point on Christmas Day, 1817. Illness had plagued his men through much of the journey, and three had died. Within a week of their arrival, Bradford's men built a comfortable log hospital for the sick and several log storehouses. Major Stephen Long, whose reconnaissance first suggested Belle Point as the best location for a post, had named his encampment Camp Smith in honor of General Thomas Smith. The general was commander of the Ninth Military District and, therefore, Major Bradford's boss. Now Camp Smith was fast becoming Fort Smith.

Major Bradford visited both Osage and Cherokee leaders during this period to urge a truce until he could investigate the conflicting charges leveled by both sides. Although Bradford attempted to be impartial, communiques between him and the War Department clearly show that Washington favored the Cherokees in this dispute. True federal impartiality might have prevented a great deal of suffering that would follow.

A delegation of Cherokee leaders traveled to Washington and told the president that the Osage Nation should give up a corridor of land so they could have safe passage to the buffalo range. There was a lot of political pressure to complete the relocation of the Cherokees from east of the Mississippi, so the president and secretary of war wanted to make every possible concession to the Cherokees, even if that meant denying justice to the Osages. This promise of support no doubt stimulated many Cherokees to move to the Fort Smith area from east of the Mississippi during 1818.

The Osage Nation was in a difficult bargaining position. Osage warriors had conducted numerous raids against Missouri settlements, and the surviving pioneers had petitioned the federal government for the Osages to make reparations for property that was stolen or destroyed during the raids. These claims exceeded the annual payments made to the tribe by the federal government, so the Osage Nation faced the equivalent of bankruptcy. Osage leaders capitulated, ceding a corridor of land to the buffalo grounds and promising to allow the Cherokees to hunt on Osage lands south of the Arkansas. The Osage and Cherokee leaders signed a treaty in St. Louis that promised perpetual peace. In return, the Cherokees promised to release the captives taken during the Battle of Claremore Mound.

These promises didn't last long. As some of the Cherokee delegation were returning home from St. Louis, they stumbled into an Osage hunting camp at the Batesville crossing on the White River. The Cherokees stole forty horses. Osage warriors responded by raiding several Cherokee hunting camps and stealing a rather large quantity of furs.

Major Bradford tried to intervene by visiting Clermont, who led the Verdigris Osages, the powerful southern branch of the Osage Nation that constituted the greatest threat to the Cherokees. Bradford promised to recover the stolen horses and force the Cherokees to release Osage hostages still being held. Clermont agreed to restrain his warriors and not sell off the captured furs until Bradford had tried his best. The Cherokees made excuses and failed to comply, since they were confident that they had the full support of the president, the secretary of war, and the governor of Missouri Territory in their conflict with the Osage Nation. Bradford was in an impossible position.

Bradford hoped his position would improve when Congress split off the southern half of Missouri to form Arkansas Territory in 1819. This development turned out to be a mixed blessing. The good news was that Bradford was appointed superintendent of Indian affairs for the new territory. This meant that he could deal more directly and forcefully with the Cherokees. The bad news was that Arkansas experienced a heavy influx of Anglo-American settlers, who increased the pressure on the local Cherokee population. The Western Cherokees became much more irritable and much more likely to break the peace. Bradford invested a great deal of creative energy, suffered a steady stream of setbacks, and struggled for nearly year before finally getting the Cherokees to honor the terms of the St. Louis treaty and return their captives to the Osage Nation.

Unfortunately, Bradford's efforts did not provide a permanent solution to the Cherokee-Osage conflict. But he did buy time—peaceful time. Minor raids and reprisals gradually resumed, but neither tribe tooled up for full-scale war.

The Osage-Cherokee conflict heated up in 1820 when an Osage named Bad Tempered Buffalo came upon Cherokees hunting bear in February. He ambushed them, killing three hunters and taking their furs. The Cherokees protested to Bradford and threatened war.

Bradford's investigation suggested that the Osage ambush was conducted in revenge for Cherokee raids, so his report to Secretary of War Calhoun supported the Osages. Calhoun continued his blanket support of the Cherokees. Nothing was resolved. The dispute smouldered and then flared into life in a series of bloody raids. Terrified settlers streamed into Fort Smith for protection when the feuding Indians turned on them as well. Governor Miller concluded that border peace was unattainable and he stopped trying. Major Bradford warned the tribal leaders to leave the settlers alone or his troops would destroy their villages, and he also tried to recover property stolen from the settlers.

The following year, a band of 300 Cherokee warriors managed to slip past Bradford's border patrols. They waged a savage campaign in which they killed and scalped twenty-nine women and old men from a defenseless camp, captured thirty women and children, and plundered great quantities of furs and other valuables. An attempt to attack the main Osage hunting camp was foiled when the Osages discovered the approaching Cherokees and attacked the invaders at night.

The Cherokee campaign had two main impacts on what followed. First, the campaign disrupted the Osage hunt, which caused great suffering in the Osage Nation. Second, it stimulated the federal government to increase the garrison at Fort Smith from a token force to one that could intimidate the warring factions. The 7th United States Infantry Regiment stationed at Fort Scott, Georgia, was ordered to the Arkansas frontier. Its commander was Colonel Mathew Arbuckle.

The movement of Colonel Arbuckle's command from Georgia to Florida to New Orleans, and up the Mississippi to the Arkansas (which was too low for keelboats when he arrived), is an adventure story in itself. The grueling process took seven months. Arbuckle arrived at Belle Point on February 26, 1822, and relieved Major Bradford of command. Bradford had accomplished a great deal in spite of many obstacles. His small command had built roads, mapped the area, nearly finished building the fort designed by Major Long, and inspected westbound trading expeditions, and Bradford had mediated the Osage-Cherokee conflict as well as he could with a small garrison and limited influence in Washington.

Yet no one lamented his departure. His men had grown to hate him because he drove them so hard. Territorial officials disliked him because he always followed the rules and would never grant special favors. Many settlers hated him because he followed orders and expelled them from Indian lands. And both the Osages and the Cherokees blamed him for not keeping the other tribe in check. Arbuckle's arrival was viewed with great anticipation from every quarter.

Arbuckle on the Arkansas

Colonel Mathew Arbuckle established a series of small outposts to minimize clashes between the Osages and Cherokees and to keep settlers off Indian lands. The main garrison at Fort Smith conducted patrols along the Osage border, mapping, surveying, inspecting the permits and cargoes of outbound traders, and guiding travelers.

Throughout this period, Arbuckle collaborated closely with a new Indian agent, Nathaniel Philbrook, who worked diligently to win the trust of Osage and Cherokee leaders and then hammer out a just resolution to their conflict. Arbuckle invested a lot of time communicating with the various tribal chiefs, and was especially gracious whenever leaders of either tribe visited the fort. His hospitality always included a tour of the post, so the Indians could see the vast buildup of men and weapons. The message was subtle but unmistakable. The army had the power to punish violators of the peace. This was the kind of diplomacy that Teddy Roosevelt would later describe as "Walk softly and carry a big stick."

The combined work of Philbrook and Arbuckle led to a treaty restoring the peace between the Cherokee and Osage Nations. Tribal leaders signed the pact at Fort Smith on August 9, 1822. Thanks to the big stick, both sides returned all captives by the end of September. Both the Osages and the Cherokees appeared to be satisfied. It was a remarkable achievement. Even the cynical governor of Arkansas Territory believed the Treaty of Fort Smith would secure permanent peace along the border.

Matthew Arbuckle.
—Arkansas History Commission

Winning the Peace

Ironically, peace along the border led to trouble on the post. Because fewer border patrols were now required, the soldiers began to spend more time at the fort. Arbuckle increased the amount of garrison activities such as drills and inspections. This elite unit chafed at garrison duty. The men wanted either action in the field or duty at a post that was closer to the cultural and recreational advantages of real towns.

Morale of the officers plummeted as Congress kept cutting their salaries in an effort to reduce military expenditures. Promotions within the enlisted ranks ground to a halt, eliminating the prospect of upward mobility. This was a critical problem for enlisted morale since only noncommissioned and commissioned officers merited the few perks and privileges that made military life worth living.

These new facts about army life in the 1820s spread quickly through the civilian population as frustrated soldiers mustered out of the army. The recruitment of competent men—of any men—began to dry up. The army steadily lowered its standards until the typical recruit was an illiterate subsistence farmer seeking a better life, or a man trying to escape troubles with a woman. More than 40 percent of these new recruits were drunk when they took their oath. One critic of this policy observed that recruits were either the "scum of the population of the older states or of the worthless German, English, Polish or Irish immigrants."

As Fort Smith began to fill its ranks with this new crop of soldiers, maintaining discipline became increasingly difficult, primarily due to the excessive consumption of whiskey.

The problem had two causes: the new recruits were hard drinkers, and a growing crop of taverns appeared in the neighboring civilian settlement, where a soldier could buy a pint of whiskey for 25 cents. The soldiers smuggled the whiskey onto the post. Consumption in their quarters soon escalated to consumption while on duty, in spite of efforts to confiscate the contraband. A bad batch of whiskey sent a large number of soldiers on sick call. Arbuckle concluded that several mysterious deaths were related to drinking on duty.

This series of developments so outraged Arbuckle that he declared war on the taverns and other civilians supplying whiskey to his soldiers. Arbuckle asked the adjutant general for permission to destroy the settlement and send the tavern keepers packing. Instead, he received orders in April 1824 to abandon Fort Smith. Arbuckle was delighted, since he had proposed moving his garrison to a more strategic location several years earlier. The areas to the west were heating up with clashes between rival tribes, and with raids by renegades on trappers and white settlers.

Arbuckle headed west with his entire command only seven days after receiving his orders. He established Fort Gibson on the east bank of the Grand River, about three miles above its confluence with the Arkansas River.

In 1831, the Choctaws were to relocate under terms of a new treaty, and those who would pass through Belle Point needed to be resupplied with food. Therefore, a small army detachment under the command of Lieutenant Gabriel Rains reoccupied Fort Smith on April 26, 1831. Rains prepared storehouses for the supplies they would need. The army really did try its best, but the arrival of the Choctaws added a dark chapter to the history of Fort Smith. The Choctaw migration seemed doomed from the start, as their journey became a trail of tears.

The Trail of Tears and the Great Whiskey War

About 7,000 Choctaws assembled in the fall of 1831 at Vicksburg for the journey west. About 500 were wealthy enough from the sale of their farms to travel first class at their own expense. The rest would travel with government agents. This larger group boarded steamboats for transport to Arkansas Post. A smaller steamer, the *Reindeer*, would ferry them to Little Rock, where they were to rest before continuing their journey. Unfortunately, the Choctaws contracted cholera at Vicksburg, and news of the epidemic preceded them to Arkansas.

Folks living along their planned route panicked. To make matters worse, the water level of the Arkansas dropped so much that the *Reindeer* wasn't able to transport the Indians from Arkansas Post to Little Rock. A great number had to walk the whole way. Many died before they were able to reach Little Rock, and more died along the Arkansas.

The Choctaws were quarantined until the epidemic passed. Then they continued overland toward Fort Smith in groups of 600. These were relatively wealthy Indians with cash in their pockets. Seeing an unparalleled opportunity for profit, traders descended upon them with whiskey and other enticements at Belle Point. The Indians quickly drew their supplies and moved on into the wilderness, but several hundred stayed behind and were shamelessly exploited. Belle Point traders established taverns within 100 yards of the Choctaw line and within 200 yards of the army landing at Fort Smith. Lieutenant Gabriel Rains declared war on the whiskey trade.

Rains energetically deployed his troops to interdict whiskey traders headed for Choctaw camps and Indians headed for the town's taverns. But his tiny detachment just didn't have the manpower for the job. The law-abiding civilians of the area became quite alarmed at the violence that grew apace with the consumption of alcohol. People began to die. Then three public buildings in town were accidentally set afire by drunken Indians.

Rains turned to the courts for help, but a federal grand jury in Little Rock determined that existing federal law only permitted prosecution if traders were caught in the act of selling whiskey to Indians inside Indian Territory. Because most whiskey sales were made inside the boundaries of Arkansas Territory rather than inside Indian lands, the grand jury could only issue a scathing report that condemned local merchants and called for a full investigation by the Crawford County Circuit Court.

The report outraged the Belle Point businesses, who counterattacked with ads in the *Arkansas Gazette* that condemned both the grand jury and Lieutenant Rains. The federal government did not like the adverse publicity from the escalating war of words. It was not that authorities in Washington, D.C., were concerned with Indian welfare; they simply feared that such publicity would discourage tribes in Alabama, Florida, Georgia, and Mississippi from relocating west of the Mississippi River. Congress quickly passed legislation to control illicit trade in Indian Territory to protect the federal land grab east of the Mississippi.

Armed with new authority and formal orders to interdict the flow of alcohol into Indian Territory, Colonel Arbuckle dispatched a larger detachment to Fort Smith under the command of Captain John Stuart. His men were able to stop the flow of alcohol on the Arkansas River, so the whiskey traders took to the growing network of roads and trails that led to the Choctaw and Cherokee settlements just inside Indian Territory. The local courts provided no help at all, even when Stuart attempted to prosecute miscreants under Arkansas laws. But the most infuriating development was that tavern keepers openly sold whiskey to Indians in full view of the captain's quarters, which sat less than 100 yards from the saloons. Stuart took this as a personal insult. He was particularly pained because he especially admired the Cherokees. He found them to be an "infinitely . . . better and more orderly people" than the Anglo-Americans living along the Arkansas border.

When Stuart's command at Fort Smith dramatically slowed the flow of whiskey past Belle Point, whiskey traders merely moved their base of operations a few miles to Van Buren. The whiskey runners became unstoppable when they started operating as mere suppliers and let the Indians do the actual smuggling. The Indians proved to be very stealthy smugglers, for they knew the lay of the land and obscure trails much better than the soldiers. Arbuckle and Stuart could do little more than mildly inconvenience the traders.

The army's most aggressive adversaries during this campaign against illicit trade were not the Indians. They were a pack of frontier lawyers, who had long hunted the frontier towns and army posts like jackals, looking to sink their teeth in any suitable prey. Army officers were their prey of choice. The scam worked like this. An enlisted man would intentionally grossly insult or otherwise provoke an officer, who might manhandle the miscreant to get his attention. A lawyer would then sue the officer for assault and battery. The lawyers would even pay soldiers handsomely, in advance, to initiate such an incident. Once the illicit whiskey trade became big business, the lawyers began to increasingly provide their services to the whiskey traders.

If, for example, Captain Stuart had an armed party board a riverboat in search of contraband whiskey but failed to find a violation of the law, the vessel's lawyer would sue him for unwarranted interference with commerce. Stuart finally had to transfer title of all his property to a relative for safe keeping. But he kept doing his job. His men inspected every wagon headed down the military road into Indian Territory.

The whiskey traders and their lawyers tried new tactics, waging a series of vicious campaigns on the pages of the *Arkansas Gazette*. They forwarded a steady stream of signed petitions and resolutions to Congress to have Captain Stuart's command removed from Fort Smith, and to have a new and better road built into Indian Territory. When attempts to remove or circumvent Stuart failed, the traders tried to get Stuart replaced with a much larger contingent on the grounds that the Indians were out of control and preying upon innocent civilians with impunity. An enlarged post would bring more military customers to the local taverns, which would compensate for Stuart's disruption of trade with the Indians.

Stuart counterattacked, saying "The Indians in this country are . . . on the most perfect friendship with the Whites . . . and according to my opinion the Cherokees are a more orderly and respectable people, than three fourths of their White neighbors." He went on to point out that stationing more troops at Fort Smith would actually be counter-productive. Stuart explained that "if Troops are ever Stationed in this Territory, for the avowed purpose of giving protection of the White inhabitants against the neighboring Indians . . . the depraved portion of the Whites, feeling themselves Protected by the Military will commence their lawless outrages on the Indians, by Killing and Stealing their property and often molesting their person." Stuart went on to emphasize that impartiality was the only way to preserve the peace. Everyone must believe, he said, that "their future . . . happiness will alone depend on their . . . conduct towards each other, and that both will be alike, protected by the military."

This was a novel concept for federal officials, who had displayed a long history of favoring one group at the expense of another. The bureaucracy bowed to local schemers in May 1834 and ordered Colonel Arbuckle to abandon Fort Gibson and Fort Smith and relocate his soldiers to Swallow Rock on the Poteau River, where they could not interfere with local commerce. The Great Whiskey War was over. The lawyers and the whiskey traders had won. The soldiers and the Indian culture had lost.

The fort at Belle Point remained unoccupied until 1838, when the army returned to Fort Smith. Two companies of soldiers arrived to conduct patrols, build roads, and repair the facilities at Belle Point. Their most important service, as far as the local civilians were concerned, was that the soldiers fueled the lagging local economy. Civilian contractors were eventually hired to refurbish and enlarge the post to support a major garrison at Fort Smith. Despite a great deal of friction between military officials and some local citizens, labor problems, and a host of other difficulties during the next eight years—the construction program was finally completed. The 6th Infantry moved into Fort Smith on May 15, 1846, and Fort Smith became the focal point for activities on the southwestern frontier.

Gateway to the Southwest

From 1846 until the outbreak of the Civil War, Fort Smith flourished as the most important post in the Southwest. It got a big boost in 1848, when the discovery of gold in California spawned a westward rush of unprecedented proportions. Heading west via Fort Smith—rather than over the more northerly route starting at Independence, Missouri—held several significant advantages for immigrants to the Far West. The Fort Smith route largely avoided mountains, which made travel by wagon much easier. Furthermore, the southerly route had a longer growing season, so grass was available to feed livestock four to six weeks earlier.

A detachment of Colonel Arbuckle's troops accompanied the first California-bound wagon trains from Fort Smith. While the obvious mission of the military escort was to protect the travelers from Indians, the soldiers ranged a day ahead of the wagons to select the best route, marking fords and smoothing steep grades. The first wagons set out from Fort Smith on April 10, 1849. By the end of the month, 400 wagons had outfitted in Fort Smith and headed west. Wagon trains were organized at Fort Smith throughout the spring and summer. The rush to California resumed the following spring. Even after the gold rush petered out, Fort Smith remained a popular gateway for overland travel to California throughout the 1850s.

Covered wagons such as this one passed through Fort Smith in great numbers during the mid-1800s. –Arkansas History Commission

Suddenly Colonel Arbuckle found himself engaged in the last battle of his career. This war began with the election of General Zachary Taylor to the presidency of the United States in 1848. Taylor hated Arbuckle. The animosity dated back to the early 1820s, when Arbuckle's charisma with beautiful ladies vastly outpaced Taylor's. Taylor was an intensely ambitious man who viewed himself as a far superior officer to Arbuckle, which made Arbuckle's prowess with the opposite sex especially maddening.

Taylor had attempted to inconvenience and sabotage Arbuckle's career at every opportunity. Now Taylor was commander in chief. He used his new powers to close the post at Belle Point and force Arbuckle's command to move back to the very Spartan accommodations of Fort Gibson. It was a personal vendetta, pure and simple. Arbuckle tried to get the order changed, but was unsuccessful. Taylor died in July 1850, and the Arkansas delegation to Congress immediately requested that Arbuckle's command be returned to Fort Smith. They succeeded. Arbuckle's troops returned to Fort Smith in February 1851. But thirty years of hard service on the frontier and this final battle had drained the energy from Colonel Mathew Arbuckle. He died in the relative comfort of Fort Smith on June 11.

As technology became more advanced in the 1850s, Fort Smith became even more important as a communications center for the Southwest. Small steamboats began to expedite the movement of people, supplies, and mail. Stage service increased. And the telegraph arrived in 1858.

That same year, Fort Smith became the focal point for overland mail service to California. Mail was carried by the stagecoaches of the Butterfield Overland Mail over two routes to Fort Smith—one from Memphis and one from St. Louis. Stages then carried the mail from Fort Smith to El Paso and on to California in a mere fifteen and a half days. (Back in the early days of Fort Smith, it took forty to ninety days for a letter to reach Washington, D.C., from Belle Point.)

By this time, Fort Smith was a thoroughly bustling community of 2,500 with two newspapers and a hotel. The post at Belle Point had become increasingly important as a supply depot for garrisons throughout the Southwest. As the national political scene heated up following the elections of 1860, secessionists began to view Fort Smith as a worthy prize by virtue of its strategic location and its storehouses (which were packed with food, supplies, and munitions).

The Butterfield Overland Mail Company stopped throughout northwest Arkansas in the 1850s as it carried freight and passengers along a route between St. Louis and San Francisco. —Special Collections, University of Arkansas Libraries, Fayetteville

A House Divided

South Carolina withdrew from the Union on December 20, 1860. Six more states followed and adopted a new constitution for the Confederate States of America on February 7. That same day, the Choctaw Council voted to support the Confederate cause. But most people in northwestern Arkansas wanted to remain in the Union.

Support for either the Confederacy or the Union was a patchwork pattern throughout Arkansas, and the political patchwork was based more on topography than whether an area was in the northern or southern part of the state. Highlanders tended to be subsistence farmers and woodsmen who had different ethnic, economic, and religious roots than the lowlanders. Many hill folk saw no reason to protect the slave-dependent plantation economies of the lowlanders.

Nevertheless, separatist sentiments were strong and spreading. Secessionists seized the army arsenal in Little Rock weeks before a state convention overturned their previous vote to remain in the Union and subsequently voted to secede. Separatists seized other federal property in Arkansas, so the War Department ordered federal troops to abandon Fort Smith while they still could. Local residents were horrified. They wired the secretary of war to keep the troops at Fort Smith to defend the area against violence, mob rule, and secession. The secretary relented, allowing federal troops to remain at Fort Smith until Arkansas seceded. As soon as that happened, Captain Samuel Sturgis was ordered to abandon Fort Smith and withdraw into Indian Territory (now called Oklahoma), where he was to deploy his men where the Texas Road crossed the Arkansas River.

Confederate batteries opened up on Fort Sumter on April 12, 1861, inflaming passions in Arkansas. Governor Henry Rector put out the call for 5,000 volunteers, who would be under the command of former U.S. Senator Solon Borland. The first mission for Borland's troops would be to seize Fort Smith. Word of this enterprise reached Belle Point before the expedition left Little Rock.

Federal scouts from Fort Smith reported that two steamboats with Colonel Borland's troops had landed at nearby Van Buren. Borland informed the editor of the Van Buren newspaper that his 300 troops had eight pieces of artillery and plenty of munitions for taking the fort. He then ordered the local militia, called the Frontier Guards, to join his march on the fortifications at Belle Point. The steamers *Frederick Notrebe* and *Tahlequah* ferried this combined force the few miles to Belle Point. The steamboats simply tied up to the wharfs at Fort Smith, and the troops took the facility without firing a shot.

Forewarned, Sturgis had immediately taken his two cavalry companies and a wagon train well into Indian Territory, crossing the Poteau

River by 9 P.M. He had reluctantly left behind his sick, who were tended by a hospital steward, a laundress, and Captain Alexander Montgomery (the post's quartermaster). Colonel Solon Borland declared that the Federals were prisoners of war, even though—at least technically—Arkansas was still part of the Union.

The convention in Little Rock reconvened and voted to secede from the Union on May 6. Now Arkansas was officially at war with the Union. With the advent of hostilities, Fort Smith became the base of Confederate operations in northern Arkansas until Union forces recaptured it in August 1864 without firing a shot. Fort Smith would remain a Union garrison for the remainder of the war.

After the war finally ended in the spring of 1865, Fort Smith continued to bustle with activity. The Federal garrison relocated refugees, supervised the surrender and demobilization of Confederate troops, and conducted patrols to protect the populace from renegade bands of guerillas. By midsummer, the demobilization of Federal units at Fort Smith began, followed by the auctioning off of surplus stores and livestock at Fort Smith. Jayhawkers and Bushwhackers had stolen virtually every head of livestock in northwestern Arkansas, so local folks were particularly interested in the sale of horses and mules from the government stables.

Soon all the Federal troops had been mustered out, all the surplus materiel had been disbursed, and the town's economy went into a severe slump. Several buildings on the post burned down in 1870, and the War Department decided to abandon the fort once and for all. But before the land could be appraised and auctioned off, trouble on the frontier once again created a mission for the old post. Former Jayhawkers and Bushwhackers, who plagued Arkansas and other frontier areas during the war, continued to ravage the countryside. Now they robbed banks, trains, stagecoaches, and businesses. They rustled cattle. They robbed and killed anyone who crossed their path.

These desperados became a formidable plague upon western Arkansas, raiding with impunity and then escaping into the refuge of Indian Territory. Fort Smith was strategically located for launching a war on these desperados. Congress began its offensive on March 3, 1871, establishing a federal court at Fort Smith that would have authority in Indian Territory. Judge William Story and his federal marshals began the process of restoring order.

In a few short years, the Western District Court of Arkansas would become the most notorious courtroom in the world, thanks to the judge who came to Fort Smith from Missouri on May 2, 1875. Judge Isaac Parker quickly became known as the Hanging Judge.

The Hanging Judge

Judge Isaac Parker is probably the most misunderstood man in Arkansas history. Some writers have claimed that he was a mean-spirited, bloodthirsty, vengeful man. Others insist that he was a man of gentle disposition and impartiality, who simply sought to serve justice in the most desperado-infested area in the country. Substantial evidence can be produced to support both views.

Parker's frightening reputation began during his first murder trial. Daniel Evans was charged with killing a nineteen-year-old man, and Parker believed he was guilty. He lectured the jurors that Evans was guilty and the guilty must be punished. The jury convicted Evans after a deliberation that lasted only a few minutes. When Parker pronounced sentence, he denounced the accused in a long and bitter harangue, which he delivered in a cold, harsh voice. Parker concluded his speech, "I sentence you to hang by the neck until you are dead, *dead*, **dead!**"

That one repetitive proclamation established the tone for his first term on the bench. His court convicted fifteen of the eighteen people accused of murder during that first term, and Parker sentenced eight of them to death. The judge decided that a mass, public execution

The only known photograph of the inside of Judge Parker's courtroom while in session. –Cravens Collection, UALR Library Archives

The first six men hanged by Judge Parker in 1875 were hung in a group to send a message to the area's desperados. Clockwise from the top are Whittington, Fooy, Evans, Moore, and Man Killer. Campbell is in the center. —Cravens Collection, UALR Library Archives

would send a stern message throughout Arkansas and the Indian Territory that The Law had finally arrived on the scene. While these men awaited execution, one was killed while trying to escape and another's sentence was commuted to life imprisonment by the president. A giant scaffold was erected at the southern end of the old post, and a huge crowd gathered to watch the mass hanging on September 3, 1875. The carnival atmosphere and macabre spectacle certainly added to Parker's bloodthirsty reputation.

Perhaps Parker's disposition softened over the years. Ada Patterson, who was a famous female reporter for the *St. Louis Republic*, visited Fort Smith in the 1890s to interview Judge Parker. She found him to be "the gentlest of men, this sternest of judges. He is courtly of manner and kind of voice and face, the man who has passed the death sentence on more criminals than any other judge in the land."

Patterson went on to quote Parker's personal views on crime and punishment. "I have been accused of leading juries," he admitted. "I tell you that a jury should be led! They have a right to expect it; if they are guided they will render justice, which is the great pillar of society." Parker also addressed his nasty reputation. "People have said that I am a cruel, heartless and bloodthirsty man, but no one had pointed [out] a specific case of undue severity. . . . I have ever had the single aim of justice in view. No judge who is influenced by any other consideration is fit for the bench. 'Do equal justice' has been my motto, and I have often said to grand juries, 'Permit no inno-cent man to be punished; let no guilty man escape.'"

So perhaps Parker did soften over the years. Or perhaps he was a more complex man than most people have observed. Although Parker denounced Daniel Evans when he pronounced sentence, another of the men sentenced to death during that first term received a very different sort of speech. While drunk, John Whittington had murdered an old friend for his money. In his long sentencing speech, Parker admonished Whittington to review what he had done and how his actions would affect both the victim's family and his own wife and child. He then suggested that Whittington use his remaining time to take religious instruction from a local minister, so he could repent and save his soul. Whittington took that suggestion to heart, and even wrote a story called "How I Came to the Gallows," which was pub-lished widely as a warning to parents and children on the evils of alcohol. (Temperance would become a common theme in Judge Parker's pronouncements over the years.)

Judge Isaac Parker was clearly a man of contradictions, mercilessly attacking one convicted murderer with words, while showing com-passion for another. Throughout the twenty-one years Parker sat on the bench at Fort Smith, he presided over the convictions of 9,500 criminals. Several respected historians have reported that Parker sen-tenced eighty-eight desperados to death by hanging, although this number is now open to debate. Whatever the actual number of hang-ings, Judge Parker tamed the seemingly untamable Arkansas frontier along with the Indian Territory. But he didn't accomplish this task alone.

Federal marshals ranged far and wide to capture these outlaws. Sometimes, desperados were brought to Fort Smith by posses of citi-zens, or by mounted police from one of the Indian nations. On one occasion, the father of a seventeen-year-old murder victim tracked a cowboy named William Brown for 600 miles through Indian Territory. After a hard chase lasting twenty-eight days, the father finally caught up with Brown in Texas. He manacled the cowboy, padlocked a heavy harness around his neck, and led him back to the stern justice that awaited in Judge Parker's court.

Congress began to nibble away at the jurisdiction of Parker's court in 1883, and this process continued throughout the following decade. The last execution on the gallows at Fort Smith took place on July 30, 1896. A month later, Parker's court lost its remaining jurisdiction west of Arkansas. Three judicial districts now divided the territory once presided over by the Hanging Judge.

Isaac Parker died six weeks later. Word of his demise quickly spread through the prison population at Fort Smith, and the prisoners began to shout their joy with such energy that the guards feared a riot might develop. The prisoners quieted down without incident. Soon thereafter, Congress voted to get rid of the old post. The federal government kept the jail and barracks, and donated everything else to the city of Fort Smith.

While the old post at Belle Point became moribund, the city of Fort Smith prospered. The city's population reached 11,587 by the turn of the century, making it the second largest community in Arkansas. Only Little Rock was bigger, with a population of 38,307. (The definition of a city in those days was any community with a population of 2,500 or more.)

Miss Laura Ziegler gave Fort Smith its most significant cultural attraction about the turn of the century, when she opened a bordello that quickly became one of the most celebrated sporting houses in the Southwest. In fact, Miss Laura's became the first bordello to be listed on the National Register of Historic Places. The original building on North B Street has now been restored to its original ambiance and is used as the Fort Smith Visitor Center.

Miss Laura's and the Row

As soldiers, traders, cowboys, pioneers, outcasts, entrepreneurs, and desperados began to form a new community on the American frontier, one of the rarest and most desirable diversions was female companionship. Ladies of negotiable virtue quickly arrived to fill this need. These ladies might entertain company at their small cabins, but this industry usually evolved into a more organized enterprise. A number of ladies would live and work out of a social club operated by a madam. This provided more protection and more respectability. A state license for working in a bordello cost $5 at the turn of the century in Arkansas.

Many girls working in the classier sporting houses would marry well and become the matriarchs of respected old families. Such matriarchs are relatively common to frontier towns outside Arkansas. In one town, for example, a substantial number of the oldest city streets were named after the girls who worked in the local bordellos. Unfortunately, few ladies from this era still survive and none cares to have her story told on the record.

That's a shame, for these women did a lot more to civilize the wilderness than written histories will ever record. Stories of great courage and great humanity will not be told. Fort Smith has the honesty and good grace to admit and preserve this important and fascinating facet of its past. The Row not only provided Fort Smith with desirable notoriety around the turn of the century (which was good for "legitimate" business), it also constituted one of the city's most prosperous commercial districts in its own right. The first real star on the Row was Pearl Starr, the daughter of the notorious outlaw Belle Starr.

Pearl Starr certainly had her mother's spunk, but she demonstrated a lot more common sense by entering a less violent occupation. (Belle died from two shotgun blasts while riding along the Canadian River in Oklahoma.) Miss Pearl opened a bordello and prospered. Well respected by local bankers (possibly for more than her excellent line of credit), Miss Pearl ran the most successful of five sporting houses on Front Street, which were collectively known as "the Row." At least, Miss Pearl was the most successful until an ambitious young lady from Vermont arrived on the scene in the late 1890s.

Laura Zeigler promptly moved into a house at 215 Front Street and opened a bordello. She developed a reputation for her elegant style, and her business flourished. Soon she needed larger accommodations and a better location. A local banker and lumberman loaned Miss Laura $3,000 to buy the Riverfront Commercial Hotel, which had been built in the late 1800s.

Miss Laura completely renovated the baroque Victorian building and moved her girls to 125 Front Street in 1905. The two-story structure featured a mansard roof with three cast-iron dormers containing *oeil de boeuf* (eye of the ox) windows. Carved scroll ornamentation decorated the circular windows. The social club downstairs included a room with a bar, a room for dancing that boasted the town's first player piano, a kitchen with pantry, a bathroom, and five other rooms. Nine rooms upstairs provided individual accommodations for each of the ladies who lived there. Each girl's name was etched in glass above the door to her room. The outside of the building was painted forest green with cream trim. Each room featured unique, decidedly feminine wallpaper with motifs such as pink or blue flowers, or babbling brooks. Elegant Victorian furniture graced every room.

Clients might come for a drink and conversation, a game of cards, or a visit to one of the nine rooms upstairs where the ladies provided personalized entertainment in their own living quarters. Everyone had to be on their very best behavior when in the public rooms downstairs. The upstairs bathtub generally was not available for bathing on Friday and Saturday nights because Miss Laura liked to fill it with ice and champagne. She would serve the bubbly free to clients. Her flair for elegance and refinement became legendary. Miss Laura's became one of the most widely known and respected establishments of its kind in the South. Regular clients came from a six-state area.

Laura Zeigler paid off the loan within seventeen months, and the future seemed bright indeed. It became brighter than anyone expected on the night of January 7, 1910. A large storage tank at the south end of Front Street containing five railroad cars of fuel suddenly exploded, sending a giant fireball rolling into the sky and shattering windows for miles. Men and women frantically abandoned the buildings along the Row clutching hats and whatever clothing that came quickly to hand, fleeing for their lives. One local wag dubbed the incident "the night of the lingerie parade." Remarkably, no one was injured and the flames began to dim without reaching the Row. But then the supports to a nearby water tank gave way, dumping a vast quantity of water into the burning oil and creating an awesome eruption of sparks that rained down on the Row.

Two once-glorious houses run by Dora Gaston and Jessie Collins burned to the ground. Miss Dora particularly grieved for the loss of her two electric pianos, which were worth more than $1,600. The fire spread to within seventy-five feet of Miss Laura's, but then a sudden shift of wind saved her house, which remained completely untouched.

Perhaps sensing that the days of legal prostitution were numbered in Fort Smith, Miss Laura sold her property the following year to one of her former girls, Bertha Gale, for $47,000. Miss Bertha became the new madam, and Laura Zeigler left Fort Smith for parts unknown.

The house went through a series of owners over the following years, and fell into accelerating neglect and decay until the house was scheduled for demolition in 1963. Donald Reynolds, founder of the Donrey Media Group, bought the structure, restored it, and got the house placed on the National Register of Historic Places a decade later.

A restaurant operated out of the restored building for a time, but then the building remained unoccupied for several years. Under a lease agreement with Donrey Media, the Fort Smith Convention and Visitors Bureau took over the building in 1992 for its visitor information center. Some ninety volunteers staff the center and provide helpful information about the fascinating past and present Fort Smith. The fact that the building is now nicknamed the "Hello Bordello" would no doubt bring a smile to Miss Laura. It is a fitting tribute to her contribution to the colorful history of Fort Smith.

The Rebirth of Fort Smith

After the demise of Judge Parker's court and the Row, the only significant period of activity at Belle Point occurred when the Arkansas National Guard used the old jail and barracks during World War I. Following the war, the federal government gave up on Belle Point and donated the remaining property to the city. Soon new warehouses and a sprinkling of other businesses sprouted on the old post grounds. Because two railways formed a sort of barrier between Belle Point and town, the site literally went to seed. The riverbank became a tangle of brush and trees, creating a jungle habitat for hobos and local derelicts. The townsfolk began to call the area "Coke Hill," because the denizens of the area commonly used cocaine and other narcotics (as well as moonshine and even canned heat).

A local group of women founded the Old Fort Museum Association and established a display of pioneer and military artifacts in the old

Ben Walker and the Fort Smith city bloodhounds. –Cravens Collection, UALR Library Archives

197

commissary building in 1911, but Coke Hill remained populated by hobos and derelicts until 1957, when the city cleared the hovels and sponsored an archaeological excavation of the fort's original foundations. The city also restored the barracks built in 1851 that later served as Judge Isaac Parker's courtroom. This restoration program proved so popular that the city asked Congress to incorporate Fort Smith into the national park system. The Belle Point post has been a national historic site since 1961.

Thanks to this interest in preserving the old post at Belle Point, Fort Smith today stands as a monument to the soldiers, lawmen, and judges who tamed a bloody frontier. The historic communities of Fort Smith and neighboring Van Buren now actively promote and preserve their rich heritage, and an increasing number of visitors come to partake of that history each year. They learn the tough, turbulent history of northwestern Arkansas. And they learn how the West was won.

–RUSSELLVILLE–

Located eighty-five miles southeast of Fort Smith and seventy-eight miles northwest of Little Rock on I-40, Russellville is best known today for the nuclear power plant on Lake Dardanelle, Arkansas Tech University, Whataburger (the state's best drive-in), and POM (Park-O-Meter, which was the first company to make a parking meter). This spot along the Arkansas River became a focal point for human activity long before the first European explorers ventured into the region, since an old Indian trail forded the Arkansas River here. In more recent times, Russellville has certainly contributed its share of interesting people who have gone on to change the course of Arkansas history.

The Russellville story really begins back in the 1820s, when a third of the Cherokee Nation lived in the St. Francis River valley and around Russellville. Cherokee leader George Guess—better known by his Cherokee name, Sequoyah—would make an unprecedented contribution to history by becoming the first person to single-handedly invent a written language.

Sequoyah

Sequoyah was born about 1770 in the Appalachian Mountains where Tennessee, Georgia, and North Carolina join. His white father left his Cherokee mother when the boy was still small. From an early age, he had a dream of making Cherokee letters that would work like the Roman alphabet. He served in the War of 1812, and came to Arkansas

Cherokee leader George Guess—better known by his Cherokee name, Sequoyah—made an unprecedented contribution to history by becoming the first person to single-handedly invent a written language.
—University of Arkansas Fayetteville Museum

Territory with Chief John Jolly and 331 Cherokees following the treaty of 1817. They settled at Galla Rock in what is now Pope County.

Although the members of his tribe viewed him as an idler, Sequoyah devoted himself to creating a written language for the Cherokees while living at the present-day site of Russellville. He developed a syllabary for the spoken Cherokee language that worked like an alphabet. The eighty-six characters were so simple that a person could master the written language in a few days.

Sequoyah gave his people the gift of literacy. He began by teaching his syllabary to his small daughter, Ahyoka. Next, he taught the written language to the tribe led by Ta-ka-to-ka, and then other members of his tribe. Everyone learned to read and write very quickly. He persuaded them to write letters to their kin who still lived east of the Mississippi as an incentive to persuade the Eastern Cherokees to learn the syllabary. The plan worked. Sequoyah returned to Arkansas after enough Eastern Cherokees had mastered reading and writing to teach the rest of their neighbors. Soon the Easterners not only read the letters from their kin in Arkansas, they had also written their own letters back.

Sequoyah returned to settle near what is now known as Scottsville. He took up the blacksmithing and silversmithing trades, and also mined salt. Others used his language to translate books into the Cherokee language, including the Bible. Sadly, Sequoyah never did learn English, so much of his personal history was lost to historians. The great evergreen tree now known as the sequoia was named in honor of this great Cherokee leader.

The Cherokees left the Russellville area after a treaty in 1828 pushed them to lands farther west. Except for the Dwight Mission and a few Indian agents, Anglo-American history of the Russellville area really begins in 1828, when pioneers from Tennessee (along with a smattering of folks from other places) quickly moved into the newly vacated valley, stimulating the creation of a new county just a year after the Cherokees left.

The Birth of Pope County

The burgeoning population of the area caused the territorial legislature to lop off a portion of Crawford County to form Pope County in 1829. The county was named after the new governor of Arkansas Territory, John Pope, who got the job because he had supported Andrew Jackson in the 1828 presidential election, even though his brother-in-law was John Quincy Adams. The third territorial governor served from 1829 to 1835, and—unlike his two predecessors—he brought his family to Arkansas. A temporary county seat was established at the home of John Bollinger until commissioners could be elected to determine a permanent county seat.

Scotia became the first permanent county seat in 1830, where the county's first post office was established that same year. Part of Pope County got lopped off in 1833 to form part of the new Johnson County. The following year, the Pope County seat was moved from Scotia to Dwight Mission, and J. C. Hollander built the first house at the future site of Russellville.

The hand-hewn log house contained five rooms on the first floor and two rooms on the second. An open hall or "dogtrot" divided the home into two halves. Two-room dogtrot houses were a common architectural style throughout Arkansas during those days. Five rooms and two stories suggested a man of means. Hollander sold his house in 1834 to Dr. Thomas Russell, who would figure prominently in the history of the place. That same year, the county seat changed once again, this time moving to Norristown on the Arkansas River, just opposite Dardanelle Rock.

Thomas Russell

Dr. Thomas Russell was born in Durham County, England, in 1801. After graduating from the Royal College of Surgeons in London, he traveled throughout Europe to study at a variety of hospitals. Then he joined his two brothers who were living in Illinois, where he met and married Mary Ann Graham. They moved to Pope County and purchased the Hollander house, which would remain a landmark until 1898. (The house was located at the present corner of Main and Huston Streets.)

Russell became greatly admired as the area's premier physician and surgeon. He traveled on horseback over a wide territory even during winter, when he donned heavy clothing and wrapped his feet and legs with heavy paper to keep out the cold.

The county seat moved once again in 1841, from Norristown to Dover, about eight miles north of an embryonic community sprouting up around Dr. Russell's house. Jacob Shinn opened the first store at the crossroads there (now Main and Denver Streets). When the settlers decided to name the community in 1842, folks proposed to name the town after one of the two leading citizens: Russellville or Shinnton. Russellville won by a single vote.

Russell amassed a considerable fortune by the time of the Civil War, but most of that wealth was invested in land and slaves, which he lost during the war. Everyone in Pope County suffered greatly after General Thomas Hindman abandoned northwestern Arkansas, leaving them prey to Bushwhackers and Jayhawkers. Russell continued practicing medicine until April 1866, when he contracted pneumonia and died. The decade following the Civil War proved to be a very dark time in the Russellville area. While many local men had fought for the Confederacy, many others had fought for the Union. Every family had been victimized by the Bushwhackers or the Jayhawkers. Passions ran high, exploding into violence with alarming regularity.

The Pope County Militia War

The first sheriff following the war, Dodson Napier, fell victim to those passions. Captain Napier, who had commanded a company in the Union army during the war, was shot for his sins while riding down a road near Dover. Both the sheriff and his deputy died in the ambush. The first county clerk after the war, William Stout, was killed in his house. The next sheriff, Morris Williams, was killed while plowing his field.

Wallace Hickox replaced the slain sheriff in 1866, and was backed up by two companies of army troops who were stationed in Dover in the spring of 1867. They stayed for eighteen months, and hostilities seemed to cool. The soldiers went out of their way to be courteous to everyone, and they made friends with folks of every persuasion. But trouble erupted again as soon as the soldiers left following the 1868 election.

Sheriff Hickox was the archetypal reconstructionist, consolidating his power by riding roughshod over anyone who had supported the Lost Cause. He would disenfranchise old residents using the most trivial of pretexts. When J. H. Williams replaced Hickox as sheriff, Hickox continued on as his deputy.

On July 10, 1872, J. H. Williams and Hickox formed a posse of twenty-five to thirty men to avenge the death of Morris Williams. They tried to arrest Matt Hale, but he was not at home, so they arrested Hale's brother (William) and father (Jack). Then the posse arrested Liberty West at Scottsdale and Joseph Tucker at Dover. They also wanted to arrest a number of other Dover residents but failed to find them. The posse brought the prisoners to Shiloh Creek, near Russellville, and opened fire.

Joseph Tucker and William Hale died in the fusillade. Jack Hale escaped by putting spurs to his horse. Liberty West was saved when his mule threw him out of the line of fire, and he was able to hide from the posse.

Jack Hale returned to Dover and raised the alarm. Outraged citizens raised companies of militia in Russellville, Dover, Scottsville, and other areas of Pope County. The Militia War erupted in earnest. W. H. Poynter killed Hickox on August 31, and the militia began to kill off every member of the posse that murdered Joseph Tucker and William Hale.

Then Acting Governor Hadley entered the fray, sending 700 state troops to fight against the Pope County Militia. For a time, it looked as though every former Confederate soldier in the county would be hunted down and killed by the state troops. Fortunately, Hadley fired the local sheriff and replaced him with Absalom Fowler from Little Rock. Passions gradually began to calm over the next several years. After a few more outbreaks of violence, peace finally settled on Russellville and the surrounding county.

Soon thereafter, the Brooks-Baxter War would erupt in Little Rock. Many Southerners would view this conflagration as the event that returned true home rule to Arkansas. Quiet times came to Russellville, although Jesse James did manage to liven up the place one summer evening in the early 1870s.

Jesse James

Isham and Martha Ann Albright were sitting quietly on the front porch of their log home just south of Russellville, watching the sunset. The sound of hoofbeats preceded the appearance of three riders, who stopped at their well. One man asked permission to water the horses. Isham Albright shouted his permission and walked down to meet the men.

Sweat caked the horses' flanks, suggesting the men had driven their horses hard all day. The riders were friendly enough, but since each carried a revolver, Albright didn't ask any questions. He did, however, invite the men to stay with his family for supper and spend the night.

The strangers maintained a lively conversation throughout the cold supper, showing particular courtesy to Mrs. Albright. They casually asked if it was true that they could ford the Arkansas River near the Albright home. It was. The strangers retired for the evening soon thereafter.

After breakfast the next morning, the three men tried to pay the Albrights for the meals and lodging. Mrs. Albright replied, "We don't have many visitors through here and it is our custom never to charge for their keep." Nevertheless, the apparent leader of the group gave a gold ring to their daughter Annie. The men saddled up. As they rode through the gate, the leader drew his revolver and emptied it into the large gatepost by the well. Then they rode off toward the river.

A posse appeared two days later, led by a U.S. deputy marshal. He asked the Albrights if they had seen three riders recently. The Albrights admitted that they had. The marshal explained that the riders were the gang led by the notorious Jesse James. After the posse left, something inspired Isham Albright to examine the bullet holes in the gatepost. The holes formed a neat *J*.

Life in Pope County settled into a normal routine until 1887, when Russellville became the latest in a long line of county seats. The town prospered as a commercial and transportation hub with the coming of the railroad, while the river port of Norristown withered away. The ferry service between Russellville and Dardanelle could not keep up with the increasing demands on its services, so private investors built a floating toll bridge in 1878, which was believed to be the longest

Jesse James (from J. W. Buel's The Border Outlaws, *published in 1882).*
—Mary Hudgins Collection, Special Collections, University of Arkansas Libraries, Fayetteville

pontoon bridge over flowing water in the world. A more durable pontoon bridge replaced the original in 1891. The structure was 2,208 feet long, 18 feet wide, and was supported by seventy-two pontoon boats. Although the bridge carried a great deal of commercial traffic (including 24,000 bales of hay in 1894), the toll bridge never became a commercial success.

Then, just after the turn of the century, the town's very own Jeff Davis became governor for three fiery terms and a hero to the forgotten poor of rural Arkansas.

The Firebrand from Russellville

It is ironic that an urban lawyer would come to dominate Arkansas politics for a decade by praising poor white farmers and lambasting rich white city folk and blacks. But the political ascendancy of Jefferson Davis (not to be confused with the president of the Confederacy, who had the same name) was inevitable for two reasons.

Small farmers were going through desperately hard times. They had lost all hope because the politicians in power did not seem to care about them at all. They equated any city dweller with the bankers and other "rich folks" who seemed to oppress them. The small farmers were angry, and they wanted to strike back at the system.

Jeff Davis had the ability to speak to the very soul of these powerless farmers, appealing to them at gut level with his vicious attacks

Governor Jeff Davis.
−Arkansas History Commission

on bankers, businessmen, blacks, news editors, and the political status quo. Davis was a brilliant orator, with an uncanny knack for spellbinding an audience. He coined the term "redneck" as a badge of honor to distinguish the hardworking farmers from the bankers and other citified oppressors who wore high starched collars.

"I am a Hard Shell Baptist in religion," Davis said of himself. "I believe in foot-washing, saving your seed potatoes, and paying your honest debts."

Although he was not related to the man of the same name who had been president of the Confederacy, many people assumed that he was. Jeff Davis did nothing to dispel that belief. He wove the ideas of the old Populist and the new Progressive movements into his speeches, along with a large measure of folksy banter. Davis delivered his oratory with an awesome force and energy. His chosen audience found him charismatic in the extreme.

"The papers say that no one will vote for me except the fellows that wear patched britches and one gallus [suspender] and live up the forks of creeks, and don't pay anything but their pole tax," Davis declared. "I want to tell you that there is no great reformation that ever originated on this earth that did not come from the ranks of the humble and lowly of the land."

Every speech attacked the perceived enemies of the poor white farmer. "The fight is on," Davis said. "It is between the trusts and the corporations and the people. If I win this race, I have got to win it from 525 insurance agents . . . every railroad, every bank, two-thirds of the lawyers and most of the big politicians; but if we can get the plain people of the country to help me, God bless you, we will clean things up."

Jeff Davis was elected to the first of three terms as governor in 1901, but he was not able to effect much change. While he is remembered for reforming the disgraceful prison system, he achieved those reforms as the state attorney general before the 1901 election.

Although Jeff Davis had attacked blacks during the course of his first gubernatorial campaign, it was a black lawyer in Little Rock who convinced Davis to reform the prison system several years earlier. The original problem with Arkansas prisons was that the state rented or leased convicts to railroads, coal mines, and other businesses. Many businessmen worked the convicts like slaves, whipping them and feeding them poorly. As many as 25 percent of these convict laborers died each year. Two-thirds of the convicts were blacks who might have been convicted for such heinous crimes as selling cotton after dark or buying whiskey. Six percent of the convicts were between the ages of nine and sixteen.

A scandal in 1887 finally forced the state to adopt a system of penal farms to replace the practice of renting out prisoners. The idea was that prisoners could pay off their fines by working for 50 cents per day on the penal farms. The problem, as Little Rock lawyer Scipio Africanus Jones explained to Attorney General Davis, was that the prisoners were charged room and board for every day they didn't work. Since Sunday was a scheduled day of rest, convicts had to pay the state 50 cents. If rain prevented working in the fields or they were injured on the job, the prisoners had to pay room and board for every day they couldn't work. The net result was that a prisoner could be forced to stay in prison for years to pay off a $50 fine.

Davis saw the validity of the argument presented by Jones, who had long provided a powerful voice for the black community in Arkansas. Davis reformed the system so convicts earned 75 cents per day whether or not they worked. He started a reform school for boys so convicted youngsters did not have to serve time with adults. And as governor, he pardoned hundreds of black convicts. But he remained an unrepentant racist.

"I stand for the Caucasian race," Davis declared during the 1904 campaign, "and I say that [Negro] dominion will never prevail in this beautiful Southland of ours, as long as rifles and shotguns lie around loose, and we are able to pull the trigger."

Davis continued to do everything in his power to disenfranchise blacks, and was outraged when President Theodore Roosevelt invited Booker T. Washington to lunch at the White House. When Roosevelt later visited Little Rock in 1905, Davis presented a formal speech welcoming Roosevelt to Arkansas, but he used the opportunity to defend lynching. Roosevelt abandoned his prepared remarks and condemned the lawlessness Davis advocated.

Davis was elected to the U.S. Senate in 1906, but his personal style did not work there. He was so out of his element that he stayed in Little Rock for most of his term. He barely won reelection in 1912, and died of a heart attack on the first day of 1913. His funeral was the largest in Little Rock history.

In 1897, while Jeff Davis was pursuing a political career in Little Rock, Russellville became an incorporated city with a population of 275. A fire destroyed twenty-one businesses in 1906, but the city bounced back and grew to a population of 5,000 by 1919. The town had three banks, a creamery, a large foundry and ironworks, a roller flour mill, two wholesale houses, the largest horse and mule market in the state, waterworks, a power plant, a theater, and a hospital. The community boasted of wide streets and well-kept homes. A steel bridge replaced the old pontoon bridge between Russellville and

Dardanelle in 1928, sealing the town's success as the trade center serving Arkansas from the Ozarks to the Ouachitas. Coal mines, lumber mills, and new industries fueled the town's growth. However, the fuel that really put Russellville on the modern map was not coal. It was uranium dioxide.

Arkansas Nuclear One

Back in the 1960s, the Entergy Corporation selected a 1,100 acre site on the northern shore of the Dardanelle Reservoir as the best location for the first nuclear-fueled power plant in the Southwest. Located about five miles from Russellville, the facility known as Arkansas Nuclear One Steam Electric Station actually has two nuclear reactors, each with its own turbine generator system.

The Bechtel Power Corporation began construction of Unit 1 in the fall of 1968. Unit 1 uses a Babcox & Wilcox reactor (a barge delivered the 320-ton reactor vessel via the Arkansas River) and a Westinghouse turbine generator. The system began commercial service in 1974 with a capacity of 836 megawatts, enough power to meet the entire electrical needs of Little Rock during peak demand in the summer, when electrical use is the greatest. The system is cooled by drawing (and returning) 760,000 gallons of water per minute from Lake Dardanelle. That works out to about 300 bathtubs per second.

Bechtel began work on Unit 2 in 1971, this time using a reactor designed by Combustion Engineering and a turbine generator built by General Electric. Like Unit 1, the newer system incorporates a 320-ton reactor vessel for its pressurized water reactor. To minimize thermal pollution of Dardanelle Reservoir, Unit 2 does not draw cooling water from the lake. Instead, the system uses a cooling tower that looms 447 feet above the landscape. That's as tall as some forty-story buildings. The system began commercial service in 1980 with a rated capacity of 858 megawatts.

Together, the two units of Arkansas Nuclear One can provide about half the power needs of Arkansas Power & Light, a wholly owned subsidiary of the Entergy Corporation based out of New Orleans. Arkansas Nuclear One employs about 1,400 people and provides business to about 450 contractors.

Following the nuclear accident at Three Mile Island in Pennsylvania, the Entergy Corporation extensively modified Arkansas Nuclear One to take advantage of the lessons learned from the accident. One of the additions to the facility was a 72,000 square foot Nuclear Training Center built on a hill north of the power plants. The center serves as both a training facility for plant personnel and an operations base during emergencies. Arkansas Nuclear One has an expected operational life of thirty to forty years, so uranium dioxide will continue to provide electricity to Arkansans into the first or second decade of the twenty-first century.

Russellville–Little Rock
78 miles

The seventy-eight from Russellville to Little Rock covers the most populated portion of the Arkansas River valley. The clash of opposing political philosophies and frustrated political aspirations provides the cornerstone for the rich history of the area. This segment of central Arkansas has changed the history not only of Arkansas, but the history of the entire nation as well.

The valley abounds with unlikely but true stories. An important county was named after a fiddle player and teller of tall tales. A seventeen-year-old civilian became the state's most revered hero of the Civil War. Two men vying for the governor's office in 1872 argued over the results of the election, recruited and armed their own militias, and launched a miniature civil war inside Arkansas that ended Reconstruction with a bang—and substantial bloodshed. The man who founded Conway and worked for aspiring railroad robber barons saw his "little stumptail railroad" destroy the presidential aspirations of the Speaker of the U.S. House of Representatives. A frightened teenage girl changed the political history of the entire nation. And a former Rhodes Scholar, draft dodger, and admitted pot smoker became president of the United States. These are just a few examples of the remarkable history that has been written by Arkansans in this short stretch of river valley.

The story begins somewhere near Toad Suck, on the Arkansas River.

—CONWAY—

Where is Conway? "Halfway between Pickles Gap and Toad Suck!" as anyone who lives in Faulkner County can tell you. For those who prefer to take their bearings from the interstate, Conway is forty-nine miles southeast of Russellville and thirty-one miles north of Little Rock on I-40. Today, it is known as a college town and a bedroom community for Little Rock. While Conway has only about 36,000 residents, it supports three colleges: the University of Central Arkansas,

Hendrix College, and Central Baptist College. That's quite an achievement for a town that started, like so many others in Arkansas, as a railroad depot.

The history of railroad development in Arkansas could yield enough tales of political machinations, graft, greed, and nobility to fill a lively book. Such a volume would begin in 1853, when the Cairo & Fulton Railroad received its charter, and continue to the modern day, when the trains roaring through the heart of Conway seem to claim a life or two every year. A suitable proverb might be: "The railroads giveth, and the railroads taketh away."

Indeed, much of the history of Arkansas between the Civil War and World War II could be written as a history of the railroads giving and the railroads taking away. The railroads certainly changed the economic and population patterns of the state. Many small farmers, for example, flocked to the new railroad towns to work for wages. Communities that depended on the commercial traffic along the waterways or the primitive road system withered and died if bypassed by the tracks. Without the completion of the Little Rock & Ft. Smith Railroad in the early 1870s, the lively community of Conway would never have appeared.

This "little stumptail railroad," as historian Ellis Oberholtzer called it in the 1920s, exerted an influence far beyond the Arkansas River valley. Although the Little Rock & Ft. Smith Railroad gave life to Conway and brought commerce to Fort Smith, it also sealed the political death of James C. Blaine, who might otherwise have become president of the United States. But that's getting ahead of the story. The founding of Conway and the ultimate success of the railroad can be traced to the energetic leadership of one man: Asa Robinson.

Asa Robinson

Born in Connecticut, raised in Newburg, New York, and educated as a civil engineer at Yale University, Asa Robinson gained his experience surveying for the Erie Railroad and later working for the Missouri, Kansas & Texas Railroad Company. Forty-seven when he arrived in Little Rock in 1869, he faced a lot more challenges than the merely mathematical problem of laying track along the best route through the terrain for the Little Rock & Ft. Smith. He also faced a host of logistic, climatic, and social problems.

During the grueling and chaotic process of building this railroad, Robinson developed a fondness for a particular spot along the right of way several miles south of Cadron, which was originally a trading post and later became a stopping place for boats plying the Arkansas River. Robinson liked this stretch of land around Conway Station

Colonel Asa P. Robinson founded Conway along the railroad line he built.
—J. N. Heiskell Collection, UALR Library Archives

because it lay on open prairie dotted with clusters of trees. He actually received the deed to this square mile of land from the railroad in lieu of salary on July 6, 1871. Contrary to local lore, Robinson received his deed *after* Conway Station had been built, although there is some evidence to suggest that he lived on the land before he gained ownership. Curiously, the railroad's ledger actually shows a payment of $2,991.93 for the land, although this may have been merely a bookkeeping formality. Robinson filed a plat for a town named Conway on August 1, 1871, and began to build a house in September. But the railroad's fortunes as well as his own were soon to bottom out.

The state treasurer confiscated the railroad after the company defaulted on interest payments on its bonds, which were now worthless. This is where the Little Rock & Ft. Smith (LR&FS) began to profoundly influence national politics. Speaker of the House James Blaine had used his substantial political clout to sell these now worthless bonds to investors in Maine, who lost everything. When Blaine sought the Republican nomination for the presidency in 1876, letters revealing his close relationship with the railroad were made public. It became obvious that Blaine had used his public office for personal financial gain, and the GOP denied his bid for the nomination. The furor eventually quieted down, so Blaine prepared to challenge Grover Cleveland in the 1884 presidential race. But those damning letters surfaced once again, and Blaine's presidential aspirations died once and for all.

Meanwhile, Robinson's new town had begun to take shape. By the end of 1874, the railroad was operating from Huntersville to within a few miles of Fort Smith, and Conway began to prosper as a transportation center. Land values increased. That same year, Asa Robinson married Mary Louise de St. Louis of Montreal, Canada. (Robinson's first wife had died in 1859, leaving five children behind.) After a trip to Europe, the couple returned to Conway and settled into the fashionable home of local white pine Robinson built at the end of the only road in town. Not surprisingly, Robinson served as the town's mayor. He also donated the land for the courthouse, and he developed a cattle ranch that became renowned for its shorthorn and Jersey cattle.

Asa Robinson founded the town and named it after the depot—but where did the depot's name come from? There are a variety of explanations for its origin. Some folks suggest the depot was named for the Conway family, which produced two Arkansas governors. Another source points out that railroad locomotives were named in those days, and the first LR&FS locomotive was called the *Conway*. This is a persuasive argument since Mayflower got its name from the Pullman car used as the mobile headquarters for the railroad during construction. The car was named *Mayflower*, and that was also its cable address for telegrams. The name continued to be used for that location after the Pullman car moved on.

It is also possible that the depot was simply named for the county it served, for Faulkner County was not carved out of Conway and Pulaski Counties until 1873. Whatever the immediate source of inspiration may have been, it is safe to say that the ultimate inspiration for the name would trace back to the illustrious Conway family that figured so prominently in the early history of Arkansas.

Conway received a big boost in 1873, when the railroad began to handle commercial telegraph business for the Western Union Telegraph and Cable Company. The new telegraph office at Conway Station became a gathering place where people could learn the latest news. The biggest news of the year came when the legislature created Faulkner County and named Conway Station the temporary county seat until commissioners could find a permanent location. By the time the commissioners had studied all the possibilities, the town of Conway was getting on its feet. So the commissioners suggested Conway, and it has remained the county seat ever since.

Most counties are named after war heroes or influential politicians. Faulkner County was named after a fiddle player and teller of tall tales. (Lest any resident of the county take offense at this revelation, I should point out that the state capital of Alaska was named after the town drunk of a nearby trading post.) Colonel Sandy Faulkner achieved his notoriety in Arkansas not for his service as a Confederate ordnance officer, but rather for writing a lively fiddle tune in the 1830s that captured the imagination of folks for the rest of the century. He called his tune and its accompanying tale the "Arkansas Traveller."

Colonel Sandy Faulkner and the "Arkansas Traveller"

Sanford Faulkner was born in 1803 in Georgetown, Kentucky. After a brief stay in Texas, he moved to Arkansas in 1829 and spent his early years as a planter in Chicot County. Faulkner traveled around Arkansas throughout 1830 on a campaign tour with Governor William Fulton, Archibald Yell, Chester Ashley, and A. H. Sevier. (Each of these men would ultimately have an Arkansas county named after him.) Sandy Faulkner's fame resulted from an incident he experienced on that campaign trail. He wove the incident into a story that he narrated (rather than sang) as he played the fiddle tune he wrote to commemorate the event.

Colonel Sanford C. Faulkner, circa 1873, about the time Faulkner County was named in his honor.
—J. N. Heiskell Collection, UALR Library Archives

Faulkner's story told of a weary traveler who was lost in the woods. Night was nearly upon him when he stumbled upon a squatter sitting on the porch of a ramshackle cabin, playing the same tune over and over. During the next half hour, the traveler kept asking if he could get food and lodging for the night. The backwoodsman showed no interest in helping the man as he kept playing the fiddle.

"Why are you playing that tune over so often for?" demanded the traveler.

"Only heard it yisterday," the squatter replied as he kept playing. "Fraid I'll forget it."

"Why don't you play the second part?" the traveler asked.

"It ain't got no second part," the squatter replied.

"Give me the fiddle," the traveler demanded. He tuned the fiddle briefly and then began to play the second part. The squatter jumped up and began to dance, waking up his sleeping hound, which began to hop up and down and thump his tail on the porch. The backwoodsman's wife even came out and smiled, though her muscles were unaccustomed to that activity. The squatter was so entranced by the music that he had his wife fetch deer meat and his old black jug for the stranger, and he even said the traveler could sleep in the cabin on the dry spot.

The Arkansas Traveller, *by artist Edward Payson Washbourne.*
—Arkansas Territorial Restoration

The tune and the tale were widely performed over the next fifty years. They were even used in a New York play called *Kit, the Arkansas Traveler,* which delighted audiences in the 1880s. Faulkner's creation was immortalized in a painting by Edward Payson Washbourne called *The Arkansas Traveller.* Reproductions of that painting were distributed widely (including on the cover of this book), which made the tune and story even more famous. The original painting can be seen at the Arkansas Territorial Restoration in Little Rock.

Faulkner achieved a great deal of fame during his lifetime from the "Arkansas Traveller." The manager of the St. Charles Hotel, for example, lettered the title in gilt over a room that remained permanently reserved for Faulkner's visits to New Orleans. A better tribute was paid a year before his death, when the legislature created a new county and named it after Faulkner. By this time, Sandy Faulkner had fallen on hard times, forcing him to work as the doorman at the hotel where all out-of-town politicians stayed while the legislature was in session. Yet Faulkner remained the embodiment of the quintessential Southern gentleman, and was widely liked by everyone. A clever legislator solved a bitter impasse over naming the new county by suggesting that it be named after Colonel Faulkner. Everyone agreed with enthusiasm. But perhaps the best tribute to Sandy Faulkner was that the

Front and Oak Streets in downtown Conway, looking east down Oak as farmers bring cotton to market. –UCA Archives

colonel's fiddle tune and tale became the cornerstone of Arkansas folklore.

Farming had long provided the economic base of the area. Cattle and grain were raised, but cotton had come to dominate the economy by 1860. While cotton production had not recovered to antebellum levels by 1870, production dramatically exceeded antebellum levels by 1880. The railroad and gins at Conway not only facilitated the movement of cotton to market, but the railroad also permitted the birth of the timber industry and market farming of fruits and vegetables in the county. Conway became the trade and transportation center for all of this commerce. Wagon yards became the hub of this economic activity and provided the major social environment as well.

Conway's Caravanserai

Without wagon yards, it's hard to imagine how any market town could have survived before pickups and trucks replaced buggies and wagons. Wagon yards developed to meet the needs of farmers and other folks who had to spend the night in town and either could not afford to stay in a hotel, or needed to tend their vehicle and draft animals. The wagon yard was an American version of Middle Eastern caravanserai, a cross between the modern motel and a campground.

The typical wagon yard was a huge, barnlike building made of wood, sheet metal, or brick designed to cover the maximum amount of space with the minimum amount of money. Large doors would open onto one or more streets to handle the wagon traffic. Stalls were provided around the outside walls for the teams. The better wagon yards provided separate bunkhouses for the men and women. Others provided bunks only for the women, and the men had to sleep in their wagons.

Inside the typical bunkhouse, wooden bunk beds lined the walls two to three beds high. A large stove provided heat and a place to cook. Neither bedding nor cooking utensils were provided, however. Everyone brought their own. The wagon yard did provide a watering trough for the stock and toilet facilities for the patrons. Although rates varied over the years, the cost for a driver to stay overnight with a wagon and team commonly ran 25 cents plus feed for the draft animals.

The wagons were parked in the central portion of the wagon yard, although "packed" is probably a better description, because the tongue of each wagon was slid under the wagon in front of it. This process did not create the gridlock one might expect, since each wagon was met by an attendant who asked when the wagon driver wanted to leave. The attendant then parked the wagon with others that would leave at a similar time. Remarkably little reshuffling would be required the following day.

Most of the patrons were cotton farmers, and most of them came between August and March, after the harvesting of one crop but before the planting of the next. The farmers would haul their raw cotton to one of Conway's gins and sell the processed bales to one of the local buyers. By 1909, Conway had five buyers who collectively paid more than $1 million for 25,000 bales of cotton that year. Cotton would remain king in Faulkner County until federal programs and a plague of boll weevils forced the diversification of farming in the 1920s.

Although local residents commonly referred to Tuesdays as "Hog and Whore Day" thanks in part to the weekly livestock auction, most farmers came to Conway on Friday, bringing their families along for the adventure. Sitting on bedding softened the harsh riding characteristics of the wagons, and sometimes kitchen chairs were placed in the wagon so family members could have a more comfortable ride. As one wagon met another and then another, the farmers would form caravans for companionship. Sometimes the conversation between wagons would lose some of its levity when a team followed so close that the animals began eating from the feed box at the rear of the wagon they were following.

The Workingman's Restaurant in Conway, circa 1920. –UCA Archives

The farmers began to trickle into the wagon yards about 3 P.M., and arrivals continued until about 9. Although many families brought food from home, others liked to treat themselves at the local grocery and bakery, where a pound of sausage cost 8 cents and a loaf of bread cost a nickel. Sometimes farmers would splurge and eat at the local restaurants and boardinghouses, which provided family style, all-you-can-eat meals for a quarter.

Not all diversions were family style. Although Conway was a dry county, like-minded farmers would band together and send someone ahead to Little Rock for a group purchase, which would be distributed discretely among the investors at a wagon yard. While Haynor whiskey was commonly the refreshment of choice, frugal individuals purchased grain alcohol from a pharmaceutical supply in Little Rock for their mixed drinks. Friday nights were spent playing cards in the bunkhouse and telling tall tales. Some farmers liked to participate in the occasional fight, and some liked to visit the local sporting house with its ladies of negotiable virtue.

Everyone who stayed at the wagon yards generally concluded their business on Saturday and headed home after stocking up on supplies (often loading the wagon with enough flour, clothing, and other essentials to last a year). The wagon yards were quiet by Saturday night.

Cotton yard in Conway, circa 1930. –UCA Archives

It's hard to overstate the importance of the wagon yards to Conway. The town had at least a dozen such establishments when Conway's population was only 3,000. Considering that each could accommodate from 15 to 125 wagons (with their occupants and draft animals), the importance of the yards becomes apparent. The yards remained a lively part of the Conway scene from the early days of the town until well after World War I.

By the late 1920s, however, the internal combustion engine was replacing the horse and mule in rural Arkansas. Farmers anywhere in Faulkner County could reach Conway in an hour instead of a day. There was no need to stay overnight, and the wagon yards went out of business. Several of the buildings were converted to other uses, but most were torn down. By 1935, every wagon yard had passed into history and then even the phrase "wagon yard" disappeared from the collective Conway vocabulary.

Whereas the wagon yards provided much of the social and financial energy of Conway's early years, the community's three colleges constitute the heart of the town now.

Hendrix College

The history of Hendrix College begins in 1876, when the school was called the Central Institute. Originally located at Altus (in Franklin County), the Central Institute began life as a primary school for about twenty students. The school prospered and added a secondary program. Then Episcopal minister Isham Burrow (who owned the school) added a college program in 1881, and changed the school's name to the Central Collegiate Institute. Three years later, several Methodist groups purchased the school, but bitter personality conflicts soon led to the resignation of the entire faculty.

The Reverend Alexander Miller became the new president of the institute. He hired new faculty members and tried to upgrade the program in 1889 by eliminating primary education and changing the name to Hendrix College (in honor of Eugene Hendrix, the Methodist bishop of Kansas City). The 500 residents of Altus developed an immediate dislike for Miller and his new faculty members, whom they viewed as meddlesome Northerners. So the board of trustees voted to move the college to a larger and friendlier community.

Seven towns courted the college, and Conway won when local people pledged $55,000 to help build the school about a mile north of Conway Station. Hendrix College had 158 students during its first year in Conway, but only 25 were in the collegiate program. College students would not outnumber secondary students until 1911.

219

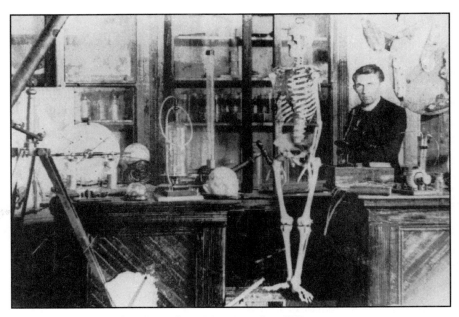

Hendrix College science laboratory, circa 1892. –UCA Archives

Hendrix was officially a male-only college of the Methodist Church. Conway got a female-only college sponsored by the Baptist Church in 1892, which dramatically improved the morale among the male students at Hendrix. (The Central Baptist College for Women no longer exists, having closed its doors after the 1947 graduation.) Hendrix finally began to recruit female students in 1918, but the first black student would not appear until 1965.

The Great Depression hit Arkansas colleges hard. The Methodist Church supported two other colleges in Arkansas besides Hendrix: Henderson-Brown College in Arkadelphia, and Galloway Woman's College in Searcy. The church merged the three colleges in 1929 into the Conway facility, which was briefly called Trinity College until the name reverted back to Hendrix College in 1931. The consolidation of the colleges plus the sale of bonds by the Conway Corporation (which operated the Conway water and power utilities) enabled Hendrix to prosper and grow during a time of great adversity.

Today, Hendrix is widely respected as an outstanding liberal arts school (and Henderson-Brown operates independently as a state-supported school in Arkadelphia). A national guide to colleges ranked Hendrix as one of the 300 toughest schools in the country in terms of competitive admission requirements, and another guide rated it as one of the 300 best liberal arts colleges in terms of providing a high-quality education at an unusually low cost. Enrollment averages about 1,000 students at Hendrix, which remains the only nationally ranked liberal arts college in Arkansas.

University of Central Arkansas

The University of Central Arkansas began life as the Arkansas State Normal School in 1908, with an enrollment of 170 students. The early years of the school were plagued with serious financial problems because state appropriations always fell very short of student needs. This problem was shared by every educational program in Arkansas. Fortunately for the state, the people of Conway and Faulkner Counties always went out of their way to support institutions of higher learning.

The construction of Old Main, which remains the centerpiece of the campus today, shows just how this grassroots support worked. The legislature only appropriated about half the money needed for the building, so a faculty member wired the building for electricity to cut costs. The contractor had to leave the ground floor unfinished when the funds ran out, but local residents contributed the shortfall plus enough money to equip the building. This kind of community support explains why Conway ultimately became a college town instead of merely another market town along the railroad.

The curriculum matured and enrollment increased, but Arkansas Normal's focus remained the education of teachers for rural public schools. The institution changed its name to Arkansas State Teachers College in 1925. At about that time, the school needed a new library for its students as well as to receive accreditation. The state government was unable to provide any financial support, but the governor ruled that the school could go into debt to build the library. Once again local support provided a solution. Hiegel Lumber Company built the library in 1929 with the understanding that payment might take awhile. Hiegel quietly waited until 1946 for compensation. When a new library was built in 1963, it took the name of the old Torreyson Library, and the original building was renamed Harrin Hall.

The college fared remarkably well in the Great Depression. The federal public works programs of the New Deal created a building boom on campus. Federal agencies built McAlister Hall, the gymnasium, Ida Waldran Auditorium, and even the president's home. This expansion encroached on the college's agricultural program, so the Conway Corporation donated 240 acres on the south edge of campus. The corporation had donated $215,000 the previous year to the other colleges in town (Hendrix College and the Central Baptist

College for Women), so this land grant provided a similar level of local support to the Arkansas State Teachers College. How many other small towns in the depths of the Great Depression gave this much support to higher education? Conway has really earned the right to be a college town.

Although the college weathered the Great Depression with remarkable grace, World War II proved a very difficult time. Enrollment plummeted, and the facilities fell into disrepair. Arkansas State Teachers College was in no shape for the explosive increase in student enrollment after the war, which was funded largely by the GI Bill.

The school gradually began to shift its emphasis in the late 1940s and early 1950s away from training teachers and toward the liberal arts and sciences. Nevertheless, the school added its first graduate program in education. The college began a program of racial integration about the same time, although the official state charter prohibiting black students was not changed by the Arkansas legislature until the early 1990s. The change in academic emphasis came to a conclusion in 1967, when the school changed its name from Arkansas State Teachers College to State College of Arkansas. It became the University of Central Arkansas in 1975. The school embarked on a long-term program to upgrade the quality of the faculty and to recruit high-school students more aggressively.

This program finally reached critical mass in the late 1980s, igniting an explosive period of growth at UCA. Enrollment jumped from 6,698 in 1988 to 9,567 in 1993, a growth of 43 percent in just five years.

Aerial view of Arkansas State Teachers College (now the University of Central Arkansas), circa 1947. –UCA Archives

Central Baptist College

The history of Central Baptist College dates back to the late 1940s, when the new Arkansas Missionary Baptist Association (now called the Baptist Missionary Association of Arkansas) was created to foster Christian education at the college level. The organization began its effort by opening an extension of a Texas Baptist college in Little Rock. As support for the program grew, the group began to search for a place to build a permanent campus.

Conway was the clear choice for several reasons. The town was known for its enthusiastic support of its colleges. It was centrally located. And, best of all, the town had a vacant eleven-acre campus that had not been used since the Central Baptist College for Women closed its doors in 1947. After a year of fund-raising, the association purchased the vacant campus and opened the school in September 1952 as Conway Baptist College.

Funding fell far short of needs at first. Such simple things as books for the library and heat for the buildings depended on a continual string of fund-raising drives. Remarkably, the school had somehow managed to pay all of its bills when the academic year concluded the following spring. Conway Baptist College expanded its curriculum, added faculty, and completely paid off the loan used to purchase the campus in just a decade. The college purchased an additional ten acres on German Lane. Its focus evolved and broadened, so the name was changed to Central Baptist College in 1962. Enrollment is now about 275 students.

Toad Suck and Pickles Gap

Since the residents of Faulkner County are so fond of explaining Conway's location by saying it is halfway between Pickles Gap and Toad Suck, no discussion of Conway would be complete without a few words about these two fascinating place-names.

Located about five miles west of Conway where Arkansas 286 crosses the Arkansas River, Toad Suck inspires more curiosity about its name than any other place in Arkansas. Local legends provide several different explanations for the origin of the name, but the two most accepted stories involve the copious consumption of whiskey or moonshine at that location on the banks of the Arkansas.

The oldest story dates back to the early 1820s, when men laboriously poled keelboats upstream against the current, and a ferry began to provide a crossing of the Arkansas River for the new postal route to Hot Springs. That first ferry was a small skiff that was just big enough to accommodate a horse and rider, plus the ferry operator. An eddy just below a big bend in the river provided a convenient

223

place for keelboat crews to rest or wait until the water level would rise enough to continue upriver. Given either excuse, the boatmen would pass the time by pulling out their jugs to "suck up whiskey like toads" or "have themselves a regular toadsuck." By about 1830, a tavern at the Toad Suck ferry crossing catered to those traveling by trail and water, more or less formalizing the tradition.

There is also a possibility that the place was named in part for the eddy itself, since any swirling vortex of water was called a "suck" in the early nineteenth-century vernacular of Tennessee and Kentucky. Another story dates to the mid-late 1800s. Folks would gather every Saturday, as this story goes, to race horses, gamble, and suck up whiskey until they swelled like toads.

Which alternative origin of "Toad Suck" is the real one? The answer remains as muddy as the Arkansas River. Perhaps each story has a grain of truth. In any event, folks have a long tradition of sucking up whiskey at this spot along the Arkansas. There may even be a tradition of sucking up toads!

Traveling medicine shows and snake-oil salesmen frequently used toads to demonstrate the efficacy of their potions, since folks generally believed that toads were poisonous. The snake-oil salesman would have a shill (usually a half-witted lad) eat or pretend to eat a toad, and then effect a miracle cure of the poisoned individual with his proprietary potion. Because local folks had a long tradition of gathering at the ferry crossing for horse racing and other merriment (Conway was not yet established), this would be a logical place to set up a medicine show.

A tavern later established at Toad Suck did a thriving business until Faulkner County "voted dry as long as they could stagger to the polls," as historian Robert Gatewood put it. But an enterprising riverboat owner converted his boat into a saloon ship, which was safe from local lawmen as long as the boat never touched the shores of Faulkner County. Over the years, patrons reached the saloon ships by crossing a log, walking up a wooden ramp, or taking a small boat.

As the years passed, the Toad Suck ferryboats became bigger and more sophisticated. When the ferry was powered by oars, the passengers as well as the crew would put their backs into the enterprise. When the water was swift and high, the effort required two men per oar. At other times, the water would be so low that the traveler could walk across the river. After the establishment of Conway Station, farmers on the west side of the river would bring their wagonloads of cotton and corn to market over the Toad Suck ferry. By 1904, a cable stretched over the river to guide the ferry. Folks used slotted sticks to grab the overhead cable and pull themselves across. This was a

Toad Suck ferry, circa 1960, before construction of the bridge, lock, and dam. —UCA Archives

big improvement over previous systems when the current was strong or the wind was high.

The ferry was commonly owned by private citizens such as Cordell Chapman, Marion Padgett, Ernest Taylor, and Irvine Gilbert. The last owners were Guy Jones, Paul Van Dalsem, and Dave Ward. Van Dalsem was also a representative in the Arkansas legislature. He and Senator Guy Jones introduced a bill in the 1940s to appropriate $25,000 for the purchase of a new ferryboat for Toad Suck. The bill failed, but Jones kept trying to upgrade the crossing over the next decades. A new bridge, lock, and dam were eventually planned as part of a federal river navigation project that would extend from the mouth of the Arkansas River all the way up to Tulsa. But Congress eventually cancelled the funds for the Toad Suck portion of the project. Jones fought back and won when he got Senator Wilbur Mills, who was chairman of the Ways and Means Committee in Congress, to fund the project using an obscure old law as justification.

Construction on the bridge, lock, and dam began in 1964. By the time the project was completed at a cost of $28 million in 1969, the facility had become one of twelve Arkansas and five Oklahoma lock and dams in the McClellan-Kerr Navigation System on the Arkansas River. The following year, the Arkansas legislature voted to give the facility the traditional name for the area, so now the place is known as the Toad Suck Lock and Dam. Every spring, Conway celebrates the zany history of this place by holding a festival called Toad Suck Daze.

Toad Suck Lock and Dam uses the traditional name of this site along the Arkansas River, where early Arkansans consumed copious quantities of whiskey and moonshine.
—Henryetta Vanaman

Pickles Gap, located about two miles northeast of Conway on US 65, is a small settlement at a break in a ridgeline. Pickles Creek runs through the gap. Some folks believe the gap was named after the creek, which was named after a family named Pickle. Others believe a barrel of pickles rolled off a wagon negotiating the ridge and broke open at that site.

Whatever the real origins of these place-names, Toad Suck and Pickles Gap have become the essential ingredients in the Pavlovian response to the question, "Where is Conway?"

Cadron

During territorial days and the early days after statehood, Cadron was one of the most important settlements in Arkansas. The diffuse settlement extended for several miles above and below the mouth of Cadron Creek on both sides of the Arkansas River. Now little remains of Cadron, except for a small park on the National Register of Historic Places. The inexorable waters of the Arkansas River have eaten away

Dedication of the blockhouse at Cadron Settlement Park in 1976. –UCA Archives

some lots, the McClellan-Kerr Navigation System inundated others, and the mouth of Cadron Creek now enters the Arkansas a quarter-mile farther upriver. Cadron Bluff is the geographic center of Arkansas, and the small park lies just outside Conway. Take US 64 about two miles west of Conway and then take Arkansas 319 another mile west to the Arkansas River.

The origin of Cadron's name can be traced back to the 1770s, when French traders established a trading post at the mouth of a creek. A letter from that period referred to the trading post as *le Qaudrant,* meaning "a quarter of a circle," which described Cadron's topography as seen from the river. The name remained even after the French abandoned their trading post. *Le Qaudrant* became Anglicized to "the Quadrant," which appears on a map dated 1816. The Quadrant became corrupted over the years to Cadron. This is the most common explanation for the name.

It is also possible that early French hunters and trappers named this place after Charles Cadron, commandant of the old post at St. Phillippe in Illinois during 1762. But known letters and maps do not support this alternative explanation.

The first Anglo-American settlers arrived in 1808 under the leadership of Alexander McFarland, who lived along the shore of the Arkansas River across from the mouth of Cadron Creek. John McElmurry settled in the area about 1810, platted the town of Cadron (as opposed to the larger and more diffused settlement), and began the cumbersome process of securing patent to the land, which was not issued until 1830—three years after his death.

Cadron lay on the border between the Osage and Quapaw nations. McElmurry was on good terms with the Quapaws, but the Osages presented a very real threat, so he built a blockhouse as both a home for his family and a fortified refuge for his neighbors. The U.S. Army Corps of Engineers and the Faulkner County Historical Society built a replica of this cedar blockhouse at Cedar Park (which was part of the original town site). While a fire destroyed the handsome structure in the early 1990s, plans are afoot to rebuild the blockhouse.

In 1818, McElmurry sold quarter interests in the town (not lots per se) to Jonas Menifee from Cape Girardeau in Missouri, Jason Chamberlain, and Thomas Tindall. Naturalist Thomas Nuttall visited Cadron in March 1819, and observed that the only residents of the town were John McElmurry and his family. Although McElmurry had managed to sell some lots with the help of Richard Menifee (a relative of Jonas), and while the cove at Cadron provided both an excellent harbor and landing—Nuttall concluded that this was not a viable town site since the area's hills and ravines provided "scarcely a hundred yards of level ground."

When Nuttall returned in December, he found four families living in "this imaginary town," although he fails to mention a dozen or so other families living in the larger Cadron settlement. Cadron now had a tavern, which was the cornerstone of a successful frontier town. But Nuttall remained underwhelmed. The tavern was "very ill provided, was consequently crowded with all sorts of company. It contained only two tenantable rooms, built of logs, with hundreds of crevices still left open, not-withstanding the severity of the season." Nuttall went on to grumble that the tavern was a "vortex of swindling and idleness" where the only amusements were dram-drinking, gambling, and horse racing.

Cadron got a big boost in June 1820, when Governor James Miller approved an act of the territorial legislature to move the Pulaski County seat from Arkansas Post to Cadron. The legislature authorized the building of a jail and a courthouse at Cadron, which were not to exceed costs of $1,000 and $400, respectively. Court was held at the Cadron tavern until the courthouse was built. But the courthouse was never begun.

The political climate changed profoundly once Little Rock became the territorial capital. Political momentum built to locate the county seat in Little Rock as well. Since a jail and courthouse had not been built at Cadron within the specified time limit of eight months, the movement to shift the county seat gained more support. The county seat relocated from Cadron to Little Rock in March 1822, and the little town's fortunes continued to decline. The post office moved from Cadron to Point Remove in 1824. A month later, Thomas Tindall and his wife, Sinai, sold their house for $200 and moved in with the David McElmurry family.

Cadron briefly became the seat of the newly created Conway County in 1825, but this was only a temporary measure until an election could be held to select three commissioners who would determine a permanent county seat. All sorts of complications finally required the intervention of the legislature, which established a temporary county seat at Harrisburg. (Lewisburg became the permanent county seat in 1831.)

The loss of the Conway county seat doomed the town of Cadron. Many local families moved to Washington County. After the death of John McElmurry in 1827 and his wife in 1825, their children moved to Monroe County, except for David, who moved to Hardin Township and took in Thomas Tindall and his wife. The bad luck continued when both wives died within six days of each other during the Christmas holidays of 1830.

The sense of doom deepened in 1834, when low water forced a party of emigrating Cherokees ashore at the mouth of Cadron Creek. They camped at the old town site, but then spread out through the woods when a cholera epidemic broke out on April 15. The Indians were already weakened by measles, a poor diet, and the many other hardships encountered on the Trail of Tears. They died in droves.

Lt. Joseph Harris, who was in charge of this party of Cherokees, wrote, "My blood chills even as I write, at the remembrance of the scenes I have gone through today. In the cluster of cedars above the bluff which looks down upon the Creek & river, and near a few tall chimneys—the wreck of a once comfortable tenement, the destroyer has been most busily at work." Headstones and footstones of native rock were used to mark the dozens of graves scattered through the hillsides. A bronze plaque at Cedar Park now lists the names of those who died in the epidemic. It is the final epitaph not only for the Indians who died there, but for the little town of Cadron, which never saw its aspirations fulfilled.

—LITTLE ROCK—

Little Rock lies 31 miles south of Conway, 159 miles southeast of Fort Smith, and 127 miles southwest of West Memphis on I-40, 143 miles northeast of Texarkana on I-30, and 149 miles northwest of the

Louisiana line via US 65. That puts Little Rock in the central portion of the state.

Early French explorers, however, knew this spot was one of the first two rock outcroppings encountered when traveling up the Mississippi and Arkansas Rivers from New Orleans. According to legend, Jean-Baptiste Bernard de La Harpe referred to this landmark as *Le Petit Rocher*—"The Little Rock"—when he passed it in 1722. But there is no written documentation to support this claim. Here at *Le Petit Rocher*, the Ouachita escarpment reaches the south shore of the river, and the terrain changes from the Mississippi alluvial plain to Ouachita highlands. Big Rock (which La Harpe called *Le Rocher Français,* "The French Rock") referred to a large rock formation just upstream from *Le Petit Rocher* on the north shore of the Arkansas. The earliest written appearance of the name "Little Rock" comes from a land deed dated 1814 and recorded in 1821 that refers to "little rocks bluff."

Although French hunters and trappers camped at *Le Petit Rocher* throughout much of the 1700s, the first settlers did not appear until 1806, when John Gozel led seven families to the area from Carolina. Thus, Little Rock may well be the only city in the country that was named a century before the first home was built at the town site.

Two brothers, John and Jacob Pyeatt, settled about twelve miles north of Little Rock at Crystal Hill in 1807. The settlement they founded was called Pyeattstown. Some of the first residents of Pyeattstown included William Lockwood, Rev. John Carnahan, Edmund Hogan, and James Miller (who would later become governor and try to move the capital to Pyeattstown). Jacob Pyeatt moved to a new settlement upriver at the mouth of Cadron Creek in 1815. These settlements were so isolated that they didn't learn about the War of 1812 until three years after the onset of hostilities.

The Early Days of Pulaski County

Pulaski County was one of five counties created by the Missouri legislature in December 1818 back when Arkansas was part of Missouri Territory. The county was named in honor of Count Casimir Pulaski, a Polish nobleman who had participated in a failed revolt against the king of Poland and then escaped via Prussia and Turkey to France. Pulaski joined the American Revolution in 1777, and was commissioned as a brigadier general even though he was only twenty-nine at the time. He fought with distinction, formed a cavalry unit, and was killed during a charge at the Battle of Savannah in 1779.

Upon the formation of Pulaski County, the home of Samuel McHenry served as the temporary county courthouse. Congress split off the southern half of Missouri to form Arkansas Territory in 1819, and

Cadron became the temporary county seat in 1820. The Arkansas legislature appointed a three-man commission to select a permanent county seat in 1821, and Little Rock received this honor in 1822.

Three years later, a printer from Boston named Hiram Whittington wrote home about his visit to Little Rock, giving a fascinating portrait of the community. Little Rock, he wrote,

> is situated on the South bank of the river and contains about 60 buildings—6 brick, 8 frame, and the rest log cabins. The best brick building is the one occupied by the paper [the *Arkansas Gazette*] and is as good a one as you will see in Boston. The Little Rock Academy is in a log hut, and the State House is a little narrow low wooden building about 10 feet by 10 feet. The town has been settled about 8 years and has improved slowly. Instead of streets, we walk from one cow path to another from house to house. The town is inhabited by the dreggs from Kentucky, Georgia and Louisiana, principally Kentucky. It is a famous place for parties. We had a violin and danced all night.

The people of Little Rock devoted considerable energy to their politics as well as their parties. Edmund Hogan, for example, began his political life as one of the county's original five justices of the peace. President Monroe appointed Hogan to be brigadier general of the territorial militia in 1821. Finally, Hogan beat Colonel Alexander Walker and Judge Andrew Scott in an election to the territorial senate in 1827. The victory, however, would be the death of Edmund Hogan. The campaign made Hogan the mortal enemy of Judge Scott, who killed the new senator the following year. Murders, stabbings, and sundry mayhem had become commonplace on the dusty streets of Little Rock by this time. Few individuals ventured about unarmed. The death of Edmund Hogan spawned a crackdown on the violence, and his murderer was executed at the town's first public hanging. The event attracted the largest public gathering in territorial history, and gradually law and order began to take root.

The riverfront town prospered with the growth of steamboat traffic. Local merchants catered to the needs of plantation owners, travelers, and steamboat crews. Freighting companies, mercantiles, and grocery stores took root along the waterfront, but so did cheap hotels, restaurants, saloons, gambling establishments, dance halls, and bordellos. Respectable businesses commonly occupied the ground floors, while less respectable enterprises operated upstairs. Particularly rambunctious areas of the waterfront came to be known as Battle Row, Fighting Alley, and Hell's Half Acre.

The best-known denizen of Battle Row was Kate Merrick, who owned a saloon and dance hall called the Ocean Wave. She also served as den mother for numerous ladies of negotiable virtue who worked the waterfront. When the Ocean Wave burned down in April 1879, the catastrophe sucked the vitality out of Battle Row. By the time railroad tracks cut through the heart of Battle Row a few years later, the patient was nearly dead anyway. The name "Battle Row" quickly disappeared from the community's lexicon, and a colorful period of Little Rock faded into obscurity.

Rough-and-tumble enterprise was not restricted to the riverfront during the heyday of Battle Row and Hell's Half Acre. Yet by 1835, a newcomer named Albert Pike could proclaim "there was not a more peaceable town anywhere than Little Rock." Pike went on assert that "there is no more intelligent, shrewd, sensible, and at the same time, generous and hospitable community in the world." Clearly, a man capable of expounding such bombastry belonged in politics (or the literary field), so it should not be surprising that Pike would figure prominently in the Arkansas political arena in the following decades. He would also write a lot of poetry. The following year—on June 15, 1836—Arkansas achieved statehood, satisfying the aspirations of many Arkansans.

It was hard for black residents to have aspirations, however. Yet, contrary to some reports, slaves could indeed work for wages during their spare time. The main caveat was that, strictly speaking, no white could purchase the handiwork or services of a slave without the owner's consent. Moreover, even free blacks were required by town ordinance to work with slaves on public street projects. Furthermore, free blacks living in the city limits were required to "bind out" their children from the ages of seven to twenty-one. This meant that the parents had to formally hand over their children to become apprentices to tradespeople via a binding contract filed in the county court minutes. It remains unclear, however, how thoroughly these restrictions were actually enforced.

In spite of such heavy-handed laws and the fact that antebellum Arkansas never had more than a few hundred free blacks, white townsfolk and even the *Arkansas Gazette* viewed free blacks in Little Rock as the town's greatest nuisance. The unstated logic behind such views was that the very existence of free blacks was a threat to slavery. Free blacks defied the planters' assertion that blacks were incapable of living independently and, therefore, needed masters to feed and clothe them. This intolerance would eventually grow to the point that virtually all free blacks had left Little Rock by the end of the antebellum era. Yet at least one free black managed to prosper and earn many friends within the white community of Little Rock.

Nathan Warren

Born in 1812 in Maryland, Nathan Warren came to Little Rock in 1834 as a slave of Robert Crittenden. Although some accounts claim that the Crittenden family freed Warren, Warren's descendents believe that he bought his own freedom. In either event, Nathan Warren became a free man sometime between 1834 and 1840. He married a slave named Anne, who was the cook for one of the wealthiest men in Arkansas, Chester Ashley. Anne already had a son when she married Nathan. Because the status of a black child was determined by the mother's status, the nine children Nathan and Anne had together became slaves owned by the Ashley family.

Nathan Warren was a talented man who worked very hard to amass enough money to begin buying the freedom of family members. He became Little Rock's confectioner, when the town's previous candy maker—Henry Jackson, who was also a freed slave—invented a cookstove that proved to be much more profitable than making candy. Warren took over the two-story frame building that housed the confectionery, and soon had the community eating out of his hand. He was especially famous for his tea cakes, and he also provided a wide range of delicacies for weddings. Warren was also a gifted fiddler who was always in demand for social events of all sort.

A man of tremendous industry, Nathan Warren also worked as a barber, handyman, and carriage driver. By 1842, he owned three lots in Little Rock. More importantly, he and his free brother Henry (who worked in Washington, D.C.) were able to pool their resources and buy the freedom of another brother, James, from Timothy Crittenden and his brothers, although the complex negotiations took from 1844 to 1850.

In spite of Warren's growing success, Little Rock was not a hospitable environment for free blacks, and Arkansas was becoming less congenial by the day. The confectionery suffered a serious fire just after midnight on March 19, 1852. Warren was convinced the fire was caused by arson, but the *Arkansas Gazette* reported that it was either accidental or caused by carelessness.

When Nathan's wife, Anne, died, he married Mary Elizabeth, who was another Ashley slave. Their daughter Ida May was born a free person in 1856 because Nathan had purchased his wife's freedom some months earlier. As part of the deal, Mary Ashley also threw in Nathan's seventeen-year-old daughter, Elizabeth, who had been born to his previous wife. This was not particularly magnanimous on Ashley's part, since the girl was sickly, half blind, and not expected to live much longer.

The *Arkansas Gazette* and other newspapers in the state were publishing a torrent of editorials urging the legislature to evict free blacks from the state. The writing, as they say, was on the wall. So Nathan Warren left Arkansas about a year before the legislature passed a law on February 12, 1859, requiring that all free blacks either leave the state or become slaves once again.

Nathan and Mary returned to Little Rock after the war and established their home at 1012 Ringo. Warren reopened his confectionery, which was quite popular but not popular enough to provide a steady income. To make ends meet, he worked as a grocer and baker. By 1873, he was operating a fruit stand. He worked at the confectionery owned by Francis Ditter in 1878, and opened a new candy shop with business partner W. C. Gibbons in 1880. By 1881, the partnership had dissolved and Warren continued the enterprise alone at the same location.

Neither Nathan nor his children held any government office during Reconstruction, but other relatives did. Hugh Newsome, who married Nathan's daughter Ella, became the city marshal of Little Rock. Another son-in-law, A. L. Richie, was alderman from Little Rock's third ward in 1872 and a member of the school board in 1873. W. A. Rector, who was the son of Nathan's first wife, served as a city collector, city marshal, and constable of Big Rock Township. Nathan himself was ordained an elder in the African Methodist Episcopal Church in 1882, and he went on to serve as the pastor at the Bethel A.M.E. church at Ninth and Broadway in Little Rock.

It seems that everyone in Little Rock knew Nathan Warren. All the blacks in town addressed him as "Father Warren," and the whites called him "Uncle Nase." He was widely respected and widely loved. Nathan Warren had come a long way from his roots in antebellum Little Rock.

Antebellum Little Rock

Little Rock's future seemed bright for most of the town's 2,167 citizens in 1840. Little Rock was one of the largest communities west of the Mississippi. While St. Louis and New Orleans were much larger, Memphis only had 268 more residents than Little Rock. Houston had less than half the population. More importantly, Little Rock appeared to have the perfect location to capitalize on the anticipated western expansion. The community straddled both the Southwest Trail from St. Louis to the Southwest and the trail to California that ran from Memphis through Ft. Smith. Furthermore, the great westward push would have to depend heavily on the Mississippi River and its tributaries (referred to as the trans-Mississippi), so the Arkansas River provided a westward access not afforded by the larger cities on the Mississippi.

This westward focus gave the Little Rock of this period a more western than southern character. Somehow the concerns of plantation owners on the alluvial plains of Arkansas seemed remote to the residents of this town perched in the foothills of the Ouachita Mountains. People in Little Rock tended to be Whigs rather than Democrats. They viewed their economic future in terms of building Little Rock's role as a transportation and industrial center. Part of the plan worked, and part of it didn't.

While Little Rock certainly attracted a number of skilled artisans, the town never did attract much industry. By 1860, the community only supported fourteen manufacturers, which employed a mere seventy-three people. These fourteen companies included a foundry, a furniture company, a slate quarry, and a lead mine. Little Rock did, however, manage to grow as a transportation center.

In 1830, the town was lucky to see one steamboat per week. By 1858, about ten boats per week brought goods into Little Rock and loaded up Arkansas's two exports: cotton and corn. Furthermore, riverboats had become much larger and much more luxurious, so their economic impact far exceeded the number of boats making the trip. Nevertheless, the best boats avoided the treacherous Arkansas River. Insurance rates for boats were higher on the Arkansas than on any western waterway except the Red River. Pilots demanded more money, too. The solution was to employ somewhat smaller and cheaper steamboats, and to increase freight rates to a profitable level. Imported goods were expensive but available in quantity, and the Little Rock economy prospered.

Unfortunately, attempts to truly diversify the town's economy largely failed. Part of the problem was the lack of suitable banks. Another factor was the rampant fraud and skulduggery that plagued the financial life of the community. For example, Little Rock Mayor Samuel Trowbridge was arrested for counterfeiting in 1842. And the two banks chartered by the legislature upon statehood—the Arkansas State Bank and the Arkansas Real Estate Bank—collapsed and closed their doors in the mid-1840s. Private bankers tried to fill the void without any real success, so Little Rock never did experience the economic boom it wanted.

Nevertheless, Little Rock grew steadily to a population of 3,727 in 1860. Residents viewed their home as a successful, modern town that could boast of a "free" school (open to white male students), the Little Rock High School for Girls, St. Mary's Academy, St. John's College, gas lights, and an improved street program. A telegraph was even in the works. But political events were about to overtake the economic and cultural life of the community.

As political rhetoric heated up throughout the land and regional views became more polarized after the election of Lincoln to the presidency, Little Rock was hardly a hotbed of secessionist fervor—even after South Carolina left the Union in December of 1860 and Mississippi, Florida, and Alabama followed suit in January 1861. Georgia, Texas, and Louisiana seceded, but the residents of Little Rock tended to keep their high regard for the Union, although the *Arkansas Gazette*'s support began to cool in March.

Yet support for secession had been developing slowly in Arkansas, as evidenced by the appearance of a secessionist newspaper, *The Southern States*, in mid-December 1860. This Little Rock paper issued a barrage of attacks on the evils of Unionism. Emissaries from states that had already seceded arrived to extoll the benefits Arkansas would reap from leaving the Union. Harried legislators decided to avoid the problem by calling for a popular election on February 18 to determine if a convention should be held to decide if Arkansas should secede from the Union.

A group of ardent secessionists did not wait for the February election. They armed themselves and marched on the U.S. Army Arsenal in Little Rock. Captain James Totten surrendered the arsenal without a shot to avoid bloodshed. He was allowed to leave town with his sixty-five men, and the separatists secured the arsenal's valuable supply of weapons and munitions.

The February election authorized the convention, which began on March 4, the very day Lincoln was sworn in as president. After two weeks of debate, the delegates decided to stay in the Union by a vote of thirty-nine to thirty-five. That pro-Union sentiment changed abruptly when the U.S. Navy tried to reinforce Fort Sumter in the mouth of Charleston Harbor, and South Carolina forces fired on the ship. In April, Lincoln declared that an insurrection was under way and called for volunteers to put down the rebellion, essentially declaring war on the secessionist states. Arkansas Governor Henry Rector refused to provide Lincoln with volunteers.

This changed the issue completely for most Arkansans. Slavery was no longer relevant to the debate. With war visited upon the people of Arkansas, the issue became which side to fight on. Judge David Walker reconvened the delegates in Little Rock on May 6, 1861. The family roots of most participants reached back to places like Kentucky and Tennessee, so it should not be surprising that, after several hours of debate, all but five delegates voted to join the Confederacy. Walker called for a second ballot to make the vote unanimous.

Only one man, Isaac Murphy, voted to remain in the Union. While Murphy outraged his fellow delegates, Mrs. Frederick Trapnall of Little Rock tossed him a bouquet of flowers from the upstairs gallery to show her admiration for his courage.

War Comes to Little Rock

The residents of Little Rock believed they were quite safe from Federal attack immediately after Arkansas seceded from the Union. The state was surrounded on three sides by Confederate states, and the chronically low water of the Arkansas River would stop Federal gunboats from reaching Little Rock more effectively than the ample batteries of Vicksburg. Any invasion would likely come from Indian Territory (now called Oklahoma). But the Indians viewed the bloodless capture of the Little Rock arsenal as a sign of Federal weakness, so they sided with the Confederacy and protected the state's western flank. Arkansas in general, and Little Rock in particular, seemed safe from attack by the Federals. The year 1861 ended without any fighting on Arkansas soil, and some folks feared that the war would be over before they got a chance to participate. They need not have worried on that account.

General Thomas C. Hindman. −Arkansas History Commission

More perceptive residents began to note with alarm that the Confederate government was stripping the state of men and materiel for the eastern front, making Arkansas increasingly vulnerable to attack. Memphis and New Orleans fell to the Federals in 1862, and the nightmare began for Arkansas. Incompetent military leaders who had bungled their assignments in Virginia were transferred to Arkansas, where they did little to bolster confidence or improve the state's defenses. Generals such as Thomas Hindman and Theophilus Holmes were subjected to daily ridicule by newspaper editors and common citizens alike, particularly in Little Rock, which served as the headquarters of the Trans-Mississippi forces. One newspaper editor published a long and caustic condemnation of Holmes, concluding "In justice, we must add, that Gen. Holmes is a man of most excellent heart, kind disposition and a gentleman in all things, and it is not his fault that he is not a General."

At first, the town emptied out as its men rushed off to fight in the East. By the middle of 1862, so many refugees and drifters and unassigned Confederate officers had appeared in Little Rock that housing was scarce indeed. One wag observed that no town could possibly have more generals than Little Rock and went on to suggest that the Confederacy should raise a regiment of captains for The Cause from the unassigned officers in the community. Meanwhile, the Union blockade of the Mississippi strangled commerce and the availability of supplies. A Texan soldier wrote that by December 1862, there was not a single egg or pint of whiskey left in the city. Everyone assumed it was only a matter of time before Federal gunboats steamed up the Arkansas River.

The first blow came in January, when Union General John McClernand temporarily diverted his forces from Vicksburg to attack Arkansas Post, which lay on the Arkansas River about fifty miles upstream from its confluence with the Mississippi. After taking Arkansas Post, he intended to steam upriver to Little Rock, but low water foiled his plan, so McClernand returned to continue his siege of Vicksburg.

The residents of Little Rock took heart when the widely admired General E. Kirby Smith replaced Theophilus Holmes as the commander of the Trans-Mississippi Department. Spirits sank to a new low when Kirby Smith abruptly moved his headquarters to Alexandria, Louisiana. Little Rock's fate now became married to the fate of Vicksburg.

Vicksburg fell in July 1863, and Ulysses S. Grant assigned Major General Frederick Steele the task of leading the campaign to seize Little Rock. Ironically, the chain of command for this Federal campaign remained rather muddy, and Steele found himself subject to the conflicting demands of three different superiors. Furthermore, Steele had no idea if Kirby Smith would use his full resources to defend the city, or whether the defense would be left to local Arkansas troops already in place. This allowed Confederate Major General Sterling Price time to gather about 8,000 troops from eastern Arkansas to defend Little Rock before the Federal juggernaut began grinding its way toward the state capital. Fort Smith to the north and Monroe, Louisiana, to the south fell to the Federals, which certainly undermined the long-term ability of the Confederates to hold Little Rock.

Resistance to the advancing Federals stiffened about twenty miles south of the city, but Steele's columns nevertheless began to approach the outskirts of Little Rock on September 10. Union cavalry swept aside resistance along the river, forcing General Price to vacate his remaining defensive positions in the city. The Federals fully occupied Little Rock by nightfall and immediately began reinforcing the extensive fortifications just abandoned by the Confederates. Steele then established garrisons at key points along the river. These measures kept the Confederates from attempting to retake their former capital.

Steele's troops occupied empty homes and public buildings, and the Federal occupation began to stimulate the local economy. Some

This 1910 painting by Stanley M. Arthurs shows Federal troops entering Little Rock in 1863. –UCA Archives

commercial goods once again appeared on merchants' shelves. The town adapted quickly to Federal control, thanks in large measure to Steele's conciliatory policy toward the residents. For example, Steele immediately brought in sutlers (contractors who supplied the military) to feed the city's hungry population. Then he brought in skilled hospital personnel to relieve the exhausted local ladies who had been tending Confederate and Union wounded for months. Any former secessionist who would swear an oath of allegiance received a full and immediate pardon, which alienated those hard-liners who had steadfastly (if quietly) supported the Union even when the Confederates ruled Little Rock. These hard-liners launched a vociferous campaign against Frederick Steele and his conciliatory policies.

Steele then lost the moral high ground as far as many folks were concerned with the death of a young lad named David Owen Dodd.

The "Boy Hero" of Arkansas

David Dodd was born in Victoria, Texas, in 1846 and moved with his parents and two sisters to Benton in 1858. The family moved to Little Rock in late 1861 or early 1862, where David enrolled at St. John's Masonic College until malaria forced him to discontinue his studies. He went to work at a local telegraph office until his father, Andrew, took a job in Monroe, Louisiana. David tagged along and worked part time at the telegraph office, where he was sometimes left in charge. But business was slow. The lad became bored and then homesick. He missed his family and friends in Arkansas.

When Andrew Dodd was hired as the sutler servicing the 3rd Arkansas Infantry, then stationed in Mississippi, David joined his father in Jackson. Andrew Dodd went on extensive buying trips through Alabama, Mississippi, and Louisiana, and relied on his son to sell his merchandise to the Arkansas soldiers. After the fall of Little Rock to Union troops, Andrew asked David to retrieve the family and bring them to Mississippi.

David collected his mother and sisters, and took them by train to DeValls Bluff, where they boarded a riverboat. They were harassed and insulted by Federals on the boat, so Mrs. Dodd demanded that her family be immediately put ashore, and the group returned to Little Rock. David's father somehow managed to reach Little Rock himself sometime around December 1, and took his family to Camden by wagon. But in his haste, he had left unfinished business in Little Rock. Andrew Dodd asked David to return and conclude his affairs. The timing of the request suited David, for the trip would give him the opportunity to visit friends in Little Rock for the Christmas holidays.

But David would need a fair amount of paperwork to make the trip. His father gave him a handwritten birth certificate to demonstrate that he was not old enough for military service and took him to the Confederate headquarters at Princeton (just outside of Camden) to obtain a travel pass. There Major General James Fagan apparently asked the young man to bring back information on the Union troops in Little Rock. Finally, Andrew gave his son several letters to people who might like to send funds via David if they wished to invest in tobacco. With these documents in hand, David rode to Little Rock, arriving Christmas Eve.

David attended parties, went for walks with lady friends, and concluded his father's business. He departed for Camden on the morning of December 29, stopping his mule at St. John's College to obtain a Federal travel pass from the Union provost marshal. Dodd showed the pass to the Federal guard at the city limits and again at a checkpoint eight miles out of town. Private Daniel Olderburg asked Dodd where he was going and how he was going there. Because the entire route was through Confederate territory, Olderburg told Dodd he didn't need the Union pass anymore, and the bluecoat tore up the document.

Unfortunately, the young traveler decided on the spur of the moment to visit his uncle, Washington Dodd, who lived eighteen miles from Little Rock. That decision would be the death of David O. Dodd.

When David left his uncle's home the next morning, he took a shortcut that crossed the road to Benton, which placed him back in Union territory. As soon as his mule walked onto the Benton road, Dodd was challenged by a mounted Union picket. The odd direction of Dodd's travel made it appear that the lad was attempting to cross the Union lines en route to Camden. This aroused the suspicion of the detachment's commander, who arrested Dodd when he could not produce a Union travel pass. The prisoner was immediately transported to regimental headquarters, where his memorandum book was discovered to contain mysterious markings. The markings turned out to be the numbers and disposition of Federal forces in Little Rock, written down in Morse code.

Dodd was formally charged with spying. A Union court-martial convened on December 31. After a trial lasting several days, the court convicted David Dodd and sentenced him to death.

Many friends of the Dodd family appealed to General Steele for clemency because David Dodd was so young. But as far as Steele was concerned, the court-martial had found the lad guilty, and he would have to pay the price. Furthermore, a lot of seventeen-year-olds were fighting in both the Union and Confederate armies, so requesting leniency on the basis of age was a weak argument. There is credible evidence that Steele did offer to free Dodd if he would name the person who gave him the list to carry back to Camden, but the boy refused.

On January 8, 1864, David Dodd wrote a farewell letter to his family just before he was brought to the gallows, seated on a coffin in the back of a wagon. The execution took place in front of St. John's College, just east of the arsenal grounds that are now known as MacArthur Park. About 6,000 military and civilian spectators had gathered, filling the yard and nearby trees. Union infantry surrounded the scaffold on three sides. Cavalry—five deep—formed the fourth side.

The wagon backed under the noose. A young Union orderly used a telescope to view the execution from the college's north tower. "I turned my glass upon the man seated upon his coffin," Charles Lake wrote home in a letter. "His countenance was a little pale—but perfectly composed. The condemned cast his eyes to the rope and seemed perfectly composed and indifferent. He sat looking at the crowd, just as calm as could be." The hangman told David to stand on the tailboard of the wagon, where he bound David's wrists and ankles. The executioner had forgotten to bring a blindfold, so the prisoner told him, "Sir, you will find a handkerchief in my coat." Those were David Dodd's last words.

The hangman was not very competent. The weight of David's body stretched the rope until his toes touched the ground. Instead of instant death from a broken neck, David slowly strangled over the course of several minutes. His body was cut down and taken under heavy guard to Barney Knighton's house at Sixth and Rock Streets, the severed rope still around his neck. He was buried the following day in Little Rock's Mount Holly Cemetery. General Steele only allowed two civilians to attend the funeral, which further alienated many Arkansans.

David's father held General Steele personally responsible for the death of his son. In a long, terribly bitter and articulate letter to the *Des Arc Citizen*, Andrew Dodd concluded, "I leave it to an impartial public to say who was most disgraced, the boy who died for his principles or the General who murdered him."

Although a flurry of newspaper articles flayed Steele alive, there was no general uprising of Little Rock citizens. No one marched in protest to Steele's headquarters after the execution. Many were clearly and vociferously outraged, but folks had grown bone-weary of the war. They were coming to terms with the hopelessness of the Cause. They mourned David Dodd, but they realized he was simply one among a host of casualties who steadily filled the cemeteries of Arkansas.

David O. Dodd, executed by Union troops while a teenage civilian, became the most famous hero in Arkansas during the Civil War. –Arkansas History Commission

After the execution of Dodd, the Federals turned their attention to their spring offensive, which would come to be known as the Red River Campaign (see Part 2). Steele marched southward from Little Rock with his 9,000-man army on March 23, and Brigadier General John M. Thayer left Fort Smith on the same day with his 5,000-man Frontier Division. Steele's objective was Camden, the second largest community in Arkansas and the most formidable Confederate stonghold in southern Arkansas at that time. Although Steele did capture Camden, a series of bloody engagements and a critical shortage of supplies eventually forced his retreat back to Little Rock.

The failure of Steele's offensive, combined with his pro-Union, hardline critics in Little Rock, sealed the general's fate in Arkansas. Steele was transferred out of the state. Friends of the general would later relate that the execution of David Dodd preyed upon his mind on a daily basis until Steele's death, not long after the war ended.

Although Steele had been the archenemy of Confederate Arkansas, subsequent events would prove that he had been the genuine friend of occupied Little Rock. Steele's replacement, General J. J. Reynolds, would rule with both a lack of skill and an iron fist. Life in Little Rock became rather grim.

Black refugees streamed into the city to secure their status as "freedmen," and white refugees appeared in great numbers to escape starvation and the depredation of Southern partisans. There simply wasn't enough food for everyone, so General Reynolds shipped about 2,000 refugees out of Arkansas during the first three months of 1865. This eviction still left far too many destitute people for the city's resources. Local citizens were impressed into forced labor by the Union commander. Confederate deserters began to appear in numbers. Everyone was hungry. And the pervasive gloom deepened with the news of Lincoln's death.

As bleak as things were, the ravages of war had never really been visited upon Little Rock, despite the fact that 2,073 Union and 2,062 Confederate dead lay in local cemeteries (more people than the population of Little Rock in 1860). The town had not suffered the ravages

Mustered-out Union Negro volunteers at Little Rock in 1866. –UCA Archives

of siege and bombardment, fighting in the streets, or the wanton depredation inflicted by Jayhawkers and Bushwhackers throughout vast stretches of Arkansas.

Little Rock did, however, experience a dramatic ethnic change. Blacks accounted for 23 percent of the town's population in 1860 and 43 percent of the population in 1865. Furthermore, many Union troops remained in Little Rock after they mustered out of service, adding to the community's diversity. While a lot of private property remained in Federal hands after the war, Little Rock seemed to be remarkably well poised to rebuild and return to normalcy. Although Reconstruction was a traumatic time in Little Rock, the town's collective experience was probably typical of similar communities throughout the South.

The events that brought the postwar era to a close in Little Rock, however, were remarkable. In a curious twist of fate, Reconstruction would die in a struggle between two of the state's most ardent reconstructionists, Elisha Baxter and Joseph Brooks.

The Brooks-Baxter War

Many problems argued for political change with the dawn of the 1870s. Back in 1867, Brevet Major General E. O. C. Ord, commander of the Fourth Military District, directed Governor Isaac Murphy to inform Arkansas legislators that their plan to reconvene would violate the Voter Registration Act recently passed by Congress. Having eliminated the Arkansas legislature, Ord began to transform Arkansas government on a large scale. The cornerstone of his efforts was the voter registration drive of 1867. Officials could deny registration to anyone who publicly supported the Confederacy, whether or not they actually bore arms in the process. Some Democrats boycotted the registration drive because they felt the process was clearly unconstitutional. The net result was that about 25,000 people remained disenfranchised when their neighbors voted for or against holding a constitutional convention in 1868. Another problem arguing for political change with the dawn of a new decade included oppressive taxes, which had risen by more than 1,000 percent. Furthermore, political incompetence and corruption within the Republican government, as well as outright fraud, had generated runaway government debt. Then, in 1868, cotton prices fell to less than half their previous level. The future promised little but grief to many people in Arkansas.

Divisions began to appear within the Republican ranks when the Republican-controlled assembly elected Governor Powell Clayton to the U.S. Senate in 1869. With the departure of Clayton, who had been a brigadier general in the Union army during the war, O. A. Hadley

Powell Clayton.
—Arkansas History
Commission

became the governor until the 1872 election. Political change became possible in 1872 because Congress passed the Amnesty Act, which restored voting rights to disenfranchised whites throughout the South.

Clayton and his followers threw their support in the gubernatorial election to Elisha Baxter of Batesville, who had been a staunch supporter of the Union before and during the war, and a committed backer of Reconstruction after the war. A reform-minded faction within the Republican Party backed Joseph Brooks, a Methodist minister who came to Arkansas as the chaplain of a black Union regiment. Although anti-reconstruction Democrats had begun to build their political power base, they could not field a serious gubernatorial candidate. So the Democrats supported the reform-minded Brooks, who had made a name for himself prosecuting Senator Clayton and Congressman Edwards for election fraud.

The results of the November election were so close that both Brooks and Baxter claimed victory, each accusing the other of election fraud.

Elisha Baxter.
—J. N. Heiskell Collection,
UALR Library Archives

A detailed analysis of the balloting published by the *Daily Republican* in December said that Baxter beat Brooks by an official count of 41,681 to 38,415. But Brooks and his supporters still asserted that systematic fraud—namely the disenfranchisement of qualified voters by election officials (who were all Clayton's men)—had altered the outcome of the election. The most glaring example of election tampering occurred when these officials threw out the ballots from four counties undoubtedly carried by Brooks. Analysis by Brooks supporters determined that he should have won the election by 1,500 votes, instead of losing by 3,000 votes.

Tensions mounted steadily as Arkansans awaited the convening of the legislature on January 6, 1873. Governor Hadley became so worried about rumors that Brooks might try to establish a rival state government by force of arms, that he called out the state militia to preserve the peace. John McClure, the editor of the *Daily Republican* and chief justice of the state supreme court, presided over the legislature as it deliberated the outcome of the November election. The legislature certified Baxter's victory, and McClure promptly administered the oath of office.

Joseph Brooks sought redress in the courts, and Governor Baxter tried to strengthen his position by courting the state's Democrats. He appointed Democrats to public office and awarded the lucrative state printing contract to the Democratic newspaper, the *Arkansas Gazette*. Such actions, along with Baxter's opposition to an expensive bill to support the railroads, alienated many hard-line Republicans, who began to think that perhaps Brooks should be declared the legitimate governor of Arkansas.

Events came to a head in April 1874, when a Pulaski County court determined that Joseph Brooks was the legal governor of Arkansas. Brooks immediately raised a band of armed supporters and marched on the statehouse, where they threw Baxter out. The Brooks-Baxter War had begun.

Elisha Baxter retreated a few blocks down the street to the Anthony House (a well-known hotel of the day), where he began to raise

The 1874 Brooks-Baxter War in Little Rock, from a painting by C. Kendric. –UCA Archives

and arm his own volunteers. Brooks barricaded the grounds of the legislature and began to strengthen his defensive fortifications. Soon each of the opposing armies had swollen to about 2,000 men. Each commander continued to claim he was the rightful governor of Arkansas and asked government officials to declare their support. Little Rock's postmaster artfully dodged such requests by holding all mail addressed to the governor until the issue was settled once and for all. Remarkably, Powell Clayton threw his support to Brooks. However, many of the best legal minds in Arkansas supported Baxter, including Augustus Hill Garland, who would later become governor himself.

Skirmishes between the opposing armies inevitably followed over the next month, but a full-scale civil war never did develop. Nevertheless, bloody clashes in Little Rock, Pine Bluff, and along the Arkansas River left hundreds dead. Most Arkansans had the same opinion as W. H. Furbish, the black sheriff of Lee County. He sent a telegram to President Ulysses S. Grant that said, "We do not care . . . who is governor; all we want is peace. The people will obey. Answer."

Grant answered that Baxter was the rightful governor of Arkansas, and a Congressional review later concurred with that decision. The

An engraving from Frank Leslie's Illustrated Newspaper *(May 2, 1874). The caption read: "The Baxter-Brooks imbroglio—the capitol building at Little Rock defended by the troops of Pseudo-Governor Brooks"* –UALR Library Archives

This political cartoon from Harper's Weekly *(May 14, 1874) entitled "A plague o' both your houses!" suggests that not all Arkansans joined one of the factions in the Brooks-Baxter War.* —UALR Library Archives

Brooks-Baxter War and Reconstruction were over. Reconstruction had burdened the state to the point that a new constitution was developed during the summer of 1874 to reduce the power of the governor, to fill key government offices by election rather than appointment, to limit the growth of taxes, and to take other measures to avoid the problems of the past. While this document has seen many subsequent changes, the 1874 constitution is still the law that governs Arkansas.

Little Rock's economy gradually began to improve somewhat throughout the remainder of the decade, and a small but successful black middle class began to emerge. The last two decades of the nineteenth century would see Little Rock prosper in a big way, thanks in part to the burgeoning railroad service connecting the community to the rest of the country. The population would triple, and the growing economy would bestow upon the residents of Little Rock the fruits of the Industrial Revolution.

This may have been a time of progress in Little Rock, but it was a time of hardship for the 90 percent of the state's population who lived on farms. Cotton was the dominant cash crop throughout Arkansas. While the price of cotton had been 25 cents per pound in 1860, the price fell to a mere 5 cents by the mid-1890s thanks to a glut of the world market. It cost most farmers more than 5 cents a pound to produce cotton, so many Arkansans faced financial disaster. The falling price prompted farmers to organize and become politically active. The net result of this activity was a set of laws in Arkansas and other southern states that disenfranchised blacks and thus removed their political power. These so-called Jim Crow laws ushered in an era of social segregation that would last until the civil rights movement of the 1960s.

Black society responded by establishing fraternal and self-help societies, schools, churches, and small businesses. The life of one black veteran of the Brooks-Baxter War provides an interesting insight into this important chapter of Little Rock history. The name will be familiar to the residents of Pulaski County, even if they have no idea who the man was, since Gillam Park and Gillam School were named after his family.

Isaac T. Gillam

Isaac Gillam was born in Hardin County, Tennessee, about 1839 and probably came to Arkansas as a slave with his mother when he was eight years old. He appeared in Little Rock three days after the Federals captured the city in 1863, and he immediately enlisted in the 2nd Arkansas Infantry, African Descent. Because Gillam displayed leadership potential and perhaps some education, he eventually rose to the rank of sergeant. After mustering out of the army three years later as a first sergeant, Gillam settled in Little Rock and soon married Cora Alice McCarrall.

They started what would become a large family. Gillam became a blacksmith to support them, since this was one of the few skilled trades that was wide open to blacks at that time. Gillam also raised horses as a profitable sideline, and he occasionally worked as a policeman and a guard at the Little Rock jail. His hard work enabled him to purchase a comfortable home in a good neighborhood and serve on the board of trustees for the Bethel African Methodist Episcopal Church, which played a prestigious role in the life of the emerging black middle class. Gillam also was active in the Masons (not to be confused with the white organization), which was one of several important fraternal organizations of the day.

While blacks were active in Arkansas politics for the twenty-five years following the Civil War, Isaac Gillam entered the political arena with a flair that was all his own. He must have been active politically by 1872 when he was a jailer, since this job was awarded in those days on the basis of political patronage. The job of policeman was also a political appointment.

Isaac T. Gillam, circa 1900. He served as a state legislator, Little Rock city councilman, and Pulaski County coroner. –UCA Archives

Two years later when the Brooks-Baxter War erupted, Gillam sided with Brooks and was given a rank of captain in the militia. The end of the Brooks-Baxter War and Reconstruction by no means heralded the end of active black participation in Arkansas politics. Gillam won election to the Little Rock City Council in 1877 as a Republican. Mayor John Gould Fletcher was a Democrat, yet he thought enough of Gillam to appoint him to the important Ways-and-Means Committee.

As Isaac Gillam's political goals evolved, he developed the habit of changing party affiliation. He ran for the state house as a member of the Greenbacker Party, which swept the election that year in Little Rock. Gillam served simultaneously as a city alderman and a state representative until the next election, when he lost his reelection bid for the city council. In 1882, Gillam switched to the Democratic Party to run for Pulaski County coroner, and he won that election. Two years later, Gillam jumped to the Populist Party in a bid to be reelected coroner, but he lost. While this defeat ended Gillam's political career, it did not end his political involvement, which eventually included a return to the Republican Party.

Isaac and Cora Gillam instilled in their children a respect for education and community involvement. Matthew became a minister. William became a musician. Cora taught at Shorter College in North Little Rock. Mary taught in local elementary schools and eventually became a principal. Isaac Gillam Jr. graduated from Howard University and went on to further his education at Yale University, the University of Chicago, and the University of Cincinnati. He returned to Arkansas and served as the principal of Gibbs High School for more than fifty years. The Gillams contributed a great deal to Little Rock through the years of political turmoil, disenfranchisement, and segregation.

Isaac Gillam Jr. would also help Dr. J. M. Robinson and several other leaders in the state establish the Arkansas Negro Democratic Voters Association in the 1940s. This primed the pump for an outpouring of political change that would wash over Arkansas in the 1950s and 1960s. Little Rock would again provide the stage for a great political drama.

The Road from Central High to Winrock Farm

To set the stage, it is necessary to develop a feel for life in Little Rock in the early 1950s. While black and white residents still pretty much kept apart, segregation was beginning to weaken. The important stores in Little Rock removed the "white" and "colored" signs from their drinking fountains. The Rock Island Railroad stopped seating passengers based on race. But segregation was still the law of the land.

The aspect of segregation that irritated the black residents of Little Rock most was not the fact that black and white schools were separate. The real problem was that the black schools were by no means equal. The biracial Little Rock Council on Education concluded that the only workable way to achieve an equally good education for black children was to integrate local schools. Other groups in other places started to come to the same conclusion, and lawsuits began to challenge the legitimacy of segregated school systems.

A number of these suits reached the U.S. Supreme Court, which combined them as *Brown vs. the Topeka Board of Education*. The court ruled in 1954 that the current system did not provide all children with equal educational opportunities, and the next year ruled that the country's school districts had to integrate with "all deliberate speed." Within ten days of the ruling, the Little Rock school board passed a plan to integrate local schools gradually. But the plan had major flaws. It only focussed on Central High in a lower income part of the city, and it ignored the wealthier western part of the city. Furthermore, the black community objected that plan was too slow and too limited in scope.

Unfortunately, the politics of the coming gubernatorial election transcended the immediate issue of segregation. Governor Orval Faubus, who had a moderate-to-liberal record on race relations, became concerned at the growing political activism and power being wielded by segregationists during his 1956 reelection campaign against Jim Johnson. Faubus concluded that he needed the backing of the segregationists to win the election. He pledged to support them if they would back his proposal for a tax increase to improve education and social services. The tactic worked; Faubus won another term in office.

In the fall of 1957, the school board went ahead with its original plan to admit nine black students to Central High. Claiming (without any evidence whatsoever) that both black and white students had guns, Faubus ordered the Arkansas National Guard to surround Central High on September 1, the day before classes were scheduled to

Governor Orval Faubus.
—UCA Archives

254

open. The soldiers had orders to keep the nine black students out of the school.

Eight of the students tried to enter the school by a side door on September 4 and were turned back by a guardsman. The ninth student, Elizabeth Eckford, never learned that the rest of the students had gathered into a group for the attempt. So she came to school by herself and walked right up to the front door, where a guardsman barred her way.

Clutching her books in her arms, fighting back tears, she walked back to the bus stop through a block-long mob of a thousand angry whites who screamed abuse at her. She held her head high as she marched through that terrible gauntlet, and photos of her ordeal appeared throughout the country in a matter of hours. The photos shocked America. The courage of a frightened teenage girl in a very real sense began to change white attitudes throughout the land toward civil rights.

A federal court ordered Governor Faubus to withdraw the guardsmen from Central High, and he complied. President Dwight Eisenhower assumed command of the National Guard and sent units from the U.S. Army's 101st Airborne Division into Little Rock to uphold the authority of the federal court. Paratroopers escorted the "Little Rock Nine" to school. Some white students were helpful to the new black students, others were confrontational, and most simply ignored the Little Rock Nine. It was not a graceful beginning to desegregation. But it was a beginning, nonetheless.

Support for civil rights finally became politically acceptable among a broad spectrum of white politicians when Winthrop Rockefeller beat Jim Johnson in the gubernatorial race of 1966. Rockefeller became the first Republican governor since Reconstruction. In a sense, this election was the natural conclusion to Rockefeller's falling out with Orval Faubus and Jim Johnson over the Central High issue a decade earlier.

Rockefeller brought Arkansas politics into the modern era with a media blitz that was fueled by a lot of money, informed by polls, and organized with computers. The owner of Winrock Farms near Morrilton, this transplanted easterner traversed the state trying to be one of the boys. Rockefeller never developed the ability to relax on public occasions, but he did manage to convey a powerful sense of personal integrity. He also took the unprecedented step of directly appealing to the growing number of black voters for their support.

Jim Johnson, on the other hand, ignored black voters. He devoted his energies to personal attacks on Rockefeller, damning him for divorcing his first wife and for his drinking, and casting aspersions on

the man because of his wealth. It is not clear whether the electorate voted *for* Rockefeller or *against* Johnson, but perhaps that doesn't matter.

Rockefeller tried his best to reform government. He attacked organized crime and political corruption. But the heavily Democratic legislature resisted the Republican governor at almost every turn. He did manage to secure a minimum wage law and a so-called "sunshine law" which exposed the conduct of state business to public view. He also used existing statutes to reform the state's prison system and clean up the corruption then rampant in Hot Springs. But most of all, he empowered the black electorate. They mattered, and politicians would never again ignore their concerns. That's not a bad legacy for any politician.

It can be argued that Winthrop Rockefeller brought Arkansas politics into the twentieth century. It can also be argued that Bill Clinton brought Arkansas politics onto the national stage, when the forty-second governor of Arkansas became the forty-second president of the United States.

The Making of a President

Born in Hope and raised in Hot Springs, Bill Clinton entered politics at an early age. After the former Rhodes Scholar served as attorney general, he ran in the 1978 gubernatorial election. At the age of thirty-two, Clinton became the youngest governor in the land and began to work on improving the state's education, highways, and industry.

Clinton lost his 1980 bid for reelection, however. Political pundits cite a host of problems that irritated the Arkansas voters and stimulated a more conservative mood among the electorate. The license fees for cars and pickups increased dramatically to finance his highways program, whereas the licenses for the commercial trucking industry did not go up much at all. Thus, average voters believed they were shouldering an extremely unfair share of the burden.

Then Democratic President Jimmy Carter sent 15,000 Cuban refugees to Fort Chaffee (located in Fort Smith). Some folks feared the Cubans would take jobs away from Arkansans, in spite of the facts that their presence actually provided an economic boost to Fort Smith

Bill Clinton speaking at a victory ball on the night of his first election to the presidency. –Polly Walter

257

and the Cubans generally left Arkansas as soon as they found sponsors elsewhere. Concern skyrocketed when some Cubans, frustrated by their long internment and the slow road to freedom, rioted. They caused neither injuries nor substantial property damage, but the flood of angry, shouting refugees into a nearby community really frightened the residents of western Arkansas.

The final straw for the good ol' boys was that Governor Clinton's wife used her maiden name for professional purposes in her law practice, so media coverage referred to "Governor Clinton's wife, Hillary Rodham." In reality, she had taken the name Hillary Rodham Clinton when she married Bill while he was attorney general, but the public perception during Clinton's first term as governor was that she had not taken his surname. Back in those days, it was considered suspect in rural Arkansas (a Democratic stronghold) when a wife did not use the surname of her husband. "If Bill isn't man enough to make Hillary change her name to Clinton," the good ol' boys complained, "then he sure as hell isn't man enough to run the state of Arkansas."

Republican Frank White condemned Clinton, attacking him in what came to be known as the Car Tags and Cubans Campaign, warning black voters that the Cubans would take their jobs. White defeated Clinton in the election and became governor in 1980. He is remembered as only the second Republican governor since Reconstruction.

Clinton's friends and advisers told him to go into law practice, work in the real world (he taught law only briefly after college), and earn a few gray hairs before returning to politics. Bill Clinton had other ideas. Hillary announced that she was now Hillary Clinton, not Hillary Rodham. The ex-governor jumped on the Baptist redemption-and-forgiveness wagon and started apologizing to any Arkansan who would listen that he was sorry for all his mistakes. He asked their forgiveness and said he would henceforth always go to the people for their input before making any political decisions. Within six months of losing the election, Bill Clinton was stumping once again for the governor's office, and his political rehabilitation was well under way. He returned to the governor's office in 1982, where he remained until the 1992 elections.

The 1992 presidential campaign finally succeeded in removing Bill Clinton from the governor's office. The same consensus-building style that resurrected his political career in 1982, and saw him through his subsequent career as governor, proved to be effective in the presidential race as well, enabling him to beat incumbent Republican George Bush.

During the campaign, President Bush once remarked that his opponent came from an obscure little state somewhere between Oklahoma and Texas. Bill Clinton gave George Bush a rather memorable geography lesson and succeeded in placing Arkansas on the national political map once and for all.

—NORTH LITTLE ROCK—

North Little Rock is located directly across the Arkansas River from Little Rock, on a vast alluvial plain that sweeps across the state from the north bank of the Arkansas to the mighty Mississippi. Interest in settling the area developed in 1839, a year after a steam ferry began crossing the Arkansas River between Little Rock and the wooded north shore. A U.S. Army officer surveyed a town site west of present-day Main Street in North Little Rock, calling the embryonic town DeCantillon after himself. Richard DeCantillon Collins attracted few settlers, partly because a cypress bog covered much of the town site.

Interest returned to the north shore with the construction of the Memphis & Little Rock Railroad in the 1850s. The north shore became the terminus for the railroad and was named Hunterville after William Hunter, the superintendent of the line. Soon wood homes and boardinghouses sprang up around the depot, and the nearby ferry

Missouri Pacific locomotive at coal chute in North Little Rock.
—Arkansas History Commission

transported people and freight between the railroad terminus and Ferry Street in Little Rock. Most of the land on the north shore was owned by the Newton family, which operated a large farm on the rich alluvial soil.

The farm was surveyed for a town site in March 1866 and broken up into lots. Colonel Richard Newton named the village Argenta because he believed that the nearby Kellogg Mine contained argentiferous (silver) ore. The glittering name didn't help the village develop, however, because the area began to earn a bad reputation during Reconstruction. Steamboat roustabouts and tough freed slaves gave the community a rambunctious and somewhat unsavory reputation. Nevertheless, the village had grown to the point that Argenta was incorporated as a town in 1871.

Argenta

The town got a boost when English banker Alexander Baring financed the construction of a railroad and vehicular bridge between the north shore and Little Rock. The Baring Cross Bridge was completed in 1873. A village called Baring Cross soon developed at the north end of the bridge. Argenta eventually absorbed Baring Cross as it had Hunterville, and the bridge continued in service until a flood washed it away in 1927.

Hamilton Hardware Store in Argenta, circa 1910. —UCA Archives

The residents of Argenta tried to incorporate their community as a city in 1890, prompting a horrified Little Rock City Council to annex the heart of Argenta (between Clendenin Hill, Thirteenth and Main Streets, and the river) as the Eighth Ward. Community leaders on the north shore fought the annexation in the county and state courts without success. But the political battle was just beginning.

The Eighth Ward continued to develop its unsavory reputation until Argenta was known as the toughest town in the state. While trains brought civilian patrons to the saloons, gambling houses, and bordellos, the U.S. Army declared Argenta off limits to military personnel—a sure sign that a good time could be had by all. Argenta also provided employment to many residents of Little Rock, who used the Baring Cross Bridge to reach their jobs at the railroad yards and other establishments on the north shore. Argenta continued to grow, but local residents believed that they were not getting their fair share of services.

For example, Argenta had the dubious distinction of harboring one saloon for every six permanent residents. But the Eighth Ward did not have a school nor the paved streets, concrete sidewalks, or electric streetlights that the residents on the south shore were beginning to take for granted. The Eighth Ward began to view itself as Little Rock's threadbare stepchild. Community leaders, who were chafing under the yoke of rule from the south shore, finally came up with a plan for their political emancipation. Rather than attacking the Little

Argenta Community Band, circa 1920. –UCA Archives

Rock City Council head-on, a flanking attack was launched by electing William C. Faucette to the state legislature. It was a brilliant strategy.

Argenta's Coup de Main

William Faucette helped draft and pass a bill that was ostensibly designed to solve annexation problems between the communities of Hoxie and Walnut Ridge. The power brokers of Little Rock never realized that the bill was actually designed specifically to enable the Eighth Ward to win its independence. The bill allowed the residents of a community facing annexation to vote on which incorporated municipality they wished to join.

Once this bill passed, the residents of the independent section of Argenta incorporated themselves as the city of North Little Rock under the ruse of forming a new school district. Then, using the Hoxie-Walnut Ridge Bill as justification, an election was called to determine if the residents of the Eighth Ward wanted to remain annexed to Little Rock or cast their lot with North Little Rock. The stunned Little Rock City Council tried to obtain a court injunction to stop the election. When that failed, the council immediately approved the funding to pave the streets in the Eighth Ward, and planned to add concrete sidewalks and streetlights, as well.

It was too little, too late. The residents of the Eighth Ward overwhelmingly decided (by a vote of 475 to 44) to be annexed by North

Little Rock. The new administration began a vigorous program to clean up and modernize North Little Rock. Bars came under local regulation and schools appeared. But community relations with Little Rock remained less than amicable. One curious development of the rivalry was that the residents of Little Rock were encouraged to dump unwanted dogs and puppies on the north side of the river. After several years of this biological warfare, North Little Rock had become so overrun with feral dogs that the community had acquired the nickname "Dogtown." The name stuck long after the north shore eliminated the plague of canines. Perhaps Dogtown was the easiest name to remember, since North Little Rock changed its name back to Argenta a year after its incorporation.

Arkansas voted to go dry in 1916, so Argenta's many saloons closed their doors. The face of Main Street abruptly changed as new businesses moved into the vacant facades. Then local businessman and mayor Jim Faucette (the brother of legislator William Faucette) conceived a scheme to improve the value of the community's real estate. He got the idea from a small town near Hollywood that renamed itself West Hollywood to capitalize on the name recognition. Land prices tripled. Faucette suggested that Argenta change its name back to North Little Rock for the same reason, and the town changed its name for the final time in 1917.

North Little Rock has continued to grow and now has a population nearly half as large as its sister city across the river. Old-timers who remember the feuds with the capital city still like to call the other side of the river South Argenta. The tremendously successful malls and shops of North Little Rock have replaced the saloons and gambling houses of Argenta as a powerful draw to lure the residents of Little Rock across the Arkansas to spend their hard-earned cash. There is a certain historical symmetry and poetic justice to the phenomenon.

—Part Four—

THE OUACHITAS

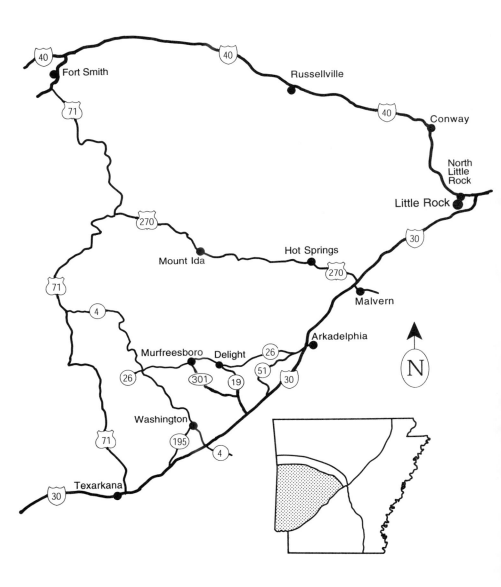

Malvern–Mount Ida

Ranging through the heart of the Ouachita Mountains, this journey takes the traveler through some of the liveliest history and greatest recreational possibilities that Arkansas offers. Here history abounds with compelling conflicts, heroic women, and great men of both noble and dastardly disposition. Malvern and Hot Springs, in particular, have seen a turbulent times swirling with glamour, gangsters, and even a G.I. revolt.

–MALVERN–

Located 45 miles southwest of Little Rock and 103 miles northeast of Texarkana on I-30, Malvern began when Captain W. H. Cooper built a store on a hill above the newly laid Cairo & Fulton Railroad (later called the St. Louis, Iron Mountain & Southern; and then the Missouri Pacific) in the early 1870s. A town site along the tracks was surveyed and named Malvern in 1873 after a town of the same name in Virginia. The railroad stimulated the birth of the timber industry in Hot Springs County but caused the almost overnight demise of Rockport, the county seat, which the route bypassed. Whole buildings in Rockport were disassembled, carried by wagon to Malvern, and reassembled. Rockport became a ghost town in a matter of months. Then on January 15, 1874, Jesse James added a bit of history to the Malvern area.

Jesse James

The stage from Malvern to Hot Springs loaded fourteen passengers and a number of mail pouches at 11 A.M., and disappeared down Hot Springs Road. Four hours later, the driver stopped at the Gaines place to water the horses. Five men rode past, but the driver didn't pay much attention.

This was a good time and place to stage a robbery. During winter, thick curtains would be drawn over the stagecoach's open windows, so horsemen could approach unseen even during daylight hours. Furthermore, people traveling to Hot Springs for medical treatment or a vacation would probably stay for some time, so they would be carrying a lot of money.

The stage had only continued on about half a mile past the Gaines place when four masked men rode up behind the coach and ordered the driver to stop. The desperados were heavily armed, so the driver had little choice. He stopped.

This drawing from J. W. Buel's The Border Outlaws *(published in 1882) inaccurately depicts Frank and Jesse James, plus the three Younger brothers, robbing the Hot Springs stage.* –Mary Hudgins Collection, Special Collections, University of Arkansas Libraries, Fayetteville

Jesse James lined up the passengers in a semicircle and ordered everyone to "shell out." A badly crippled man was allowed to remain in the coach, and he wasn't robbed. Everyone else was. Cole Younger and Clem Miller collected the booty—some $3,000 to $4,000—and put it in a sack. They took all the gold watches from the passengers but let Charles Moore keep his silver watch. The gang then slit open the mail pouches and searched for registered letters, which often contained cash. A package to the Southern Express Company yielded $435.

Just before the gang departed, James asked if anyone had served with the Confederacy. G. R. Crump of the Memphis Cigar Company replied "yes" in a strong southern accent. Not fully satisfied, James demanded his rank, commanding officer, and regiment. Crump supplied this information and James returned all of the man's money and valuables, saying "We do not rob Confederates."

Encouraged by this turn of events, T. A. Burbank (the former governor of Dakota Territory) pleaded for the return of his papers, which would have no use to anyone else. James squatted and rifled the papers, then stiffened and said, "Boys, I believe he is a detective. Shoot him!"

The only people Jesse James hated more than Yankees were Pinkerton men. Three guns pointed at Burbank's head. But James changed his mind at the last minute, saying, "No, he looks all right. Let him go." Perhaps this was an example of what passed for the

*Joseph "Diamond Jo"
Reynolds, wearing his famous
diamond.* —Mary Hudgins
Collection, Special Collections,
University of Arkansas Libraries,
Fayetteville

humor of Jesse James. The gang kept Burbank's gold watch, diamond stick pin, and $840.

The accent of a man from Massachusetts infuriated the gang, so he claimed to be from St. Louis. This was not a smart choice. James concluded that he was a Republican newspaperman from the hated *St. Louis Democrat,* which supported the carpetbaggers. The gang members began to wager how close to his body they could shoot though his clothing without hitting flesh. The man began to tremble uncontrollably. They finally laughed and left him alone.

The James Gang then rode away. Local legend claims that the desperados hid the money from this holdup in a rattlesnake-infested cave near the Ouachita River. Some historians, however, believe this was one of a series of robberies that was actually committed by a group other than the James Gang.

The Diamond Jo Railroad

A year after this spectacular robbery, Malvern got a big boost from Chicago grain mogul Joseph Reynolds. Reynolds was called "Diamond Jo" because he marketed sacks of grain stenciled with his company trademark—the word "Jo" surrounded by a diamond—and because he always wore a large diamond on his shirt. Reynolds got his start as a cabin boy on a riverboat. He later bought his own boat, which soon parlayed into a fleet that hauled a great deal of grain. Getting directly into the grain business seemed like the logical next step. By 1870, Reynolds was a multimillionaire.

Diamond Jo liked to vacation at Hot Springs. The only way to get there was to take the railroad from Chicago to Malvern, and then ride a stagecoach over twenty-five miles of extremely rough roads through the Ouachita Mountains. After a particularly difficult journey that included the breakdown of the coach and a heated argument with the very rude driver, Diamond Jo resolved to establish a more satisfactory way to reach Hot Springs. He built a narrow-gauge railroad from Malvern to Hot Springs.

While the Diamond Jo Railroad was one of America's shortest railroads (twenty-two miles), it was also one of the most romantic. A pigmy engine pulled a single baggage car and five elegant passenger coaches on miniature tracks. The narrow tracks wound through

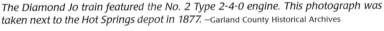

The Diamond Jo train featured the No. 2 Type 2-4-0 engine. This photograph was taken next to the Hot Springs depot in 1877. –Garland County Historical Archives

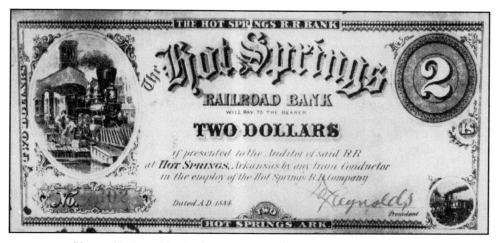

Diamond Jo Reynolds gave free rail passes to his friends. They were printed to resemble money so their use would not alienate the paying passengers on his Malvern–Hot Springs railroad. —Mary Hudgins Collection, Special Collections, University of Arkansas Libraries, Fayetteville

narrow valleys, up steep grades, and over rapid streams through handsome scenery. Diamond Jo demanded superb engineering as well as careful attention to aesthetics. For example, the rails were made from the finest steel (which soon saved many lives). The engines sported silk curtains, a hand-polished walnut cab, and gleaming brass worthy of a millionaire's private coach. The engineers and firemen kept the locomotives polished with beeswax, and they frequently entertained famous passengers who would rather ride in the engines than in the luxurious coaches with imported appointments. Best of all, the fare was only a third the cost of the stagecoach.

Something about the tiny train bred an air of informality. When the crew stopped the train to "wood up," the passengers commonly piled out of the train to help, laughing as they loaded four-foot logs. Even the rich and famous helped, including the likes of Phil Armour, Jay Gould, Captain (later Admiral) Dewey, General John Logan (who later established the army and navy hospital in Hot Springs), John Sullivan, and even a Harvard-educated Japanese prince.

The railroad's yin and yang of elegance versus informality matched the man known as Diamond Jo. Folks simply addressed him as Jo— not Mr. Reynolds. Once he arrived late in Malvern, missing the train to Hot Springs, so he decided to buy a few sandwiches and walk the twenty-two miles to the resort. That way, he could inspect the state of the roadbed. He was past middle age at the time, so someone decided Reynolds was being overly confident, and contacted engineer J. H. Ryan in Hot Springs to back the engine down the line to pick up Diamond Jo. Ryan later recalled:

> When I found him, where do you think he was? He was this side of Butterfield, sitting on a log between two tramps. The three of them were calmly eating the lunch he carried. And the diamond he was wearing in his shirt front, gleaming like a headlight. He wouldn't admit it, but he was tired. As he climbed into the fireman's seat beside me, I tried to give him the cushion on which I sat. He wouldn't have it. He said I was doing the work, and I was the one to be comfortable.

Ryan was a man of character as well. One gray dawn, he began the trip from Malvern to Hot Springs unaware that a fire had completely burned away the supports of a bridge. Only a few charred ties continued to hold the rails together, and the bridge itself was gone. A blind curve hid the calamity from view as the train approached at a substantial speed. Ryan noticed the glowing embers only a hundred feet from the chasm. There was no chance to stop. He opened the throttle wide to full power and shot ahead. The train somehow roared across the unsupported rails and reached the safety of the other side before the rails disappeared into the chasm. Totally unnerved, Ryan stopped the train. Everyone piled out and stared in silent awe at their miraculous deliverance. One survivor was a baseball player for the Chicago White Stockings, who told Ryan, "it must be that God still has some mission for persons on this train to perform. It is up to each one of us to find out what that mission is." Billy Sunday would leave baseball and enter the ministry.

Another measure of Diamond Jo, the man, came in the 1880s. Hard times strangled the Reynolds shipyards. Instead of laying off workers, he sent them to Hot Springs to build a new depot. While he was at it, Diamond Jo donated a great deal of granite and had his workmen build an imposing wall around the city park being built across the street from his depot. (The city hall, post office, and chamber of commerce buildings were later built over that park.)

Malvern prospered with industry and commerce. Then a disastrous fire in 1896 destroyed most of the businesses in town. Malvern lay in smouldering ruins from Third Street to the depot on both sides of Main Street. The ashes of the old wood-frame structures were replaced with brick buildings almost before the smoke cleared.

Diamond Jo widened his narrow-gauge railroad to conventional width in 1898 to better carry freight. He died several years later, and the line was swallowed up by the Chicago, Rock Island & Pacific. Diamond Jo and his romantic railroad passed into history.

Malvern continued to prosper as the seat of Hot Springs County. Agriculture began to change from row crops to the production of livestock and poultry. The social and economic changes spawned by World War II shifted interest from small farms to industry. Today, Malvern is home to the Ouachita Vocational Technical School and claims the title "Brick Capitol of the World." The community celebrates an annual Brickfest on the last weekend in June. In addition to the usual food and music, the festival features brick-throwing contests, running events, and arts and crafts.

—HOT SPRINGS—

Located 21 miles northwest of Malvern on US 270, 53 miles southwest of Little Rock via I-30 and US 70, and 109 miles southeast of Fort Smith via US 71 and US 270, Hot Springs may have received its first European visitor in 1541. In that year, some folks believe, Hernando de Soto discovered the geothermal springs that would eventually give this community its name. Yet the human use of this area dates far back into antiquity. The restorative benefits provided by bathing in the hot springs made this hallowed ground to the Indians of the Mississippi basin, who called the valley Man-a-tak-a, the Place of Peace, according to local lore.

Soon after the early French settlement of Louisiana, trappers and traders began to visit the hot springs, where the Indians welcomed them in peace. The first permanent settlement appeared in 1807 thanks to the efforts of Emanuel Prudhomme, who was a successful planter of tobacco and indigo from Louisiana. (Cotton had not yet been introduced to the area.) Friends among the Natchitoches Indians suggested that he accompany them to bathe in hot springs to the north. Prudhomme was so enchanted by the place that he built a small cabin there. He remained about a year, until the demands of his flourishing plantation required his return to Louisiana.

Antebellum Activities on the Ouachita

Two trappers from Alabama appeared soon after Prudhomme built his cabin. John Percival and Isaac Cates came specifically because they had heard of the medicinal value of the hot springs, which lay about a mile from the Ouachita River. Cates constructed a wooden trough in which a person could lie while the water flowed over his body. When Prudhomme returned to his plantation, he simply gave his cabin to Percival. More folks began to come to drink and bathe in the waters of the creek and pools fed by hot springs. Visitors during that period limited their stays to the spring and summer. The valley was virtually deserted in the winter.

European visitors tended to build cabins. They would give the cabins to Percival when they left, since he supplied them with game and other provisions. Percival fell in love with the daughter of a family visiting the springs in 1812, and Sarah Lemon stayed behind to marry him. Between twenty and thirty cabins dotted the valley by 1814 for Southern gentlemen seeking "a delightful and rational amusement," according to Thomas Nutall in his *Journal of Travels into the Arkansas Territory During the Year 1819*. The year after Nutall's visit, Joseph Millard built a dogtrot-style log house, which was the first structure at Hot Springs that might be termed a hotel.

Interest in Hot Springs continued to grow. After several newspapers published descriptions of the hot springs, the number of visitors began to increase. The creek became especially popular with European invalids. Since its temperature varied gradually along its length, the visitor could easily select an agreeable spot.

By 1828, the little village growing up around the hot springs was known by the name of Thermopolis, while the entire valley was known as Hot Springs. The lack of facilities and accommodations discouraged many prospective visitors. When Ludovicus Belding brought his family to the valley from Boston for their health, he saw the profitable potential of the place. He settled his affairs in Massachusetts and built a hotel. When not taking the waters, the guests amused themselves by hunting, walking, and playing cards. The summer of 1832 proved to be the first real resort season at the hot springs. Many planters from neighboring states brought their families. General Sam Houston stayed for a month to take baths for an ulcer on his head.

The hot springs became much more accessible in 1835, when stage service from Little Rock was initiated. The trip took four days under ideal conditions. That year, Governor James Conway leased the hot springs and opened a resort run by Samuel Reyburn. They provided excellent accommodations, both refitted and new bathhouses, a well-furnished bar, and plenty of horse feed, according to the *Arkansas Gazette*. Pioneer John Percival died at his home, and his widow sold out a few months later. New accommodations and facilities were built to serve the increasing number of visitors during the spring and summer months. By 1846, demand prompted several hotels to remain open throughout the entire year.

Hot Springs was incorporated as a town in 1851, but it remained little more than a struggling village. The community consisted of two rows of bathhouses, hotels, saloons, stores, and a recent addition—doctor offices.

Development remained at a fairly primitive level, however, partly because legal ownership of the hot springs remained in question.

Franklin D. Roosevelt visited Hot Springs in June 1936.
—Garland County Historical Archives

Everything to do with the hotels and bathhouses remained crude and temporary. For example, with ownership unclear, no one was willing to upgrade the baths so bathers could adjust the water temperature. Nevertheless, the hotels accommodated as many as 500 people at a time from nearly every state in the country. The hot waters were said to help people with diseases of the skin, obstinate ulcers, chronic rheumatism, mercurial diseases, and syphilis.

The future of Man-a-tak-a promised sanctuary to a growing number of pilgrims and invalids. But then war clouds gathered, raining down a torrent of roving marauders who would finally violate this sanctuary. Bands of Jayhawkers, Bushwhackers, and brigands brought such death and desolation that the area was completely depopulated by the end of the war. A sense of sanctuary would return as the Spa City matured and hosted the likes of both Franklin D. Roosevelt and Al Capone. Old-timers will comment, off the record, that the presence of famous gangsters in the 1920s and 1930s actually brought the community its most crime-free period in modern times. But that's getting ahead of the story.

War Comes to Hot Springs

When war erupted, the men of Man-a-tak-a and the surrounding areas flocked to Rockport, which was then the seat of Hot Spring County. Companies were organized and marched off to join the Confederate army in Little Rock. Most became a part of the Third

275

Arkansas Cavalry. Residents in the northern part of the county enrolled at Mount Ida in Montgomery County, and were mustered into Confederate service in Missouri. More than a hundred men left Mount Ida for war. Only a dozen or so would return.

Not everyone in the area supported the Confederacy. Many hill folk supported the Union, and some families were split down the middle. George Blocker, for example, became an officer in the Union army, but his half-brother William Gray joined the Confederate army. One fellow, Montgomery Owen, ultimately became a veteran of both armies.

When Union General Samuel Curtis invaded northern Arkansas in 1862 and captured Batesville—a scant 100 miles from Little Rock—Governor Henry Rector feared the Federals would march on the state capital next. Not waiting for authority from the legislature, he ordered that the most important state records and archives be loaded onto a steamboat so they could be transferred to Hot Springs. The boat ascended the Arkansas River as far as Dardanelle, where it proved to be very difficult to find enough wagons to carry nearly 18,000 pounds of poorly packed documents over the mountains.

Somehow the task was completed, and Rector set up a temporary capitol in a two-story home he owned on the site of the present-day park across from the Arlington Hotel. When the danger had passed toward the end of July, Rector's government and paperwork returned to Little Rock. This was the highlight of the Civil War for Hot Springs, which was never occupied by either Union or Confederate troops during the conflict. But by the end of 1863, skirmishes erupted throughout the countryside, and both sides maintained an almost constant pressure on the area.

After Little Rock fell to the Federals, a Union patrol was dispatched to Hot Springs in January 1864. Union soldier Wade Beach described that patrol's activity in a 1926 interview. "It was cold, I can tell you. There were just a few ramshackle places, and a stream of water with steam and vapor rising from it, and ran down what is now Central Avenue. All the hot springs were exposed. We arrested everyone we found and those who would not take the oath of allegiance we sent to the penitentiary in Little Rock."

The soldiers confiscated all the food and forage they could find. Yet they produced much less suffering than the lawless bands who never joined either army, but roamed the area robbing, burning, and murdering in the name of the Union or the Confederacy. These Jayhawkers (pro-Union marauders) and Bushwhackers (pro-Confederate marauders) plunged the land into the darkest anarchy. They killed each other and civilians with abandon, raiding far behind the

recognized battle lines. Normal society collapsed entirely, and virtually everyone had deserted Hot Springs by the fall of 1863.

Hot Springs Rebuilds

After the war ended in 1865, former residents began to return from
Louisiana and Texas to rebuild their lives. Soon settlers appeared
from the northern and eastern states, and business began to boom
as visitors once again trekked to Hot Springs to drink and bathe in
the legendary waters.

By 1870, the population of Hot Springs had increased sixfold over
the population when Arkansas seceded from the Union. The demo-
graphics of the antebellum and postwar populations were, however,
quite different. The postwar population boom in Hot Springs was fueled by men of military age (eighteen to forty-five), who presumably
had seen the area during the war. Many of these men came from states
that had not been a part of the Confederacy, and many foreign-born
settlers began to appear for the first time. This diverse group of individuals poured their energies into transforming a burned-out, remote
village in the Ouachita wilderness into the nation's dynamic Spa City.

Spa City's Golden Age

Two problems limited the economic potential of Hot Springs. First,
the area was relatively inaccessible. Second, the courts had never
established who actually owned the springs. The Diamond Jo Railroad (see Malvern) solved the first problem. A solution to the second
problem proved elusive until the mid-1870s, when the federal government took over the administration of the land and water rights
under the aegis of the Hot Springs Reservation.

Four square miles of adjacent forest were cleared so a separate
town could be developed to accommodate visitors. A survey reserved
the mountains for the federal government and divided the new town
site into blocks. Some lots were donated for public buildings and some
were reserved for sale to the public. Because all prior deeds and claims
to the land were disallowed, some folks—who had in good faith purchased land and lived on it for three generations—suddenly found
they had to repurchase the land from the federal government or leave.
As painful as this process was, the arrangement finally resolved the
crippling problems of uncertain land ownership and water rights.
Eliminating these chronic impediments to growth permitted steady
progress and development of Hot Springs throughout the rest of the
century.

Soon after Diamond Jo provided comfortable and affordable transportation to Hot Springs, the nation's wealthy and famous began to

view it as one of their favorite destinations. When the Chicago White Stockings became the first baseball team to head south for spring training, they chose Hot Springs. Other northern and eastern teams quickly followed suit, and Hot Springs became the off-season capital of baseball.

People taking the waters had a lot of time on their hands between baths, so gambling quickly became a growth industry in Hot Springs. By 1884, gambling had become so profitable that operators of the town's many gaming establishments split into two factions. Frank Flynn led one. Major S. A. Doran led the other. Conflict between the two seemed inevitable.

The Flynn-Doran War

Frank Flynn was a Canadian of slight build and delicate features, thinning black hair and darting black eyes. Flynn visited Hot Springs during the town's renaissance following the Civil War. Like many visitors of that period, he decided to stay. Over the years, he gained such control over gambling in Hot Springs that folks started calling him Boss Gambler. He controlled five of the seven big gambling houses on Central Avenue: the Arlington, Billy McTague's, the Owl, the Ozark Club, and the Office (which was Flynn's headquarters). Every gambling establishment had a similar two-story layout: a saloon on the first floor, and gaming rooms upstairs.

Jim Lane owned the other two first-class gambling houses on Central Avenue: the Palace and the Monarch. A "sporting man" from Cairo, Illinois, he resisted Flynn's attempts to control him. Flynn's overtures became threats. Finally Flynn and his thugs invaded the Palace, destroying all of the gaming equipment, throwing tables out the windows, and chasing out all the customers. Lane's dealers resisted and even managed to kill one of Flynn's henchmen. But the assault worked, and Lane scrambled out of town in fear for his life.

In the months that followed, Major S. A. Doran decided to challenge Boss Gambler. Doran's military bearing derived from his service as a major in the Confederate army. His six-foot, three-inch stature and 220 pounds added to his authoritative presence. Doran began to quietly refurbish the plundered Palace. Meanwhile, Flynn's arrogance soared to new heights. He became quite testy whenever a customer quit gambling after a winning streak, especially if the patron was a Texan. When one young Texan left a seven-up game with a pocketful of money, Flynn warned him, "Young man, you haven't won enough to pay your fine for gambling." The young Texan thought he was kidding, laughed, and walked out the door. Under orders from Flynn, the local lawman promptly arrested the Texan and fined him heavily for gambling. Flynn was known neither for his magnanimity nor his sense of humor.

Major Doran steadily resisted Flynn's attempts to bully him into submission. Flynn decided he needed more muscle than his two brothers, Jack and Billy, so he began to recruit gunmen from Texas and the western territories. Doran responded by hiring his own gunmen.

When Doran's restoration of the Palace neared completion early in February 1884, he announced a grand opening and invited the leading citizens of the community. He even hired a brass band to serenade his guests at the festivities. Lawyers, doctors, bankers, and all the beautiful people of Hot Springs packed his gaming rooms to sip whiskey or eat chicken salad and sandwiches, which they washed down with champagne. Even the tough guys who attended were on their best behavior, since the major had his army discretely distributed throughout the crowd. It should have been a peaceful party. And it was.

But the Palace's patronage fell precipitously on the following nights. So did the attendance at every other gaming establishment in Hot Springs, since everyone believed that one faction would surely attack the other at the earliest opportunity. Every faro dealer at the Palace kept a Winchester rifle beside him at the gaming table for three nerve-wracking days. Then on the morning of the fourth day, veteran gambler Tom Dale walked into the Palace and talked quietly to Doran. The major lit a cigar and followed the gambler downstairs. Dale and Doran walked out of the Palace onto Central Avenue.

"Omaha Frank" Borland, who was playing poker at the Palace when the major left, claimed that Dale had brought Doran a challenge from Flynn to settle their dispute *mano a mano* in the fashion of the Old West. Gunfire erupted ten or fifteen minutes later. Then Major Doran appeared at the head of the stairs, his cigar still clenched in his teeth.

According to one report, Doran spotted Flynn on a street corner and warned him to draw. Flynn fired and missed. Doran's gun misfired, so he threw it down and drew another. Doran hit Flynn in the chest and Boss Gambler staggered back into a doorway. Doran holstered his gun and returned to the Palace, where he complained that Flynn must have been wearing a coat of mail. "I know I hit him once over the heart," the major complained. I saw the dust fly off his coat. Next time I hit him, I'll plug him in the eye."

Flynn's camp offered a somewhat different version of events. They claimed Major Doran fired without warning, wounding Flynn slightly before he could even draw his gun. They went on to say that Flynn only wore a buttoned greatcoat, not a coat of mail as the major claimed.

279

Public opinion initially favored Flynn. Although he was a rascal of the worst order, at least he was a local lad. Major Doran was still viewed as an outsider. Public opinion shifted, however, when Flynn rented a room at the Arlington Hotel across the street from the Palace. Flynn and a number of riflemen occupied all the windows overlooking the entrance to the Palace, so they could ambush Major Doran as soon as he tried to set foot outside. A crowd of spectators gathered on the balcony of Billy McTague's saloon to watch events as they unfolded. But the Hot Springs sporting set was outraged by Flynn's intended ambush; it just wasn't . . . *sporting*. Flynn's snipers finally gave up and left the Arlington Hotel.

The next move belonged to Major Doran, who decided he would have to neutralize Flynn and his thugs in order to survive. The major's men struck on a cold, drizzly winter morning as Frank, Jack, and Billy

Billy Flynn. –Garland County Historical Archives

Flynn were riding in a horse-drawn cab near the south end of Bath House Row. Seven or eight gunmen, who were deployed along the plank sidewalks and in doorways, loosed a fusillade that killed the driver and Jack Flynn. Frank and Billy Flynn jumped out of the cab to return fire, but both were hit by the second volley.

The terrified horses bolted as the driver fell into the mud. Billy struggled onto the sidewalk in front of the Visitors' Home across from the Rammelsburg Bath House. Frank apparently took refuge in the lobby of the Hot Springs National Bank, where a doctor came to dress his wounds.

Chief of Police Tom Toler arrived and began to disperse the crowd that had gathered. Only then did he learn that several innocent people had been caught in the ambush. A man standing in the doorway of a barber shop was severely wounded, and the driver of a freight cart was killed.

The townsfolk decided it was time to stop the violence, which was not only striking innocent people but frightening away spa patrons. The citizens organized a Committee of Twelve, which resolved within hours of the shooting to drive out of town every gambler associated with Flynn or Doran. The committee drew up lists of known gamblers and visited each one in turn, ordering him to leave town within twenty-four hours. Several failed to comply. Men armed with bayoneted rifles packed their bags, bought them tickets on the Diamond Jo Railroad, and escorted them onto the train.

Frank Flynn stood on the rear platform of an outbound train shaking his fist and shouting obscenities. Major Doran left quietly for Fort Smith, where he was killed several years later in a quarrel over a woman.

The gaming houses promptly reopened, but under official supervision. Local officials warned that anyone who cheated at gambling or any establishment that ran a dishonest game would be treated harshly. Gambling once again became a popular diversion for patrons of the spas at Hot Springs, and the community continued to grow in size and glamour.

Fires, Floods, and Feds

The town enjoyed an impressive pace of progress, although it did experience a few cataclysmic setbacks. Fire devastated Hot Springs in 1878, 1905, and 1913. Residents solved this problem by abandoning wood-frame construction in favor of more durable building materials. The community still suffered though periodic flash floods, however. The worst roared through town in 1923. The plucky resort community always rebuilt with unbridled confidence in a brighter future.

The flood of June 1910 inundated Hot Springs. This buggy in front of Albright's on Bridge Street is up to its hubs in water. –Garland County Historical Archives

Smoke engulfs the Arlington Hotel in April 1923. –Garland County Historical Archives

The local economy got a big boost in the 1880s, when the federal government established the Army and Navy Hospital in Hot Springs to take advantage of the therapeutic value of the waters. It might be hard for the beneficiaries of modern medicine and wonder drugs to understand that bathing in the hot springs really did help people with rheumatism and skin diseases. A series of expansions would ultimately increase the hospital's capacity to 1,500 patients. Yet from the Elegant Eighties through the Roaring Twenties, most folks came to Hot Springs for the spas and the gambling.

Casino gambling remained a major institution in Hot Springs. From time to time, a politician running for state office would rail against the evils of gambling, and the casinos would obligingly shut down until after the election, when they would resume business as usual. Local residents remained indifferent to organized gambling, but visitors saw it as a major attraction. The Illinois Club, the Southern Club, and especially the posh Belvedere teemed with high rollers from Little Rock, Dallas, and Chicago. Major mobsters such as Frank Costello came for the horse races and nightlife. Gambling, girls, and booze fueled the local economy. No one really objected until veterans

The Hot Springs Street Railway Company used horse-drawn wagons after the fire of 1913 destroyed much of the city's core. –Garland County Historical Archives

returning home after World War II took on the 1940's version of Boss Gambler: Mayor Leo Patrick McLaughlin.

The G.I. Revolt

Leo McLaughlin grew up in Hot Springs, went to law school, and was elected city attorney about the time he was old enough to vote himself. McLaughlin was elected mayor in 1927 and immediately began to consolidate his power. He gradually melded politics and gambling into a unified, well-financed machine. He affected an exuberant, outgoing manner complete with fashionable attire and a red carnation in his lapel at all times. He would frequently drive through the streets of Hot Springs in his horse cart, pulled by two magnificent steeds named Scotch and Soda.

McLaughlin had a flair for public relations and power politics. His machine was so strong that anyone running for even the most minor public office needed his backing. He maintained his power by controlling payoffs from illegal casinos, and by forcing people who depended on him to buy quantities of poll tax receipts. (In those days, a citizen had to pay a poll tax to have the right to vote in Arkansas.)

Hot Springs Mayor Leo McLaughlin drives a surrey behind his famous horses Scotch and Soda. –Garland County Historical Archives

The McLaughlin machine could control the outcome of an election by handing out poll tax receipts—with $2 bills attached—to petty criminals, town drunks, and prostitutes who would vote as directed. One local madam had to buy hundreds of poll tax receipts for the right to stay in business.

The veterans who challenged McLaughlin in 1946 didn't object to gambling per se, but rather to gambling's stranglehold on local politics. Since Mayor McLaughlin controlled local gambling, he became the focus of the energetic campaign led by a former Marine Corps officer, Sidney McMath. Like McLaughlin, McMath grew up in Hot Springs. But McMath grew up poor. He sold newspapers in the casinos, shined shoes, and boxed in local bouts. During the depths of the Great Depression, he left town with $2.50 in his pocket and hitchhiked to Fayetteville, where he began to work his way through law school.

When McMath and his fellow veterans returned to Hot Springs after World War II, they decided they had fought for freedom and honest government, not the corruption they found in their hometown.

The veterans launched their campaign against the mayor, whom they called "Der Fuhrer of Hot Springs." Soon the press had labeled their campaign "the G.I. Revolt." The reformers brought McLaughlin to trial on charges of bribery and malfeasance. Two juries acquitted the mayor, but his stranglehold on local politics was broken.

Open gambling disappeared for a time, although some believed the mayor was only a figurehead for Vincent Owen Madden, who was a well-known figure in the New York world of organized crime before he moved to Hot Springs in 1930. Sid McMath went on to become a prosecuting attorney, which served as a stepping stone to the governor's mansion. McMath won the 1948 gubernatorial election and became the youngest governor of Arkansas since the Civil War.

Bill Clinton, who went to grade school and high school in Hot Springs, would later become the youngest governor in the United States, when he was elected to his first term in 1978 at the age of thirty-two. The forty-second governor of Arkansas, Clinton went on to become the forty-second president of the United States (see Little Rock, in Part 3).

One of the most colorful residents of Hot Springs during the 1950s and 1960s was Maxine Temple Jones, who earned her place as the most successful (and toughest) madam in Hot Springs. Her autobiography, *Maxine: Call Me Madam*, not only provides a lively and compelling account of her life, it also provides a gritty look into the political corruption that ran rampant through Hot Springs and Arkansas during her heyday.

The Madam

Born in 1917, young Maxine Temple grew up as a tomboy near Warren, where her father worked as a farmer and logging contractor. Although her life with six brothers and a sister was a happy one, Maxine realized at an early age that she was somehow different. She would rather work in the fields, ride horses bareback, and hunt with her father than stay in the house with her mother and sister. Maxine did, however, develop her father's style and good taste. Quality became more important than quantity. Her father taught her the fierce independence that would become the cornerstone of her personality.

After a hitch in the Women's Army Corps—largely spent driving generals around Washington, D.C.—she returned to Arkansas and worked as a security guard at the Camden arsenal. Her father had just died, so Maxine supported the family while her mother raised the two youngest boys. Maxine's job at the arsenal disappeared with the end of the war in the Pacific, so she decided to visit her old friend Nell Raborn in Texarkana. Raborn ran a very successful bordello at

807 West Fourth Street. Maxine worked there for three years and developed a real flair for the "entertainment" business. She also discovered that she had management potential.

Maxine fell in love with the beauty and charm of Hot Springs during a visit in 1948. The place felt like home, so she stayed. She asked a handsome man at a cab stand if there were any bordellos in Hot Springs where she might get a job. She thought he was a cab driver, and only later learned Gary Mason was a sheriff's deputy. He answered "Yes, ma'am!" and walked her around the corner to a little walk-up hotel above the cab company at 105½ Prospect, where he introduced Maxine to Mary Williams, the madam of the establishment. Within a year, Maxine was driving a Cadillac and had purchased a ranch west of town. A year after that, she bought the Prospect Rooms and made the leap from labor to management.

By 1956, Maxine's business was known for its quality of service, innovative advertising, and professional management. But the location was less than ideal for a truly classy operation. So Maxine bought a magnificent old house built in 1900 from Ellis Kendall, a black doctor considered to be one of the finest physicians in Hot Springs, as well as one of the most moral and respected men in town. Dr. Kendall raised his family and ran his practice in the old house from 1922 until his retirement in 1955. Located at the corner of Convention Boulevard and Palm Street, Maxine restored and redecorated the structure to unbridled elegance to attract successful businessmen, doctors, and politicians from throughout the state. She claimed that an Arkansas attorney general, a federal judge from Washington, and even members of Congress visited the sixteen-room Mansion, which remained her fondest achievement. "Honey," she once remarked, "I like an old-fashioned whorehouse that has respect and dignity."

Those golden years lasted until 1962, when mobsters and their crooked politicians tried to coerce Maxine to join their "syndicate." She was far too independent to kowtow to ruffians and pay them a portion of her profits. But she needed some protection, so she married Worth Gregory. "Worth Gregory was the best looking son of a gun that ever walked," according to Maxine. He was a "tough dude out of Texas, a hit man with five notches on his gun." Gregory did manage to protect his wife for a time, but the syndicate eventually set him up for a fall. Convicted of possessing narcotics, Gregory was sentenced to prison, where he died under questionable circumstances. Maxine was convinced that the syndicate of mobsters and corrupt politicians had him silenced. Local police began to raid her bordellos and ignore all the others in Hot Springs (which belonged to the syndicate).

Deputies of the Garland County sheriff raided her business in July 1963, about a month after Gregory died in prison. Convicted of pandering, Maxine received a fourteen-month sentence to the Cummins State Penitentiary near Pine Bluff. She claims that she was denied adequate medical attention there, and she lost fifty pounds as her health steadily deteriorated. After winning an early release, she returned to Hot Springs, where she was able to get the medication she required and began a long road to recovery.

Once back on her feet, Maxine rented the Central Avenue Hotel and married a tough, admitted bank robber, Edward Jones, for protection from the syndicate. "He was the only guy I ever loved in that special way," Maxine said. Edward Jones spent a lot of time in and out of jails, but mobsters feared him so they never directly attacked Maxine. The madam wrote that they simply hired police and politicians to harass her. One day Edward Jones turned up dead in a motel. According to his wife, Jones was poisoned by someone he trusted, with the apparent complicity of *his own mother*. Maxine was on her own for the last time. According to her book, she was double-crossed by her own lawyer and harassed by both sides of the law. So Maxine Jones left the "entertainment" business for good. She subsequently moved to Warren to be near her family, and only visited Hot Springs when the weather was nice, even though she still considered the town her home.

Gamblers, Mobsters, and the Rise of Winthrop Rockefeller

Following the G.I. Revolt, mobster Vincent Madden lived the life of a model citizen throughout his tenure in Hot Springs. Former mayor Leo McLaughlin quietly lived out his life in Hot Springs until his death in 1958. In 1959, a prominent gambler and old friend of Madden quickly became a big name in town. Dane Harris built the Vapors supper club and apparently rebuilt the gambling industry as well. He began to donate to every church fund-raiser in town. He even donated two swimming pools to the community: one for whites and one for blacks. Two years later, Congress passed a federal anti-gambling law to help local governments stamp out the practice. The U.S. Department of Justice promptly questioned Madden and mobster Joe Velachi about gambling activities in Hot Springs.

Madden didn't say much. Velachi explained that Hot Springs was popular with many known members of organized crime simply because they liked taking the waters. The Department of Justice eventually concluded that Hot Springs had the largest illegal gambling operation in the entire country, but a grand jury could find no proof of any wrongdoing.

Illegal gambling continued to flourish in Hot Springs. Dane Harris told an out-of-state reporter: "There is no reform group. There never has been. We are respected; there's no feeling that we're doing something unlawful."

Harris was wrong. Reform groups did exist. While Faubus had been governor for a decade, he never tackled the illegal gambling in Hot Springs until an outbreak of violence erupted between rival gambling factions. Bombs detonated in the Vapors supper club as well as in the homes of underworld figures. Faubus responded by ordering that the casinos close their doors. A group of legislators tried to stop Faubus by introducing a bill to legalize gambling, but the effort failed.

May 29, 1964, was the last night of casino gambling in Hot Springs. Xavier Cugat and Abbe Lane performed at the Belvedere Club in front of an audience that lacked the usual gaiety. The patrons believed this was the end of the good life in Hot Springs. One city official, however, commented to a reporter that the casinos would reopen within a year. Few people were that optimistic. Within days, the local economy seemed to go into a tailspin.

Seven large conventions quickly cancelled their reservations. Many visitors who did come to Hot Springs were quite disappointed at the lack of gambling, and they expressed the wish it be reintroduced as soon as possible. One local wag claimed that the casinos simply must be reopened before everyone starved to death for a lack of hundred-dollar bills. A reporter for the *Saturday Evening Post* observed that the "unrepentant little resort [was] fighting for its low, evil, up all night, bad-example-setting and extremely comfortable life."

Gambling promptly resumed in the big clubs of Hot Springs. Faubus decided not to run for another term, and Winthrop Rockefeller defeated the Democratic candidate in the 1966 election. Soon after taking the oath of office, Governor Rockefeller quietly attempted to pressure local law enforcement officials to close down illegal gaming houses. Quiet diplomacy failed.

Rockefeller's new head of the state police, Colonel Lynn Davis, conducted a series of raids in 1967 that seized hundreds of slot machines and other gambling devices. Davis turned the machines over to the local police to be used as evidence in criminal prosecutions. Not only did the local officials fail to prosecute, the gambling machines reappeared in the casinos, which promptly reopened for business.

Undaunted, Davis launched a new series of raids. He had the state police destroy the gambling machines they confiscated. This spawned a small manufacturing boom in Hot Springs as small shops appeared to rebuild the broken machines. This time, the state police raided the repair shops. Public opinion began to change when the state police discovered that many of the craps tables they confiscated were fitted with "juice joints," which were battery-powered black boxes fitted under the tables that allowed the croupiers to control the final position of the dice.

Colonel Davis conducted his most successful raid on the night of October 7, 1967. A local judge gave him a warrant to search the home of Harry Columbus, who owned the Southern Club. Davis asked Columbus to open a padlock on the door to a large storehouse behind the club-owner's home. Columbus refused, so the state police broke down the door. They found two truckloads of slot machines. Fifteen of those machines had received state police markings when confiscated on earlier raids, before they were turned over to the Hot Springs Police for destruction.

Davis kept those fifteen machines and had the rest taken to a gravel pit. Davis called in the media to film as a bulldozer ground the confiscated machines into kindling. The state police poured thirty gallons of diesel fuel over the debris and set it ablaze. Once the fire burned itself out, the bulldozer buried the ashes of casino gambling in Hot Springs. It was, as Davis observed at the time, the end of an era.

But that raid was not the end of gambling, for horse racing had been an accepted gaming activity in Hot Springs since before the Civil War. Soon after the turn of the century, one racetrack began to dominate horse racing in Hot Springs: Oaklawn Park.

Oaklawn Park

Horse racing started in Hot Springs well before the Civil War crushed the life out of the area for several dark years. Local farm boys would sometimes bring their fastest mounts for the amusement of locals and visitors. They gathered on the southeastern edge of town in a pasture where, according to local legend, the Oaklawn track was eventually built. Racing became more organized and formal during the Gay Nineties with the creation of a jockey club.

By 1893, Hot Springs could boast a half-mile track with 400 boxed stalls. Sportsman Park, as the track was called, was a half hour from downtown Hot Springs. The first season was most successful. Attendance and purses grew steadily larger, but anti-gambling laws began to strangle the park. The legislature repealed problem legislation in 1903, and the Jockey Club planned a real tour de force for the 1904 racing season.

290

The Oaklawn track on April 12, 1919. –Garland County Historical Archives

Racehorse Moflame is held by trainer J. P. Flynn at Oaklawn Park on March 10, 1956. –Garland County Historical Archives

The Jockey Club built a new track and grandstand near the Choctaw Railroad (formerly the Diamond Jo and subsequently the Rock Island). The railroad agreed to run twelve trains per day between downtown and the track, which was briefly called Camp Lawrence before taking the more dignified name of Essex Park. The mayor declared an official holiday on the day the track opened, and a huge crowd filled the grandstands to overflowing. The twenty-three-day season exceeded everyone's expectations by a substantial margin.

A group of turfmen from St. Louis decided to give the track some competition. The Western Jockey Club constructed a rival track at Oaklawn, which was much closer to town. Furthermore, the new track featured a glass-enclosed, steam-heated grandstand that could seat 1,500 patrons in comfort. Oaklawn became a major force in racing from its very first season in 1905.

That 1905 season was a turfman's dream, with three sets of races taking place in Hot Springs. In addition to races at Essex Park and Oaklawn Park, the Arkansas Jockey Club of Little Rock brought the Arkansas Derby to Hot Springs for the first time. Hot Springs had never seen so many horses in town.

To no one's surprise, an intense rivalry developed between the competing tracks. Oaklawn had something of an unfair advantage because the Western Jockey Club not only controlled Oaklawn, it also assigned dates for all the races in Arkansas. Naturally, Oaklawn got the best weather dates, which infuriated the owners of Essex Park.

They rebelled and created their own racing schedule, so the 1907 racing season saw a number of days with racing at both tracks. This anarchy and Oaklawn's more convenient location conspired against Essex Park, which went bankrupt. The future of Oaklawn seemed assured. But the Western Jockey Club and Oaklawn had pushed the owner of Essex Park to the breaking point. William McGuigan sold Essex Park, and joined a reform group trying to completely eliminate horse racing in Arkansas.

McGuigan was known as Umbrella Bill because he always carried an umbrella regardless of the weather. He thought it brought him luck. During his career as a turfman, he would thrust his umbrella like a rapier toward the horse he was betting on.

The anti-racing forces succeeded in banning racing for much longer than Umbrella Bill had intended—by outlawing betting on the races. Hours after the new law was passed, police raided the betting facilities at Oaklawn and arrested every Oaklawn official they found, including Louis Cella, who was on the board of trustees for the Western Jockey Club. Oaklawn was permitted to finish out the 1907 season— without any betting. Without this essential source of revenue, horse racing slipped from the scene at Hot Springs. The only activity at Oaklawn Park during that period was the state fair for a few days each year.

Then in 1916, the local Business Men's League voted 387 to 13 to bring back horse racing to Hot Springs. They planned a thirty-day season at Oaklawn Park, which would be organized as a nonprofit enterprise to avoid legal problems. The season was successful enough for the businessmen to expand the effort the following year, when the dates were divided between Oaklawn and Essex Park. Ill fortune continued to plague Essex Park, however. Fire completely destroyed the grandstand the day after it reopened. Any hope of rebuilding was drowned when the rising waters of Lake Catherine flooded part of the grounds. Essex Park passed into history. Oaklawn became the focus of racing in Hot Springs until anti-racing forces closed the track down from 1919 until the 1930s. The Prohibition Era dried up drinking and horse racing in Hot Springs.

With the demise of Prohibition in 1934 and the advent of the New Deal, the Arkansas legislature voted to restore pari-mutuel racing at Hot Springs. Under this system, everyone who bets on the winner shares the total stakes, minus a small percentage for the management. Over the decades that followed, attendance at Oaklawn Park steadily increased and the facilities were continually upgraded. Interest reached such a level in 1961 that the season was extended from thirty to forty-three days. Oaklawn bounced back from financial difficulties in the 1980s thanks to some tax relief from the state legislature and innovative amenities such as gourmet dining at the park.

By 1990, the Oaklawn season had increased to sixty-five days, from early February until late April. That year, the track instituted a summer schedule showing simulcasts of thoroughbred races at other tracks. Oaklawn Park has become thoroughly woven into the fabric of the economic and social life of Hot Springs.

Hot Springs Today

Although the spas generated most of the economic activity during the community's first century, interest in taking the waters dried up after World War II. Improved medicine and changing lifestyles doomed the spas. Vacationers would rather explore new highways in their automobiles than spend several weeks soaking and lounging around in some hotel. As America's love affair with the car increased, business at the spas plummeted. All but one closed their doors.

Hot Springs responded by attracting the burgeoning tourist traffic to the area's unique resources: three lakes with hundreds of miles of shoreline, Hot Springs National Park, a picturesque downtown, and horse racing at Oaklawn Park. Several artists visited the community and stayed, attracting more artists, until dozens of studios and art galleries dotted the landscape. While bathing in the hot springs may no longer draw many people to Hot Springs, the area's many other recreational possibilities make this one of the liveliest communities in Arkansas.

—MOUNT IDA—

Located twenty-nine miles west of Hot Springs and thirty-two miles southeast of Y City on US 270, Mount Ida has long been an important crossroads in the Ouachita Mountains. The town is now best known as the "Quartz Crystal Capital of the World." Quartz was mined commercially for more than 100 years to make numerous products ranging from crystal balls to sandpaper. These days, rock hounds do the mining at the dig-it-yourself mines that abound in the area.

The origin of the town's name is somewhat circuitous. The story begins five years before the legislature created the county, when Granville Whittington was the secretary of the meeting that petitioned Congress for statehood. Granville established the Mount Ida post office in 1842 on his farm, which was located about a mile and a half east of the present town of Mount Ida. Because the Ouachita Mountains reminded him of his native Massachusetts, Granville named the post office after a mountain he admired near Boston.

Later that year, the legislature established Montgomery County, naming it after a war hero, as was a common practice of the day. Born in Ireland in the 1730s to a member of Parliament from Dublin, Richard Montgomery was educated at Trinity College and entered the British army in 1756. He fought in America during the French and Indian War, and later participated in the capture of Havana during a campaign in the West Indies.

After mustering out of the British army, Montgomery settled his affairs in England and returned to America. He married an American from a prestigious family, and accepted the rank of major general in the new Continental army, as the second in command to General Philip Schuyler. Schuyler fell ill soon after marching on British forces in Canada, so Montgomery assumed command. He was unusually successful at building both the morale and the combat skills of his troops. Montgomery's forces captured British forts on the Richelieu River and went on to take Montreal. Montgomery then marched on Quebec in a coordinated assault with forces under the command of General Benedict Arnold, where Montgomery was killed by British artillery.

The legislature established the county seat at its present location, and the town was named after the same war hero as the county. The county court changed the town's name from Montgomery to Salem in 1850. That lasted four months. Because of pressure from postal authorities in Washington, D.C., the town's name was changed to match the name of the post office. Mount Ida was incorporated in 1854. The present courthouse was built in 1923 at the site of the original 1846 courthouse. While it may be the best example of English Adamsesque architecture in Arkansas, the building is not entirely original thanks to the construction of a modern brick addition.

Arkansas 26 and 301
Arkadelphia—Crater of Diamonds State Park
41 miles

This is a journey through small towns, with the delicious names of Delight and Murfreesboro, to one of the most unusual destinations in North America: the Crater of Diamonds State Park, where anyone can dig for diamonds with their own hands. Inside the crater is a very real field of dreams, dreams fulfilled and dreams denied. A diverse and compelling cast has written the history of diamonds in Arkansas, but the final act has yet to be conjured into life. Only the future will tell which competing dream for the Crater of Diamonds will ultimately prevail.

—DELIGHT—
Delight is best known as the hometown of singer Glen Campbell. The town was built on land owned by W. H. Kirkham, who proposed the town name because he found the area to be quite delightful. The town is in Pike County, which was *not* named after Albert Pike, who figured prominently in Arkansas politics in the middle of the nineteenth century.

Rather, the county was named after Zebulon Pike, who was a U.S. Army explorer from New Jersey. He joined the army in his teens and was commissioned by the age of twenty. After searching for the headwaters of the Mississippi River, Lieutenant Pike went on to explore the upper reaches of the Arkansas River, where he discovered a great mountain that was named after him: Pike's Peak. Zebulon Pike rose to the rank of brigadier general and was killed while fighting the British during the War of 1812.

—MURFREESBORO—

When Pike County was created from chunks of Clark and Hempstead Counties in 1833, the state legislature stipulated that a temporary county seat be established at the home of Paschal Sorrels until commissioners could be elected to determine a permanent location. That location was called Zebulon in honor of Lieutenant Pike. By 1934, Zebulon could boast a log courthouse, a small frame building for the county clerk's office, and a post office. The lots in the county seat were surveyed by Tennesseans in 1836, who reportedly suggested changing the name of the town to Murfreesboro after their former hometown.

—CRATER OF DIAMONDS—

Located about two and a half miles southeast of Murfreesboro on Arkansas 301, the Crater of Diamonds is now a state park where visitors can search for diamonds, as well as forty different kinds of semi-precious gems and minerals. This is believed to be the only place on the planet where anyone from the public at large can hunt for diamonds in their natural geologic formation. The turbulent history of

Hunting for diamonds at Murfreesboro in 1966.
—Southwest Arkansas Regional Archives

this diamond deposit reels from the clashing personalities of plain folks, thieves, and visionaries. Some found their dreams fulfilled. Some found their dreams denied. The clash of conflicting visions continues to this very day, making Crater of Diamonds more than an utterly unique experience for tourists and rock hounds. Crater of Diamonds generates lively history like a great mountain generates its own weather. This turbulent swirl of history was begun by John Wesley Huddleston, who bought the old McBrayer farm early in 1906.

Diamond John

The son of a sharecropper, John Huddleston had spent most of his life as a wandering backwoodsman who spent more time looking for Indian arrowheads than he did working for a living. He was a massive man—several inches over six feet tall, with huge paws for hands, long arms, sloped shoulders, and a hard expression in his dark eyes. A harelip, which was largely hidden by a big black moustache, impaired his speech and probably contributed to his unfriendly attitude toward strangers. This attitude contrasted with his companionable, if eccentric, behavior when among friends. One day in 1906 he finally realized that he had a wife and four daughters to support, so he reluctantly decided to settle down and raise hogs.

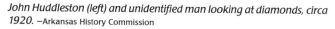

John Huddleston (left) and unidentified man looking at diamonds, circa 1920. –Arkansas History Commission

Huddleston made a deal to buy 160 acres for $1,000. But he didn't have the $100 down payment requested by the owners, so he offered a mule instead, which was accepted. Huddleston couldn't read or write, so he simply put his X on the papers. On August 8 of that same year, he discovered two white diamonds on his farm. Prior to Huddleston's discovery, a few scattered diamonds had been found in placer deposits left by glaciers from Hudson Bay to Wisconsin. But no diamond had ever been recovered from its natural geologic formation in North America. Those 3 and 4.5 carat Arkansas diamonds created such a stir that Huddleston was able to sell his 160-acre farm for $36,000. He figured that $6,000 apiece would last himself, his wife, and each daughter for the rest of their lives.

Soon after he earned the moniker "Diamond John," he brought the first automobile to Pike County. Resembling a high-wheeled buggy, it could not negotiate the muddy wagon tracks that passed for roads in those days. Then the automobile suffered a flat tire while Diamond John was driving south of Delight. It proved to be the final insult. Diamond John got out of the car, looked at it with disgust, and walked back to town. He never made any attempt to recover the car, and finally someone hauled it away.

His wife died soon thereafter, and his notoriety as Diamond John quickly attracted a young blonde carnival girl whom he met in Arkadelphia. They moved to Murfreesboro, and he bought his bride a Model T Ford coupe. He was very proud of his wife, who would drive him around the town square most evenings. One evening, when he got out of the car to buy a cigar, she drove westward out of town and was never seen again.

Diamond John's fortunes continued to decline. He had purchased several properties around the Murfreesboro town square as well as several farms near Arkadelphia. He had placed only minimum down payments on each property, and soon he was having trouble keeping up with the payments. He lost his investments. But he remained a trustworthy resource when one of his friends needed a helping hand. Diamond John did, however, sometimes display a certain impatience with adversity.

Once, for example, a buzzing wasp awakened him while napping on his front porch one warm afternoon. He spied a wasp nest under a corner of a roof, so he stomped off, grabbed his shotgun, and blasted that nest—and a substantial part of the roof—into oblivion. Normally he showed a bit more finesse. He could pick off a wasp with a single shot from his .45 caliber pistol. Yet it is interesting to note that, with all his faults and eccentricities, his friends remembered Diamond John as a likeable man and an entertaining conversationalist.

When his daughters reached marriageable age, he declared that a $1,000 dowry went with the hand of each daughter. The first three daughters did get their dowries, but his fortune had completely disappeared by the time Huddleston's fourth daughter married. Pike County lore is filled with fascinating stories about Diamond John, who is still remembered fondly.

Samuel Rayburn, who was president of the Union Trust Company in Little Rock, purchased Diamond John's farm. Rayburn solicited 600 investors from Little Rock to New York and formed the Arkansas Diamond Company. They commissioned a former manager of the African diamond mine Dutoitspan to test the commercial potential of the property in 1909. John Fuller sunk a test shaft 205 feet into the greenish clay known as kimberlite.

The shaft produced twenty-one carats of diamonds for each hundred tons of clay. South African deposits varied from six to forty-two carats for the same amount of clay, and a yield of ten carats was considered profitable at that time. So Rayburn's diamond deposit was quite viable commercially. Furthermore, if similar structures in South Africa were any indication, the Arkansas diamond deposit could extend to a depth of 5,000 feet or more. That was the good news.

The bad news was that Rayburn's tract of land only contained forty-nine acres of the deposit. A large parcel was owned by a neighboring farmer who was also county clerk: M. M. Mauney. Both of these tracts are now contained in the Crater of Diamonds State Park, but this consolidation only occurred recently, after a long and turbulent conflict between rival owners. From a geological perspective, the two tracts of land—which came to be collectively known as the Crater of Diamonds many years later—proved to be a single volcanic pipe.

The Crater of Diamonds

The volcanic pipe forming the Crater of Diamonds carried molten rock up to the surface of the earth from a depth of perhaps 100 miles, where virtually pure pockets of carbon formed crystals known as diamonds. During the Cretaceous period, the molten rock formed a mound, which subsequently eroded down to the present ground level over many millions of years. The mineral filling the old volcanic pipe is a variant of peridotite known as kimberlite, which is named after the famous Kimberly Mine in South Africa. This greenish blue rock weathers into the soft, claylike soil seen in the Crater of Diamonds. The diamonds do not occur in the kimberlite as veins like gold or copper. Rather, the diamonds are scattered randomly throughout the deposit. This phenomenon makes recovering diamonds both expensive and labor-intensive.

But the capital required for commercial mining was no concern for M. M. Mauney. He continued working as the county clerk and held weekend ice cream socials, where 50 cents would pay for ice cream as well as the right to hunt for diamonds, which the finder was free to keep or sell. Samuel Rayburn and his investors, however, focussed on commercial mining of the deposit. Thus, there are really two different—and yet interwoven—histories to the Crater of Diamonds.

The Dawn of Commercial Diamond Mining

The start-up of commercial mining by Mauney's neighbor, the Arkansas Diamond Company, stimulated his dreams of wealth. Mauney sold 75 percent of his property (about thirty acres) to Horace Bemis Sr., who was a wealthy lumberman from Prescott. Mauney kept ten acres for himself. Together they formed the Ozark Diamond Mines Corporation to commercially mine their holdings. They built three processing plants, but the two men quickly developed heated differences. Their partnership dissolved just after mining operations began. Bemis died soon thereafter, and his heirs sold their thirty acres to Austin Millar for $110,000.

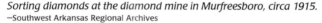

Sorting diamonds at the diamond mine in Murfreesboro, circa 1915.
—Southwest Arkansas Regional Archives

In April 1912, Mauney offered to lease his ten acres to Millar for a 25 percent royalty. Millar accepted, but then defaulted on the terms of the lease when mining equipment was not delivered in a timely manner. Mauney sued Millar and lost. So he sued again just before he died. His son, Walter, continued what would become a family tradition, suing Millar another thirty-two times without success.

Millar got into full-scale production the following year. A narrow-gauge railroad hauled ten cars of kimberlite per hour to a crushing plant. Then the ore was washed with water pumped from Prairie Creek to remove the lighter soils. The ore was then dumped into ten-foot washing wheels that contained a liquid three times more dense than water. The washer rejected those components of the slurry that floated, while retaining the dense components, which included any diamonds in the ore. The concentrated ore was then processed though a recovery plant, where the diamonds were removed using water and grease.

This interesting process merits a brief description. The process works because most gravels will not stick to grease. But untreated diamonds will. A slurry of concentrated ore and water is poured onto sloping tables covered with sheep fat. The surface structure of a diamond grabs the grease as the water washes all the other gravels off the table. After processing an appropriate amount of ore, the diamond-studded grease is scraped off the table and melted with boiling water. This final process leaves clean, loose diamonds that are ready for sorting by hand. Like the diamonds found in South Africa, about 20 percent of the diamonds are gem quality. The rest are suitable for industrial applications.

A unique property of Arkansas diamonds is that they average about 28 percent harder than most diamonds. This contributes to the yin and yang of gem-quality diamonds from the Crater of Diamonds. Their hardness makes Arkansas diamonds more brilliant, but the hardness makes the gems much more difficult and expensive to cut and polish. Such hardness makes industrial-quality diamonds from Arkansas particularly useful for use on cutting tools.

Millar recovered a lot of diamonds during the first five years of his operation, in spite of the fact that his workers were stealing diamonds at a prodigious rate. His success must have further frustrated his neighbors at the Arkansas Diamond Company, who were plagued by incompetent management. The Arkansas Diamond Company owned most of the diamond-bearing ground, yet four separate attempts to get mining under way failed miserably at substantial financial loss to their investors. Their frustration must have produced the plague that descended upon their successful neighbor, Austin Millar.

Fires broke out at all three of Millar's processing plants simultaneously on a cold January night in 1919. Everything burned to the ground except a few minor outbuildings. Even the railroad was destroyed, since the ties had been soaked in kerosene. Remarkably, there was no official ruling of arson, which brings to mind a legendary Chicago suicide in the 1930s where the victim had shot himself in the back six times.

While the fire killed off the Ozark Diamond Mines Corporation for good, Austin Millar retained ownership of his thirty acres. He continued to live on the property until his death. Folks would sneak onto his property to steal diamonds, but Millar never ran them off.

One fellow in particular lived within a stone's throw of the diamond mine. He never worked at a regular job, but he managed to raise a large family thanks to a vial of diamonds that he always had in his pocket when he walked the streets of Murfreesboro. Diamonds could be quietly purchased from individuals on the courthouse square more or less continuously over the years. But this one neighbor regularly searched the old mine and was never chased off. The Millars were tolerant folks.

Millar's son, Howard, worked at the plant until the fire, when he moved to Little Rock to work as the assistant state geologist. Millar's competition, the Arkansas Diamond Company, reorganized as the Arkansas Diamond Mining Corporation. The new company muddled along until 1929, when a lot of dreams crashed throughout the country and the Great Depression spread its malevolent tentacles across the land. The Crater of Diamonds remained a forgotten backwater of history until several years after the conclusion of World War II.

The Dawn of Tourism

In the late 1940s, Austin Millar leased his portion of the crater as a tourist attraction, where visitors could dig for diamonds all day for a fee. The operators failed to turn a profit and eventually defaulted on their lease. Austin Millar died of a heart attack at the age of ninety-three on Thanksgiving Day, 1951, and ownership passed to his son, Howard.

Howard Millar believed that using the property as a tourist attraction could be profitable if it was managed properly. A heart attack prevented him from continuing his rigorous life as a geologist and stimulated him to try a career in tourism.

Howard entered a partnership with his friend and neighbor, Mrs. Wilkinson, to start a tourist business. Her lawyer from Indiana, Joe Noel, suggested that they name the tourist attraction the "Crater of Diamonds." Mrs. Wilkinson agreed to match Millar's $20,000 investment

A family searches for gems at the Crater of Diamonds.
—Arkansas History Commission

for start-up expenses, but she only provided $3,500 at that time. The rest, she said, would be mailed later that year. The money never appeared. Nevertheless, Millar moved his family to the property in 1952 and started his business, even though he was undercapitalized by the shortfall from Mrs. Wilkinson. She eventually asked to dissolve the partnership, and Millar bought out her share of the tourist venture.

The rules of his tourist attraction were simple. Pay a small fee and keep any diamonds under five carats. The Millars would share in the profits of any stones over that weight.

Meanwhile, back on the larger tract, Art Slocum ran a wildcat mining operation from 1958 through 1962. Then a man and his wife who had worked for Howard Millar's Crater of Diamonds tourist operation

303

abruptly quit. James Johnson and his wife, Odell, leased the large tract from Mrs. Wilkinson as a tourist attraction, and opened for business two weeks later.

Millar was stunned for several reasons. As part of his earlier financial deal with Mrs. Wilkinson (which Millar recounts in his book, *It Was Finders-Keepers at America's Only Diamond Mine*), his neighbor had promised that she would never compete with Millar's tourist operation. Millar was also stunned that the couple he had taken under his wing, trained, and promoted would turn around and hurt his business.

The Johnsons called their operation the Arkansas Diamond Mine and referred to it as "the big mine." The competition was fierce and rather unpleasant at times. For example, the Johnsons surrounded and blocked Millar's signs with their own. The Johnson signs led tourists to believe that their operation produced only big diamonds. On one occasion, it appears that Mrs. Johnson actually followed several busloads of tourists into the Millars' parking lot, shouting from her pickup, "These are my customers!" Such rude competition was very hard on Howard Millar and his wife. James Johnson died a few years after starting the family business, and his widow continued the operation until both properties were sold in 1969.

Birth of a State Park

The first calm in the storm that has swirled around the entire history of the Crater of Diamonds appeared in 1969, when General Earth Minerals of Dallas purchased the crater's entire 72.5 acres along with 815 acres of adjoining lands. Everyone sold out to this company, which intended to begin full-scale mining operations.

Howard Millar moved with his wife and younger daughter to Fayetteville. The General Minerals operation fizzled before it ever got started, and the mine was simply used as a tourist attraction until the Arkansas Department of Parks and Tourism purchased the tract in 1972. The tradition of individuals hunting for diamonds that they get to keep continues. When Howard Millar retired from fifty years of experience hunting diamonds in Arkansas, he estimated that the Crater of Diamonds had produced more than 400,000 diamonds, averaging more than a half carat each.

The Crater of Diamonds has produced some impressive stones. The Uncle Sam diamond, which was found in 1924, weighed 40.23 carats. The blue-white Star of Arkansas, which was found in 1956, weighed 15.31 carats and was the size of a pigeon egg. The Gary Moore diamond found in 1960 proved to be a flawless golden canary weighing 6.43 carats. The list of famous diamonds goes on and on. Perhaps

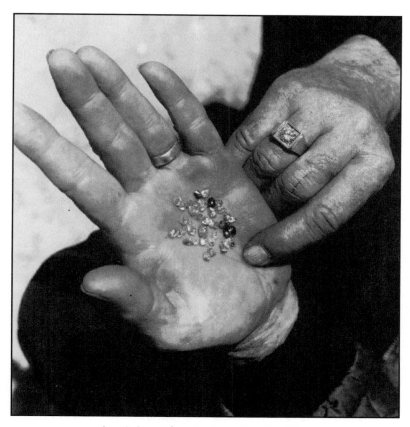

Assorted gems from the Crater of Diamonds.
—Arkansas History Commission

the most interesting was discovered in 1981: the 6.25 carat Newman diamond. This proved to be a very rare Type IIA diamond, which means that it has little or no nitrogen in the crystal. And it was graded "D" flawless. Arkansas diamonds can rival the color and quality of the best South African, Russian, and Australian gems.

Since its inception, mining companies have been interested in commercial mining of the Crater of Diamonds State Park. Some feasibility testing has been conducted. Legislation enacted in 1987 requires that any commercial operation must preserve the function of the park as a place where the public can go to hunt diamonds. One possible solution is to cover thirty-five acres with weathered, crushed, unsorted kimberlite to a depth of five feet. This public search area would be periodically replenished with fresh kimberlite. The same legislation specifies a commission empowered to accept or reject commercial mining of the park, and the legislation also specifies the distribution of royalties. The sanctity of tourist use must be preserved, whatever course of action is eventually taken.

The public seems to be quite divided on this issue, and both sides present articulate arguments. It will be interesting to see how this controversy is finally resolved.

—Part Five—
THE OZARKS

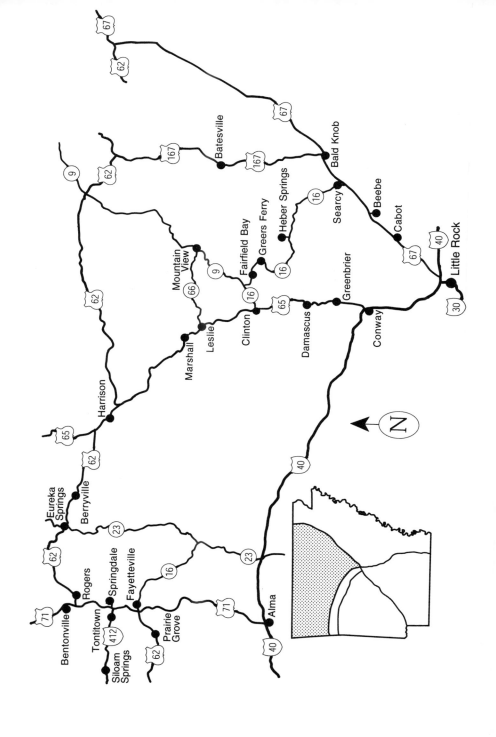

Alma–Eureka Springs
118 miles

The stretch of highway from Alma to Eureka Springs spans the western Ozarks. The history of the area features some of the most notorious desperados on the American frontier, clashing armies, gentle men, twelve governors of four states, humanitarians, charlatans, visionaries, and some of the most successful corporate moguls in American history. The western Ozarks are packed with fascinating stories.

—ALMA—

Located at the junction of I-40 and US 71, Alma was originally named Gum Town by the first settlers in the area. When residents applied to the federal government for a post office, postal officials refused to accept the name. So like the citizens of a surprising number of embryonic Arkansas communities, local residents changed the name of the town to satisfy the bureaucrats in Washington. Sam Daugherty, who was the postmaster in a neighboring community, proposed his sweetheart's name: Alma.

—FAYETTEVILLE—

Located about forty-seven miles north of Alma and thirty-three miles south of the Missouri border on US 71, Fayetteville was originally called Washington Courthouse when it became the seat of newly formed Washington County in 1828. The name created a certain amount of confusion, however, because an important community in Hempstead County was called Washington. So postal authorities requested that the newer town be renamed. Local residents decided to name the town after another hero of the Revolutionary War, French nobleman and American general Marie Joseph Paul Yves Roch Gilbert du Motier, marquis du LaFayette.

LaFayette was larger than life. Even though he was only twenty when he arrived from France to join the Continental army in 1777, Washington gave LaFayette the rank of general. This rank made sense for several reasons. LaFayette had excellent training as an officer in the French army, and he had powerful political connections in France thanks to his status within the French nobility. Americans greatly admire the man for his invaluable contributions to the American Revolution, but most folks don't realize that he also figured prominently in the subsequent French Revolution. LaFayette went on to command an army that fought against Austria. After being captured and imprisoned, Napoleon eventually freed him. As if all these achievements weren't enough, LaFayette also designed the modern French flag, known as the Tricolor. LaFayette returned to the United States in 1824, and people throughout the land greeted him with an outpouring of admiration and gratitude, naming numerous counties and communities after him.

County residents built a crude wooden courthouse on the west side of Fayetteville's town square in 1829. By 1830, Fayetteville had a population of 75, and the 2,100 residents of Washington County viewed their $50 courthouse as inadequate to the task and something of an embarrassment. Congress authorized the county to sell 160 acres of land to finance the construction of a proper courthouse. This land was sold off as town lots, so the need to upgrade the courthouse actually stimulated the growth of the community. This growth was enhanced by the fact that Fayetteville sat astride the confluence of several Indian trails that were gradually being improved into important frontier roads. The most important connected Fort Smith to Jefferson City, Missouri, and eventually came to be known as Old Wire Road. Others connected Fayetteville with Cane Hill and Huntsville, and an important trail passed through Weddington Gap to Indian Territory.

The town grew to a population of 400 over the next decade, while the county grew to more than 7,000 people. Fayetteville's population included 123 slaves, and the county's population included 880 slaves and 19 "freedmen." Slaves were rare throughout most of the Ozarks. But the land around Fayetteville was unusually good for farming, so planters imported slaves to work the land. Fayetteville merchants imported slaves to work in the stores.

Fayetteville remained very much a tough frontier town. The town got tougher in the late 1830s, when a plague of desperados descended on Washington County. A local store clerk, James Case, wrote a letter in 1840 that said, "This county and town in particular has become one of the most lawless and uncivilized in all creation. . . . Shooting, stabbing, knocking down and dragging out appear to be the order of the day. . . . Almost everyone you see is armed to the teeth." Vigilantes who called themselves the Committee of 36 finally stopped the scourge, and the vigilantes continued to operate in Washington County until the mid-1840s. The most colorful resident of Fayetteville during this period was Archibald Yell.

Governor Archibald Yell. −Arkansas History Commission

Archibald Yell

Born in Tennessee, Archibald Yell began his life of adventure when he fought in the War of 1812 at the age of thirteen or fifteen (his year of birth is variously reported as 1797 or 1799). Yell continued his military career through the Seminole War in 1818, after which he returned to Tennessee and studied law. After serving in the Tennessee legislature for several years, Yell was appointed a circuit judge based out of Fayetteville in 1831.

Yell secured this appointment in spite of the fact that his legal skills were modest at best. Simply put, the judgeship was a reward for Yell's performance fifteen years earlier at the Battle of New Orleans, in which then General Andrew Jackson had commanded U.S. forces. Yell succeeded as a judge because of his character and personality, which

311

eventually led him back into politics. He became the first congressman from Arkansas in 1836, and the state's second governor in 1840. He successfully ran for Congress again in 1844.

With the outbreak of the Mexican War, Yell resigned from Congress and returned to Arkansas, where he enlisted as a private in the Arkansas Mounted Volunteers. Mostly men in their teens and early twenties, the volunteers elected Yell as the colonel in command of the unit. These young frontiersmen were full of spunk and vinegar, spoiling for a good fight, and quite indifferent to the demands of military discipline. Yell had his hands full. His young firebrands would soon become known as Yell's Mounted Devils.

The war did not go well for the Arkansas Mounted Volunteers, who were used as scouts and as guards at scattered outposts. The Mexicans responded to the U.S. invasion with guerilla tactics, which took a particularly heavy toll on the young Arkansans. The irregulars severely tarnished Yell's military reputation when they sought revenge for the murder of one of their members. They overtook a group of Mexican peasants fleeing into the mountains and killed every man, woman, and child they found. By the time a company of volunteers from Illinois arrived and restrained them, about thirty people had been brutally massacred. One historian suggests, however, that this atrocity was mild compared to some events perpetrated by the Texas Rangers.

Yell atoned for his men's behavior a few days later on February 23, 1847, during a fight that came to be known as the Battle of Buena Vista. Santa Ana's lancers had just routed and badly demoralized the Arkansas Mounted Volunteers. Yell died while attempting to rally his men, and was buried on the battlefield. When his men returned Yell's remains to Fayetteville later that year, 4,000 people came to his home to pay their respects. The turnout was unprecedented in the annals of Arkansas.

Even Archibald Yell's political opponents liked and admired the man. Long-term political adversary Albert Pike observed that "Yell was a worthy and honorable man . . . of unblemished integrity . . . a man of kindly nature, amiable and obliging, and of heroic bravery."

Many important and influential people have called Fayetteville home, including twelve governors of four states. Even in such lofty company, it's hard to find a more fascinating and compelling figure than Archibald Yell.

Within three years of Yell's death, the population of Fayetteville had reached 600, shops offered an ever-increasing variety of products, and the streets remained as mean as they had been two decades earlier.

Antebellum Fayetteville

Perhaps the most vivid vignette of Fayetteville life in 1850 comes from Marian Tebbetts Banes. "It was a common thing to see covered wagons trailing through town, and sometimes fearful things happened. A wayfarer, begging a meal and a night's comfort for himself and his horse, then killing the man and his wife, owners of the outfit, and helping himself to their belongings."

Brigands did not, however, operate in Fayetteville without peril, as Banes observed. "Once a mob caught up with a man who had committed a terrible crime and hanged him, south of town, then cut off his head and hung it on a pole for the buzzards and for a warning."

In spite of such scenes, Fayetteville was poised on the threshold of a new era with the establishment of schools such as Arkansas College (the first school to offer a college degree in Arkansas) and Van Horne's Female Institute. The prospect of improved transportation into western Arkansas also hinted at a brighter future. In the early years, the so-called roads into the Ozarks were so poor that oxen provided the only reliable transportation into Washington County. Horses lacked the stamina, and mules were not yet abundant enough for the task.

Local doctors T. J. Pollard and Wade Pollard began operating a freight line in the 1840s that connected with steamboats on the Arkansas River, but they aspired to a more efficient mode of transportation. In 1853, Pollard and others incorporated the Arkansas Western Railroad. The goal was to build a line from Fort Smith—through Van Buren, Fayetteville, and Bentonville—to the Missouri railroad. The project stalled (and would stay stalled for three decades), so the two doctors sold their transportation business to John Butterfield, bringing Fayetteville onto the national stage.

The Butterfield Run

John Butterfield owned the Overland Mail Company, a stage line that carried mail, passengers, and freight over an increasing expanse of the country. By 1858, the Butterfield Run stretched over 2,000 miles between St. Louis and San Francisco via a southerly route that skirted the Rockies. Stages stopped at Elkhorn Tavern, Shiloh (now Springfield), and Fayetteville (among other stops in Arkansas) four times a week, bringing a steady flow of commerce and news to the relatively isolated communities. A branch line connected Evansville, Hermannsburg (now Dutch Mills), Newton (now Clyde), Cane Hill, and Prairie Grove.

The Overland Mail Company was a substantial operation for its day, employing about 800 men to operate more than a hundred expensive Concorde coaches. The company used 1,000 horses over much of the route, but about 500 mules were necessary for grueling stretches such as the Ozarks. The fare between St. Louis and San Francisco was $200 in gold, and Butterfield provided service twice weekly in each direction.

The drivers were well dressed and well paid ($20 per month). Perceived as colorful characters and men of adventure, local lasses eagerly sought their company at socials and dances. Everyone treated the drivers and even the passengers like celebrities.

The Butterfield Run provided unprecedented service. But even with a lucrative mail contract, the Overland Mail Company never did turn a profit. With war clouds looming on the horizon, Butterfield closed down the operation in 1861. This ended a romantic chapter of U.S. history and opened a new chapter of Fayetteville history characterized by the changing fortunes of war.

Changing Fortunes of War

Fayetteville profited during the antebellum years from its strategic location as a crossroads in northwestern Arkansas. But the most important military road connecting Missouri and Arkansas ran through Fayetteville, so the town's location led to a dizzying series of occupations, withdrawals, and reoccupations by both the Union and Confederate armies as the fortunes of war ebbed and flowed through the Ozarks.

Following the Battle of Wilson's Creek in the summer of 1861, Confederate forces fell back from southern Missouri and regrouped at Fayetteville. General Benjamin McCulloch quartered his men at Arkansas College and converted Van Horne's Female Institute into an arsenal. When massive Union forces approached in late February 1862, the Confederates torched the town square and the Female Institute before they retreated over the Boston Mountains. Exploding munitions at the Female Institute spread the inferno to the campus of Arkansas College. When dawn ended the nightmare the following morning, only a single brick dry goods store remained standing on the town square.

Union troops under the command of Brigadier General Alexander Asboth occupied Fayetteville a few days later. Asboth had both the will and the firepower to hold Fayetteville, but he was ordered to withdraw northward on March 4. Confederate forces reoccupied the city and struck northward, only to be defeated at Elkhorn Tavern during the Battle of Pea Ridge, which began on March 6. The Federals turned east and began a leisurely march on Batesville.

The Battle of Pea Ridge on March 7, 1862. –UCA Archives

Fayetteville residents were just beginning to recover from the Confederate torching of the town in February, when a major battle erupted at Prairie Grove on December 7. The Federals followed up their victory at Prairie Grove and occupied Fayetteville in early January 1863. Colonel LaRue Harrison commanded the Federal garrison, and Lieutenant Colonel A. W. Bishop served as provost marshal. Harrison would become Fayetteville's first mayor after the war, and Bishop became president of Arkansas Industrial University. Until this point, no fight had erupted between Confederate and Union forces in Fayetteville. That changed three months into the Federal occupation.

As April 16 dawned in the Ozarks, 900 Confederates under the command of Brigadier General William Cabell conducted a daring raid against the Union headquarters of the First Arkansas Cavalry at the home of Judge Jonas Tebbetts in Fayetteville. The house was used as the headquarters of whatever army occupied the town (located at 118 East Dickson Street, it still stands and is open to the public during the tourist season). A trench connected the headquarters with the heavy fortifications that ringed the town square.

Cabell's cumbersome artillery delayed his night traverse of the Boston Mountains until it was too late to launch a surprise attack. His cannon began a barrage from Mt. Sequoyah soon after dawn; Confederate infantry launched a diversionary attack while cavalry charged

315

Elkhorn Tavern overlooks the field where the Battle of Pea Ridge was fought. –Polly Walter

up the ravine in the eastern part of town and attacked the headquarters. Alerted by the barrage, the waiting Federals repeatedly repulsed the cavalry. Union Colonel Harrison described the "gallant cavalry charge," which the Federals met with a "galling cross-fire . . . piling rebel men and horses in heaps in front of our ordnance office." After a spirited battle lasting about an hour, Cabell withdrew his forces behind a screen of skirmishers. "By noon," Harrison reported, "their whole force was in full retreat for Ozark." The Tebbetts house still displays scars from the battle.

Ironically, the Federals were ordered to withdraw from Fayetteville a week later. The Confederates reoccupied the town, which Cabell used as a base of operations for raiding Union supply trains to the west. The Union thrust toward Fort Smith precipitated the final with-drawal of Confederate forces, who were needed to defend that post. The First Arkansas Cavalry restored Union control of Fayetteville, which lasted until the end of the war. Much of Fayetteville had been destroyed during the war, but soon the plucky community began a lively period of rebuilding, which culminated in the establishment of a university and the arrival of the railroad.

A College and Railroad Town

Six years after the end of the war during the period known as Re-construction, the legislature decided that the state needed a univer-sity. A number of communities vied for the honor by submitting bids, raising funds, authorizing bonds, and offering land. Washington County and Fayetteville pooled their financial resources and arranged for the donation of 420 acres to establish the university in Fayetteville. A former Union colonel and a Confederate judge joined forces and ramrodded the effort. The plan worked and the contract was awarded to Fayetteville.

The 160-acre farm of William McIlroy overlooked the town and seemed to provide the optimum location for the new school, so the farm was purchased and quickly equipped with stoves, chairs, and blackboards. The Arkansas Industrial University opened for business in January 1872. Despite substantial opposition, the university scan-dalized a segment of the state's population by admitting women. The first building constructed for the new school opened three years later, using wagon loads of Ozark stones pulled by oxen from a quarry sev-enty miles away. Called University Hall, the building with the twin spires is now generally known as Old Main. Those spires rise above the surrounding trees to provide a distinctive and charming landmark that can be seen from many places throughout the community.

By 1874, 146 students were taking college classes and another 198 were taking college-prep classes. By the end of the decade, the town's population had reached 2,000 and Dr. Pollard's dream of railroad ser-vice to Fayetteville was about to become a reality. The St. Louis & San Francisco Railroad began service between Missouri and Fayetteville in 1881, and extended service to Fort Smith the following year.

The university and the railroad stimulated the local economy, trans-forming the community from a tough frontier town into a prosperous economic and cultural center. Remarkably, the university—which had changed its name to the University of Arkansas in 1899—continued to grow during the depths of the Great Depression. The entire com-munity emerged from the chaos relatively unscarred by the ravages experienced elsewhere in Arkansas. Not a single bank failed in

Fayetteville. People helped each other, bartered when they didn't have money, and generally reaffirmed the nobility of the human spirit. Fayetteville had come a long way from its beginnings as a violent frontier town.

Fayetteville continues its leadership as a center of economic vitality, higher education, and college sports in Arkansas. The campus now supports about 14,000 students. The football team is known as the Razorbacks, a tradition that apparently began in 1909 when Coach Hugo Bezdek first referred to his players as "a wild bunch of razorback hogs." The steady trek of sports fans from central Arkansas to Fayetteville to watch the Razorbacks play football led to the establishment of another nickname. Most out-of-town fans travelled to the games over the beautiful stretch of Arkansas 23 that winds through the Ozark National Forest. So many folks started calling that road the Pig Trail that even the state highway department made up official signs bearing that label. The University of Arkansas at Fayetteville has certainly become a pervasive part of life in Arkansas.

—SPRINGDALE—

Located between Rogers and Fayetteville along US 71, Springdale is about fifty-four miles north of Alma and twenty-six miles south of Missouri on US 71. William Quinton originally settled on this land in 1840. The nucleus for the town was created three years later when Rev. John Holcombe founded the Shiloh Primitive Baptist Church. Interest in the area prompted Holcombe to lay out a town site in 1868, and the young community decided it needed a post office in 1875. But postal authorities pointed out that Arkansas already had a Shiloh post office, so local residents decided to rename their town Springdale because of the large spring in the center of town.

Establishment of the St. Louis & San Francisco Railroad in 1881 gave the town's economy a big boost. Today, Springdale is best known as the corporate headquarters of Tyson Foods (the largest producer of chickens and hogs in America). Cut from the same bolt of cloth as the late Sam Walton, corporate guru Don Tyson was usually seen wearing corporate coveralls with "Don" embroidered on his chest until his recent retirement. Springdale is also known for the award-winning Shiloh Museum of Ozark History, and the Northwest Vocational Technical School.

Tontitown

Located several miles west of Springdale on US 412, Father Pietro Bandini established Tontitown in 1898 to help Italian immigrants whose dream had turned into a nightmare of severe malnutrition and

Father Pietro Bandini established Tontitown in 1898 to help Italian immigrants. He also served as the town's mayor from 1909 to 1913. —Ray Watson Collection, Shiloh Museum of Ozark History

malaria in southeastern Arkansas. The catastrophe was spawned by the best of intentions.

New York millionaire Austin Corbin decided to do something about the hard life immigrants faced when they arrived at Ellis Island. Corbin came to Arkansas and purchased a tract of land in Chicot County. Next he wrote the mayor of Rome and offered homes to a hundred farm families from northern Italy, who would work as sharecroppers in Arkansas at a new village Corbin called Sunnyside. On April 7, 1895, 562 people arrived at Sunnyside. While the climate of southern Arkansas did not agree with many Italians, life there showed promise until Corbin died several years later. Then nature really conspired against the immigrants. Crops failed and malaria swept through the Italian community. Father Bandini was working in New York City for the welfare of Italian immigrants when alarming reports of sickness and starvation began to appear from Sunnyside, where the Italians worked under a system best described as peonage.

Leo Maestri General Merchandise was the first brick building in Tontitown. —Jada Maestri Collection, Shiloh Museum of Ozark History

Bandini, whom the late journalist Ernie Dean described as a Catholic priest of high birth from Italy, left for Arkansas to see how he could help. He traveled through the Ozarks on the way to Sunnyside and fell in love with the hill country, which reminded him of northern Italy. He purchased 1,000 acres of land, where he planned to relocate the unfortunate families from Sunnyside. He quickly relocated thirty-five families to Washington County and gave each family 20 acres of land, which they would buy a little at a time after each crop. He established a village and named it after Henri de Tonti—the Italian lieutenant of French explorer René-Robert Cavelier, Sieur de La Salle—who founded Arkansas Post in 1686.

Father Bandini became the first mayor of Tontitown. He helped so many Italian immigrants over the years that Queen Marghorita of Italy presented him with a beautiful set of vestments in 1895, and Pope Leo presented him with a gold chalice and another set of extraordinary vestments in 1911. Bandini died in 1911, and the residents of Tontitown raised the money to commission a monument in their cemetery, which included four statues and a cross that were made in Italy to honor Father Bandini. Tontitown became the first place in Arkansas to raise table grapes, and the town also became known for its orchards and vintners. It should not be surprising that the residents

320

of Tontitown celebrate their heritage with a grape festival every August in the town that Bandini built.

Siloam Springs

Located nineteen miles west of Springdale on US 412 at the Oklahoma border, the Siloam Springs area was settled in the 1830s by Simon Sager. The creek that runs through town now bears his name. Colonel D. Gunter established the Hico Trading Post in the mid-1840s. A village slowly appeared around the trading post and eventually stimulated the establishment of the Hico post office in 1855.

Former Union scout John Hargrove purchased a farm in the area when the war ended, and eventually ran the only general store in Hico. Samuel Box, the Hico postmaster, had fought for the Confederacy and was such an ardent supporter of the Lost Cause that he refused to surrender after Appomattox. Box escaped to Mexico and later attended the burial of the Confederate flag at Eagle Pass, Texas.

Hargrove decided in 1880 to plat a portion of his farm near a mineral spring generally believed to have medicinal value. He called the town Siloam Springs.

As Siloam Springs grew and prospered, it attracted most businesses from Hico, except for its flour mills. Hico became, in essence, a residential suburb of Siloam Springs. Nevertheless, Hico provided the only post office in the area until 1886, when John Daniel became the first postmaster at Siloam Springs.

Siloam Springs. –Special Collections, University of Arkansas Libraries, Fayetteville

Siloam Springs street scene. —Special Collections, University of Arkansas Libraries, Fayetteville

Among the early residents of Siloam Springs were the parents of Jim Reed, who is remembered as the first husband of the notorious outlaw Belle Starr. After Reed died, Belle married Sam Starr, who came from a Cherokee family of desperados. According to local legend, Belle's daughter Pearl lived with Jim Reed's parents in Siloam Springs. Miss Pearl later ran a successful bordello in Fort Smith. Belle and Sam Starr would soon figure in the death of the man who founded the town.

According to local legend, Sam and Belle Starr purchased thirteen thoroughbreds in Kentucky to start breeding horses in Arkansas. Belle developed a reputation for their horses by racing them, while Sam ran the ranch. After Belle raced a multistate circuit for two years, she decided in the fall of 1884 to challenge John Hargrove's racehorse, which had dominated racing in the Siloam Springs area. About 1,000 people showed up for the race, held where the Eastgate Motel now stands.

Belle planned more than a simple horse race, however. According to local legend, she told her jockey to win the race by the smallest possible margin. He won by a neck. Just as she imagined, Hargrove complained that his horse didn't get a good start, so they should run the race again. Hargrove was so confident of victory that he placed heavy bets with the Starrs as well as local residents. He lost the race and so much money that he wandered off and shot himself.

Today, Siloam Springs is best known as the home of John Brown University and the town's numerous historic sites on the National Historic Register.

—BENTONVILLE—

Located seventy-five miles north of Alma and seven miles south of the Missouri line on US 71, Bentonville is the seat of Benton County. It is unusual for a county and its seat to be named after the same person. The only other example in Arkansas is Perry County and Perryville. Bentonville and Benton County were named after Thomas Hart Benton, who started to earn his reputation as a rough-and-tumble frontier lawyer in Tennessee during the early 1800s.

Like contemporary Andrew Jackson, Benton developed a reputation for barroom brawling and dueling. After being involved with a shooting and stabbing in a Tennessee bar, Benton moved to St. Louis in 1815, where he became the editor of the *Missouri Inquirer*. Benton also practiced law quite successfully, which led him into politics when Missouri became a state in 1821. Benton not only became the first U.S. senator from Missouri, he would eventually become the first senator to serve in Congress for thirty years. When Arkansas legislators carved Benton County from a portion of Washington County in 1836, they named the county to honor Benton because he helped secure statehood for Arkansas earlier that year.

Artist Thomas Hart Benton is a descendent of the lawyer of the same name for whom Bentonville and Benton County are named. Here the artist and his daughter pose with his portrait of her. —Special Collections, University of Arkansas Libraries, Fayetteville

Senator Benton is best remembered for his role in helping President Jackson remove the Indians from east of the Mississippi River, reforms that helped open up lands for westward expansion, and for helping create the Pony Express. His contemporaries in Congress probably knew Benton best for his eloquent and ruthless oratory, which was fueled by his independent thinking as well as the combative personality he developed during his earlier days as a barroom brawler and duelist. Thomas Hart Benton died several years after he lost a bid for reelection.

By then, Bentonville had grown from the days in 1836 when the future town site consisted of nothing but the Osage post office. By 1860, Bentonville had grown to about 500 people. The town boasted five general stores, four doctors, several attorneys, several saloons, two hotels, two churches, a furniture store, and the county courthouse. Bentonville's slow but steady growth received a severe setback in February 1862 when Union troops burned down thirty-six buildings before their commanding officer ordered them to stop. Confederate troops retook the town, only to abandon it to the Federals once again. Before leaving, they burned down the two churches, school, jail, and Masonic lodge so the buildings could not be used by

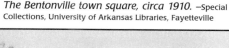

The Bentonville town square, circa 1910. –Special Collections, University of Arkansas Libraries, Fayetteville

the invaders. The county clerk loaded a stagecoach with all the county records and hid them in Texas until the war was over. That was remarkable foresight, because the Benton County Courthouse would soon be reduced to ashes. No one was sure just who burned the courthouse when the town changed hands. The Confederates blamed the Federals, and the Federals blamed the Confederates. By the end of the war, much of Bentonville lay in ruins. The rebuilding that followed the war gave the town a rich architectural heritage. Many historic homes still survive, and some are on the National Register of Historic Places. Bentonville remained a small community; the town's present population is scarcely more than double its size at the outbreak of the Civil War. The town remained small because the St. Louis & San Francisco Railroad bypassed Bentonville in favor of Rogers in 1881.

The infamous Starr family, a family of Cherokee brigands, wrote a lot of history across Indian Territory and the Ozarks in the late nineteenth century. The exploits of Henry Starr are remembered with particular interest in Bentonville, because Starr and a band of desperados robbed the Peoples Bank in 1893.

Henry Starr and the Peoples Bank

One day in June 1893, Henry Starr and five men rode into Bentonville from the west and tied up their horses behind the *Benton County Sun*, one of two weekly newspapers in town. Two men stayed with the horses, and the other four staggered into the town square like they were drunk. One man fired a rifle into the air—shouting for everyone to get off the street—while the other three entered the bank and demanded all the money. After bank employees filled two meal sacks with gold, silver, and currency, the robbers left the bank with four hostages, including cashier George Jackson, who carried part of the loot. By then, townsfolk were arming themselves and converging on the scene. Maggie Wood, who worked at the *Sun*, opened the front door to the newspaper office and shouted at Jackson. The cashier took advantage of the increasing commotion and bolted for the door with $900 in silver. The desperados had enough sense to ignore Jackson and race for their horses. Sheriff E. P. Gailbraith raised a posse, but Starr and his companions escaped with $11,000. The robbery is reenacted every May during Bentonville's Sugar Creek Days.

Sam Walton

Bentonville began its road to national recognition in 1950, when Sam Walton opened a 4,000-square-foot store on the town square. Called Walton's 5 & 10, the store featured a variety of merchandise that could be purchased for a nickel or a dime. That store is now a

Sam Walton's original five-and-dime store on the town square of Bentonville. —Polly Walter

little museum called the Wal-Mart Visitors Center, where folks can get a fascinating look at the man and his accomplishments.

The best-known resident of Bentonville, Sam Walton built his original Bentonville store into the Wal-Mart empire and became the richest person in America. By 1990, Walton's empire included more than 1,400 Wal-Marts and 127 Sam's Wholesale Clubs, and Wal-Mart had become the top retailer in the country. In 1993, Wal-Mart created more new jobs than any company in America. But that's only part of the story.

Widely admired because of his friendliness and lack of pretensions, Walton is the best part of the story. Arkansans from all walks of life still enjoy telling how Sam struck up a conversation with them and then drove off in an old pickup truck with his dog. Now Sam is gone, but having had a personal encounter with Sam Walton remains one of the best brags an Arkansan can make. Nice folks *can* finish first.

—ROGERS—

Located several miles east of Bentonville and thirty-three miles west of Eureka Springs on US 62, Rogers began life as a simple log inn on the Old Wire Road, where stagecoaches carrying passengers and mail would stop to change horses. The place was called Callahan Spring, named after the pool of water at the foot of the hill.

To encourage the building of the St. Louis & San Francisco Railroad, Robert Sikes donated right-of-way through his land, and other local farmers along the route donated $600. The railroad established a work camp at Callahan Spring, and by 1881 the location had a saloon and a post office. When the first train stopped at Callahan Spring on May 10, 1881, the town site had been surveyed and named after Captain C. W. Rogers, who was the vice president and general manager of the railroad. Many early residents lived in tents, yet the town grew so rapidly that Rogers had two newspapers by the end of the year. The *Champion* soon folded, but the *New Era* survived and later became the *Rogers Democrat*.

Esculapia Hollow—a small settlement and stagecoach stop several miles east of Rogers—withered even as Rogers blossomed. Many residents moved their buildings to Rogers, and Esculapia Hollow faded into oblivion, like so many other Arkansas towns bypassed by a railroad.

Newspapers extolled the medicinal value of the local springs, and Rogers began to see its future as a health resort. Hotels began to sprout up in Rogers and nearby Electric Springs, Frisco Springs, and Silver Springs (later renamed Monte Ne by William Hope "Coin" Harvey). Monte Ne featured the biggest log hotel in the world and a special train that took guests to Harvey's spring and its flower-covered gondolas. Constructed of 8,000 logs, Harvey's Monte Ne Hotel was 305 feet long. By 1902, Rogers was the biggest community in Arkansas that wasn't a county seat. Six years later, humorist Will Rogers married Betty Blake at her parent's home on East Walnut Street.

As modern medicine replaced nineteenth-century practice, and regular bathing became socially acceptable (a presidential candidate was once severely criticized for bathing frequently)—health resorts and "taking the waters" faded from the American culture. Investors in Monte Ne bailed out in 1910, and Harvey's resort went out of business. As the other resorts began to wither and die, the apple industry blossomed in a big way.

Boom, Bust, Boom, and Pop (or . . . from Apples to Daisies)

The local apple cider vinegar plant established in 1905 became the biggest facility of its kind in the world. By 1919, Benton County was shipping 5 million bushels of apples per year, which brought about

Will Rogers and Pine Bluff industrialist Harvey Couch.
—Special Collections, University of Arkansas Libraries, Fayetteville

$1 per bushel. Four years later, W. R. Cady suggested that Rogers should capitalize on the apple boom by hosting an annual apple festival like the big peach festival held each year in Georgia.

The annual Apple Blossom Festival soon began to attract so many visitors—up to 50,000—that special trains from Springfield, Joplin, and Fort Smith were needed to handle the demand. Torrential rains cancelled the festival in 1927, which proved to be the end of the celebration. The weather was beginning to affect the orchards as well as the festival. Late frosts, wet springs, and dry summers plagued the apple trees. Insects and blights infested the orchards. By the late 1940s, the apple industry had gone the way of the local health resorts.

About that time, a poultry boom developed when Hastings Hatchery, the biggest such company in the world, opened a facility in Rogers. Hastings began to airfreight 3 million chicks per year from Rogers. The community got another boost in 1958 when the Daisy Manufacturing Company moved from Michigan to Rogers.

Daisy started out as the Plymouth Iron Windmill Company in the 1800s. As a marketing ploy, the company started making air rifles and giving one free to every farmer who bought a windmill. These air rifles became so popular by 1885 that Plymouth stopped making windmills and concentrated on air guns. Three years later, the company introduced the Model 1888 air rifle. Plymouth's general manager, L. C. Hough, took one look at the rifle and said, "Boy, that's a daisy!" Hough had just inspired a new name for the company and the rest, as they say, is history. The Daisy International Air Gun Museum in Rogers keeps that history alive. Located next to the Daisy headquarters on US 71, the museum displays what is probably the finest collection of air guns in the world. The collection includes American and foreign air guns from 1770 to the present day.

—EUREKA SPRINGS—

Located thirty-three miles east of Rogers and twelve miles west of Berryville on US 62, Eureka Springs is probably the most picturesque community in Arkansas. Built into the sides of two mountains, the town is a veritable museum of Victorian architecture spiced by a delightful maze of switchback roads, paved footpaths, and stairways. More than 60 of the 1,200 springs in western Carroll County lie within a mile of downtown Eureka Springs. Although hunting first attracted Europeans into the area, it was the springs that put this section of the Ozarks on the map.

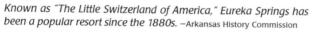

Known as "The Little Switzerland of America," Eureka Springs has been a popular resort since the 1880s. —Arkansas History Commission

Dr. Jackson's Eye Water

According to local legend, the story begins in 1834, when Dr. Alvah Jackson was hunting in the area. Besides working as a physician, he also was a hunter and trader. At this time, one of his enterprises was shipping bear oil down the White River from Oil Trough. While trading with local Indians, Jackson learned of a sacred healing spring deep in the mountains. He searched in vain until 1853, when he found the site quite by accident while hunting panther with his twelve-year-old son. The boy had a chronic eye problem, which became a crisis when the lad got dirt in his eyes while pursuing a panther up a cliff near the head of Little Leatherwood Creek. Jackson had noticed a spring at the bottom of the hill nearly covered with fallen leaves. He told the boy to go down to the spring, rake off the leaves with his hands, and wash out his eyes.

Jackson's son returned and told his father that the spring seemed to flow through a hand-carved basin. The description exactly matched what the Indians had described two decades earlier. Jackson had finally discovered the Indian Healing Spring. Each day after his son's accident, the doctor returned to the spring to fill his saddlebags with bottles of water for his son's eyes. The springwater apparently cured the boy's ailment. While this story was probably a marketing ploy, the spring itself was not a fabrication; it can still be seen. It's now known as Basin Spring, which is located in Basin Circle.

The doctor began to sell the waters from Indian Healing Spring throughout Arkansas and Missouri, marketing the bottled water—which he called Dr. Jackson's Eye Water—as a cure for a variety of eye problems.

When the Civil War descended on the Ozarks, Jackson refused to take sides. He used an old stone hunting cabin near the Indian Healing Spring as a hospital and bathhouse, and built himself a small cabin on the bluff overlooking the spring. The doctor reportedly treated both Confederate and Union soldiers throughout the war, although his meager facilities were quite overwhelmed by wounded after the Battle of Pea Ridge, which took place about twenty miles away.

The old sacred spring remained virtually unknown to the world at large until the 1870s, when Judge L. B. Saunders moved to Berryville from Indian Territory so his son could attend Clark Academy. The judge suffered from a nasty leg sore diagnosed as erysipelas, which numerous doctors had pronounced incurable. Dr. Jackson and Judge Saunders stayed in a tent near Indian Healing Spring so he could bathe his leg in the waters daily. After two months of taking the waters (and hunting for amusement), the "incurable" leg had healed. Word of the judge's miraculous cure spread so quickly that by July 4, 1879, several hundred people were living around the spring in tents to take the waters.

A Town Springs to Life

When the people living around Indian Healing Spring met to discuss establishing a town, C. Burton "Buck" Saunders suggested the name Eureka Springs (for the Greek word *eureka*, "I have found it"). Saunders was widely respected as an expert marksman. His collection of firearms and other items of historic interest can be seen at the Saunders Museum in Berryville. Within three years, a small gaggle of tents had exploded into a thriving community, and nine trains per day brought people to the town of sixty-three supposedly curative springs.

Thanks in large measure to the efforts of former Union general and Reconstruction governor Powell Clayton, the chaos of trails wandering through tents and dilapidated shanties quickly progressed into 238 named streets with real houses and permanent businesses. Because of the location's precipitous landscape, none of the original 238 winding streets had 90-degree intersections. The town's population quickly soared to 5,000—although it later evaporated to a fraction of that. Subsequent road-building robbed Eureka Springs of its distinction of having no traditional intersections.

Perhaps Powell Clayton's greatest contribution to Eureka Springs was his plan to build a grand hotel.

The Crescent Hotel

As president of the Eureka Springs Development Company, Powell Clayton secured twenty-seven acres of woodland on the highest point of West Mountain for a grand new hotel. The location would permit the building to dominate the surrounding landscape like a European castle. Isaac Stockton Tailor of Nashville designed the American Gothic structure. Huge blocks of White River limestone were transported to the construction site using specially designed wagons pulled by large teams of mules. Because this stone was unusually dense, Clayton brought in specialists from Ireland to cut and fit the slabs, so the hotel's eighteen-inch-thick walls could be joined without any mortar. This expensive technique ensured the longest possible life span of the structure. After receiving a luxurious Victorian interior and landscaping to match, the Crescent Hotel opened for business on May 1, 1886. Advertisements of the day heralded the Crescent as the most luxurious resort hotel in America.

The Crescent Hotel in Eureka Springs. –Arkansas History Commission

By the turn of the century, Eureka Springs had become a thriving year-round resort. Although the Crescent Hotel did attract its share of millionaires and influential people, neither the local waters nor the hotel's diverse entertainments attracted enough business to keep the hotel profitable into the twentieth century. The Crescent closed soon after the turn of the century, reopening as the Crescent College and Conservatory for Young Women in 1908. The school attracted students from thirty-nine states and continued in operation until the Great Depression forced it to close its doors in 1932. Residents deserted the town in droves during the Depression, transforming the resort community into something of a ghost town.

Five years later, an inventor, eccentric, and rabid enemy of organized medicine found a new use for the vacant hotel. Norman Baker opened the former hotel's doors again in 1937 as the Baker Hospital and health resort. Baker was something of a shady character and soon fell afoul of the law. In a trial of unprecedented length in 1940, a jury convicted Baker on seven counts of mail fraud for his quack cancer cures. Baker went to Leavenworth for four years of hard time, and the Crescent Hotel closed its doors once again. This time it lay vacant from 1940 to 1946, when a consortium of Chicago businessmen restored and reopened the hotel.

Eureka Springs began to capitalize on its charming scenery and architecture in the late 1940s, and the refurbished hotel did well until a fire destroyed the upper levels of the south wing in 1967. The hotel changed hands a number of times over the next several years. When Robert Feagins bought the hotel in the early 1970s, he bought it for the land and planned to demolish what he viewed as a "huge, hilltop hunk of limestone." Feagins wanted to recycle the limestone and build condominiums for expensive retirement homes. His wife, Lowana, had other ideas. She convinced her husband to restore the seventy-two-room hotel. The Crescent Hotel reopened for business eighty-seven years to the day after it first opened its doors. Ownership changed again in 1980. The hotel continued to draw celebrities such as actress Carrie Fisher, singer Willie Nelson, and the Oak Ridge Boys.

The Crescent Hotel remains open for business after more than a century, but the hotel has lost its former elegance. Yet its faded charm still attracts a lot of repeat customers who enjoy a communion with history they just can't find elsewhere. The Crescent Hotel is still a draw in Eureka Springs.

Just downhill from the Crescent Hotel is St. Elizabeth's Catholic Church. Richard Kerens, who owned an interest in the Crescent Hotel, built the church in 1907 as a memorial to his mother. He selected that spot, on a very steep slope, because it was the last place he saw his mother alive. Ripley described the church in his *Believe It or Not* newspaper feature as the only church in the world that is entered though its bell tower.

Close-up view of the dome and entrance arch at St. Elizabeth's Church in Eureka Springs. —Jesse L. Charlton, Special Collections, University of Arkansas Libraries, Fayetteville

Eureka Springs abounds with interesting places to visit and things to do for the history buff. In fact, the entire downtown is listed in the National Historic Register. Once visited, Eureka Springs tends to draw people back again and again. This charming town is addictive.

US 65
Missouri State Line–Conway
134 miles

Known to many folks as the road from I-40 in central Arkansas to the recreation center of Greers Ferry Lake (Arkansas) and the entertainment center of Branson (Missouri), this stretch of US 65 carves its way through the heart of the Ozarks. US 65 also provides part of several common routes to Mountain View, which has become the living soul of mountain culture and crafts from the nineteenth and early twentieth centuries. This area of the eastern Ozarks has a lot of history to offer.

—HARRISON—

Located 25 miles south of the Missouri border and 109 miles north of Conway on US 65, Harrison is now the seat of Boone County. The legislature created Boone County in 1869 from portions of Carroll and Madison Counties, naming it after famed frontiersman Daniel Boone according to a contemporary article in the *Arkansas Gazette*. The county used the home of Henry Fick as the courthouse until 1870, when the Harrison town site was selected and surveyed near the Crooked Creek Post Office (which had been serving the area since 1836).

By 1860, the average Ozarks mountaineer in this area had several acres of cleared land, a modest log house, no slaves, and the simple aspiration to be left alone to farm the land. The hill folk had no desire to leave the Union. Once Arkansas seceded, the average mountaineer still wanted nothing to do with the war. Yet by the end of the conflict, nearly every able-bodied man in the area had fought for either the Union or the Confederacy. For the most part, veterans returned to their homesteads and left their neighboring former antagonists in peace—the occasional fistfight notwithstanding. Several notable exceptions did, however, lead to spectacular gunfights.

334

Following the war, a former captain in the Union army from New York moved into the area from Pope County. Henry Fick would exert considerable influence on the political evolution of the area. It is interesting that some of the best friends Fick developed in those years were the very men he had fought against during the war.

Birth of a County and Town

The creation of Boone County from part of Carroll County had a substantial effect on the political and economic future of the area. The new county line ran just east of Carrollton (about fifteen miles west of Harrison via US 65, US 62, and US 412), the seat of Carroll County. But state law required that the permanent seat be within six miles of a county's geographic center. The residents of Berryville used this law to pressure the relocation of the county seat from Carrollton to Berryville. This political battle raged for six years. Finally, Carrollton lost and Berryville became the new county seat. Robbed of its political, cultural, and much of its economic lifeblood, Carrollton slowly began to lose its vitality.

Part of the plan for Boone County created by Captain Fick and his associates included building a community on the banks of Crooked Creek, where Fick owned a store and ran the post office. Fick hired an engineer to survey the town site, and offered to name the town after him in lieu of wages. The engineer was M. Larue Harrison.

Harrison lived in Fayetteville before the war, but he had been born in Michigan and frequently voiced his opposition to slavery. With the outbreak of war, Harrison raised the First Regiment of Arkansas Cavalry Volunteers to fight for the Union. Harrison commanded the defense of Fayetteville in August 1863, retired from the army as a brigadier general after the war, and then surveyed the right-of-way for a railroad line from Springfield, Missouri, into northern Arkansas. Attracted by the Ozarks, Harrison moved to Boone County. He began to advertise his services as a surveyor and civil engineer in the *Boone County Advocate*, which brought him to the attention of Henry Fick. After living for several years in the town that bears his name, Harrison moved to Chicago, where he resided until his death in 1890.

The new seat of Boone County began to grow up astride a wagon trail from Springfield, Missouri, as well as a trail connecting Carrollton with Fayetteville. But the local population continued to suffer depredations by outlaws who got their start as Bushwhackers and Jayhawkers during the war.

Many of the most notorious outlaws of the day spent some time in the Ozarks, including such desperados as Jim and Cole Younger, and Frank and Jesse James. Although many robberies and shootouts throughout Arkansas following the war were erroneously attributed to the James Gang, the following account comes from a participant, W. F. Pace, who actually knew and positively identified Jesse James.

Shootout at Gaddy's Corner

A town called Burlington, located twelve miles north of Harrison on US 65, was known as Gaddy's Corner in 1870, when four despera-dos robbed William Baker of the mail pouch he was carrying. "I was scared, all right," Baker recounted, "when the red-complected one they called Jesse pointed his pistol at me and demanded the mail pouch. They got $105 in money and some registered mail."

Baker headed north to the nearest settlement, Omaha (six miles north of present-day Burlington on US 65), where he raised the alarm. As local residents began to assemble a posse, a mail carrier rode south to Harrison to raise more men. Captain W. F. Pace put together a group in Harrison and rode north to join in the manhunt. By the time Cap-tain Pace and his men joined up with the Omaha posse and Pace had assumed overall command, a local preacher had joined the group and reported a number of suspicious riders at the old log home of a man named Perry, who lived near Gaddy's Corner.

The cabin, which stood near present-day US 65, was barricaded when the posse arrived. Captain Pace deployed his men among the stumps, logs, and trees that surrounded the structure. Pace then shouted at the men in the cabin to surrender. Someone inside yelled back that they would discuss the terms of surrender, if the posse would send a single man forward. Pace rode up to the cabin with his rifle lying across the saddle. Two men appeared at the window. Pace recognized them as Frank and Jesse James.

Jesse suggested that Pace order the posse to leave and forget the matter. Captain Pace could see a table inside the cabin that was cov-ered with loaded cap-and-ball pistol cylinders. In those days before metallic cartridges were widely available, it was quicker to swap cyl-inders than to reload each individual cylinder in a revolver with pow-der, patch, ball, and cap. Although the desperados were clearly pre-pared for a fight, Pace insisted that the men surrender.

The James brothers conferred briefly, and then Jesse replied, "If you'll send Parson New up here, we'll surrender to him." Captain Pace rode back to his men, and Parson New agreed to accept the surren-der. But as the parson rode up to the cabin, the James brothers emerged, and Jesse promptly put a bullet in the parson's head, shout-ing that he had killed the man who had betrayed him. The posse im-mediately loosed a fusillade at the cabin as Frank James drew a bead on Captain Pace. The captain's horse bucked from the sudden gunfire just as Frank fired, so the bullet hit Pace in the shoulder instead of the head. The James brothers dove into the cabin as Pace spurred his horse to cover.

The standoff dragged on, punctuated with an occasional exchange of gunfire. Someone in the posse eventually came up with the bright idea of assaulting the cabin, using a wagon as a rolling shield. But as the men rolled the wagon forward, the James brothers drilled Ace Thomason and John Hemsley, who were briefly exposed. The posse pressed forward. When they finally got within throwing distance of the cabin roof, someone yelled, "Come out with your hands up or we'll set you afire!"

"We like fire!" came the reply.

Just as the posse lit a number of torches, four men burst out of the cabin shooting their pistols at anyone who moved. Then Jesse James crowed like a rooster, and the four men escaped into the nearby woods without a scratch. "The posse," according to Ralph Rea, "was unwilling to accept a complete defeat in the fray, so they sought out the man, Perry, who was alleged to have harbored the outlaws. They killed Perry as a partial settlement for the casualties they had suffered."

Frontier justice had a downright biblical bent in those days. When the Democrats eventually came to power after Reconstruction, Pace served as the county's circuit clerk and then went on to practice law in Harrison for many years. Practicing law in a town that boasted more than twenty gun battles on its Dead Man's Corner was not always conducive to one's health, as Pace learned in the so-called Gay Nineties.

Gunfight at Dead Man's Corner

The problem started when Monroe Alderhalt had a serious falling out with his wife. Alderhalt had moved to the area from North Carolina in 1867. He began to build his reputation by surviving several gunfights with rustlers and outlaws. Alderhalt went on to acquire a 300-acre farm just west of Harrison along Crooked Creek, plus extensive real estate holdings throughout the county. He also ran one of the county's bonded distilleries for several years. Although Alderhalt was widely respected, he always carried a brace of revolvers. Folks respected his marksmanship and considered him a dangerous man to cross.

So when Alderhalt threatened any lawyer who would represent his estranged wife, the one lawyer who risked Alderhalt's wrath received a severe beating for the trouble. Alderhalt's wife then turned to Captain Pace, whom everyone knew had stood up to the James Gang.

337

Alderhalt tried to intimidate Pace into dropping the case, wounding Pace slightly in the process. Pace refused to back down and armed himself to prevent any more unpleasant surprises. Pace's three sons—Troy, Henry, and Frank—armed themselves, too.

When Captain Pace unexpectedly crossed paths with Alderhalt a few days later in the town square, the lawyer said, "Good morning, Mr. Alderhalt." Alderhalt warned the lawyer never to speak to him again. The two men parted without incident.

Later that day, Alderhalt walked from East Stephenson into the square, where he spotted the three Pace boys. Frank and Henry Pace stood at different places near a restaurant at the southeast corner of the square, while Troy stood across the street on the south side of the square.

There is no reliable account of who started the fight. Bystanders reported that both Henry Pace and Monroe Alderhalt began shooting at each other before anyone realized there was a problem. Pace hit Alderhalt, who collapsed into the street just as Frank ran to the corner. Alderhalt fired three rounds that whizzed past Frank's head into the restaurant wall. In response, Troy approached from across the street and fired a single shot at Alderhalt, who passed out from his wounds just as Captain Pace appeared after a mad ride toward the sound of gunfire. Alderhalt died soon thereafter.

At first, townsfolk split pretty evenly over the issue of who started the fight. But as more facts came to light, sentiment swayed in support of the Paces and against Alderhalt. Although a grand jury did indict the Pace boys for murder, the judge assigned to the case disqualified himself so he could testify in support of the Paces. A second judge resigned for the same reason, so a special judge had to be appointed. Sheriff Ceaf Parker also intended to testify in support of the Paces, so a special sheriff had to be appointed as well. Frank eventually went to trial and was acquitted. The cases against Troy and Henry were subsequently dropped.

As the new century dawned, Harrison remained a rough-and-tumble town. Harrison popped into the national headlines again in the 1920s with the death of a notorious desperado who had also been a movie star.

Last of the Oklahoma Desperados
Born in 1873 near Fort Gibson in Indian Territory, Henry Starr came from a long line of Cherokee desperados. His family tree included the notorious outlaw Belle Starr, who reigned as the bandit queen of Indian Territory until she ran afoul of the Hanging Judge in Fort Smith. She later died from two shotgun blasts while riding along the Canadian

Henry Starr was both a notorious bank robber for many years and a star in silent movies. This photograph was taken in 1892. –
Cravens Collection, UALR Library Archives

River in Oklahoma. Henry Starr was the last of the Oklahoma desperados, as well as one of the most successful. He probably robbed more banks than anyone in the history of the United States. A complex and relatively educated man, Starr eventually had the good sense to try going straight by starring in several movies about bank robbers. Starr essentially played himself and quickly discovered that there was more money to be made as a reel bandit than a real bandit.

Unfortunately, there was also more money to be lost. Starr helped underwrite a movie about his life called *A Debtor to the Law*. The movie ran into financial difficulties, and Starr found himself more than $6,000 in debt. Rather than plead for more time to cover these debts, the old desperado decided to rob one more bank to save both his financial reputation and his career as a movie star. That would prove to be a fateful decision.

On February 18, 1921, Starr and two other bandits cut the phone lines on each side of Harrison and then entered the People's National Bank just after it opened. A fourth man waited in the getaway car. Brandishing .45 caliber handguns, they forced cashier Cleve Coffman

339

Belle Starr and Blue Duck.
—Cravens Collection,
UALR Library Archives

to open the safe. Starr began to scoop up the cash while the other two men watched the bank patrons and staff.

Bug Eagle, a local customer, entered the bank without knowing a robbery was in progress. Eagle initially refused to put up his hands, which distracted the attention of the three robbers. This enabled W. J. Myers, a former president of the bank, to back into the vault and retrieve the .38/.40 caliber Winchester rifle kept there for just such an emergency. Myers quietly removed the rifle and shouldered it, waiting for the appropriate moment to fire.

Once Starr's two accomplices had gained control of Bug Eagle, Starr squatted in front of the safe and reached into it with his right hand while he held his pistol in the left. Myers carefully aimed just above Starr's hips so he would sever the spine or hit a kidney if he jerked the shot. The vault magnified the roar of the Winchester, and Starr collapsed onto the floor. His accomplices immediately raised their pistols at the cashier, but Starr called out, "Get out of here, boys! I'm done for."

The two men grabbed customer Ruth Wilson as a shield from Myers's Winchester and backed out the front door of the bank. An impromptu posse set out in hot pursuit, but the bandits soon abandoned their car and escaped into the woods. They were eventually captured and sentenced to prison.

Henry Starr lingered on the brink of death for four days, wracked with convulsive pain and retaining consciousness to the bitter end. He asked to see the cashier, who thanked the desperado for saving

W. J. Myers, the man who shot Henry Starr during an attempted bank robbery. —Boone County Heritage Museum

People's National Bank in Harrison. —Sammie Rose

Charles Myers studies the the Boone County Heritage Museum display that chronicles the day his great-grandfather, W. J. Myers, shot bank robber Henry Starr inside the People's National Bank. —Sammie Rose

his life by stopping Starr's accomplices from shooting him. Starr then told Coffman that he wanted the cashier to have his pistol. He expressed no animosity toward Myers, who had shot him. "I do not blame him at all," Starr said. "He was at one end of the game, and I was at the other."

The last of the Oklahoma desperados was scarcely in the ground when violence erupted once again in Harrison—this time over a strike against the Missouri & North Arkansas Railroad. Then life in Harrison finally calmed down once and for all. Today, Harrison is best known as the home for the Twin Lakes Vocational Technical School, the North Arkansas Community College, and the charming Boone County Historical and Railroad Museum.

–MARSHALL–

Located thirty-eight miles south of Harrison and twenty-seven miles north of Clinton on US 65, Marshall was known as Raccoon Springs when the community was settled in the early 1820s. Raccoon Springs would eventually take two more names and become the seat of Searcy County, after the legislature created the county in 1838 from a portion of Marion County. Ironically, Marion County had itself been called Searcy County from 1835 to 1836, so the legislature revived the original name when it drew the new boundary. The county and the seat of White County were both named in honor of Richard Searcy (see also Searcy). A highly regarded lawyer from Batesville and later a territorial judge, Searcy died in 1833, so he never knew about the town and the county named to honor him.

After temporarily holding court in the home of James Eagan, the commissioners of the new Searcy County selected Lebanon as the permanent county seat. Lebanon was located along a tributary of the Buffalo River about five miles west of present-day Marshall. In 1855, the residents of Lebanon split over the issue of moving the town to a more favorable location. The following year, about half the townsfolk moved to the present location of Marshall, taking the county seat with them. The fracas didn't end there.

Some people wanted to rename Raccoon Springs "Burrowsville" after John Burrows, who donated eleven acres of his homestead for the town site. Some folks fiercely opposed the name, claiming that Burrows never actually transferred title to the land. Finally, the legislature had to step in to solve the problem by declaring that the county seat would be called Burrowsville. That lasted until 1867, when the town was renamed Marshall in honor of John Marshall, who was one of the most influential men in U.S. history.

Marshall was born to a frontier family in 1755. His Virginia mother was related to such important colonial families as the Jeffersons, Randolphs, and Lees. The eldest of fifteen brothers and sisters, John Marshall began his public service in Washington's Continental army during the Revolutionary War. He then served in the Virginia legislature, in the U.S. Congress, and as commissioner to France. While serving as the secretary of state, Marshall was appointed chief justice of the U.S. Supreme Court. Marshall fundamentally defined the role of the Supreme Court by establishing its right to review both federal and state laws, and to establish the constitutionality of those laws. It is hard to overstate the depth and breadth of Marshall's impact on American law due to his broad interpretation of the Constitution.

—CLINTON—

Located about forty-four miles north of Conway and ninety miles south of the Missouri border on US 65, Clinton has no relationship to Bill Clinton, who became the forty-second governor of Arkansas and the forty-second president of the United States. Settlement of the area dates back to the early 1800s, when pioneers surged into Arkansas to escape the effects of the New Madrid earthquake, which devastated southern Missouri. Most of the early settlers in the Clinton area, however, were folks from Tennessee who came from English, Scottish, and Irish stock. Subsequent settlers included a substantial wave of German immigrants as well as people of diverse backgrounds from Kentucky, the Carolinas, Mississippi, Georgia, Illinois, and Missouri. The hill country was particularly attractive to settlers because swamp fever (now called malaria) epidemics were ravaging low-lying areas throughout much of the South at that time.

Some folks opted for the healthy climate of the Ozark hills in spite of the poor and rocky highland soil, rather than risk the ravages of swamp fever that plagued the fertile lowlands. The area now known as Van Buren County became an early focal point for people of this new American subculture, who came to be known as "ridge runners" or "mountaineers." Settlement in this area began in the 1820s, just after Arkansas Territory split off from Missouri Territory. The future location of Clinton was then part of Izard County.

As the population grew, the demands for more efficient government stimulated the creation of Van Buren County (named after then Vice President Martin Van Buren) from parts of Conway, Independence, and Izard Counties in 1833. The home of Obadiah Martin became the temporary county seat until commissioners selected Bloomington as the seat of justice. The small settlement lay along the Little Red River about eight miles below present-day Clinton.

That same year, Russell Bates opened the Clinton post office along an old ox trail that ran from Old Lewisberg on the Arkansas River to Batesville on the White River. The post office was named in honor of DeWitt Clinton, who served as mayor of New York City for many years and went on to become the governor of New York. He is best remembered for his leadership role in the building of the Erie Canal and the Champlain-Hudson Canal. The seat of Arkansas County, DeWitt, was also named after him.

The 1835 territorial census revealed that the population of Van Buren County was 855 people, including 10 slaves and one free black. An election that year to determine if residents wanted Arkansas to become a state produced the following tally. Of the 123 votes cast, 61 supported statehood, and 62 opposed the idea. The entire territory, however, voted 1,942 for statehood and 908 against, so Arkansas Territory became the twenty-fifth state the following year.

By 1840, Van Buren County supported 243 families and a total population of about 1,500 people, which included 59 slaves. George Counts established a forty-acre homestead between Archey Creek and the south fork of the Little Red River in 1842. Counts donated six acres for a new town, which took the name of the older post office. Two years later, the county seat moved to Clinton, where it remains to this day. The first courthouse in Clinton was a small log house, and

the present sandstone courthouse—which was completed in 1934—
is the smallest in Arkansas. The county population nearly doubled in
the 1840s. By the end of the decade, the county had 448 families and
a population of 2,756. Then settlement slowed as the better land was
cleared and farmed.

By the end of the century, farming remained the principal occupation, and cotton was the principal cash crop. After processing at local gins, farmers loaded their wagons and made a three-day journey
to market at the nearest railroad town. A big achievement in the 1890s
was the establishment of more than a hundred one-room school-
houses throughout Van Buren County, so students would not have to
walk more than three miles to school. Otherwise, life remained much
as it had been in the days of the pioneer. The coming of the railroad
changed all that.

The Railroad Revolution

The new Missouri and North Arkansas Railroad from Leslie to Cotton Plant came through Shirley (about nine miles northeast of Clinton
on Arkansas 16) in 1908. Shirley became an important transportation
hub for the railroad, which opened up markets for local farmers and
permitted a substantial growth of the timber industry. Corn joined
cotton as an important cash crop, but timber really fueled the growth
of the county. The region witnessed an explosive growth of sawmills,
and factories producing barrel staves and railroad ties appeared in
towns like Shirley and Clinton. Majestic virgin mixed-hardwood forests soon became reduced to tangles of brush. Banks, newspapers,
and other manifestations of progress began to appear during the first
really prosperous period in the history of Shirley and Clinton.

Farmers became increasingly frustrated trying to raise cotton on
the rocky hills. They began to focus more on raising corn, wheat,
oats, alfalfa, sorghum, and dairy cattle. By the end of the 1920s, specialists brought into the area to foster new farming techniques stimulated interest in terracing farms and the 4-H Club. With the onset of
the Great Depression, cotton prices fell to a mere 5 cents per pound.
Combined with hot winds from Texas and a plague of boll weevils in
1931 and 1932, county cotton production fell dramatically. With the
demise of the timber and cotton industries, Clinton, Shirley, and the
rest of Van Buren County fell on very hard times indeed.

The onset of war in 1941 stimulated the farming industry, as demand increased for beef, poultry, peanuts, beans, and other vegetables. Nevertheless, people began to leave the county to work in
war-related industries, beginning an exodus that would continue until 1960. The county population plummeted from 12,500 to less than

7,500 during those two decades. Soon after the end of World War II, local business leaders successfully pressured the State Highway Commission to improve the roads. But then the cumulative curses of inadequate revenues, mismanagement, inhospitable terrain, and labor problems forced the Missouri & North Arkansas Railroad to stop its operations through Shirley in 1949.

While farming shifted from crops to dairy and beef cattle, and poultry—many of the local farmers began to retire. With few youngsters willing to farm the rocky Ozark hills, grass and brush began to cover an increasing number of fields. By 1990, only 17,000 of the 133,000 cleared acres in Van Buren County were actually under cultivation, and most of that acreage was used for hay. Just as the economy was bottoming out in the late 1950s, the U.S. Army Corps of Engineers resurrected an old plan to build a dam across the Little Red River in Cleburne County, just east of Heber Springs. The dam would generate hydroelectric power for the central Ozarks, and its reservoir was expected to create recreational opportunities and related jobs.

Greers Ferry Lake

Ironically, it was the demise of the Missouri & North Arkansas Railroad that enabled the economic revitalization of Van Buren and Cleburne Counties. During the Depression, the U.S. Army Corps of Engineers unveiled a plan to build a dam across the Little Red River, creating a vast reservoir extending thirty-five miles upriver to Choctaw (five miles south of Clinton on US 65). That reservoir would have cut the railroad, however. So the project remained on hold until the railroad went out of business, removing the only serious obstacle to the plan. The corps began construction of the dam in 1959 under legislation passed in 1938.

The five-year project profoundly changed the face of Van Buren County, displacing about thirty families during the first year. Workers relocated thirteen cemeteries containing 1,482 graves to the new Eglantine Cemetery and to the Huie Cemetery near Choctaw. Residents of Choctaw and Eglantine had to abandon their villages, which were buried by the reservoir. With the establishment of three marinas and fourteen campgrounds in the area, the recreation industry boomed and land prices increased dramatically. The assessed value of property in the area increased by more than 50 percent in a decade.

The big boom really came to Van Buren County with the development of Fairfield Bay community on the north shore of Greers Ferry Lake (about thirteen miles east of Clinton on Arkansas 16). Fairfield Bay tripled the assessed value of property in the county.

Fairfield Bay

A corporation based in Little Rock called the Fairfield Communities Land Company began to develop retirement communities in Arkansas, Arizona, and Tennessee in the mid-1960s. It began to purchase large tracts of land along the north shore of Greers Ferry Lake in 1966. By 1975, the company had paid more than $4.2 million for about 12,000 acres of relatively undeveloped land, most of it in Van Buren County. The corporation then invested another $6 million into building roads, a marina, several swimming pools and tennis courts, and a golf course. Soon the embryonic community included a medical clinic, bank, post office, grocery store, restaurant, beauty parlor, and community sewerage and water systems.

This level of services, plus the beauty and year-round recreational opportunities of the area, stimulated the construction of 451 houses and 240 condominiums. Largely built by local workers using local vendors, these new homes were collectively worth more than $14 million. By 1974, more than 600 people called Fairfield Bay home, representing about a fourth of the county's population growth since 1965.

Since then, many less expensive homes have sprouted throughout the area surrounding Greers Ferry Lake. The public marinas and swimming areas are used to capacity during the warm months, and the area has become a favorite recreational area for people from central and northern Arkansas. Many retirees live around the lake, as well. This is perhaps the only example in Arkansas where the demise of railroad service actually helped a local economy. The decade of the 1980s did not, however, go as smoothly as the 1970s.

A Bang and a Scream

The 1980s began with a bang when a 150-ton Titan II missile exploded in a silo near Damascus, which lies about nineteen miles south of Clinton on US 65. Located just west of US 65 about four miles north of Damascus, this was one of eighteen such facilities in the area. Air Force Sergeant David Livingston and a maintenance crew from the Little Rock Air Force Base were trying to repair a fuel leak in the chronically hazardous Titan, when a maintenance worker dropped a wrench socket down the 155-foot-deep silo. The socket pierced the thin skin of the Titan's fuel tank just as a fresh crew was entering the silo at 3:01 A.M. The vaporized fuel ignited in a flash that illuminated the countryside like daylight, sending an orange fireball hundreds of feet into the sky and quakelike tremors through the central Ozarks. The tremors woke up people as far away as Conway and Heber Springs, where residents emerged to a deep rumbling and an ominous glow in the sky.

The explosion killed Sergeant Livingston and injured twenty-one other workers at the silo. The blast destroyed the 740-ton reinforced concrete doors, which were designed to survive a nuclear attack, and reduced the entire silo to rubble. One report said the ten-megaton warhead (the largest in the U.S. arsenal) was blown out of the silo and landed three miles away. An acrid reddish orange cloud spread out from a gaping hole in the earth. Because the fate of the warhead was unknown at the time, the authorities evacuated about 1,400 residents from Van Buren, Faulkner, and Conway Counties until the atomic device was located and it was determined that no nuclear material leaked from the warhead. Folks were allowed to return to their homes after about twelve hours, but a stretch of US 65 near the silo remained closed for several days.

A flood two years later left downtown Clinton under several feet of water and washed out bridges and roads throughout the area, generating millions of dollars in damages. The flood stimulated the relocation of Clinton businesses to land along US 65 after a small Wal-Mart store opened across from the hospital. Two years after the flood, on March 15, 1984, a tornado touched down at Eglantine, screamed through the hills of Fairfield Bay, careened across the lake, and finally destroyed the Edgemont Bridge. While the tornado destroyed more than fifty homes, remarkably no one was killed.

These natural disasters failed to slow the exuberant growth around Greers Ferry Lake, which has become one of the great playgrounds and retirement areas in Arkansas.

Mountain View

When the legislature carved Stone County from portions of Independence, Izard, Searcy, and Van Buren Counties in 1873, local residents built a temporary county seat a quarter mile east of the present courthouse. Folks placed potential names for a new post office in a hat, and the drawing produced Mountain View, an apt name for a location high in the Ozarks. A town grew up next to the courthouse and post office, taking the same name. Mountain View is thirty-seven miles northeast of Clinton on Arkansas 9 and thirty-three miles east of Marshall via US 65 and Arkansas 66.

Throughout the years, Mountain View remained a quiet, traditional Ozarks community. It didn't even earn a place in *The WPA Guide to 1930s Arkansas*, which provided an exhaustive travel guide to the state as it was prior to World War II. The town's only claim to fame was that actor Dick Powell, who was immensely popular in the 1940s and 1950s, came from Mountain View.

Jimmie Driftwood, who wrote a song called "The Battle of New Orleans," founded the Ozark Folk Center in Mountain View.
—UCA Archives

When the early 1960s heralded a revival of traditional folk crafts and music throughout the Ozarks, Mountain View remained—as the writer Ernie Dean once observed—unspoiled by progress. The town had only been connected to the rest of the world by a paved road for a few years. Electricity had not reached everyone in the surrounding hills. The local economy was not exactly robust.

More important, "there were men and women, and young folks, too, who had been brought up on the old music and songs, and could produce them in an absolutely authentic way," Ernie Dean wrote in the *Springdale Daily News*. This was a time when the Ozarks' own Jimmie Driftwood had a song called "The Battle of New Orleans," which was getting a lot of play on the radio. Local musicians realized they had a marketable property as well: traditional mountain music. That led to the first folk festival in Mountain View in the spring of 1963. It turned out that people from diverse backgrounds longed to hear *real* mountain music. Folks flocked to the annual festival to get their fill of instrumental music, songs, dancing, food, and the spectacular spring-time scenery.

The May family, shown here with guitars and a violin on the family homestead, played the sort of traditional Arkansas music preserved by the Ozark Folk Center. –Southwest Arkansas Regional Archives

Although the spring folk festival remains a popular annual event, the town's role as the center of mountain music and crafts was institutionalized with the establishment of the Ozark Folk Center. Originally developed by Jimmie Driftwood to preserve and perpetuate local crafts and music from 1820 to 1920, the Ozark Folk Center is now a state park. The heart of the fifty-building complex is an auditorium that features performances of traditional music throughout the day, plus a more substantial program in the evening that includes jig dancing, square dancing, and clogging. Many of the other buildings feature people working in traditional crafts such as blacksmithing, gunsmithing, printing, furniture building, pottery making, and wood carving, among others. Additional exhibits of folk crafts, a traditional herb garden—plus food shops and a restaurant—make the Folk Center a friendly place for families to learn about and enjoy Ozark traditions.

Mountain View with its Ozark Folk Center has become a living museum dedicated to the rich heritage of Ozark mountain culture. Arkansas is certainly richer for the effort.

Little Rock–Batesville

93 miles

US 67 and 167 between Little Rock and Batesville approximately follow an ancient Indian path that diagonally crossed what is now Arkansas from Hix's Ferry on the Current River in the northeast, along the foothills of the Ozark and Ouachita Mountains, to the Red River in the southwest. Called the Southwest Trail by early pioneers who widened and improved the trail, the route skirted hills, avoided swamps whenever possible, and crossed rivers at the best fords. At the end of the eighteenth century, this was the closest thing to a road cutting through the Arkansas wilderness (see also the Southwest Trail, in Part 2).

The modern incarnation of this route along US 67 and 167 skirts the western edge of the Mississippi Alluvial Plain—through Cabot, Beebe, and Searcy—and climbs the eastern edge of the Ozarks to Batesville, which figured prominently in the early history of the state. From Batesville, the old Southwest Trail extended northeast to Hix's Ferry (later called Pitman), which is now a forgotten backwater on the Missouri border about four miles northwest of Success. Hix's Ferry lies about fourteen miles west of where US 67 crosses the Arkansas-Missouri border.

—CABOT—

Located about twenty miles northeast of Little Rock and seventy-three miles southwest of Batesville on US 67, Cabot was born as a railroad town in 1873. The birth of Cabot as a water and fuel stop for the Cairo & Fulton Railroad signaled the demise of Austin (which was previously called Oakland Grove, Sandersville, and Atlanta, and now appears on maps as Old Austin several miles east of Cabot on Arkansas 38).

Old Austin (not to be confused with modern Austin, which lies along the railroad just east and north of Cabot) began life as the Oakland Grove post office in 1830. The town grew up at a crossroads frequented by stagecoaches running between Little Rock and Searcy, freight wagons running between Des Arc and Little Rock, and travelers heading west from Memphis. A measles epidemic during the Civil War killed 430 Confederate soldiers encamped nearby, who were reburied at the Camp Nelson Confederate Cemetery around the turn of the century. Old Austin withered and died a decade later when the railroad bypassed the town.

The first residents of Cabot were a handful of railroad workers, who lived in huts near the track and probably named the town after a railroad engineer. Cabot grew rapidly despite such humble beginnings, adding a church within a year, and then a school the following year. By 1889, the town had six general stores, five churches, two blacksmith shops, two drugstores, a railroad depot, livery stable, cotton gin, post office, free school, and a lawyer. Two years later, Cabot incorporated and became the 139th city in Arkansas. The town prospered, supplying local farmers with everything they needed and serving as the transportation hub for shipping produce to market.

Modern conveniences such as telephones and automobiles began to appear in Cabot after the turn of the century, but life remained close to the soil as it had always been. The main cash crop continued to be cotton until the 1940s, when it finally became apparent that dairy farming was better suited to the hilly terrain around Cabot.

Soon after the end of World War II, US 67 was paved all the way between Cabot and Little Rock, rural electrification had reached Lonoke County, and the horse-drawn wagon had virtually disappeared from local streets. Within a decade, Cabot residents had gas and sewer service. When the US 67 and 167 corridor eventually became a four-lane highway, the town increasingly became an attractive bedroom community for people working in Jacksonville and Little Rock, spawning a period of growth. This proved to be the proverbial calm before the storm. On March 29, 1976, a tornado chewed its way through Cabot, destroying or damaging about 200 homes as well as much of the downtown area. Five people died. Mayor Willie Ray devoted as many as eighteen hours per day to the cleanup and helped secure millions of dollars in federal grant money to rebuild the town. The new community center was named in honor of the mayor after his death.

Rebuilding after the tornado spawned a real sense of community spirit among the residents, and that spirit reached a high point when Terri Utley won the Miss USA title in 1982. Cabot's morale remains high long after the residents conquered the effects of the tornado.

—BEEBE—

Located about twenty-seven miles northeast of Little Rock and sixty-six miles southwest of Batesville on US 67, Beebe is typical of many Arkansas railroad towns. When the railroad bypassed Stony Point in favor of a route about three miles to the east, most of the town merchants moved their businesses to high ground along the railroad between Cypress Bayou and Bull Creek. The time was April 1872. Most residents of Stony Point quickly moved to the new town,

352

Roswell Beebe, president of the Cairo & Fulton Railroad.
—Arkansas History Commission

This locomotive of the Cairo & Fulton Railroad, photographed in 1872, was called the Roswell Beebe. —UCA Archives

which they named after Roswell Beebe, who was the first president of the Cairo & Fulton Railroad. The town prospered sufficiently to support the establishment of the Beebe Junior Agricultural College in the late 1920s, which has subsequently evolved into a branch of Arkansas State University.

—SEARCY—

Searcy lies about fifty miles northeast of Little Rock and forty-three miles southwest of Batesville on US 67. The recorded history of the place actually dates back to about 1820, when a bear hunter discovered mineral springs there. Hunters increasingly stopped at Sulphur and Shalybeate Springs, which quickly earned the much more pronounceable name of White Sulphur Springs. In 1834, an article in the *Arkansas Gazette* reported on the apparent medicinal value of bathing in the springs, where a fellow named Gray opened a crude hotel. The following year, the legislature created a new county from portions of Jackson, Pulaski, and Independence Counties.

They named the new county after Hugh White, a U.S. senator from Tennessee who lost the 1836 presidential election to Martin Van Buren. The home of David Crease served as the temporary county seat for two years, while commissioners looked for a suitable site for a permanent seat in the central part of the county. White Sulphur Springs was a prospering little community, and Crawford Walker donated the required ten acres of land adjacent to the springs, so White County finally got its seat. Israel Moore platted the new town, which was called Searcy, and named the streets after the streets of Philadelphia.

The town name honored Richard Searcy, a tall redheaded frontier lawyer with piercing gray eyes who was widely admired. This lawyer from Batesville later became a territorial judge and particularly distinguished himself in the land fraud cases that choked the legal system in those days.

The Southwest Trail—also known as Old Military Road and later as the National Road—did not pass through Searcy, but the road did run about seven miles to the west. Local settlers benefitted from the dawn of steamboat service into Arkansas in the 1840s. The first steamer journeyed up the White River and then up the Little Red River as far as the mouths of Gin and Deener Creeks in 1849. That spot quickly became known as Searcy Landing.

Unfortunately, the water in the Little Red River was frequently too shallow for small steamers to make it all the way to Searcy. But the riverboats could usually reach a nearby landing, which lay a handful of overland miles to the southeast or twice that distance downriver. The steamers brought goods directly from Memphis at less cost than goods shipped overland from Little Rock. W. C. West surveyed a town site at the new boat landing, which took his name. By 1860, West Point had become the second largest town in White County. Searcy continued to be the largest town in the county, with a population of about 700.

The Civil War

Searcy lawyer Danbridge McRae became the town's best-known veteran of the war. Commissioned as a captain, he quickly rose to the rank of brigadier general after leading troops at Springfield, Wilson's Creek, Pea Ridge, and Corinth. He then led a brigade under General Thomas Hindman and participated in the unsuccessful Battle of Helena.

The war finally reached Searcy in 1862 after the Federals marched down from Missouri and captured Batesville on May 4, in a drive they hoped would take them to Little Rock. About 20,000 Federals camped several miles away on the far side of the Little Red River (near present-day Judsonia) and sent foraging parties throughout the countryside. A sizeable group of Federals camped on a hill near the future site of McRae Elementary School and set up a cannon to cover the approach.

A small Confederate reconnaissance party was spotted, and during the resulting skirmish a cannonball struck the house of Israel Moore (at the future intersection of Moore Street and Arkansas 16), where a slave was cooking a meal and tending an infant, Elizabeth Moore. The baby lay in a cane basket on the floor in front of the fireplace. The cannonball whizzed through the kitchen, narrowly missing the infant, and lodged in a wall without hitting anyone or exploding. The Moores left the ball sticking out of the wall for years as a conversation piece.

Small Confederate units continued to worry the Federal flanks and supply lines. The first sizeable scrap in White County occurred on May 18. The fracas came to be known as the Battle of Whitney Lane, although it was really more of a spirited skirmish than a full-scale battle. Texas Dragoons and the Searcy Home Guards temporarily drove back a group of Federals until they received reinforcements. This resistance, combined with constant harassment by small units and rumors of pending large-scale reinforcements spread by agents working for General Thomas Hindman, managed to convince Union General Samuel Curtis that the time was not propitious for a strike against Little Rock.

The war returned to Searcy in August 1863, when the Federal gunboat *Cricket* steamed up the Little Red River and captured the Confederate transports *Tom Sugg* and *Kaskaskia* at Searcy Landing. The

Federals burned the bridge to cut off Brigadier General John Marmaduke's forces, who were on the east side of the river. A company of Federals made a sweep through Searcy and then returned to the boats. When the *Cricket* and its two prizes turned back downriver and passed West Point, about 500 of Marmaduke's men opened up from a distance of only about thirty yards. The furious fighting only lasted for about twenty minutes, but the relics of the engagement lasted for many years after the war. Many local homes displayed bullet holes, and the scars of shrapnel and cannonballs, as constant reminders of the spirited skirmish at West Point.

After the end of the war, Searcy entered a period of doldrums in which everyone displayed a profound lack of energy. The town fell into such a deplorable state of disrepair that ladies would not attempt to travel afoot down the city streets. All that remained of the successful antebellum spa was an old shed at the sulphur springs.

Rebirth of a Town

Bathing in the sulphur springs was no longer possible in the years immediately following the war because of debris and the glut of horses watering at the springs. The city council cleaned up Spring Park, passed an ordinance against watering livestock from the springs, and planned to build two bathhouses. Soon the springs attracted a steady stream of visitors. They even inspired poetry.

The vitality of the community permitted it to respond when Western Union decided to bypass Searcy. Local merchants put up substantial subscription money to tap into the main telegraph line at West Point, and other Searcy residents donated 250 twenty-four-foot oak and sassafras posts for the branch telegraph line. Steamboat traffic increased to Searcy Landing and freight rates dropped considerably, which helped fuel the reviving local economy.

Then Searcy faced its greatest economic challenge when the Cairo & Fulton Railroad (later the St. Louis, Iron Mountain & Southern; now the Missouri Pacific) decided to bypass the hilly country surrounding the town in favor of a cheaper route through flatter lands a few miles to the east. The town council decided to build a railroad spur between Searcy and Kensett to connect the town with the Cairo & Fulton. Building a spur with steel rails proved to be prohibitively expensive, so the town came up with a decidedly zany solution.

The Mule and Oak Railroad

The plan was to build a railroad using rails made of three-by-five-inch white oak, which were fastened to oak cross-ties with a half-inch steel rod to maintain a constant gauge of three feet. The line would have one freight car and one passenger car, which would be pulled by a team of draft horses rather than a steam locomotive. The Searcy Branch Railroad was completed with $6,900 in cash and an $8,000 bond issue.

A passenger who took the Searcy Branch in 1877 wrote the following account of his trip soon after the city sold the line to W. A. and A. W. Yarnell.

> [The] Kensett to Searcy connection is made by a wooden tramway, dignified by the name horse railway. It is a very rough, shake-up and jugglety affair; an excellent remedial agent for dyspepsia but withal a pleasant route of travel and of great convenience for those who wish to transport goods from the depot at the station town four miles away. . . . The rolling stock of this road consists of one passenger coach and one freight car. The engines consist of three mules, named respectively, Madam, Muggins, and Hun. We had the pleasure of riding behind Madam, a brownish sun-colored animal with a gait like that of an old clothes peddler, a paint brush tail, and a look of wicked intelligence. Madam is honored by being the passenger engine and is kept in a little better repair than Muggins and Hun, who [are] compelled to haul freight.

Going downhill on a mule-drawn train proved to be tricky. The drivers soon learned to unhitch the mules at the top of a grade and coast downhill. The train often coasted "engineless" into Searcy with the driver rubbing a long sapling against the ground as a makeshift brake. As crude as the Searcy Branch Railroad was, it enabled local residents to easily connect with a modern railroad and travel to Memphis or Little Rock with unprecedented speed, economy, and style. Either trip by rail took half as much time and money as a stagecoach. And rail passengers also had the benefit of upholstered seats, kerosene lamps for reading, and woodburning stoves for heat in the winter. They even enjoyed gourmet meals of squirrel, wild turkey, and bear at the two stops along the way.

Steel rails did eventually connect Searcy with the main line. Much of the town turned out on the evening of April 20, 1927, when the first real passenger train rolled into Searcy. The Missouri Pacific sent its Sunshine Special, complete with an observation car and a string of Pullmans. The struggle for real passenger service had taken a half century, and Searcy savored its moment of triumph. These were exuberant times throughout the nation—the Roaring Twenties—and Searcy's steel rails seemed to confirm the promise of a bright future.

The Roaring Twenties, Strawberries, and Ice Cream

Timber and agriculture fueled the economy of Searcy and White County during the Roaring Twenties. As old oaks disappeared, agriculture expanded and adapted to new cash crops including vegetables, peaches, alfalfa, and lespedeza. But the crop that really revolutionized agriculture was strawberries. White County exported 810,170 crates of strawberries during the Roaring Twenties. This was such a valuable crop that pickers could earn three to six times the average daily wage of the time. Strawberries fed the economy to such an extent that Searcy could boast more miles of paved roads in 1929 than the entire state of Montana.

The Great Depression changed boom into bust. Searcy suffered such appalling hardships that the people of Orrick and Camden, Missouri, sent an entire freight car of food and clothing to help the desperate people of White County. Although magazines of the day published articles on painless ways to commit suicide, some bright and fearless people did manage to prosper in Searcy. Ray Yarnell, for example, purchased a dairy business from Ben Grisham to start the Yarnell Ice Cream Company.

Just after the deal closed, the infamous "bank holiday" of March 1933 froze all the capital Yarnell had raised to operate the business. Yarnell somehow managed to borrow more money. But the economy was so bad that sometimes the company didn't sell a single item from a production run. Ray Yarnell did not draw any salary himself during those dark days, but his grit and determination enabled the Yarnell Ice Cream Company to survive the depths of the depression and become an Arkansas institution. The gathering of war clouds in the late 1930s fueled the economic recovery, although the 1940s brought a new series of economic challenges to Searcy and White County.

Hot War, Cold War

Because transportation corridors—whether railroads or highways—tend to make or break local economies, the Arkansas State Highway Commission outraged local residents in 1941 when it decided to bypass Searcy by three miles when building US 67 and US 64. This was the last in a series of economic insults that had plagued Searcy for a century. Snubbed by the National Road in the early 1800s and the Cairo & Fulton Railroad in the mid-1800s, this latest insult was almost too much to bear. More than a hundred concerned citizens protested the decision in testimony before the highway commission, proposing an alternative route for US 67 that would touch the eastern city limits and keep the county seat on the highway. Congressman Wilbur Mills threw his support behind the plan, despite

The Searcy Courthouse is best known for its attractive lighting during the Christmas season. —Jimmy Weatherley

the fact that the residents of Batesville opposed the additional six miles the new route would add to the overall length of the highway. US 67 was built through the outskirts of Searcy, and US 64 terminated at Bald Knob.

Searcy's population increased by almost 50 percent during the war. In order to provide petroleum to fuel the convoys to Europe and actual combat operations in that theater, Congress decided to build a pipeline from Texas to New York. The contract for building the portion of the pipeline from Texas to Illinois went to the Oklahoma Construction Company, which established its headquarters in Searcy. But as construction was completed and other wartime industries (not to mention the military services) attracted workers from Searcy, the area developed an acute labor shortage. Lakeside Lumber in Doniphan, the White County Motor Company in Searcy, and local farms all desperately needed workers.

Yet Searcy effected such a strong economic revival after the war that a 1950 issue of *Forbes Magazine* reported on the city's remarkable growth. That growth continued as the icy realities of the Cold War replaced the smouldering embers of World War II. In 1960, construction began on six Titan II missile silos around Searcy. Although the new economic activity helped local businesses, many residents

359

feared that the silos made Searcy a prime target in the event of a nuclear war.

The finicky, liquid-fueled Titan missiles proved to be dangerous in peacetime as well as in war. An explosion at Launch Site Four, about eleven miles north of Searcy, killed fifty-three civilian workers in 1965 as they were repairing the plumbing, air-conditioning, and exhaust systems in the silo. Only two workers survived the explosion, which was the worst disaster in the history of the ballistic missile program. This would not be the only explosion in a Titan II silo. Decades later, when the cold war began to thaw, the air force gratefully decommissioned the trouble-prone Titan missile silos.

By this time, many residents of Searcy and White County were taking advantage of highway improvements in the 1970s to commute to jobs in Little Rock. Today, Harding University and the Foothills Vocational Technical School provide promise for the future. The old buildings of downtown Searcy (some dating back to the mid-1800s) provide a constant reminder of the community's long and interesting history.

—BALD KNOB—

Located about fifty-seven miles northeast of Little Rock and thirty-six miles southwest of Batesville on US 67, this railroad town took its name from an acre-sized rock that had been a landmark in the area for generations. Known variously as the Knob, Big Rock, or Bald Knob Rock, the layered brown sandstone outcropping shaped like an up-side-down washtub dominated the surrounding landscape at the dawn of railroading in White County. To the east and north, virgin stands of oak, hickory, elm, sweet gum, and cedar sheltered abundant wildlife. To the south, vast canebrakes carpeted the bottoms along the White and Little Red Rivers. Two log sheds and cattle pens near the knob stood vacant most of the year.

Before the railroad came, most folks lived several miles northwest of the knob, centered around the Shady Grove church, which also served as the local school. Residents of the area were mainly subsistence farmers who raised cattle as their cash crop. Every winter, they drove their cattle into the canebrakes south of Big Rock, where the cane provided both forage and shelter from the bite of harsh winter winds. The farmers built the cattle pens at the knob for spring round-ups, when they branded new calves and culled out animals to sell. As late as 1876, the future site of Bald Knob lacked a single real building. Sylvester Barnes observed that the only board to be found at that location was a sign reading "Bald Knob." Benjamin Franklin Brown apparently stuck that sign in the ground next to the new railroad tracks to designate where trains should stop to off-load passengers and freight.

The area around Bald Knob had remained isolated because of the area's lack of roads and navigable waterways until the railroad suddenly connected it with the outside world. The Cairo & Fulton Railroad Company merged with the St. Louis, Iron Mountain & Southern Railroad in 1876, taking the latter's name. Much of the old Cairo & Fulton's roadway still required ballasting the ties, which would require a tremendous volume of rock. Railroad officials began to eye Bald Knob, and soon leased the area around the rock from Michael Howard and B. D. Turner.

The railroad opened up vast tracts of forest to exploitation. John Kerr brought a sawmill from Canada and began the local timber industry. John Bradford added another mill. But the thing that really spawned the creation of a town was the knob itself. Workers flooded into the area to help quarry material from the rock between 1876 and 1878. The first workers lived in tents near the quarry. Then the railroad provided cars outfitted with sleeping quarters.

Lunsford Worthington built the first house in town, and he used the log structure as both his home and a post office. When he petitioned the U.S. Postal Service in 1878 to give the village a post office, he listed 158 families who would be served. Soon boardinghouses and hotels appeared to provide more suitable shelter for the quarry workers. The workmen brought their families, spawning the appearance of stores, and a real community was born. Gradually the population of Shady Grove moved to Bald Knob.

The 1880 census listed 221 residents of Bald Knob. Fifty-seven of that number worked at the quarry. The community included saloons, boardinghouses, hotels, blacksmiths, stores, churches, teamsters, a doctor, druggist, butcher, and tailor. The following year, local voters decided to incorporate Bald Knob, making the town's birth official. Workers continued to harvest a living from the knob over the next several decades, feeding the railroad's need for ballast. They continued the process until nothing remained of the acre-sized rock that once dominated the landscape at the end of present-day Center Street, just south of Arkansas 367.

Now Bald Knob Rock lives on as an amorphous part of the Missouri Pacific right-of-way, and as the name of the town it gave life. Bald Knob serves as the western terminus of US 64 and the southern terminus of US 167 (which approximates the route of the old Southwest Trail to Batesville).

—BATESVILLE—

Perched on the north bank of the White River where it emerges from the Ozarks, Batesville is a town with a particularly long history. In fact, Batesville has the oldest post office in continuous operation in all of Arkansas.

French explorers in the late 1600s named the waterway *Rivière Blanche*, which means White (or Clear) River, because the water was so transparent that they could see the rocks in the bottom of the river. Batesville is about ninety-three miles northeast of Little Rock via US 67 and 167. The town is also sixty-one miles south of the Mammoth Spring (at the Missouri border) via US 167, 62, and 63.

The Batesville story begins just before 1808, when the Osage Indians agreed to a treaty that ended their claims to the lands north and east of the White River. Before the treaty, John Lafferty poled a keelboat up the White River to trade with the Osages for furs. He fell in love with a spot on the south side of the White River, just across from the mouth of Polk Bayou (which was also known as Poke Bayou, Polk Creek, and Poke Creek). After the treaty, Lafferty left for Kentucky and returned with his family, the James Trimble family, and John Austin to settle at the mouth of Poke Creek in the fall of 1810. Samuel Miller arrived in 1813 and built a place three miles east of the Poke Bayou encampment along a creek that now bears his name. Samuel's grandson William would later become governor of Arkansas.

Meanwhile, John Lafferty went off to fight in the War of 1812. He returned home to find that the settlement he founded was growing but still had not attracted a doctor. The village did have a store, fur trader, blacksmith, and about a dozen homes. A German ran a trading post for a company in St. Louis. But without proper medical attention, Lafferty languished and eventually died in 1817.

By that time, Poke Bayou was part of Lawrence County in Missouri Territory. The Missouri territorial legislature created Independence County (which was much larger than today) from Lawrence County in 1820 in recognition of the growing local population. The home of Charles Kelly became the temporary county seat until officials could select a permanent site. Kelly served as the first sheriff and the second postmaster of the county. (Peyton Tucker became the county's first postmaster when he established the White Run post office at the mouth of Salado Creek ten months earlier.) Kelly's house appeared on maps of the day as Napoleon, which was about a mile downriver from Poke Bayou (Batesville).

Kelly lobbied for making Napoleon the permanent seat, but the landowners of Poke Bayou objected that Napoleon only had one building, whereas they had a prospering village. Although a map of the day described the location of the post office as Napoleon, the official postal designation was Poke Creek, and the village a mile upriver remained Poke Bayou. When officials platted the town the following year, the deed establishing the county seat at Poke Bayou referred to the village as Batesville. The name of the post office did not change to Batesville until 1824, when that facility finally moved to the permanent county seat and Hartwell Boswell became the new postmaster.

The county seat was named in honor of James Woodson Bates, who grew up in Virginia, attended Yale, and graduated from Princeton in 1810. Bates moved to St. Louis in 1816 and established a law practice at Arkansas Post in 1820. Widely liked and respected, Bates became the first territorial delegate to Congress in 1821. Defeated for reelection by Henry Conway in 1823, Bates moved to the town that was named in his honor. There he practiced law and later served as a territorial judge until 1830, when his judicial appointment expired. Bates then moved to Crawford County. He went on to serve as a delegate to the first constitutional convention in Arkansas and subsequently as the land office register at Clarksville. Bates died in 1846.

Soon after Bates moved to Batesville in the early 1820s, settlers in the surrounding countryside had cleared enough land to begin raising cash crops. Cotton provided the most income per acre. Local farmers shipped more than 100 bales of cotton down the White River in 1826. Five years later, Captain Philip Pennywit and Captain Todd Tunstall piloted the steamer *Waverly* up the White River to Batesville. This first steamboat to reach Batesville heralded the dawn of a new economic era for the more than 2,000 residents of Independence County. A month later, the steamer *Laurel* landed at Batesville. For the next half-century, steamers would provide the area with its main transportation link with the outside world.

Independence County grew gradually in the 1840s, but the population jumped from 7,767 to 14,307 in the 1850s. This mirrored a similar trend statewide, when the state's population more than doubled, largely because of a substantial migration of people from the southern states to Arkansas. Tennessee provided most of the newcomers to Independence County, which remained an area of small farms rather than large plantations. In 1844, Batesville produced the first of its three state governors, Thomas Drew, who served in that office until 1849.

Batesville was no longer a frontier town, thanks to an abundance of businesses, doctors, and lawyers. The town boasted a new brick courthouse and a three-story brick building called the Batesville Institute (located on Main Street between State Street and Central

Avenue), which housed the city offices and library, and provided a place for fraternal meetings and public entertainment. Probably the first three-story structure in the state, the Institute lasted for less than four months. A fire that started in a neighboring building on the morning of January 16, 1859, destroyed the uninsured Institute as well. A smouldering debate over secession would soon reduce any hope of rebuilding the Batesville Institute to ashes.

Although the debate over secession inflamed passions throughout the South, there wasn't much anti-Union sentiment in Batesville or Independence County. Only 221 county residents (about 2 percent of the white population) owned slaves. A mere nine people owned a fourth of the slaves. So it should not be surprising that only about 300 of the county's voters wanted to leave the Union in February 1861. That opinion changed abruptly when President Lincoln called for volunteers to restore the Union after the fall of Fort Sumter.

The Civil War

Captain William Gibbs, a Batesville lawyer, raised the county's first Confederate company within a month after Arkansas left the Union on May 6, 1861. Two months after that, the company fought at Wilson's Creek near Springfield, Missouri. Job Neill, the brother of the company's first sergeant, died in that battle and Captain Gibbs disappeared. Ernest Neill, the son of First Sergeant Robert Neill, believed that Gibbs actually deserted because of his humiliating performance during the course of the battle. Many officers during the early part of the war attained their rank because of their political or financial standing, rather than any military training or skill.

Independence County would eventually raise twenty-three companies for the Confederate army. Many of these volunteers viewed themselves as home guards who would protect their farms and families from northern invaders. But most were sent off to fight in distant places like Virginia, Georgia, and Mississippi. Some soldiers eventually deserted to stay near their families. Furthermore, loyalties remained quite divided. Although Independence County raised 1,525 men for the Confederate army, it also provided 815 men to the Union army.

The first Federal volunteers stepped forward soon after Union General Samuel Curtis marched down from Missouri after his victory at Pea Ridge in March 1862 and captured Batesville on May 4. Curtis hoped to continue his drive all the way to Little Rock. The Confederates occupying Batesville withdrew without a fight when Curtis appeared. Curtis stayed in Batesville for several months, recruiting 365 enlisted men and 14 officers before retreating back to Missouri.

Small Confederate units reoccupied Batesville after the Union withdrawal until January 1863, when Brigadier General John Marmaduke and Brigadier General J. O. Shelby arrived. In an interesting touch of irony, Marmaduke commandeered the Ewing house as his headquarters—the same house that Curtis had used as *his* headquarters. (The Ewing house stood on Main Street where the parking lot for the First Methodist Church is now located.) Shelby used the home of F. W. Desha as his headquarters. The main body of troops wintered near Oil Trough Bottom.

About a thousand Federals under the command of Colonel R. R. Livingston returned to Batesville on Christmas Day, 1863. Colonel Elisha Baxter (see also Brooks-Baxter War under Little Rock, in Part 3) raised about 450 men for the Union army from the Batesville area and organized them into the Fourth Arkansas Infantry Volunteers by the end of the year. The Federals remained for about five months, and then moved on to Jacksonport when they exhausted the food and forage around Batesville.

It was during this period that the only serious fighting erupted in Independence County. A Federal wagon train was hunting forage north of Bethesda, when Confederates under the command of Captain George Rutherford launched a surprise dawn attack at Waugh's farm on February 18, 1864. The Confederates killed a number of Federals, including their commanding officer, and escaped across the White River with 200 Union horses and mules. Although local farmers lost livestock, food, and forage to Federal and Confederate forces confiscating supplies throughout the war—the real hardships came from the Bushwhackers and Jayhawkers who robbed and killed civilians with impunity. The experience of Edwin McGuire and his family, who owned a substantial farm near Oil Trough, provides a compelling look at the suffering visited upon innocent civilians by roving bands of guerillas.

Emeline McGuire wrote the following letter to her son after Jayhawkers drove the family off their land, and they temporarily escaped to Kentucky. The letter tells the human side of war in Arkansas with all its pathos.

Oldham County Kentucky
August, 1864

My Dear Son,
How to commence this letter to you I don't know. I have so much melancholy things to tell you about. In the first place, I know you will think it strange, when you look at the heading of my letter, that

your Ma is in Kentucky. Well, I will tell you how it was that we came here. We have had first the Confederate soldiers and then the Federals changing first one and then the other ever since war commenced, and last winter a band of Jayhawking thieves came into Independence and all the adjoining counties, going to people's houses of nights and demanding all their money and threatening to kill them if they did not and they did kill some.

One night three men rode up to our gate and hallowed and your Pa went out thinking it was some of our neighbors wanted something, when to his surprise they took hold of him and said he was their prisoner. They were all armed and he had only an old pocket knife. They took him nearly a mile into the woods and asked him for a large sum of money. Your Pa told them they would have to kill him then for he had not near much money. They told him he had to give all he had. They then searched his pockets and then brought him back to the house and told me to bring out all the money or they would burn the house. I took the money out and they released your Pa.

About three weeks after that a gang of those thieves came to our house about eleven o'clock at night. We had our doors locked and Pa had his guns and pistols loaded. They did not say a word but commenced trying to burst the doors open. Finding the doors too strong, one of them came to the window and burst the shutter off. Just as he did so your Pa shot and killed him. He loaded his gun again and went into the cellar with the intention of trying to get out. Knowing they had got all the money before, your Pa believed they had come with the intention of killing him, and he was determined to sell his life as dear as he could.

As soon as this man was killed, they made the negroes carry him to Lamburtons and they set the house on fire. They put the fire at the end of the old store room and the house was all in flames before I knew it. Your Pa managed to get out of the cellar but not until he was wounded in the left arm above the elbow and he killed another one of those thieves.

He then had to run through the open lot and them following him and shooting at him all the time. Just as he jumped the lot fence by the negro cabin, they shot him a second time in the same arm which I fear will make him a cripple for life. But he succeeded in getting away with life for which I am thankful to my blessed Savior, for I know it was nothing but his interposition that saved him. Our dwelling houses, kitchen, smoke house with everything that was in them burned up with the exception of a few things Auntie and myself carried out. A few days afterward our mill and gin was burned and all our negroes left us and went to the federals except Jo. Our house was burned on the fifth night of December [1863]. . . .

Your mother, Emeline McGuire

Such depredations were common throughout Arkansas during the war. Some local people were members of the Jayhawkers and Bushwhackers and preyed upon the civilian population. This activity generated feuds, reprisals, and hard feelings that sometimes lasted for generations after the war. Even when members of a community fought on different sides in the organized armies, old friendships rarely recovered. Batesville and Independence County, however, somehow managed to promptly return to normalcy and old friendships despite divisions produced by the war. Batesville became a bastion of brotherhood where bygones could truly be bygones.

A Bastion of Brotherhood

One reason Batesville quickly returned to normalcy after the war was that no military government was ever imposed on the local population, and few carpetbaggers appeared in the area during Reconstruction. Although the county provided a substantial number of troops to both armies, the area experienced few of the reprisals against returning soldiers and their families seen elsewhere in Arkansas. Veterans of both sides renewed old friendships without regard to former military affiliation. In fact, Batesville veterans of both the Confederate and Union armies organized a common fishing club soon after the war.

Another reason Batesville citizens quickly put the war behind them was that most local officials elected to office in the decade following the war had been born and raised in the area. That was a relatively uncommon phenomenon during Reconstruction in Arkansas. Furthermore, many of those officials had fought for the Confederacy. For example, three of the four sheriffs who served the county from 1865 to 1874 had supported the Lost Cause.

Freed slaves also fared better in the Batesville area than in many areas of the South. The Freedmen's Bureau opened a tuition-free, government-sponsored school for blacks in November 1868. At first, the school struggled because of apathy and inadequate government funding—a not uncommon experience in Arkansas during Reconstruction. What makes the Batesville experience interesting is that local white citizens (many of whom had supported the Confederacy) began to support the school and it prospered. This success stimulated the residents of Batesville to open the town's first public school for whites in 1871.

When Elisha Baxter returned to Batesville after the war, he returned to the practice of law. He also tried to heal the religious divisions created by the war. The slavery issue had divided the Methodist, Baptist, and Presbyterian churches into Northern and Southern branches. The Methodists split over this issue in 1845, and Batesville had separate pro-slavery and anti-slavery Methodist churches before the outbreak of war. Baxter led the struggle to reunite the two branches of the Methodist Church. He went on to become the second resident of Independence County to be elected governor of Arkansas, serving from 1872 to 1874. The two Methodist churches in Batesville finally buried the hatchet in the early 1880s, although the national organizations didn't reunite until 1939. The Presbyterians reunited even later, while the Baptists never did.

Batesville education got a boost in 1872 with the founding of Arkansas College. The school admitted both boys and girls to a curriculum that ranged from first grade to the college level. The same year, the Male and Female Academy opened at Sulphur Rock. Several years later, the third resident of Independence County to become governor of Arkansas entered the statewide political arena.

William Miller, the grandson of pioneer Samuel Miller, was born on Miller's Creek in 1823, and began his political career as the county clerk. Miller then moved to Little Rock, where he served several terms as the state auditor before passing the bar and returning to Batesville to practice law. He eventually returned to Little Rock to serve another term as the state auditor before running for the governor's office. He served two terms as governor, from 1877 to 1881. He died six years later. His tombstone in Mt. Holly cemetery proclaims that William Miller was the state's first native-born governor. Because he knew he would be buried amid a lot of politicians and bankers, Miller directed that his tombstone include the inscription, "An Honest Man."

The arrival of the St. Louis, Iron Mountain & Southern Railroad in 1882 stimulated an economic boom in Batesville and Independence County. Although cotton and timber fueled much of that growth, the mining of manganese, lime, and phosphate became a major economic factor as well. The railroad extended a spur to the mines in 1886. The mines also spawned the birth of a new town, Cushman, the following year.

One of the most unusual industries to develop in the 1880s was the dredging of mussels from the White River. Some mussels contained beautiful pearls that could fetch $300 to $500. The shells proved valuable for making buttons, although forty carloads of shells were needed to make one carload of buttons. The business flourished until the Great Depression.

Meanwhile, downtown Batesville was growing rapidly. Several large fires had made building with sandstone and brick increasingly attractive. Many of the old sandstone and brick buildings on lower Main Street date to this economic boom of the 1870s and 1880s. Batesville

Until the Great Depression, the Batesville area supported a button-making industry that used mussel shells harvested in the White River.
—Arkansas History Commission

was quite a modern town during this period, boasting the arrival of electric lights in 1881 and telephones in 1887. The advent of the railroad in the 1880s led to the decline of the steamboat. The last steamboat to land at Batesville off-loaded its cargo in 1907.

Soon after the turn of the century, the railroad added a spur to the marble quarries owned by the Pfeiffer family north of town. Batesville marble became widely known throughout the United States because of its beauty and because of the great skill of the craftsmen at the Pfeiffer Stone Company. Batesville marble was used in the state capitol building in Little Rock, in the trim on the White River Regional Library, for the columns in front of the First United Methodist Church on Main Street, and in the Confederate monument in front of the Independence County Courthouse. Many tombstones found throughout the county are also made from Batesville marble.

Looking toward Batesville on the White River, circa 1905. –Arkansas History Commission

The new century dawned bright with promise for Batesville and Independence County, but the coming decades would periodically cloud that future with one dark, turbulent storm after another.

Fires, Floods, Emigration, and Immigration

Massive flooding along the White River in 1914 and 1915 hit local farmers hard, destroying all the crops in the bottoms. Water spread out three to ten feet deep for miles and even covered the railroad tracks at Newark. An even worse flood hit in 1916, but it actually did much less damage since the flooding occurred during the winter after farmers had harvested their crops.

Soon after the area dried out, fires began to plague the county. An overheated iron started a fire in 1920 that destroyed a house on Vine Street in Batesville. Flames quickly spread up Vine, Boswell, and College Streets as far as St. Louis Street. The inferno gutted at least eighty homes and left 300 people homeless. The community rallied around the victims and found everyone a place to stay as they began to rebuild their lives.

The Great Depression inflicted more pain upon the Batesville area. One of three local banks failed, and its depositors eventually recovered only 35 cents on the dollar. Local businesses began to close as farm incomes plummeted. Many folks pulled up stakes and moved to the West or the North in search of jobs. But the county did experience some progress during those dark days. J. K. Southerland started the poultry industry that is now a mainstay of the local economy. And the University of Arkansas established its Livestock and Forestry Experiment Station near Bethesda.

The outbreak of World War II accelerated the exodus from the Batesville area. Some residents went off to join the military, and many others moved away in search of well-paying jobs in defense plants such as the big Boeing Aircraft factory at Wichita. Few of these people returned to the Batesville area after the war. The population of Independence County showed a significant decline from 1940 to 1950, and this trend continued through the 1950s. Severe droughts from 1952 to 1954 forced many small farmers out of business and out of Arkansas to look for jobs. By 1960, the population of Independence County was the lowest since 1880. But Batesville bucked this trend by attracting new industries to town, and by capitalizing on the growing publicity that the Ozarks were a good place to retire. Batesville began to grow again.

The complexion of the agricultural industry in the Batesville area changed dramatically during this period. The farms were growing larger. And by 1974 the cash crop that had long fueled the county economy—cotton—completely disappeared from local fields. The area's last cotton gin, which Desha Lester built at Desha in 1936, closed down in 1970. It signaled the end of one era and the beginning of another. Batesville continued to attract new industries, the county population continued to grow, and the White River Medical Center

Binding wheat near Batesville in the 1930s. –Arkansas History Commission

371

(which opened in 1975) began to draw patients from a broad area of north-central Arkansas.

The 1970s brought two very different waves of immigrants into the Batesville area. Many people who had moved away to find jobs years before returned to retire in the Batesville area. In many cases, their friends came from places like Michigan and Illinois to retire in the county, too. Then local families and churches began to sponsor Vietnamese refugees who were being temporarily housed at Fort Chaffee (near Fort Smith). That capped a tradition, more than a century old, of embracing the veterans of painful wars. Whether starting a fishing club that welcomed both Union and Confederate veterans, healing religious differences spawned by the issues leading to secession, or opening the community's arms to dispossessed Vietnamese, Batesville has a long and venerable heritage as a bastion of brotherhood.

Batesville is also becoming known as a bastion of education. Arkansas College developed a solid reputation as a liberal arts school and began a six-year program to expand its curriculum. This precipitated a 25 percent increase in applications to the school in 1993. As part of this expansion program, Arkansas College changed its name to Lyon College in the spring of 1994. The community has come a long way since fire destroyed the Batesville Institute in 1859. James Bates would be proud.

RECOMMENDED READING

The following list is by no means comprehensive. Rather, it is a highly subjective collection of books that I recommend to friends and readers as worthy of their time and effort.

Arnold, Morris. *Colonial Arkansas, 1686–1804: A Social and Cultural History.* Fayetteville: University of Arkansas Press, 1991. 232 pp.

> Few Arkansans know much about the history of Arkansas before the area's incorporation into Missouri Territory. Arnold does a thorough job of bringing this story together in accessible and readable form. It remains the classic reference for the period of colonial rule by the Spanish and French. Arnold even discusses the only battle of the Revolutionary War to be fought west of the Mississippi. To say the text is well documented is an understatement. Arnold assembles all the footnotes from each chapter in the back of the book, along with useful appendices and an index, which together constitute 24 percent of the volume. This arrangement satisfies scholars while making the text less intimidating to the casual reader.

Baker, T. Harri, and Jane Browning. *An Arkansas History for Young People.* Fayetteville: University of Arkansas Press, 1991. 429 pp.

> Although written as a classroom text for students in the eighth grade, this volume should not be overlooked by adults. Simply stated, this is the best and most readable comprehensive history of Arkansas ever published. It should be used as the model for other history texts. Most history texts are stodgy and boring, some are biased, and few inspire an interest in history. I developed an interest in history in spite of history texts, not because of them. Baker and Browning have created a history that even adults will find compelling. Only a few elements in the book will seem condescending or simplistic, and even fewer textbookish features will distract the casual reader. This is an outstanding history of Arkansas.

Baskett, Tom, Jr., editor. *Persistence of the Spirit: The Black Experience in Arkansas,* second edition. Helena, Ark.: Delta Cultural Center, 1991. 48 pp.

This inexpensive magazine-sized booklet contains five excellent essays by seven authors who chronicle the black experience from the days of black pioneers and slaves, through the nineteenth and twentieth centuries, to the present day. This important work makes a good read for anyone and is worth the price just for the section at the end, which provides an annotated bibliography on black history. This booklet can be ordered directly from the Delta Cultural Center, 95 Missouri Street, Helena, AR 72342.

Bearss, Edwin, and Arrell Gibson. *Fort Smith: Little Gibraltar on the Arkansas,* second edition. Norman: University of Oklahoma Press, 1979. 351 pp.

This is an excellent history of a community. The book tells the larger stories of the initial exploration and homesteading of the American West, the pressures driving the Indian nations westward, and the post's pivotal role in western military history. The book focuses primarily on the post rather than the civilian community of the same name that grew up around it, describing the post's role in bringing law and order to a turbulent frontier at the end of the nineteenth century. That law and order was personified in Judge Isaac Parker, who soon earned the moniker "The Hanging Judge." The book concludes with the establishment of the fort as a National Historic Site in 1961. This book is required reading for anyone with an interest in how Arkansas helped open the western frontier. I also recommend reading any scholarly articles by Edwin Bearss, such as those in the *Arkansas Historical Quarterly* and similar journals. His articles on military history are wonderful.

Bolton, S. Charles. *Territorial Ambition: Land and Society in Arkansas, 1800–1840.* Fayetteville: University of Arkansas Press, 1993. 152 pp.

Using county tax records, census counts, and period manuscripts, Bolton analyzes the development of Arkansas society in the first four decades of the nineteenth century. This was a time of rapid upward mobility for many pioneers, who earned their fortunes through fraudulent land speculation, politics, or the accumulation of land and slaves (which together constituted most of the taxable wealth in antebellum Arkansas). Bolton describes the forging of Arkansas and its culture, and places the process into perspective. He explains the development of common myths; some are vindicated, and some are brought into serious doubt.

One acquaintance described this well-researched and well-written book as dry. Such an assessment is wide of the mark. Bolton's book is meaty—not dry—and 100 percent fat free. It may not be the ideal book for the casual reader, but anyone with an interest in the pioneers who transformed Arkansas from a wilderness to a state will thoroughly enjoy sinking their teeth into this delicious morsel. Although this is a scholarly work, the reader doesn't need to be a rocket scientist or closet scholar to enjoy it. This is a very important book that should be required reading for anyone with a serious interest in the history of Arkansas.

Dean, Ernie. *Arkansas Place Names.* Branson, Mo.: The Ozarks Mountaineer, 1986. 201 pp.

> This little volume merits a place on every Arkansan's bookshelf. It is a book to be perused over the years rather than read cover to cover at a single sitting. Writing about everywhere from Apt to Zink, the late Ernie Dean describes how and why places got their names. Using the research skills and reverence for facts of a scholar, and the whimsy of a humorist whenever possible, Dean provides a unique look into Arkansas history. Yet *Arkansas Place Names* provides more than the opportunity for small talk on subjects other than sports and the weather. This book provides the sense of place, the sense of roots, necessary to really feel a part of the flow of Arkansas history. This inexpensive book can be ordered from Ernie Dean Books, 910 Arlington Terrace, Fayetteville, AR 72701.

_____. *Ozarks Country.* Branson, Mo.: The Ozarks Mountaineer, 1988. 200 pp.

> Although this book does not provide a comprehensive history of the Ozarks, it does paint intimate vignettes of the people, customs, events, places, and natural history of the mountains the late Ernie Dean knew and loved since he first visited them as a lad in 1930. The charm and insight of these vignettes end up providing a more intimate understanding of the Ozarks than more comprehensive volumes published on the subject.
>
> Dean was able to attain such intimacy because he knew that magnificent hill country in the days before the inexorable march of progress eradicated the area's unique language and lifestyle. Throughout the 1970s and 1980s, Dean chronicled Ozark life as it was and had been, as well as the changes sweeping through the mountains. Although some of the changes were not to his liking, Dean also reported on the renaissance of mountain culture and folkways, which now provide a substantial spiritual and economic foundation for the Ozarks. This inexpensive book is one of the best-kept secrets on the Arkansas bookshelf, and it can be ordered from Ernie Dean Books, 910 Arlington Terrace, Fayetteville, AR 72701.

DeLano, Patti. *Arkansas: Off the Beaten Path.* Old Saybrook, Conn.: Globe Pequot Press, 1992. 158 pp.

This book lets readers write some history of their own as they explore the back roads and unique places that help give Arkansas its charm. This is a modern travel guide for people who don't like divided highways and fast food, but prefer to travel kinder, gentler byways whenever possible. This charming book would make the perfect companion volume to *Roadside History of Arkansas* as one explores the past and present delights Arkansas has to offer.

Dougan, Michael. *Confederate Arkansas: The People and Politics of a Frontier State in Wartime*. Tuscaloosa: University of Alabama Press, 1976. 165 pp.

Well written but with a somewhat academic ambiance, this book provides the best understanding of the politics that led to secession when most Arkansans wanted to stay in the Union, as well as the political turmoil that plagued Arkansas throughout the war. Dougan describes the ebb and flow of military fortunes in their political context. The author also gives the reader a gut-wrenching sense of the depredations by foraging armies, Bushwhackers, Jayhawkers, and bandits on the innocent civilian population during the war. This book is required reading for anyone with a serious interest in this turbulent chapter of Arkansas history.

Fletcher, John Gould. *Arkansas*. Fayetteville: University of Arkansas Press, 1989. 348 pp.

This reprint of Fletcher's 1947 classic shows the delightful consequences when a great poet turns his pen to history. This immensely readable volume gives the reader a rich sense of history that oozes deep into the bones to become part of one's tribal memory. Harry Ashmore's introduction to the reprinted volume provides an analysis of both Fletcher and his history from a modern perspective. From the explorations of de Soto, through the settlement of a rowdy and often lawless frontier, to the Confederacy, and then to homegrown populists, Fletcher provides an entertaining view of Arkansas history through World War II.

Hanson, Gerald, and Carl Moneyhon. *Historical Atlas of Arkansas*. Norman: University of Oklahoma Press, 1989. 160 pp.

This book provides a unique view of Arkansas history by using seventy-one maps to illustrate the state's geography and natural history, settlement patterns, political evolution, civil war politics and battles, and economic and political growth into the 1980s. Each map has a corresponding block of text on the facing page to further explain important aspects of the subject at hand. This work is a useful reference for serious students of history and supplements more comprehensive and readable volumes like *Arkansas* by John Gould Fletcher and *An Arkansas History for Young People* by T. Harri Baker and Jane Browning. My only complaint with the *Historical Atlas of Arkansas* is that the maps of Civil War battles do not convey as much information as they should, and the information they do contain is not clearly explained.

Harington, Donald. *Let Us Build a City.* New York: Harcourt Brace Janovich, 1986. 475 pp.

This book shows what can happen when a talented novelist decides to write a book of history. Harington has produced an absolute jewel of literature. It is a lively, eccentric journey through the back roads of Arkansas, a history unlike any other in American literature. Starting with the premise that the builders of more than a thousand towns in America ostentatiously placed the word "City" in the names of their embryonic communities, Harington chronicles the stories of eleven of the thirty-six "cities" in Arkansas that didn't quite live up to expectations.

The story is told through the eyes of his researcher, Kim, who visited towns that have declined into obscurity and others that were "never anything to begin with, despite the brave dreams of their founders." Kim ferreted out interesting people with enchanting stories, and the author wove these stories into a remarkable adventure. At the end of it all, the author and his researcher fell in love. This book is a remarkable achievement and a wonderful read. Unfortunately, the volume was never given a chance to succeed in the marketplace, thanks to divisive federal tax laws that penalize publishers with a lot of inventory. This volume was dumped just a few months after it was published. *Let Us Build a City* will be hard to find but worth the effort.

Jones, Maxine Temple. *Maxine: Call Me Madam.* Little Rock: Pioneer Press, 1983. 194 pp.

This lively book describes the life and times of the most successful (and toughest) madam in Hot Springs during the 1950s and 1960s. Writing in a conversational style that gives a real sense of her personality, Jones not only provides a compelling account of her own subculture, but also provides a gritty look into the political corruption that ran rampant through Hot Springs and Arkansas during her heyday. Although out of print, this book is highly recommended and worth the trouble to find.

Lancaster, Bob. *The Jungles of Arkansas.* Fayetteville: University of Arkansas Press, 1989. 231 pp.

To simply describe this book as a collection of ten essays about particularly interesting aspects of Arkansas history is to undervalue the style, grace, wit, and outstanding writing that make this book sing to the reader. Rarely seen in bookstores, this thoroughly enjoyable volume deserves much better exposure than it has received. The book's title was inspired by a put-down from that late, great, master curmudgeon H. L. Mencken, who once wrote about the "miasmatic jungles of Arkansas" to emphasize the state's relative obscurity. Lancaster brings forth ten steaming, savory slices of history with the mastery of Vino's pizzeria in Little Rock. The two spicy dishes complement each other well.

Rafferty, Milton D. *The Ozarks, Land and Life.* Norman: University of Oklahoma Press, 1980. 282 pp.

This is the best book on the Ozarks, which extend through northern Arkansas, southern Missouri, eastern Oklahoma, and a wee bit of Cherokee County in Kansas. The book's layout, footnotes, and references at the end of every chapter give the volume an academic ambiance. But Rafferty writes in an accessible style as he describes the history and contemporary life of the Ozarks.

Shea, William, and Earl Hess. *Pea Ridge: The Civil War Campaign in the West.* Chapel Hill: University of North Carolina Press, 1992. 417 pp.

Masterfully and extensively researched from Connecticut to California, this volume demonstrates that academicians *can* write with vitality, sensitivity, and style. Although the authors footnote their text with the thoroughness of scholars, the text itself is written with the panache of a novel. The result is a compelling history similar in ambiance to the remarkable history of the Civil War written by novelist Shelby Foote. Shea and Hess describe a crucial campaign that erupted into one of the earliest intense battles of the Civil War. Pea Ridge stands as one of the largest battles fought on the western frontier, a battle that changed the balance of power in the trans-Mississippi region. The book not only describes this ferocious battle in detail, but also explains the grueling campaigns that led to the fight at Pea Ridge, as well as the battles that followed as an immediate consequence of the Union victory at Elkhorn Tavern.

Whayne, Jeannie, and Willard Gatewood, editors. *The Arkansas Delta: Land of Paradox.* Fayetteville: University of Arkansas Press, 1993. 321 pp.

This collection of essays by a variety of historians focuses on the history of the Delta, which can be viewed as a microcosm of the

Southern experience. The authors view this experience as a struggle between competing forces such as man versus nature, blacks versus whites, rich versus poor. Although a scholarly work published by a university press, the volume is not plagued with the stodgy writing and disjointed format often characteristic of histories written for historians. The ten individual essays are well written, and together they give the reader a substantial sense of place and the forces that have shaped the flow of history in the Delta.

Much of this history was driven by agriculture, which has a legacy of wealth and poverty, as well as privilege and exploitation. The authors view the history of the Delta as the one of a rich land and poor people. Plantations no longer exist, for the very word itself reeks of exploitation. Agricultural holdings are now called "farms" regardless of size, and large farms control much of the wealth. The book concludes, "Delta towns reflect the poverty of the region, with vacant stores along main streets staring back like empty sockets. Today's Delta is still the product of its past. Its agricultural legacy of wealth and poverty, of privilege and exploitation, still hangs over the region's future." The book certainly has a strong point of view.

Writers' Program, Work Projects Administration. *The WPA Guide to 1930s Arkansas.* 1941. Reprint, Lawrence: University of Kansas Press, 1987. 447 pp.

> Although generally stodgy and dated, *The WPA Guide to 1930s Arkansas* gives a capsulized history for many communities in Arkansas and describes the local points of interest. The authors wanted to provide a portrait of the cultural, political, and economic histories of communities as well as a sense of local architecture, geography, musicians, and writers. They succeeded in providing an interesting slice of Arkansas life in the 1930s. The authors organized their stories into seventeen automobile tours through most areas of the state. The reprint is worth buying just for the twenty-two-page introduction written by historian Elliot West, who skillfully places both the book and the overall history of Arkansas into perspective.

Young, Gloria, and Michael Hoffman, editors. *The Expedition of Hernando de Soto West of the Mississippi, 1541–1543.* Fayetteville: University of Arkansas Press, 1993. 311 pp.

> It seems as if nearly every community or county in Arkansas has claimed, at one time or another, that "de Soto slept here." Therefore, it can be hard to separate fact from folklore. Even an attempt by scholars decades ago to develop the definitive story on de Soto has since proven to be inadequate. Although it's hard to sleuth out verifiable facts and produce the last word on the subject, this book is the best attempt in a long time. It's a shame that bookstores and

average readers seem to be intimidated by the fact that this volume is actually the proceedings of two symposiums held in 1988 and 1990. Even an appalling number of local libraries in Arkansas do not have this fascinating volume in their collections.

Yet anyone who is a history buff or who likes good detective stories should find a wealth of fascinating reading here. The book gives a compelling glimpse of how working historians attempt to solve seemingly unsolvable problems, how their thought processes evolve over the years, and how they can abandon their own theories gracefully and even gleefully when someone produces a better bit of detective work. I came to particularly admire the skill, grace, and wit of Charles Hudson in his quest to accurately determine de Soto's route west of the Mississippi. You'll never think of history or historians in the same way after reading this book. If this volume is not available at your local library, it's certainly worth getting on interlibrary loan. But be forewarned: you may get hooked and decide you're going to have to buy a copy for yourself.

INDEX

382

We encourage you to patronize your local bookstores. Most stores will order any title that they do not stock. You may also order directly from Mountain Press by mail, using the order form provided below or by calling our toll-free number and using your Visa or MasterCard. We will gladly send you a complete catalog upon request.

Some other Roadside History titles of interest:

_____Roadside History of Arizona (paper)	$20.00
_____Roadside History of Arkansas (paper)	$18.00
_____Roadside History of Arkansas (cloth)	$30.00
_____Roadside History of California (paper)	$18.00
_____Roadside History of California (cloth)	$30.00
_____Roadside History of Florida (paper)	$18.00
_____Roadside History of Florida (cloth)	$30.00
_____Roadside History of Idaho (paper)	$18.00
_____Roadside History of Idaho (cloth)	$30.00
_____Roadside History of Nebraska (paper)	$18.00
_____Roadside History of Nebraska (cloth)	$30.00
_____Roadside History of New Mexico (paper)	$18.00
_____Roadside History of Oklahoma (paper)	$20.00
_____Roadside History of Oregon (paper)	$18.00
_____Roadside History of South Dakota (paper)	$18.00
_____Roadside History of Texas (paper)	$18.00
_____Roadside History of Texas (cloth)	$30.00
_____Roadside History of Vermont (paper)	$15.00
_____Roadside History of Wyoming (paper)	$18.00
_____Roadside History of Wyoming (cloth)	$30.00
_____Roadside History of Yellowstone Park (paper)	$ 8.00

Please include $3.00 per order to cover shipping and handling.

Send the books marked above. I enclose $_____

Name_____

Address_____

City_____State_____Zip_____

☐ Payment enclosed (check or money order in U.S. funds)
Bill my:☐ VISA ☐ MasterCard Expiration Date:_____

Card No._____

Signature _____

Mountain Press Publishing Company
P.O. Box 2399 • Missoula, MT 59806
Order Toll Free 1-800-234-5308
Have your Visa or MasterCard ready.